THE POVERTY AND EDUCATION READER

THE POVERTY AND EDUCATION READER

A Call for Equity in Many Voices

Edited by

Paul C. Gorski and Julie Landsman

STERLING, VIRGINIA

Published by Stylus Publishing, LLC
22883 Quicksilver Drive
Sterling, Virginia 20166-2102

Library of Congress Cataloging-in-Publication Data

The poverty and education reader : a call for equity
in many voices / edited by Paul C. Gorski and
Julie Landsman. -- First edition.
pages cm
Includes bibliographical references and index.
ISBN 978-1-57922-858-3 (cloth : alk. paper)
ISBN 978-1-57922-859-0 (pbk. : alk. paper)
ISBN 978-1-57922-860-6 (library networkable e-edition)
ISBN 978-1-57922-861-3 (consumer e-edition)
1. Children with social disabilities--Education--United States.
2. Poor children--Education--United States. 3. Educational
equalization--United States. 4. Poverty--United States. I. Gorski,
Paul C., editor of compilation. II. Landsman, Julie, editor
of compilation.
LC4091.P64 2013
371.826'94--dc23

2013024438

13-digit ISBN: 978-1-57922-858-3 (cloth)
13-digit ISBN: 978-1-57922-859-0 (paper)
13-digit ISBN: 978-1-57922-860-6 (library networkable e-edition)
13-digit ISBN: 978-1-57922-861-3 (consumer e-edition)

Printed in the United States of America

All first editions printed on acid-free paper
that meets the American National Standards Institute
Z39-48 Standard.

Bulk Purchases

Quantity discounts are available
for use in workshops and for staff
development.
Call 1-800-232-0223

First Edition, 2014

10   9   8   7   6   5   4   3   2

To Althea and Bobby with love and respect.

—Paul

With gratitude to the students who raised me, their parents who were patient with me, and my fellow teachers who fight for equity and go the distance every day in schools all across this country.

—Julie

CONTENTS

PART THREE: MAKING CLASS INEQUITY VISIBLE

PART FOUR: INSISTING ON EQUITY: STUDENTS, PARENTS, AND
COMMUNITIES FIGHT FOR JUSTICE

PART FIVE: TEACHING FOR CLASS EQUITY AND
ECONOMIC JUSTICE

In one of the most bizarre developments in education in our lifetimes, public schoolteachers are becoming the focal point of attacks on public schools. Little notice has been paid to the fact that as income and wealth inequality grew, so grew the dismal disparities in graduation rates and reading and math achievement. As more adults have lost their jobs, as homelessness has increased, as services for low-income people have been discontinued because of spiraling state budgets, standardized test scores fell. As programs that had helped students from families in poverty get into college were discontinued, as tutoring diminished or was taken over by for-profit companies that had little knowledge of students or their communities, as class sizes became larger and larger, schools and their teachers were blamed for the results of this economic trickle-*up* debacle. For eight long years federal, state, and local funding dwindled further and further in many of the communities—rural and urban and suburban—that needed funding the most.

Oddly, in our experience, conversations about the education of poor and working-class youth, often focused largely on those pesky standardized test scores, rarely include any serious consideration of these bigger concerns. How often do we imagine how educational outcomes might be different if every child had access to regular health care, if no child had to live near toxic waste sites, if rural Mississippi schools were funded at the same rate as those in the suburbs of Chicago, if all parents and guardians had access to living-wage work so they could spend more time helping their children with schoolwork? We understand, of course, that most teachers and school administrators, however empathetic we might be to low-income families, do not see health care access or the availability of living-wage work as within our purviews. Unfortunately, as several of the authors in this volume attest, these issues can have a tremendous impact on the day-to-day lives of our students. In many ways, those test scores, if they measure anything at all well, do a decent job of measuring opportunity: What level of access has this student enjoyed to high-quality preschool, to health care, to a computer and the Internet, to tutors and academic camps? But just knowing this—just looking on at a slightly new angle—might be all some of us need to see low-income students as resilient rather than deficient.

Making matters worse, as the recent economic crisis and teacher-blaming have reached their peaks, many educators have been trained to view low-income youth through a fictitious "culture of poverty" lens and, as a result, to pass the blame along to working-class and working-poor students and families. Today, when people aren't blaming teachers for achievement gaps that really could better be described as *opportunity* gaps, they (and sometimes *we*, the educators) insist that low-income families simply do not care about education—an assertion absolutely disputed by decades of research demonstrating that poor and working-class families have the *exact same attitudes* about the value of education as their wealthier counterparts. As a young high school student said two weeks after Hurricane Katrina buried the ninth ward of New Orleans in waves of water and debris, "It seems if you are poor they treat you like you are a criminal."

Take a couple steps back and the picture becomes bleaker: increases in rates of unemployment as jobs are sent overseas, a lack of preventative medical care suffered by so many low-income communities, the lack of a real increase in the minimum wage, and an epidemic of new jobs paying below living wages. Meanwhile politicians and businesspeople, most of whom never have known poverty, who often have attended and sent their children to fenced-in private schools, who often have no connection to the challenges faced by people who work multiple jobs and still need food stamps, are making educational policy decisions that affect the lives of students and teachers. We believe that this mismatch between education policy makers and people who spend their lives in the everyday world of low wages and precarious living situations has exacerbated the complex and challenging job of creating schools and agencies that ensure educational equality. In many ways, even as teachers and administrators are disempowered by the pressures of high-stakes testing, the imposition of scripted curricula, and expectations that we will "teach to the test," we are our most economically vulnerable students' last line of defense against educational policies and practices imposed by people who do not necessarily have their best interests at heart.

Remarkably, often absent from this narrative of neglect and marginalization experienced by low-income students and their families is the tremendous resiliency and creativity of low-income youth and their parents or guardians and teachers who are working with local communities to mitigate educational and societal inequities. We regularly are stunned by the great things teachers and schools are doing in partnership with low-income families despite growing class sizes, the imposition of rote pedagogical models in high-poverty schools, teach-to-the-test mandates, and the denigration of the teaching profession. We are inspired by the passionate engagement of poor and working-class families who, despite the popular notion that they don't care about school, are standing up for the rights of their children. And we are energized by low-income youth who are voicing their concerns, demanding better school conditions. Gaps are closing, art is flourishing, some schools are becoming service sites where students are fed three meals a day, and graduation rates are improving. All this is happening, we're afraid, in a somewhat piecemeal fashion as teachers and administrators scrape together resources or receive grants, but the word is getting out about some of these small victories despite the odds.

Still, we are disheartened by the popular deficit-laden perception of students from low-income families. It sometimes can feel as though those of us who believe that poor and working-class students bring resiliency, creativity, compassion, and amazing energy to schools are in the minority. We hear from teachers in high-poverty schools who want to incorporate art and music into their curricula as a way to motivate students and encourage complex thinking—a strategy that research clearly shows can be highly effective for low-income students—only to be told their ideas are not appropriate for "those kids." We have heard from teachers and school-level administrators attempting to create, in high-poverty neighborhoods, schools that are centered around project-based and other student-centered learning—based on research demonstrating the effectiveness of dialogic pedagogies when it comes to engaging (and even increasing those pesky test scores of) low-income students. Unfortunately, in many cases their ideas are squelched by state administrators who declare, against decades of scholarship to the contrary, that poor children need rigid and what we would describe as militarized schooling focused on regimented math and reading instruction. Just as often, though, we hear from teachers and administrators who are finding ways within their spheres of influence to do amazing educational things with low-income kids and their communities. This book is full of examples of students being taught to think and act and advocate for themselves, of low-income parents and guardians organizing to advocate for better schools for their children, of youth and teachers together researching and responding to economic injustice in their own communities.

In essence, the purpose of *The Poverty and Education Reader: A Call for Equity in Many Voices* is twofold. First, the authors whose chapters fill these pages roundly reject the deficit view of low-income youth and families. We are very conscious of the popularity of books and workshops that, purposefully or not, support a deficit view by suggesting that we fix educational disparities by fixing poor and working-class people. We have gathered here chapters ranging from personal narratives and poetry to syntheses of research on poverty and schooling that, together, demonstrate the destructiveness of the deficit view. Part of this focus includes raising questions about the efficacy of policies and practices, from No Child Left Behind to tracking, that have had disastrous effects on our schools, especially for low-income students.

Second, and just as important, when we imagined the possibilities for this book, we wanted most of all to provide space for the voices of people who have lived in poverty or who have worked directly with low-income youth and who are involved in local initiatives for educational equity. Rather than responding to the deficit view purely from a philosophical or theoretical place, we were determined to include counterstories from people who know the strain of poverty and the resilience of low-income communities.

This is not an academic book—not in the traditional sense, at least. It is driven, most of all, by on-the-ground narratives. Contributors were urged to write for a broad audience of teachers, administrators, public school advocates, and other people who are on the ground, knee-deep in the day-to-day muckiness of public schooling. However, we were careful, as well, to ask contributors to provide evidence for their arguments so that nearly every point about poverty and schooling made in this book is supported by at least one personal narrative and at least one reference to research findings that illuminate authors' suggestions for realizing educational equity. No stone was left unturned. Teach for America, charter schools, direct instruction, the popular "culture of poverty" view of poor people, educational funding: Questions are raised about all of this and more in these pages. And the broadness of the range of issues covered in this book is similar to that of the range of voices and genres of the chapters. We have included memoir chapters from people who grew up poor in Appalachia and from those who grew up poor in cities and towns, all of whom were marginalized by school. Also represented are analyses of how schools are funded, of how race and poverty interact, of the perceptions of people who never knew what it is like to work with their hands, and of the curricula that, for better or for worse, are used in some high-poverty classrooms.

We recognize, of course, that it can be very easy to criticize—to list all of the ways in which schools disenfranchise low-income families. Our most important commitment as we imagined this book, then, was to balance every criticism or concern with a recommendation or vision. Nearly every chapter in this book contains on-the-ground strategies for mitigating the effects of educational inequality on low-income students and families.

Having said that, we are under no illusion about the enormity of what is needed to restructure schools and educational opportunity to be truly equitable. We know that there are some teachers who do not belong in classrooms and should be counseled out of the profession. However, in our experience, this would be relatively few teachers, so school "reform" efforts that focus largely on nudging out rather than empowering teachers tend to be less about improving teaching than about diverting attention from the underlying causes of outcome inequalities, such as unequal school funding. We know that corporate billionaires and the politicians whose campaigns they finance, for-profit organizations, and other power brokers have their hands in educational policy, and more, and are driving the administration of public education. We also know that some of these individuals and agencies appear intent on undermining the whole idea of public education. Others are oblivious to the challenges faced by communities from which low-income students come, yet they believe that they know best how to structure schools to ensure that no child is left behind. Yet others advocate this or that magic bullet—the one program or strategy that will close the opportunity gap, whether it be charter schools, alternative paths to licensure that circumvent teacher education programs, homeschooling, or new, clever forms of tracking.

We also are not under any illusion that a single program or policy or pedagogy can undo the inequity in access to basic resources like health care experienced by low-income families, nor do we believe that teachers ought to be held responsible for counteracting larger societal inequities. But we do believe that there are students and teachers, principals and social workers, organizers and city council members who have important and relevant ideas for challenging and changing the disparities they see in their communities.

In the end, *The Poverty and Education Reader* is our modest attempt to provide a platform to those creative and committed voices, a place where students, teachers, and other people dedicated to educational equity are in conversation with one another in the voices and genres they choose for the task at hand. It is a collection of poems, memoirs, research, and wonderfully odd and poignant combinations of the three—a compendium of lived experiences, deep reflections, and thoughtful recommendations. We see the fruits of the contributors' labors as a frame within which we might plot and create the conditions for children to succeed and dream in the spaces that comprise our spheres of influence, no matter the income level of their parents or the color of their skin, even as we recognize the need to expand those spheres.

Previewing the Remainder of *The Poverty and Education Reader*

This book is organized into six parts, each of which includes chapters from a wide variety of contributors writing in a wide variety of genres. The parts are roughly thematic, although many of chapters quite easily could have been placed into multiple sections.

Part One, which we titled "Counterstories: Insiders' Views on Poverty and Schooling," consists of one poem and six first-person narratives from people who have experienced school as low-income students. Notably, each of the authors with a chapter in this section later became a teacher, several choosing to teach in high-poverty schools.

In Part Two, "Identifying the 'Problem': From a Deficit View to a Resiliency View," contributors challenge deficit-laden perceptions of low-income students head-on, often by pointing to the gifts and resiliency that poor and working-class families—often the authors' *own* families—bring to school.

Contributors to Part Three, "Making Class Inequity Visible," uncover the social and school conditions against which low-income families demonstrate resilience, from unequal access to high-quality curricula and pedagogies to unjust school and social policies.

Chapters in Part Four, "Insisting on Equity: Students, Parents, and Communities Fight for Justice," challenge the popular assumption that poor and working-class families do not value education by highlighting students' and families' demands for educational equity. This section also contains recommendations from students and families on how to get us there.

Part Five, "Teaching for Class Equity and Economic Justice," contains practical strategies and approaches for effectively teaching low-income students, including ideas for how to teach *about* poverty and economic justice.

Finally, in Part Six, "Poverty, Education, and the Trouble With School 'Reform,'" contributors raise important questions about the diversionary nature of many popular "reform" initiatives that, as they explain, are deteriorating, rather than improving, schools in high-poverty communities.

PART ONE

Counterstories
Insiders' Views on Poverty and Schooling

FIRST GRADE LESSON

Sandy Nesbit Tracy

Rain left a puddle in the schoolyard—
shiny, flat water reflecting tall green trees
and two-story red brick building
in Springdale, Arkansas, in 1951.

That September morning dawned cool.
I wore a flour-sack dress my mother made,
white socks handed down from my sisters,
too-small brown sandals with buckled straps.

Margaret and Connie were in the yard
in their store-bought dresses with white collars.
Margaret's was pale pink with a ruffle;
Connie's was light blue and yellow plaid.
Margaret's socks were pink;
Connie's were blue with yellow flowers.
They both wore new saddle shoes.

"Walk through the puddle," they dared me.
I hesitated.
"Watch us—we'll walk through the water."
I watched.

I started walking through the water.
The cold wet soaked into my socks.
The bell rang.
Margaret and Connie hurried away.
I lagged behind.

Slosh, slosh, slosh sounded my
wet socks in my sandals.

"Sandra, why are your socks all wet?"
said Miss Jean Clinkscales,
tall, thin teacher of first and second grade.

"I walked through the puddle in the front yard.
Margaret and Connie told me to."

Miss Jean looked down at me.
My face burned.
"They did it, too."

Miss Jean sniffed.
"It's all right for Margaret and Connie
to walk through the puddle.
See how substantial their shoes are.
But you—[she sniffed again]
you only have on those flimsy sandals.
Now take off your socks."

I unbuckled my sandals and pulled off
the muddy wet socks.

Miss Jean gingerly picked them up
and hung them on top of the tall windows
above the blinds
for all to see.

2

ON LILACS, TAP-DANCING, AND CHILDREN OF POVERTY

Bobby Ann Starnes

Every spring, I turn over a new leaf (so to speak), vowing that *this* year I will garden. Last Saturday, the warm sunshine and light breeze made it the perfect day to make good on this year's promise. So I donned my rubber gardening shoes, pulled out my color-coordinated gardening tools, and headed out to plant flowers along the bank of the creek that runs through my yard. I suppose that in the spirit of full disclosure I should say that "creek" is the word my landlord uses to describe the little stream of muddy water. A cartographer would more likely refer to it as a drainage ditch. Whichever name is more accurate, I'd decided to plant day lilies along its bank. I dug carefully spaced holes to exactly the depth prescribed by the planting instructions and then packed dirt around each flower. After repeating the process several times, I stood to admire my work. Looking at the meager amount of work completed and pondering all the holes yet to be dug, I wondered why I had ever thought this was a good idea. Just then, something brought me to an abrupt stop.

It was the lilacs. A gentle wind had carried their aroma across the creek. Seemingly overnight the buds had transformed from the promise of bloom into full, thick blossoms. As my lungs filled, my body sank to the ground, and I closed my eyes and gave myself over to the lilacs' magic. I was transported back in time and found myself standing in front of the three-room tar-paper house on Ottello Avenue where I grew up.

It was not a happy place, and I was not a happy child. Life was full of extremes—too many people in too little space, never enough to go around, but far too much for a child to experience far too soon. There was little safety to be found on Ottello Avenue. But there were the lilac bushes. It was safe there.

About four feet from our house, a long row of lilac bushes separated our yard from our neighbor's. Those lilacs flourished there where it seemed nothing else could. Untended, their branches grew wildly and, heavy with blooms, drooped to the ground, creating a hideaway for two young children. There, surrounded by thick, rich lilac bushes, my brother and I spent long days immune to all that occurred outside their boundaries.

My mother worked all night in the fireworks factory, and my father worked all day operating an elevator in the local General Motors plant. Their schedules left my brother and me on our own. Long before the term *latchkey* was invented, we took care of ourselves from early morning until late in the evening.

The image of that house was hard for me to revisit, but the lilac bushes reached out for me and invited me inside. My imagination pulled a lilac-laden branch aside, and I peeked in. That's when my mind gave me the gift of a memory so real it was as though I could reach out and touch it. I could see us, my brother, Tom, and me, there in all our childish glory. My blond hair jutted out wildly, as was its tendency, especially on mornings when I couldn't find a comb to provide its curls at least some guidance. And there was Tommy standing shirtless and barefoot, his blond hair cut close to his head, his cotton shorts twisted crookedly around his waist. I smiled at the memory. He was always such a dork. Yet Tommy was a remarkable person. At 4, he was a regular reader of Superman comic books and could reasonably explain how archenemy Mr. Mxyzptlk traveled from the fifth dimension to torment the Man of Steel. As for me, well, I had managed to finish the first grade without learning to read much of anything. But I had other skills. One was preparing escape routes.

On that day, we were deeply engaged in one of my favorite escape scenarios—the Hollywood discovery. I'd heard stories of people like us who were just minding their own business when a talent scout happened upon them and bing-bang-boom, those people were rich and famous. I wanted us to be ready when the scout showed up on our little street in Dayton, Ohio.

Tommy and I held long sticks that we called canes, and we were deep in conversation. His eyes were sharp and clear, and his attention was focused completely on me as I choreographed the dance we would perform for the talent scout. As I enthusiastically pointed my "cane" here and there, Tommy nodded his head obediently. My brilliant plan fully articulated, we began.

Standing side by side, we wildly twirled and whirled. And as we tap-danced ourselves into a frenzy—or did what we thought was tap-dancing—we began to sing a song we had practiced hundreds of times before. It was our song, and we knew every word.

"Oh, we ain't got a barrel of money," we sang more loudly than well. "Maybe we're ragged and funny. But we'll travel along, singin' a song, side by side." I watched with anticipation for the big finish I knew was coming. "Through all kinds of weather," we sang in unison as we planted our canes firmly on the ground in front of us and came to a hard stop in our routine.

"But, Bobby," Tommy said seriously, "what if the sky should fall?"

"Oh, Tommy," I replied in feigned amusement. Then we sang the last line together with all the gusto we could muster: "As long as we're together, you know it really doesn't matter at all." We ended our song and dance with the two of us standing, legs apart, bent at the waist, our chins resting on the top of our canes.

"Oh, it was beautiful," we told ourselves, certain that when we were discovered, our performance would delight audiences everywhere. But we did not rest on our laurels. We practiced over and over again for days and weeks to come—two barefoot children together, hidden from a hard world under the lilac bushes.

The future had seemed so distant, but the dream of a better life sustained us. I thought Tom and I would always be side by side, but a few years back, the sky did fall when Tom died unexpectedly.

As I thought about those two children and what lay ahead of them, my mind drifted to a conversation I'd had with Marsha, a teacher friend, after she attended a Ruby Payne workshop. Ruby Payne wrote the highly popular and heavily criticized *Framework for Understanding Poverty* and parlayed it and the ideas it espouses into a highly lucrative consulting business. Today she and those who work for her offer hundreds of workshops for teachers, administrators, and community members around the country every year.

I remembered Marsha telling me that the workshop had changed everything for her. At last she understood something about the children she had been teaching for more than 26 years. Her students' families experience extreme financial stress and are of a cultural and ethnic minority. Having grown up in a middle-class, White family, Marsha has always struggled to understand the community, families, and children she teaches and has always been frustrated that she could not. Still, she has always tried. Marsha tells me she has even prayed for understanding.

I suppose it shouldn't be surprising that Marsha and teachers like her are seduced by Payne. She promises clarity—a clarity even Marsha's prayers have failed to deliver. And it is so simple. Payne has mapped out all the strategies for Marsha. The trick, Payne's approach says, is to teach children in poverty to play by middle-class rules. So if Marsha follows Payne's directions, she can "solve the problem" of poverty and the families who live in it. All she has to do is to "un-teach" the "hidden rules of poverty" that prevent her kids from succeeding. Why wouldn't Marsha try? She really loves the kids she teaches. She wants their lives to be richer, fuller, less troubled. If only it were that easy.

Much has been written about Payne's work. Critics point out that she never addresses the unequal education poor kids receive and that she preaches a deficit model. We don't have to change society or schooling—just poor people. Sitting there on the bank, I realized that my real concern about this message is that it never could account for those two tap-dancing children, the promise that existed for their futures, or the ways we could help them prepare. I don't recognize the families Payne uses as "case studies" in her books, except as the stereotypes I have fought most of my life.

The thing is, I told myself, economic distress and the situations it creates are as varied and complex as the children who experience them. In the place where

I grew up, no one expected children to leave the neighborhood. Teachers knew—or thought they knew—what we needed, and they were determined to guide us along their path of low expectations. Fortunately for Tom and me, we didn't know that our future had been mapped out for us. We were lucky that way.

Payne seems to say that the best thing we can do is teach poor kids to act middle class. If we can only "fix" them, then the world will open up for them. But the real fix lies not in the children but in the inequalities and societal norms that prevent children from having equal access. In the small world of our class-rooms, we can get to know our children as complex individuals living unique lives and help them to build *their* dreams and achieve *their* goals, not—as Payne suggests—our middle-class expectations of success.

Lost in my thoughts, with clarity seemingly only moments away, I was snapped back into the present by the phone ringing in my kitchen. Many more day lilies needed my attention, but I'd had enough. I picked up my gardening tools and headed toward the house. "So much for that new leaf," I thought. "No wonder I don't do this more often." But after a few steps, I ignored the phone and walked across the creek to the lilac bush, gathered a branch laden with blooms into my arms, and buried my face into its blossoms. And for just an instant, it was as though I were hugging Tommy once more in the safety of our lilac fortress.

Note

Reprinted with permission of Phi Delta Kappa International, www.pdkintl. org. All rights reserved. Starnes, B. A. (2008). On lilacs, tap-dancing, and children of poverty. *Phi Delta Kappan, 89*(10), 779–780.

3

CLASS, RACE, AND THE HIDDEN CURRICULUM OF SCHOOLS

Buffy Smith

My students rarely out themselves as being poor. You could not tell they struggle financially by the papers they turn in to me or by what they say when we discuss things in my sociology classes at the University of St. Thomas. During office hours, however, students reveal to me that they grew up poor, and often they tell me that they are the first person from their family to go to college. They talk about the social distance they feel from their peers who have money. They tell me they often hang out with other poor students to avoid being reminded of what they simply don't have. Many low-income students do not own cars. They are less likely to dine at off-campus restaurants or to have an entire wardrobe of brand-name clothes. They do not go to vacation resorts on spring break. They get tired of being reminded of these differences when they are with wealthier students.

The same unease students feel with their more affluent peers can transfer over to their professors. They may not reach out to their professors when they are performing poorly in the class, fearing that they will be judged as lacking in the ability to succeed in school.

Starting in kindergarten, schools rarely reward poor students for the qualities they bring to their schools: their perseverance, compassion, flexibility, patience, and creativity, just to name a few. Instead they are judged on qualities determined by dominant cultural norms: the attitudes, preferences, tastes, mannerisms, and abilities valued by a system that never was designed to meet their needs (Apple, 1982, 1990). They find themselves at a disadvantage in such a system, and this extends into college experiences. Their teachers and college professors rarely reward them for their diversity of attitudes, preferences, tastes, mannerisms, and abilities or encourage them to draw on their own experiences to achieve in school. Social justice is rarely a subject introduced as part of their education.

The Unrecognized Strength of My Home

My own story provides an example of the complex way such a situation plays out in schools. My older brother and I grew up in a single-parent household.

I was shaped and nurtured by my mother and grandmother. My mother graduated from a Mississippi high school, and while she eventually earned a certificate in early childhood education from a community college in Milwaukee, she primarily worked at jobs that paid minimum wage. My grandmother, who had only a sixth-grade education, was a former sharecropper and domestic servant in Mississippi. They raised me to respect adults and people in authority. I was socialized to say "ma'am" and "sir" when addressing my elders. I was a quiet and shy child, and for the most part, I followed adults' instructions and rules. In this way I was raised to be compliant, one element of the hidden curriculum in our schools. This insistence on compliance is also one aspect of schooling that keeps some students from feeling they can challenge the very structures that repress them. They often feel silenced and alienated from public education at an early age.

In my household, we did not have many books. I believe my lack of books contributed to my below average reading test scores. In third grade I was reading at a second-grade level. Research indicates that social class can influence cognitive abilities because a lack of money results in fewer experiences at museums and traveling, fewer books in the home, and less access to preschool education (Bowles & Gintis, 2002; Good & Brophy, 1987). My teacher, Ms. Skinner, recommended that my mother make sure I read during the summer to improve my skills. My mother responded by taking me to the public library every week during the summer. She made sure I read three or four books each week. She also purchased a set of encyclopedias and dictionaries for our home. The following year, I was placed in the fourth-grade-reading-level class. This is what I brought to school: the support of a strong, persistent mother and grandmother. In descriptions of poor children, such remarkable families are rarely mentioned. They run counter to the deficit descriptions of poverty educators are used to hearing.

My mother and grandmother instilled in me a faith in God. They provided me with an abundance of love. But there were some things they simply could not do to prepare me to succeed in a public school geared toward middle-class and wealthier students.

The Complexity of Racism and Classism

As a youth, I was psychologically equipped to confront racism in school. I was taught by my mother to stand up for myself when people used racial slurs. She consistently reminded my brother and me that we should never feel inferior because of the color of our skin. However, I was not adequately prepared to address classism in the education system. There was no pride in being poor. In fact, I did not know anyone who marched in the streets with their fist in the air saying, "Poor is beautiful." I loved being Black, but I hated being poor.

In my early years, I was bussed with other Black students to a predominantly White school in order to further integration. For the first time, I noticed racial and class differences. Most of us who were bussed received "free lunch" tickets. White students made jokes about Black students being poor and wearing off-brand clothes and shoes. I also heard my White "friend" Steve call Rebecca, another Black girl, a "nigger." I asked why he called Rebecca a nigger. He responded, "Because she is one, but don't worry, Buffy, you are not, you are Black." The only distinction between Rebecca and me that I can remember is that Rebecca would speak loudly. She hung out exclusively with the other few Black students in school. Although I socialized with both Black and White students, I self-identified as "Black." After the name-calling, and after I realized the students who were not compliant and submissive were the ones who were ridiculed, I questioned my friendships with White students.

According to some scholars, the school system privileges individuals who comply with dominant culture, like that of middle-class and upper-middle-class teachers, professional staff, and administrators (Bourdieu, 1984, 1986; Bourdieu & Passeron, 1990; Musoba & Baez, 2009). Bourdieu suggests that these privileges are likely to be based less on merit or hard work than on the cultural attitudes, behaviors, norms, and values of dominant groups. Because Rebecca was assertive and independent, she was penalized. And of course her race made her an especially easy target. It is when these two come together that we see how poverty and race intermingle to marginalize students. Low-income students are more likely to achieve positive educational outcomes (e.g., passing test scores or graduating) once their strengths are recognized, affirmed, and rewarded to the same degree that their middle-class peers' are. Because I was respectful and did not disagree with or challenge other students or educators, teachers accepted me. I was one of the "good ones." My compliance and obedience were rewarded with good grades.

However, there were things about the hidden curriculum that became more relevant in high school. My African American teacher had suggested I take an honors class in ninth grade. The majority of the students in the class were White. Only one other person of color, a Black male, was in the class. As I listened to students talk about the different places they visited during their summer vacations, I felt more and more out of place and uncomfortable. I made eye contact with and smiled at some students, but no one reached out to me. Suddenly a short, stout, White woman approached me, introduced herself as Ms. Hill, and stated she was happy I was in her class. She introduced me to the class, directing their attention my way, and asked the students to introduce themselves to me.

As class went along Ms. Hill called on different individuals to read aloud passages from a text. Next, she asked us to analyze the passages and look for larger social meanings in them. I was uncomfortable speaking out because I did not want to make dumb comments. During the second week of school,

Ms. Hill said she wanted me to come see her during my lunch hour. Immediately, I thought I was going to be kicked out of the honors class. As I entered the room, she warmly smiled and invited me to sit in a chair near her desk. She asked me if I liked her class, and I quietly told her it was a good class. Then, she told me she believed I belonged in the class, and she wanted me to start participating in discussions. I promised to do my best. She was instructing me in a part of the hidden curriculum, that speaking up in class is important for my success.

To my own surprise, I raised my hand the next day. Ms. Hill smiled. She appreciated my remarks and agreed with many of my comments. Some of the students also remarked that they shared my perspective. After class Ms. Hill gave me a nod and wink and said, "Good job." I continued to participate in class and received Bs and B+s on my written assignments.

Ms. Hill invited me again to come to her office during my lunch period. She wanted to let me know that she noticed my progress. She also invited me to come see her any time to talk about school issues or other concerns.

Although I did not easily open up to people, I talked with her about my fears and challenges in school. I shared with her my self-doubt about my academic abilities. I also revealed to her my shame in being poor, that I shared a bedroom with my mother, and that we did not have a car. I told her I felt driven to succeed in school. I trusted her and shared stories with her I never had shared with anyone outside of my family and closest friends. I finally had found a teacher who really liked "all" of me. Ms. Hill invited me to eat my lunch in her office two or three times a week. We talked about what I needed to do to prepare for college. She promised to write a letter to the National Honor Society for me. She said that she would make a phone call to her friends in the admissions office on my behalf if I attended her alma mater, a private liberal arts college for women. She was walking me through the hidden curriculum step-by-step. From her I learned about recommendations, college essays, and making connections.

All this time I was becoming more and more comfortable in the honors class. Ms. Hill's approval and excitement over my reflections made the other students in the class acknowledge my existence. The honors students never became my friends—my friends were in nonhonors classes—but they were cordial to me.

Class and Race Together Complicate This Narrative

Unfortunately, toward the middle of the school year, all this changed. We had begun reading Mark Twain's *The Adventures of Huckleberry Finn*. The class started as usual with Ms. Hill selecting passages for students to read aloud. It appeared to me that most of the passages she selected used the word *nigger* in them. Every time one of my classmates read the passages and said "nigger,"

I became angry. I do not know if it was the tone in their voice or the fact that they would look at me before or after they said the "N word," but it made me uncomfortable and furious.

Finally I felt compelled to say something. I raised my hand and asked Ms. Hill, "Why do we have to read a book with the 'N word' in it?" She remarked that it was an American classic. I stated that just because it is a classic does not make it okay to use the "N word." I also suggested that if we must read the text, we could refer to it as the "N word." Ms. Hill gave me a long stare and then looked away shaking her head. She instructed the class to read what was written. When it was my turn to read a passage, I skipped over all the "N words."

Ms. Hill's face and neck were red, and her eyes were full of disappointment and anger. I did not know why she was angry with me. I had simply expressed my opinion about the use of racist language. She had trained us to analyze literature, and that is what I thought I was doing.

The next day, Ms. Hill did not warmly greet me at the beginning of class. I raised my hand, and she called on me last. When I shared my perspective, she was noticeably silent. She had something positive to say about everyone else's comments but mine. Soon this treatment became the new norm. I stopped meeting with her during my lunch periods. As weeks passed, Ms. Hill never gave me praise, so I became silent again. This time my silence did not matter to my classmates or Ms. Hill. No one cared. I was invisible to them. My class participation declined, as did my grades. I once was perceived as a promising college-bound student, but now I was treated as a dumb kid. I questioned whether I was academically ready for college. If I could not do well in my honors class, how could I succeed in college? I wonder whether one of the more privileged students would have been celebrated as assertive for raising the same concerns that resulted in me being seen as a troublemaker.

Lessons Learned From Ms. Hill's Class

Today, when I reflect on Ms. Hill's class, I realize that I simply did not know one of the most important aspects of the hidden curriculum: build social capital with teachers, guidance counselors, and other professional staff. If I had established a strong mentoring relationship with Mrs. Locket, who had referred me to the honors class in the first place, and with others in the building, they could have given me advice on how to handle the situation with Ms. Hill. They could also have used their relationships with Ms. Hill to advocate for me. But I can't help but wonder why this was left up to me. I was left vulnerable to a teacher who had seemed to understand me. What does this say about barriers many poor students face in our schools—that they are left to the mercy of whatever teacher happens to connect with them?

I could have approached Ms. Hill in private to express my concerns about the book instead of raising them in public. I could have talked with Ms. Hill about ways to improve my grades. But because I did not understand the hidden curriculum, I did what many young people do when they feel disconnected from their teachers: I became disengaged from the learning process. In my case the combination of race and class informed my situation. For others it may be assertive behavior related to issues of poverty that lead to teachers or administrators admonishing them. This is a dangerous reality for poor students who need support from their teachers in order to advocate for themselves and for economic justice.

Teachers can play a major role in helping students feel engaged and connected to their learning communities. First, we need to make the invisible visible—to unveil the hidden curriculum. And more important, we need to encourage students and colleagues to question the legitimacy of the hidden curriculum itself.

I was a student who would have benefited from strong academic mentoring. I did not know what I did not know. I was subject to an establishment that did not value what I *did* know: my resiliency, my outspokenness, and my other strengths.

Recommendations for My Fellow Teachers

Numerous educators, scholars, and activists support the idea that schools have a responsibility to help students acquire the cultural capital and social capital they need to achieve academic success (Arriaza, 2003; Collier & Morgan, 2008; Henningsen, Valde, Russell, & Russell, 2011; Lareau & Weininger, 2003; Smith, 2013). Many schools do an adequate job of sharing academic requirements and policies with all students, including those who are poor. The best schools provide an instructional curriculum in which students see themselves and in which students learn not just from teachers but also from adults and activists from the local community. Students in these schools feel valued for their ideas, attitudes, and skills.

Unfortunately too few schools prepare their students to understand and navigate the hidden curriculum. They rarely provide poor youth with the connections and resources to which wealthier students have access simply because they were born with money.

Starting where we are and on the basis of my lived experiences, teaching, and research, I offer the following recommendations for mitigating these disparities.

1. Elementary and secondary administrators have a responsibility to become cognizant of the hidden curriculum and to help teachers learn to identify it and understand its implications. Time and resources should be allocated not only to learning the concept but also to helping students become aware of it and how it operates.

2. We should incorporate into our teaching the assets low-income students bring to school. If poor students' resilience, flexibility, and persistence toward a goal is affirmed and integrated into the school culture, students would not drop out at the rate they do.

3. One approach to reducing structural inequality in schools is to create an activist mentoring culture in which educators model the practice of questioning and challenging the status quo. While mentors work to bolster students' academic skills, they also can be role models of activism and hope in their communities. Teachers could learn from the mentors as well, developing collaborative relationships with them. They could develop creative role-playing exercises, allowing students to develop the ability to feel comfortable in situations where they previously have been uncomfortable. Spoken-word poetry, neighborhood projects, and even political advocacy can be ways to build confidence and inspire hope for justice and real change.

4. Parents have to be an integral part of the mentoring process. They can reinforce the skills students learn at school and provide important information to teachers about the strengths of their sons and daughters. For their part teachers can help parents to help their children access scholarships and funding for summer programs and other opportunities many do not know about because they have been left out of the information loop.

In conclusion, if we do not intentionally unveil the hidden advantages that middle-class and upper-class students have over their low-income peers, we run the risk of indirectly reinforcing these inequalities in our classrooms. Many of us enter the teaching profession to challenge the status quo. Then we get swept up in rules and mandates and procedures, and we lose sight of why we went down this road in the first place. It takes courage to go on our own in a system that perpetuates itself at the expense of poor students. But not challenging this, not aligning ourselves with the strengths of the communities and neighborhoods from where our students come, is going back on our own moral center. It is, in the end, a civic responsibility to ensure that all students have opportunities to imagine lives of great hope.

Notes

1. The names of all the students and teachers are pseudonyms.
2. I provide more detailed research on the hidden curriculum, cultural capital, social capital, and mentoring process in my book *Mentoring At-Risk Students Through the Hidden Curriculum of Higher Education* (Lanham, MD: Lexington Books, 2013).

References

Apple, M. (1982). *Education and power.* New York: Routledge.

Apple, M. (1990). *Ideology and curriculum* (2nd ed.). New York: Routledge.

Arriaza, G. (2003). Schools, social capital, and children of color. *Race, Ethnicity and Education, 6,* 71–94.

Bourdieu, P. (1984). *Distinction: A social critique of the judgment of taste* (R. Nice, Trans.). Cambridge, MA: Harvard University Press.

Bourdieu, P. (1986). The forms of capital. In J. G. Richardson (Ed.), *Handbook of theory and research for the sociology of education* (pp. 241–258). New York: Greenwood.

Bourdieu, P., & Passeron, J.-C. (1990). *Reproduction in education, society and culture.* Beverly Hills, CA: Sage.

Bowles, S., & Gintis, H. (2002). *Schooling in Capitalist America* revisited. *Sociology of Education, 75,* 1–18.

Collier, P., & Morgan, D. (2008). "Is that paper really due today?" Differences in first-generation and traditional college students' understandings of faculty expectations. *Higher Education, 55,* 425–446.

Good, T., & Brophy, J. (1987). *Looking in classrooms.* New York: Harper & Row.

Henningsen, M., Valde, K., Russell, G. A., & Russell, G. R. (2011). Student-faculty interactions about disappointing grades: Application of the goals-plans-actions model and the theory of planned behavior. *Communication Education, 60*(2), 174–190.

Lareau, A., & Weininger, E. (2003). Cultural capital in educational research: A critical assessment. *Theory and Society, 32,* 567–606.

Musoba, G., & Baez, B. (2009). The cultural capital of cultural and social capital: An economy of translations. In J. Smart (Ed.), *Higher education: Handbook of theory and research* (p. 24). New York: Agathon.

Smith, B. (2013). *Mentoring at-risk students through the hidden curriculum of higher education.* Lanham, MD: Lexington Books.

4

HOW SCHOOL TAUGHT ME I WAS POOR

Jeff Sapp

"You're poor, White trash," Danny hissed as he sashayed by me on the dusty, pebble-filled playground at first recess. I started to cry, and I remember that Phillip laughed and said, "He's crying like someone just threw dirt in his eyes." And that's exactly what it felt like being told you're poor without being ready for it. I had no idea—absolutely no inkling whatsoever—that I'd spent the last eight years in poverty.

I grew up in West Virginia, where the entire state looks like a national park. And I grew up playing barefoot in rich, old-growth Appalachian forests. A feral child. Maybe growing up around such beauty, you believe you *are* rich. Danny's pejorative term, though, would be only the first inkling of what was to come. But I'll never forget that Danny started it in third grade. Third grade was a bad year. Third grade was the year I learned in school that I was poor.

The "Vorce"

I remember in elementary school when Ricky walked passed me in the hallway and hissed, "My mom says you're divorced and you don't have a father and that you're poor, White trash." I didn't know what "the vorce" was, but it sounded bad to me.

You learn in fourth-grade West Virginia history that Mother's Day was founded in Grafton, West Virginia, on May 10, 1908, and Father's Day in Fairmont, West Virginia, on July 5, 1908. But I learned in school that a father was simply one more thing that other children had that I didn't. And I learned fast that making Father's Day cards was awful. I made them silently, then obediently took them home and gave them to my bewildered mother.

Because of Ricky, I felt self-conscious about doing the family tree assignment. Everyone else's tree had beautiful, perfectly symmetrical limbs on it, a father limb and a mother limb. My fatherless tree only had a mother limb on one side, and it looked like those pine trees on top of Pikes Peak, where the wind had whipped all the limbs onto one side. My tree wasn't whole.

It wasn't until I got to seventh grade and had to take shop class that I realized how important it was to have the prerequisite of a father. What did I know of hammers and tools and woodworking? I grew timid and unsure of myself in shop class. I made the smallest project you could choose, a little kitchen match-book holder. No sturdy shelves or benches for me. I still have it to this very day, wrapped in my first-grade elf costume and tucked away in a box full of memories of school and of being poor.

Happy Holidays

It seemed fun at first. We were all given the same materials to make our valentines bags. White bags, pink and red hearts, ribbons and streamers, and, of course, the elementary staple, glitter. After the giant globs of Elmer's glue dried, all of the bags looked pretty similar. I felt good about this holiday.

Mom bought me a pack of valentines, and I carefully read each one to be sure that it went to exactly the right person. But the next day at school, the joy became pain when I saw the beautiful cards and candies that some of the other classmates brought. It made me feel like Charlie Brown. Somehow everyone else knows you're poor. How is that? You feel so different, alone, ashamed, and at a total loss of what to do about this "lack of."

Christmas was no better. I knew that our teacher would open her gifts in front of everyone. How could my hand-drawn picture of a snowman hold up against Crystal's store-bought sweater or the fancy bottle of perfume from Lois? Sometimes I would be "sick" on the day we had to bring our favorite holiday gift to school for show-and-tell. Besides the fact that I'd already eaten most of my little book of Lifesavers, I knew that the other boys would have robots that moved or race car tracks. I couldn't compete. I may as well have stood up and said, "We're poor, and a nice man from church brings us candy."

At Halloween I wore overalls and a red plaid shirt with hay coming out of my shirt. A lifeless scarecrow of a child, I was no match for the beautiful costumes purchased at local stores.

Over and over and over again, holidays seemed an endless curriculum review of how I couldn't afford what the other children brought to school. My worst school holiday memory by far, though, was Easter.

The Nobel Peace Egg

"We're going to have an Easter egg decorating contest," declared my teacher. "There'll be prizes awarded for the best decorated egg." Only a third grader would think this the equivalent of the Nobel Peace Prize. I begged my mother for the 99-cent Easter egg coloring materials. I pulled a stool up to the stove and watched patiently as my egg boiled. You've got to be hard-boiled to win the Nobel Peace Prize.

I carefully studied my color options. It seemed to me that red, white, and blue were my best choices. Like the flag, patriotic. I mixed the colors myself, and then I measured and penciled two lines that split my egg into thirds. I held the first third of the egg in the red dye with the little copper wire holder myself for what seemed like hours. Next, I held it until it dried. Then I turned the egg upside down and held a third of it in blue dye. This took an entire evening.

My egg was spectacular, and I was thrilled to carry it proudly into school the next day. And that's when I saw the other eggs. Danny's egg was dressed exactly like Abraham Lincoln. It had a top hat and a black jacket with a white shirt and stiff paper collar. Its face was painted like a china doll, and it had real hair that had been liberated from a curly-haired sister for a beard and moustache. It had its own little stand. It looked presidential.

I could feel my panic rising. Maybe I had misunderstood the assignment. Even my third-grade mind could tell that parents had helped this Lincoln get elected. I felt immense shame about my red, white, and blue egg. And then I noticed my classmates' response to my sad homemade flag. It was pity, pure and simple. It's the first time I remember feeling shame. After school that day, I threw my red, white, and blue egg into a field on the way home and busted it.

School Photographs

The older you get, the worse it is. In high school the Pences drove a beautiful little yellow Volkswagen to school. They passed me as I walked to school. Both ways. Going and coming. The teenage years are about the right clothes and fitting in, and I had hand-me-downs and felt awkward.

I remember wearing my older brother David's suit for my senior pictures. It hung on me like a droopy Halloween king-sized ghost sheet. It was obvious that it was a borrowed suit of clothing. The shirt collar hung around my neck like a necklace. I felt like a seven year old, playing dress up in the attic with a box of clothes that had been my dad's.

Even in the classroom, I couldn't get away from the sting of high-school poverty. In history when we learned about the Great Depression and the Dust Bowl, a rich student named David started calling me "Dust Bowl" as a nickname. High school algebra taught me that some people are "greater than" and others are "less than."

I didn't have the cultural capital to know where to take a date for dinner before the senior prom. The only restaurant I'd ever been to was McDonald's. In my small town, The Point of View was the fancy restaurant to go to for senior prom. Up on a hill, it overlooked the Ohio River and historical Blennerhasett Island and mansion. It was supposed to be beautiful. That's what I'd heard, anyway. I took my date, Michelle, to Shoney's, mistakenly thinking it was a high-end restaurant. What did I know of high-end restaurants? At Shoney's you had to sit down and a waiter came to your table and served you. I was so nervous that the $5.99 fried shrimp plate was wasted on me.

More Is Caught Than Taught

Imagine my surprise one day to be standing in front of a classroom of students as their teacher, returning to the scene of the crime. Over and over and over again in school I had been cued both verbally and nonverbally that I was poor. I wasn't good enough, I didn't have enough, and what I had was the wrong thing. School projects, holidays, extracurricular activities, and field trips would send a surge of panic through our house because they were yet another expense.

There are other curricula besides the one being verbalized. There are the ones in the hallways with snide remarks from peers, on the playground with put-downs learned from parents, and in the celebration of holidays at school that can completely panic a happy family. More is caught than taught.

Note

This chapter is reprinted with permission from Teaching Tolerance and the Southern Poverty Law Center.

5

THE PLACES WHERE WE LIVE AND LEARN
Mementos From a Working-Class Life

Jaye Johnson Thiel

Time passed and I grew taller, but never overtook the others; and the wrestling court was a place of grief to me, for there were people a year younger who could lift me off the ground. I no longer hoped to be seven feet tall; I wanted a foot even of six. (Renault, 1958, p. 30)

High School Mementos

There it sits on the shelf.

A book.

A reminder.

A little red engine telling me: "You should have done. You should have done."

A novel that now serves as a memento of what I promised myself I would never do again: Give up.

I first checked out the book on July 19, 1990, and again on August 1, 1990. I know this because the date-stamp card from the library still sits regally in its front cover. The book is Mary Renault's *The King Must Die*, with a copyright of 1958, the first book on a long list of summer reading for twelfth-grade AP literature. It still smells like the library, its cover crinkling in my right hand as I type these words with my left, its spine separated from the binding.

I never returned it.

I never read it.

Instead, I drove, with the book sitting shotgun in my white Chevette, dented passenger door tethered shut and broken window duct-taped gingerly, to my high school the day before Open House on a muggy late summer afternoon. The mission? To change my schedule to a regular English class.

A class that wouldn't challenge me.

A class I would pass with ease.

A class where I would reign as the "smart one."

A class that didn't have a book list.

27

It wasn't too difficult to change my class. All I had to do was walk in, ask the counselor to drop AP literature, and have a new course added to my schedule. This new schedule even afforded me the opportunity to take a work-study course so I could go to my food service job of almost four years a little earlier each day. No one questioned me like they did the year before when I wanted to move out of a drafting class into the advanced physiology course. I needed a parent to do that. Not this time. This time, no one cared. I had no intentions of college, had never taken the SAT, and had showed no signs of scholarship material, even though I was in the top 5% of my class. College was an economic luxury we could never afford. My mother, often paralyzed with fear from shyness, never had the time to come to the school, and my dad was never around. I was well under the radar. I was just another working-class girl with a peppered school behavior record and little potential past being popular, cheerleading, and . . . English . . . and . . . literature . . . and . . . composition.

I knew eventually my eleventh-grade English teacher, Mrs. Sculler, and the AP literature teacher, Mrs. Pearson, would find me and scold me for taking the easy road, especially since Mrs. Sculler had pushed for me, a girl not served by the gifted program, to be placed in such an esteemed course. But for now I was safe. Just sign the papers and show up in two days. A means to an end. A way to walk away from the fear and the possibility that I might just live up to Mrs. Sculler's version of who I was: an intelligent girl with potential beyond that of high school. What could I possibly do with that knowledge anyway? Poor Mrs. Sculler! It seems she had more faith in me than I had in myself. But the anticipated nomos of an AP literature class made me uneasy, uncomfortable in my skin, and a bit queasy in my tummy. I wasn't ready to take on that habitus, and no one was there to make me. Not even Mrs. Sculler in the long run.

I spent the year in an English class that was sufficient. I was assigned readings from Chaucer and the Brontë sisters. I wrote pretend college entrance essays and always got into the fake college that was really my high school English class in room 121. I was often the only one in our classroom accepted into this pseudo college. But no one ever encouraged me to write a real essay for a real college. There was no need. I would never go. I could never afford it.

To compound matters, I found myself pregnant by January and spent the rest of the year trying to hide my "indiscretion" from the judgments and the stares as long as I possibly could. But in a few months, I was exposed. Even Mrs. Sculler no longer made eye contact with me when I walked by her room. In fact, she stopped talking to me altogether. I was a disappointment, a lost cause, a waste of talent. Or maybe it was just too painful for her to watch me take a path she had wanted me to avoid. I never asked her. I will probably never know.

Living in the Crease

Let us imagine what it would be like if the history and culture of working-class people were at the center of educational practices. (Zandy, 2001, p. xiii)

There is a crease where I stand, a crease where the academic places and the places where I live fold back onto one another. Sometimes it is a bend of fullness and opportunity. Others a bend where I feel choked and smothered. Today it is the latter as I hover in the front of the room, readying myself to teach.

I stand here—vulnerable—staring out at a sea of faces.

For a brief second, I feel as though I am an imposter, wondering why and how it is I am facilitating this class, thinking the college, the department, must have made a mistake by asking me to take on this role. But before I allow the "not belonging" to crawl back in and usurp my body, I quickly push it away.

"If only I had my book, *The King Must Die*, sitting here beside me," I think to myself and then scoff at how absurd that thought sounds in my head, as if the book has some sort of power that I can't just muster on my own.

I really dislike these moments, and whether they are born out of my working class-ness or my gender-ness or some other -ness I haven't quite pinpointed. I do not know how they continue to sneak in and take over like a virus. All I do know is that I have to overcome the fear quickly, before it swallows me up and spits me out in chewed tiny bits and pieces, spewed all over the classroom floor. It wasn't like this with little ones. There is something so beautiful and accepting that comes with a young heart that always allowed me to feel as if I belonged. But here, with a room full of young adults, I struggle, even though most are half my age.

I call everyone to sit in a circle. Bodies move around the room. I take a breath and assess the faces as this semester's undergraduates settle next to friends. I smile. We begin introductions. I take notes. I listen. This part is easy—until the circle comes back to me. And then it is my turn. Somehow I must bridge this introduction into a lesson about the complex and intricate nature of identities and how we all bring our lives with us into the places where we learn.

I begin to tell my story.

The story of where I am from.

I share my working-class background—the trailer I lived in, the dirt road I lived on, and the winding trajectory I lived through. Things seemingly so simple, yet still so hard to reveal. I speak of my two children, one their age and one a teen—there is no other time when I must be completely aware and in control of my face, my body language as I see people gasp and scrunch faces through vocal reactions.

"But you look so young!"

"I can't believe you have children that age!"

"How old are you?"

I hold my face steady, and through smiling teeth I casually reply, "I look good for my age," and I move on to my point. All students bring the places they live into the places they learn. How can we make sure we open up a space where the two can coexist in dignified and respectful ways? That is the charge I set forth—day one.

The rest of the morning is a blur. Writing exercises, syllabus overviews, and outside readings assigned. I feel a bit raw from the vulnerability I allowed myself to steep in on this first morning of the semester. I always do.

As students leave and I pack up my belongings, I see a straggler, a student waiting in the wings, shuffling feet, seemingly nervous but anxious to speak with me. I make eye contact, and the student walks toward me with a smile.

"You told my story," the student explained.

With a bit of confusion, I responded, "I did?"

"Yes, you did."

This student proceeded to tell me about growing up working class, a rural life, living in a trailer—a connection to the personal that had never been made in the classroom for this student before. That is, until now.

And there it was. The reason why I allow myself to be vulnerable. The reason I must share. The reason why I belong here.

I watch the student walk away, and I exhale with relief—not a large breath but an exhalation nonetheless. There is always one. One student who comes forward and joins the collective working-class voice I try so hard to bring into the places I teach and learn.

It was well into my college career—my PhD program to be exact—before I heard a professor share another story like mine, before I was given working-class authors like Dorothy Allison and bell hooks to read. A new world opened for me in this discovery. Preceding this moment, I didn't know working-class literature existed on shelves, and I certainly didn't know working-class lives and memories existed inside the academy. For the first time, I was given the opportunity to see other lives like my own, and from that point on, it was important for me to make sure I became part of the collective working-class memories that intersect and collide in academic trajectories.

This intersection is important to me for several reasons. One, it opens a space where students with similar experiences are given the opportunity to hear another working-class voice, possibly allowing them to move beyond covering and passing, even if that thread shows itself only in writing and conversations with me. Second, it decenters the privileged voice of middle-class academics and gives attention to that which resides in the surrounding spaces—the lives of those often considered the Other—and begins to encourage future teachers to see children and families, no matter what social class, as possibility rather than problem. Third, it gives me a voice, a space to remain connected to a past, that I felt I needed to shed from my body and toss aside for way too long.

Back to the Book

Now as I look back on my past, I like to believe I could have aced the AP literature course I was supposed to take in high school. I may have even found a way to see my future as something different, something a little less difficult to overcome. If only I had read *The King Must Die* . . . maybe then . . . but even so . . . that wouldn't have changed who I was and where I am from. Was I the obstacle, or was the obstacle my lack of cultural, social, symbolic, and economic capital? I have come to believe it was a little of one and a whole lot of the others.

So, I keep the book where I can see it every single day. Not because I am scared to turn in a book that is over two decades past due. Not because I want to read the book one day (which is a goal I have for the future). I keep it because it serves as a beacon, a silent remembrance of what I could have done—what I should have done, if I had only believed in myself, if I had only lived in the right neighborhood with the right money, if I had only been able to take a chance, if I had only been given the right circumstances, the ones schools seemed to honor the most.

I look at the wide spine of the brown-covered book through the corner of my eyes every day. Sitting on the bookshelf on the way to my front door, it speaks to me in a whisper as I walk by:

Don't give up.

Hold your head up.

You can do it.

You are as good as they are.

You deserve this just as much.

As I write these words, the book is lying face-up to the right of my computer. Soon I will put the book back on the shelf, wedged in between a sign language dictionary and a collection of poems. But for now I will fan the pages across my face and smell the yellowed timeworn sheets as they pass by. I will take time to open the book to random passages in order to read a short line or two. I will remember that feeling of inadequacy from years ago, the same feeling that sneaks up on me week after week, day after day of my entire scholarly life. I allow the novel's pages to quietly blow away the doubt that is stamped in red indelible ink on my brain, like the due date etched in its front cover.

There it sits beside me.

The book.

The reminder.

The little red engine telling me: "Never again. Never again."

Mary Renault's typed text serves as a way to never forget a time when I traded in AP literature books for fast-food menus because anything and everything else was too high on the shelf, just out of my reach.

Being in the Present

We can always find reasons in this world to feel as if we are not good enough. Isn't it time we began to create spaces where students can sit in classrooms and feel fullness as well? As educators, it is our duty, our charge to make certain these spaces exist. We can do this through the books we read, the conversations we share, and the lived experiences we privilege. Being poor is not the problem. The vilification of the poor is. Children who grow up in working-class and working-poor families aren't looking for someone to "fix" them or their lives. They are just looking for a space—no matter how small—to feel as if they can just be enough, be validated, be dignified within the in-between creases, the place where living and learning collide.

References

Renault, M. (1958). *The king must die*. New York: Pantheon.
Zandy, J. (2001). *What we hold in common: An introduction to working-class studies*. New York: The Feminist Press at the City University of New York.

6

ALONE AT SCHOOL

Scot Allen

Have you ever been poor?

I mean really poor; not poor like a college student living on ramen or struggling-artist poor. I mean poor as in working as hard as you can your whole life and still living week to week and check to check. Have you ever been that kind of poor? I have.

When I was a child, we lived in a tin single-wide trailer that my parents bought used when they dropped out of school and got married. The place was cold in the winter, hot in the summer, and I swear you could feel a strong gust of wind when sitting in the living room with all the doors and windows closed. We had no heat other than plug-in heaters and an old propane heater that stunk to high heaven.

No air conditioning.

No telephone.

Most of our family dinners consisted of boxed macaroni and cheap hot dogs.

Still, all in all, life was great. My parents loved me, and I got along with my younger brother. In fact, the biggest downside to being poor was that my mom and dad had to work really hard.

My parents worked at the local textile mill. My mom got a job there when I was a baby and worked at the mill until she was diagnosed with a terminal disease. My father, who retired a few months before he turned 50 because of chronic back pain, still managed to spend 30 years inside the mill. For him it was a family affair; his mother worked at the same mill for the better part of her working life, his aunt worked at the mill for 40 years, and his older brother served almost 40 years there. If you're counting, that's two generations, five people, and almost 150 years of manual labor in an uncaring, unforgiving environment. *That's* what being poor meant to me.

These are the images I conjure when I hear or read about parents from lower-earning families not supplying their children with the cultural capital that they need for early success in elementary school, capital that higher-earning families are more likely to provide. I think about parents who struggle to provide, to exist.

Now that I am a teacher, I often hear stories of how this or that student is struggling, and there always seems to be a student who has problems stemming from a "lack of parental support" at home. There is always evidence of this lack of support, reasons such as "the parents don't seem to be involved academically—they never come to the school" or "academics are not being supported at home because the reading log has not been signed, even though the student claims to have read every night." Some parents don't come to school because of a hectic work or personal schedule that leaves little room for even small changes in routine. Other students may have trouble getting school items signed by a parent or guardian who works long hours or on a night shift. The point is, it can be a mistake for a teacher to make assumptions about a student's circumstances or support system without knowing the situation.

When I started school, I soon learned that being poor might mean both the things I thought it did and also something much, much worse: It meant that I was inferior to those who were not poor; I was *less than*. It's a terrible feeling to become aware at an early age that not having money somehow means that you are less deserving in the classroom than students who are more privileged, that you are less deserving of a teacher's attention or praise, that you are less deserving of good grades, that your financial shortcomings indicate that your parents have failed in some way. I remember not being spoken to—being flat-out ignored—by kids in my class when we were at lunch or recess. I would sit and wonder what it was that I could have done to make them dislike me and not want to talk to me. It was much later that I began to understand that the kids didn't have to talk to me in order to not like me. All they had to do was look at the clothes I was wearing to know that I was a poor kid, which meant that I was to be avoided.

My worn shirts and shabby jeans marked me as an outsider. Other students knew this, and I was supposed to know it. My teachers were definitely in on the deal; as long as I was quiet and didn't cause trouble, they ignored me. I made good grades and always did well on basic skills tests, but because I didn't speak up or act out very often, I was more or less disregarded in the classroom. The fact that my parents never came to school functions only exacerbated the situation.

When I think back on my time in elementary school, what stands out to me more than anything else is the feeling of being alone. Of being left alone. My younger brother and I have spoken in depth many times about this overwhelming feeling of alienation. One discussion that stands was about the time another boy in a second-grade class started a conversation with him over a sheet of stickers in one of his class folders. That conversation led to a friendship, and my brother still remembers all these long years later being happily stunned that someone outside of our immediate family showed interest in something he cared about. If a caring teacher had shown a similar interest in him, I believe he would be more self-confident as an adult.

I have a similar story that involves one of my classmates who was generally regarded as popular and "well-off." He asked me one day to toss a football around at recess. That's the first time I remember someone talking to me who wasn't poor like I was. That kid became my best friend, and he still is almost 30 years later. He never cared about how much money my parents made or what I was wearing, and eventually I came to realize that no one else had the right to judge me by those attributes either. Though we have parents who are very supportive of us, confidence is something my brother and I have struggled with since we were kids. Our early interaction with teachers and classmates at school gave us reason to believe that we just didn't matter very much.

I never had negative experiences with teachers in the early grades, but I can't remember having a positive memory-forming experience with any of my teachers in elementary school either. I believe that at least some part of the lack of encouragement and interaction I experienced was directly related to the fact that I came from a poor family. This meant that my parents were never going to make an effort to communicate with my teachers and that they would never come to the school, and for the most part this ended up being true. My mom came to school with ice cream, cake, and cola on my birthday, but she worked too late to attend PTO meetings, and because I didn't get into trouble, she was never asked to the school otherwise. No parent wants to be called to come in and talk about how his or her kid is underachieving or getting into trouble. However, I think that if a teacher had made some small attempt to communicate with my mother in a positive manner, perhaps a letter inviting her to come to the school or just an invitation for a letter in reply, it would have been a great step toward earning my mother's respect and trust. My mother, like many other mothers out there, loves to talk about her children, so I feel that she would have been very receptive to the idea.

Communication with teachers and school representatives was never an easy fit for my parents. They both had negative experiences with schooling when they were kids, and the residual feelings from those experiences, what Sara Lawrence-Lightfoot (2003) called "generational echoes," surely affected their views of interacting with school representatives.

My mother was the daughter of a sharecropper, and her family moved around often, following work where work was to be found. As a result, my mother attended nine different schools during an 8-year period, and she never felt that she was a true part of any school's community. Her family was never in one place long enough for her parents to establish a relationship with teachers. Even if they had not moved around so much, such a relationship would probably not have occurred, because my grandfather was no fan of the institution of school, having dropped out of school himself as a 12-year-old third-grade student. My grandfather told me that he attended the third grade for parts of four different years. Each year, his father would remove him from school to help work crops, and when he went back to school, he would again be placed in third grade, until he quit school completely rather than be faced with the prospect of being a teenaged elementary student.

The first time my dad came to a school function was for my eighth-grade graduation. My father cared fiercely about my schooling; along with my mother, he demanded that I be a respectful student and bring home good grades, but he wouldn't be dragged to the school unless he had to be. The son of a single parent, my father suffered an abusive home life that made him suspicious and untrusting of authority. He rarely speaks of his time in school, and when he does it is to recount the anger and embarrassment he felt about being treated by teachers and authority figures as though he was not good enough to warrant their attention.

I don't think that my teachers ever questioned *why* my parents never came to the school; they just knew that they didn't, and this led to my being allowed to fade quietly into the background in the classroom.

A Teacher's Impact

It is well documented that quality instruction has a large impact on student achievement (Clayton, 2011). However, elementary teachers have an impact on the future of student achievement that reaches beyond the classroom. We spend a great deal of time telling teachers they need an intense grounding in teaching standards and meeting requirements, but I think a quality teacher must also be caring enough to instill self-confidence in students.

Look up the word *educator* in a dictionary and you will find definitions that include teacher, instructor, and mentor. I want to teach all my students that they are no less (and no more) important than the other kids in class and that everyone they come in contact with deserves their respect, just as they deserve to be shown respect. I aim to instruct them on standards—in writing and reading, math, science, and social studies—but also standards such as valuing diversity. I mentor students by caring for what's best for them and showing interest in their lives. I do this in an attempt to provide my students with the support that I longed for from teachers when I was in school.

In my first education course in college, a teacher who *did* have an influence on the future of my education taught me that even though it may not seem so, we all have a voice that matters, one that we can use as we see fit. Some of us may have to work harder or overcome more obstacles to find our voices, but if we persist and believe, we can make ourselves heard. It is what we have to say that matters, not how much money our parents make or where we come from. Students from poor families need to be told this, and more, they need to be made to believe it.

References

Clayton, J. K. (2011). Changing diversity in U.S. schools: The impact on elementary student performance and achievement. *Education and Urban Society*, 43(6), 671–695.

Lawrence-Lightfoot, S. (2003). *The essential conversation*. New York: Random House.

7

LOW-INCOME, URBAN YOUTH SPEAKING UP ABOUT PUBLIC EDUCATION

Iabeth Galiel Briones, Diamond Dominique Hull, and Shifra Teitelbaum

There will, I am afraid, be fewer fascinating mavericks, fewer penetrating questioners, and fewer powerful dissenters coming from our inner-city schools. . . . A healthy nation needs its future poets, prophets, ribald satirists, and maddening iconoclasts at least as much as it needs people who will file in a perfect line. (Kozol, 2005, p. 106)

I work with youth who attend urban public schools in Los Angeles. I see their wit and wisdom, their potential, and the environments and circumstances in which they are expected to learn. I have seen the impact of budget cuts, standardization, and evaluation of students, teachers, and schools by test scores.

I have known Diamond Dominique Hull (18 years old) and Iabeth Galiel ("Gali") Briones (19 years old) since they started high school. I know how bright they are, and I have seen how public education has failed them. They are the students to whom Kozol refers in the opening quote, and they are increasingly isolated and marginalized as education reform initiatives quell students' individuality and creativity, particularly in low-income schools. Gali and Diamond met through their involvement with youTHink, the youth program I direct, and quickly became close friends.

Students like Diamond and Gali are critical to the conversation about inequities in public education. They have had similar educational journeys. They are both from low-income families and have attended schools in the Los Angeles Unified School District (LAUSD). Diamond is African American, and Gali is Latino. They have attended a variety of schools from local Title I, largely segregated schools, to more diverse magnet schools in middle-class neighborhoods, to largely segregated continuation high schools.

Both tested gifted in elementary school. With their inquisitive natures and keen senses of observation, both were perceived at times as threats to their teachers. Neither succeeded academically in their traditional high schools. Both were counseled into continuation schools—alternative schools for students who are behind in credits or perceived to be "at risk" in traditional high schools.

Officially speaking, continuation high schools in LAUSD use Options Learning, a program through which students are given packets of work for each course so they can work independently and quickly make up units. In reality, the majority of the students I know who have attended continuation schools, including Gali and Diamond, have not graduated on time. Many were assured they would be able to graduate early and were surprised to find out how difficult it was. Continuation schools are small, often with only a handful of teachers. As a result, many classes required for a college-ready diploma are not available.

I have talked with Gali and Diamond over the years about their love of learning and their frustrations with their educational experiences. I also have seen how disengaged they were in school, so I invited them to participate in a book group with me to explore their perceptions about education. They chose to read *Shame of the Nation: The Restoration of Apartheid Schooling in America* by Jonathan Kozol (2005). We discussed the book and its connections to their lives, using it to help them analyze their school experiences. They wrote about those experiences and how they reflected the implications of educational inequities.

These are their stories.

Diamond Hull's Story

In fifth grade I transferred from 75th Street Elementary School in my neighborhood to Brentwood Science Magnet Elementary School. My mother had not seen Brentwood's facilities or spoken to teachers and administrators there, but she sensed that since it was in a more affluent neighborhood, it would be better for me. In my class of 30 at Brentwood, there were eight Latino students, two Asian students, and three Black students; the remaining students were White. This was my first time in a class with or even in close proximity to White children. Before this, I had known only White authority figures: police officers and school and district administrators.

The economic differences between the other students at Brentwood and me made me feel like an outsider. At lunchtime, I saw things I had never seen before, like kids with prepared lunches in bento boxes with personalized chopsticks. I received LAUSD's free lunch. This made me a spectacle; children would crowd around me, asking things like, "Why don't you bring your own lunch? Your mom can't afford to buy you lunch?" When I told them my mother worked and didn't have the time to prepare my lunch, I was hit with even more questions. "Why does your mom have a job? My mom doesn't work." I don't think these things were said out of hatred, just ignorance.

Transferring to Brentwood from my home school allowed me to see the differences in schools firsthand. When I was in fourth grade at 75th Street, it was revealed that lead paint had been used on one of the school buildings.

My mother received a letter advising her to have me checked for lead poisoning. I don't recall parents protesting or collecting signatures on petitions. Like so many others, my mother and I were unaware of our power in LAUSD as a parent and student.

On the other hand, Brentwood was the "Hollywood" of elementary schools. Little differences had a big impact on me. The facilities were in much better condition. The school had a science lab where I learned to use a microscope and a Bunsen burner. Where 75th Street had asphalt, Brentwood had grass. Where 75th Street had an old metal jungle gym that gave kids rust stains on their hands and clothes, Brentwood had one of the nicest playgrounds I had ever seen. At 75th Street, I often would write on the floor and walls of the school, even spit in the hallways. At Brentwood I took care not to make a mess of anything because the school seemed so beautiful to me.

Being a poor child in a world of affluence, I became introverted because I had no one to relate to. At 75th Street I had a huge group of students to socialize with, but the performance and resources of teachers were lacking compared to those at Brentwood.

Mrs. Hahn, my fifth-grade teacher at Brentwood, was a small White woman, kind and energetic. I remember she read *Johnny Tremain* by Esther Forbes to us. One part of the book mentioned that slaves were counted as three fifths of a White person. Mrs. Hahn explained what that meant and that it was wrong. I really appreciated that. I didn't know much about my history. I knew that Black people were slaves. I knew about Harriet Tubman and Martin Luther King, Jr., but that was the first time that anyone ever gave me a lesson about slavery.

My last assignment of the year was to write a biography about a famous person in American history. The subject had to relate to us in some way, a connection we could express to the class when we presented it. I had decided to write about a Black woman, but Harriet Tubman and Rosa Parks were the only women I could remember learning about in my school's Black History Month assemblies and Black Appreciation programs at my church.

I went to Mrs. Hahn at lunch and told her my problem. We flipped through a Black history book together, and she told me tidbits about different people in the book, seeing which would interest me. We eventually landed on a picture of Madame C. J. Walker. I learned from my teacher that she was a self-made businesswoman and one of the first Black millionaires. That was enough for me to decide I wanted to do my assignment on her. Mrs. Hahn let me type my assignment on one of the class computers during recess and lunch. I had no access to a computer at home, and I arrived home from school after the public library was closed. This project was one of my more positive experiences in LAUSD.

In contrast to my learning experiences in fifth grade, in my freshman English class at Fairfax Visual Arts Magnet High School, we were discussing *The Adventures of Huckleberry Finn* by Mark Twain. I had read ahead of the class, so I held back in many class discussions. When we got to the section I was reading, I voiced my opinion. I suggested that Judge Thatcher was a surrogate father for Huck, since he was in control of Huck's money, a prominent male figure in the plot, and kinder to the boy than his drunkard father was. My teacher told the class that this was not the author's intention and that I should have read the chapter with his "study questions" in hand so I would "be on the same page" as the rest of the class.

After much frustration at Fairfax High School, I transferred to West Adams Preparatory High School, which was closer to my home. Unlike Fairfax, which was racially and economically mixed, West Adams was 88% Latino and 11% African American and 94% low-income. I fell into a pattern of truancy there and was written up for my "behavioral problems." I was failing many of my classes and was further behind in high school credits than when I transferred from Fairfax.

My counselor brought me into her office to point out my academic and social failing. She recommended that I attend Johnson Alonzo Community Day School, a continuation school. She told my mother and me that in continuation schools, students work at their own pace on accelerated programs of study. She said that at Alonzo I would get individualized lesson plans and be allowed to work alone. This seemed great because I was bored by the easy work in my classes and dreaded the mandatory group activities. The individual attention the counselor alluded to seemed perfect for me.

Alonzo CDS is located across the street from Le Conte Middle School, the middle school I attended. The neighborhood wasn't overtly unsafe or seedy. Every morning while heading to school, I would see parents dropping off their kids at the preschool down the street on their way to work. Though the place had its gangs, violence in or near the schools was uncommon.

I'll never forget my first day at Alonzo. I was born in one of Los Angeles's more dangerous neighborhoods. Seeing gang members on the street or hearing gunshots ring out in the night did not get me worked up, but walking into Alonzo and seeing classmates with ankle bracelets that monitored their locations every second of the day because they were on probation shocked me. It was common for my classmates to curse at teachers and to be violent. It was so extreme that each day I had to hand over my backpack to office staff and was allowed to carry only my binder into class because having a backpack gave me the opportunity to conceal weapons or drugs or graffiti paraphernalia. This was the explanation my principal gave me, anyway. What I didn't know until recently is that Alonzo and other community day schools are the district's dumping grounds for undesirable students: gangbangers, students who have had run-ins with the law, pregnant students, and students like me.

For the first time in a long time, I had teachers telling me I was their most well-behaved student. Though my standing in my teachers' eyes had improved, the academic quality of the classes dropped dramatically. The individual attention I was expecting was nonexistent. I would often go whole periods without once talking to a teacher unless I initiated the conversation. Where was the accelerated learning? The drastic difference between what my counselor told me and the reality left me feeling tricked. The counselor at West Adams acted not in my best interest but in the best interest of West Adams. I was shipped off to a school where I was expected to fail. If I am expected to fail by my teachers, principals, and counselors, the people who are supposed to motivate me, the ones who are supposed to guide me in my aspirations, how can I succeed?

I soon transferred to a more traditional continuation school. While it is far from accelerated learning or meaningful intellectual stimulation, I understand how the Options Learning contracts work, I do my independent assignments, and I finally am nearing graduation.

Gali Briones's Story

> *The general idea that schools in ghettoized communities must settle for a different set of goals than schools that serve the children of the upper and middle class has been widely accepted. And much of the rhetoric of "rigor" and "high standards" that we hear so frequently, no matter how egalitarian in spirit it may sound to some, is fatally belied by practices that vulgarize the intellects of children and take from their education far too many of the opportunities for cultural and critical reflectiveness. (Kozol, 2005, p. 98)*

My mother understood the state of public education, being a product of the same LAUSD schools where I was headed. She saw potential in me, so she strived to "alejarme del barrio," or take me out of the "hood."

I was bused to Windsor Hills Magnet Elementary School for fifth grade. Windsor Hills is located in an African American community significantly more affluent than my own. The teachers taught in a similar fashion to the ones in my old school, but there was much more talk of college. But the best resources and opportunities, like arts classes, were only for gifted classes, which were most often filled with the children of the wealthier parents. This experience opened my eyes to the fact that issues of educational inequity go deeper than race.

I was fortunate to have an unorthodox fifth-grade teacher, Mr. Becker, who often broke from the standard curriculum. He focused on the learning process more than the end results. He strengthened our reasoning and deduction skills with daily logic puzzles and engaged us with games like chess that required our full attention. He didn't forget about our bodies. He took time every day to have us stretch, to help us if we were antsy or tired. He was constantly scrutinized because he wasn't doing what he was "supposed" to do. He was an amazing teacher and had a big impact on my education.

My first time at Orville Wright Middle School, I was taken aback by the amount of open space on the campus. At schools back home there were tall buildings, reminiscent of the local prison towers, crowding the field and cafeteria.

Wright has a magnet school and a community school. It is located in the predominantly White community of Westchester. This was my first experience going to school with White children. It was an integrated campus because they bused kids from all over urban LA; 90% of the school's students of color were in the magnet. Most of the White students were in Wright's community school.

The teaching at Wright was more rigorous than anything I had encountered in my neighborhood. Yet as a student who was bused in to the school, I felt expendable, as if we were visitors. We were always reminded that we were on a contract, and any little mistake would land us back at our home schools. The less affluent students from outside the neighborhood only got access to the school's enrichment programs based on academic performance and what they called "exceptional character," while all the community students were entitled to everything the school had to offer.

Teachers were accustomed to docile students who learned as they were told and never got too out of hand. Intelligent students who didn't conform to the teachers' methods were cast aside as troubled. I remember one good friend in particular, Quinton, a heavyset African American student who was in the foster care system. Quinton would get to school and choose a 400- or 500-page book from the library and be on the last pages by sixth period. In class he answered any question when called upon but didn't do more than was asked of him. Teachers complained that he wasn't interested in class. They felt undermined by his constant reading. They had an issue with his excessive absences but never took into consideration his situation at home. There were several attempts to have him removed from the school. I always felt like the teachers might be afraid that Quinton would learn more on his own than they could teach him.

The local community students, who were primarily White, seemed to be the priority for faculty. Many of them had siblings who had gone to the school, and their parents had connections to teachers or administrators. These parents never missed Back to School nights, bringing along the entire family. The teachers would smile and ask what high schools or colleges the older siblings were attending. Then they would turn their attention to the young ones. "I'll be torturing you next," they'd joke. When my friends would bring their brothers and sisters, teachers rarely acknowledged them and often treated them as a disturbance. This upset me deeply. They were so nice to the White kids. I made it a point to take these little kids outside to entertain them when the teachers started shooting them dirty looks for frolicking around. I felt a need to protect them from the teachers' disrespect.

It seemed that the kids who were always getting in trouble were the bused-in magnet students. The White students in the magnet rarely got in trouble even though they were often the most unruly in class. My friends were sent to the office for "disrupting class" when we were simply talking to each other about what we were learning. When I objected, I was often sent along for insubordination.

After spending a summer at Johnny Cochran Middle School, my neighborhood school, I began to appreciate Wright more. Classrooms at Cochran also served as storerooms. Textbooks were tattered and much older than the ones at Wright. I immediately understood the disparities between the two schools and realized that they ran far deeper than aesthetics.

The teachers at Cochran expected much less from students. For me, it felt like a lack of faith in our abilities. I had to retake seventh-grade English and health that summer because of excessive absences. On my first day in summer school, I remember entering the classroom and recognizing many of the faces from my fourth-grade class, when I still attended Arlington Heights Elementary School.

On the first day of summer school at Cochran, the teacher asked for volunteers to read out loud. I was the only one who raised my hand. I read the passage loud and clear, as I would have in my regular class. When I looked up, I saw that everyone, including the teacher, was staring at me, some with open mouths. I felt very uncomfortable. After the teacher saw that he would get no other volunteers for reading, he played a tape recording of the story as we followed along. I spent the rest of my summer reading my own book and tuning in to class only when asked to complete a worksheet. I learned nothing about English but a lot about schools and the way they work. I received an A E E in that class, which is supposed to represent a present and active student. I was neither, but I did my worksheets.

My experiences at Wright and Cochran illustrate that students will go only as far as they are expected to go. If teachers don't expect a seventh grader to be able to read out loud to the class, what are they really saying about what they expect for that person's future? The teacher at Cochran did not push the students to read; he was content with open books and fingers being dragged across the text to show that we were "following along." The students in the summer class, who had been in my fourth-grade class a few years earlier, were the top-ranked students at Arlington Heights. I knew that they were capable of reading this story out loud.

In my last year at Wright, there was a push from community members to turn the community school into a charter school. I remember having a heated conversation about it with a teacher who didn't care for me. He told me the reason they wanted the switch was "to have more control over 'our' school." Apparently things were "getting out of hand with all these 'other' students coming in." I didn't fully understand it back then, but I sure felt it.

Yet I enjoyed being with other students at Wright. We did our best to get along and understand each other, even though we knew we were from different sides of the tracks. For some youth, interacting with wealthier peers can be a negative experience. It made me appreciate what I had even more. I realized that many of the values I had been raised with weren't commonplace. I took pride in my work ethic, my priorities, and my character.

That doesn't mean it was easy. I began to struggle with my identity. I started taking on what this more affluent community believed a Latino was. I began listening to Chicano rap, "sagging" my pants a little, and I became very interested in ancient Mayan cultures, the latter probably being the only thing that brought me closer to my heritage. In my neighborhood schools I was just one of the kids, but now, in this new world, I was one of the "Latino" kids.

When I was in eighth grade, my math teacher, Mr. Andrews, asked me what my "plans" were after high school. He suggested the army so I could "get the discipline I needed," and, he added, it would help me out with college, "if I should want to go." I became angry and bitter with this teacher. He knew very well that I had aspirations for college just like the other students in my class.

My excessive absences led him to accuse me of cheating and truancy. The reality was, if I missed my school bus, it was nearly impossible for me to get to school. It wasn't until the last semester of eighth grade, after much trouble, that I mastered the 2.5-hour public bus route that would bring me near the campus, followed by a mile-long walk. His accusations were due to my high test scores. How could I learn the material if I "wasn't in his class enough"? I loved math, and at that level it came pretty easily to me.

Even though I wasn't in my neighborhood, I was still bound by the limitations imposed on people of my cultural and economic background. I realized I would encounter these stereotypes anywhere I went. Even in spaces that claim to be accepting of all people, it doesn't mean they're going to treat you equally.

The last school I attended was Walt Whitman Continuation High School. I felt like I was back at Cochran. I was surrounded by intelligent students of color who weren't being challenged or motivated.

Sadly, it was the most academically deficient school I attended. But for once I was allowed to take a greater part in my learning. I worked *with* my teachers, not *for* them. As a self-driven program, Options Learning can be very beneficial. The problem is that students are sent to options schools because they are believed to lack motivation.

Like I experienced with my eighth-grade math teacher, expectations of students like me were low. Whether through direct comments or subtle hints about one's place in society, faculty downplayed students' talents. Very few students argued because they had heard it their entire lives.

I am coming to understand the concept of entitlement. Growing up, I was instilled with the belief that I deserve nothing; everything I get in life I must earn by working hard. If I work hard enough, by someone else's standards, then I will be rewarded. If not, I am to continue working until I am granted what I want. To take was wrong, to assume that you were entitled was wrong, and to assert yourself made you a troublemaker. This was the general understanding in my family and community, and it was applied to every situation in my life. I understood it as work ethic. Now I'm beginning to ask myself who my work is benefiting and how my experience fits into a bigger picture.

In 1954, in *Brown v. Board of Education*, the U.S. Supreme Court ruled that "separate but equal" public schools were unconstitutional. My experiences of public education were very different from what I believe *Brown v. Board of Education* envisioned, yet they taught me so much. Most students don't attend a good school with students from different backgrounds. I think most Americans have given up on integration. Now they just hope to create good schools in "less fortunate" communities. We are creating a way for upper- and middle-class communities to shut out our children.

The Students' Final Reflections

Upon hearing that their stories were going to be published, Diamond and Gali had additional thoughts to share.

Diamond's Final Reflections

I haven't fully digested the fact that someone out in the world will read what I have to say. For my entire life I've done assignments for a grade, writing on topics I had no interest in and turning papers in to teachers who didn't have any real interest in reading my work. This was a totally different experience; I got to choose what I would write and why. I am completely invested in this piece of work because this piece is me. Even though I don't have a solution for the problems in public education, I know where I stand, With my head held high, I can start down this path of demanding change.

Gali's Final Reflections

Through this project, I've refined my understanding of the education system. Exposure to writers like Jonathan Kozol and Paulo Freire, who have dedicated time and research to understanding educational structures, taught me to see these structures more clearly and articulate my opinions of them. For a long time I felt like I was simply complaining about a bad situation. Now I have gained an understanding of these issues on a macro level. While these issues are greater than my experiences, I know my experiences are also a part of the big picture. In choosing to speak up and address the elephant in the room, I hope we can raise awareness and educate our communities. I hope to be a part of the wave of young people who inform our communities. We have a voice as well, if we choose to use it.

Conclusion

I have seen Gali, Diamond, and other students from low-income communities go to great lengths to acquire a merely adequate education. Getting a quality education should not require heroics, especially when it is so readily available to more affluent youth; this is not equity. Students from low-income communities are blamed far too often for their circumstances when structural inequality is to blame.

Diamond and Gali's stories illustrate the disparities in public education. While their local, segregated schools may have serious limitations, integrated schools are not doing enough to create inclusive learning environments to help low-income students feel seen and respected as full members of their school communities.

So what are the implications of these stories for teachers? We live at a time when teachers are blamed for far too many of our education system's and society's failings. But there are lessons we can take from Gali and Diamond's stories that can make us stronger educators:

- *Bring students' lives into the room.* School curriculum is more meaningful and engaging when students can connect it to their own lives and when the whole student is welcome in a classroom. Students' perspectives about current events, literature, history, and other topics are informed by their lived experiences and can enrich the curriculum for everyone.
- *Name the elephant.* Even if it's not part of your curriculum, if you have students from diverse cultural backgrounds, economic classes, and neighborhoods, name these differences diplomatically and create safe opportunities for students to talk about them. In more homogeneous classes, name *that* reality. Where are the other students? Why aren't they here? What might they teach us?
- *Recognize structural, systemic issues.* The more you understand the ways that poverty, racism, and other structural inequities affect our society and our students' lives, the better you can help students see and understand them, too.
- *Think about the students who trigger you.* There are always some students who are harder for us to reach. It is critical that we reflect on which

ones trigger us and why. Might it be that they ask questions that are hard for us to answer? Might their attitudes reflect anger or frustration about the ways that education has failed them before they even arrived in our classes? Are we equating compliance and cooperation with intelligence and potential? It might be easier, but it is unfair to write students off rather than understand them and figure out how to reach them.

- *Find support.* None of us should do this alone. Whether battling structural oppression, engaging students, or creating a safe and inclusive learning environment, we must seek out peers, in our schools or beyond, who can support us, brainstorm with us, point out things we might not see, and help us continue the process of becoming the best teachers we can be.

References

Freire, P. (2000). *Pedagogy of the oppressed* (30th anniversary ed.). New York: Continuum.

Kozol, J. (2005). *Shame of the nation: The restoration of apartheid schooling in America.* New York: Three Rivers Press.

PART TWO

Identifying the "Problem"
From a Deficit View to a Resiliency View

8

SAVE YOU OR DROWN YOU

Stacy Amaral

My name is Zuleta Concepción, and I was asked by my old (well, not old but "ex") school counselor to write about being poor. Now I am in college, though I wasn't always "going to college," if you know what I mean. Being poor and going to school can either save you or drown you. It wasn't clear which was which for me until I learned some things, so I will tell you about those things. Living poor creates chaos, spills oil on important papers, forgets to sign permission slips, and robs you of the road to knowledge, which is the worst thing.

Well, maybe the worst thing is having to leave your own life to get anywhere, and no matter what, you miss your people.

I only now am learning how much I didn't know. Of course there were many things I did know, but they didn't help to write papers, buy the right clothes, or speak "good" English. I can cook. I can take care of kids and figure out how the hell to get out of my house, a boring class, or a relationship with a boyfriend. These only get you so far. And, anyway, who will have your back when you go to a new place? Who will tell you the truth?

* * *

Of course it goes without saying that if your parents are poor then you will be poor too. Yet there is always hope that somehow you'll escape. You hear about those rap stars and movie stars who want to buy their mothers beautiful houses. Of course, who wouldn't want their folks to have a great house with a kitchen to feed everyone? Most moms in my neighborhood feed everyone as best they can no matter what their kitchen looks like. For years our kitchen had broken linoleum and a stove with two working burners. My mother always had food going.

Of course, it was always the same food. Why was the variety so limited, you ask? Well, there wasn't a lot of time to try new recipes or money to buy special ingredients. I noticed this later, how people with money have all kinds of spices and flours, herbs and things I had no idea how to use. We had no cookbooks. Cooking was cooking, not a hobby.

* * *

Everything is limited if you are always worried about having enough. There are places we don't go because maybe it wouldn't be worth the money you would need to spend to get in. Better to go where you know what you'll get, like the carnival instead of the crafts fair. Do you see what I mean? All this limits your vocabulary along with your knowing.

* * *

As we all know vocabulary is the key. You read about these famous poor people like George Washington Carver, who learned a new vocabulary word every day. I thought about this for the SATs. How do we cram for an entire life of vocabulary in a few months? Impossible.

Vocabulary is like ingredients; some people feel more comfortable sticking to what is usual for them. I had a teacher once in a bilingual class who wouldn't let us use the words *el deso*, which is like saying *thingamajig*. I thought she was ridiculous. Now I know. The more specific you are, the more you are understood and life runs more smoothly. This is what I know now.

* * *

The other hard thing about having poor parents is that they can't help you with things that they never learned, like applying to college, dealing with the financial aid mess, asking for references, and all that. My parents are smart but not school smart and not in English. Some people say that they'll help you, but then you feel judged by them. Some people want to do it *for* you and that feels like you are not good enough to do it on your own. You do, though, have to find that help—that bridge to get from one place to another.

* * *

I've noticed that poor people have more plastic things while wealthier people have more wooden things. Toys, for example. Plastic things break more easily. What we would get for Christmas didn't last but a few months at most, and then, toy parts all over the place. You lose the pieces to games and puzzles. There are fewer places to put things, and so there is more of a mess and things get lost. Shelves take up space, and there were several of us sharing a room.

* * *

That is something to consider: Not enough room. Important papers get lost when you don't have places to put them. Not that poor people are slobs by any means. I have been in the houses of some people with money that would make you worry for your health.

I have done cleaning and babysitting. And I study what is around me. One of my best teachers taught me to be observant. I tell my mother that being observant and being nosy are not the same. She thinks that I'm too interested in other people's ways of life.

* * *

You see, my mother worries a great deal about how people will think of us, her kids. Did she raise us right? Do we act right? Do we dress right?

* * *

My father says that people who ask too many questions—me, for example—are rude. My teachers say that you *should* ask questions; it's a sign of intelligence. I think that some of the difference has to do with the fact that my parents are not from this country and so are not always sure of what is "right" here. I wish there were a class for poor parents in which they'd learn how schools work and that it is just fine to ask questions and stand up for their children when they are not given what they need to learn.

* * *

There is an idea floating out there that poor people don't care whether their kids do their homework. My parents would tell us constantly, "Do your homework." But they didn't know what to look for, and it was easy to get over on them. "I did it in school." "I don't have any." A kid could feel powerful getting over on their folks for a bit, but then there is the reality of terrible grades and the possibility of a meeting at school.

I have had to go to interpret in meetings in which teachers and others are talking about poor students and their behavior. These are awkward to say the least. It would be good if school people used language that everyone knows. I mean everyday kinds of English. It would be good to ask if a parent needs an interpreter.

* * *

I will tell you what did help me get used to college: the Upward Bound Program. I got to live in a dormitory for a few weeks every summer I participated in the program. I only had to share a room with one roommate. It took a while to get used to sleeping with someone who wasn't family, but it sure was interesting.

Let me tell you that my roommate took better care of her hair than anyone I know. My hair isn't that good, but I just put it up. We do that in my house due to the problem of lice. When my little sister got them, I had to stay home from school to comb her out. They wouldn't let her back until every one was gone. Anyway, staying in that dorm with my roomie, I learned about more than hair. It was fun.

* * *

There was another program there that helped Latino students with tutoring and such. They included parents in their program, which I have to say is so necessary. Lots of Latino parents I know don't want their kids going away and sleeping out of the house. If you are from another culture, it can be hard to "read" people, so it is hard to figure if there is some danger in a stranger's house.

It was hard to study in my house with everyone in and out and my brothers practicing what they call their "act." Don't even ask about it; I'll just tell you that it's *loud*. I'll give it to them, though. They made us laugh.

* * *

My father wanted me to commute to college, and so I did for the first year. The next year I moved into the dorm. I didn't have to pay board because I was an assistant to the residence counselor. I had to listen to a lot of sad stories, though: Girls freaking out about all kinds of misery. There were many who left school. Too much pressure.

One kid from my neighborhood who was number one in the class had trouble staying. Could be something in the water: Very few of us make it through. Did we miss home? Or did we miss the neighborhood, our families and friends? We weren't prepared.

* * *

I was nervous about bringing my new college friends home to meet my family. The one time I did it was because this girl pushed me into it by saying that she had never met anyone who lived in a two-family house.

I noticed that in some people's homes there was so much space. There were rooms to play in, rooms to study in, rooms to sleep in, and rooms to be a family in. In my house we were always tripping over ourselves. We couldn't leave things out because all the space was needed for living. The winter was the worst.

Then going outside was not always possible. The boys got in trouble with a neighbor for making noise. My father didn't want us out too much. He was concerned about the number of halfway houses for ex-cons that were in our neighborhood. He didn't have anything against them personally, but we all wondered why they did not put some of those houses out in rich neighborhoods.

* * *

We never did live on the first floor either. Everything had to be carried up at least two flights of stairs. When my grandmother came from Puerto Rico, she could hardly go out because of her heart. The stairs bothered her. She could not go out until my father came home to carry her downstairs. She wasn't heavy. She was little and thin, but still it was impossible to get her down there very often.

* * *

We moved a bunch of times too. Once because the landlady wouldn't let my mother keep her mad-big stroller for the twins in the hall. Then we moved because the house was sold, then again because they found out it had lead paint. For a while we lived in the projects, but then my parents made too much money.

* * *

Too much money! I don't know how they figured that. I was glad though. I never did like the projects. The buildings and the halls felt like they had the ghosts of all the people who had ever lived there. These people had worked hard and had hopes. And frequently the landlords did not respond to their problems. And it felt sad to me when my father would organize people to get what we needed and the rental company got angry with him. We moved back to the old neighborhood, and we were all glad even if the rent was more.

* * *

Not enough of some things and too much of others. Say, funerals, for example. Poor kids go to more wakes and funerals than richer kids do. In some ways the wakes were like get-togethers. We'd hang out in front of the funeral home and hold each other up.

One of the kids who I counsel in the dorm came to me crying the other night. Her grandmother had died, and she was worrying about going to the funeral. She had never been to one. Another world.

* * *

So, these are some of the differences I see between growing up poor and having money. I hope some day to have enough money to buy a house; well, two houses, really, one for me and one for my family. No, I do not want to live with them in the same house. Enough is enough.

I hope to be able to have enough to take my kids on trips. I promise that I won't be on them all the time about how easy they have it compared to me.

I hope to finish college and get a job. Sometimes I think about teaching, but the money is not all that great, and I wonder if I have had enough with kids.

I think about being a librarian. There is a Puerto Rican children's librarian in my city who has helped me a lot. Maybe this is actually my strength: to organize kids, to give them the power to learn.

I know I have choices, and I know also I miss kids when I am away from home. I will just have to see, just have to decide when the time comes.

9

ON GRIFTERS, RESEARCH, AND POVERTY

Bobby Ann Starnes

On a dreary, rainy day last week, I sat in front of my TV aimlessly switching channels. Nearly brain-dead, I did something quite unusual for me. I stopped on the channel showing *Dr. Quinn, Medicine Woman*. Somehow the mindlessness of the show appealed to me at that moment. In this episode, a snake oil salesman enters Colorado Springs, home to Dr. Quinn, her love interest—the hunky and enigmatic mountain man Sully—and her three adopted children. The snake oil salesman, a self-proclaimed doctor and self-proclaimed celebrated healer, hawks his wares, as snake oil salesmen do, knowing that his potion would not cure any ailments except that of his empty wallet. Unfortunately, the townspeople jump on the bandwagon and turn away from Dr. Quinn's legitimate treatments. She warns them, but they can't resist the promise of a quick cure. Alas, she is proven right. The grifter steals away in the middle of the night clutching his ill-gotten gains, heading for another town to employ his scam.

It occurred to me that education, particularly since No Child Left Behind, has more than its fair share of modern-day snake oil salespeople. They tend to come in the form of panacea programs, consultants, and testing companies. Each packages its own particular elixir, making big promises and claiming their research proves the effectiveness of their special treatments. Like the traveling doctor of old, these salespeople with their dubious credentials, their big-bang marketing hype, and their pseudoscientific research claims swoop into town, sell their wares, and leave town pocketing the profits.

I grew up poor. We were not the romanticized poor but proud family. We struggled. It was hard, harsh, and often ugly. As an Appalachian child trying to make my way through a school system where my culture, values, dialect, and traditions were daily points of jokes, teasing, and pranks, I quickly learned that being poor was an offense to those around me. But being Appalachian, well, that was reprehensible.

My teachers wanted to help me, but they had no real-life experience with people like me. They'd grown up in privilege. Not wealthy, but privileged nonetheless. They thought, as the helping class often does, the best thing they could do for me was teach me to be like them—or as one teacher actually suggested in her kindest teacher voice, I needed to "learn to act White." I knew what that meant. If I wanted success, I'd have to adopt their language and culture and deny my own. I did what they asked; I learned to pass. Passing is a treacherous road to travel.

As a teacher, I've always thought my experiences with poverty and the choices I made to adopt ways that weren't my own could serve me in my work with marginalized children. And I vowed I'd never require children to deny who they were. We'd find other roads to success, roads that build on their strengths and use their cultures and experiences as a starting point for learning rather than impose middle-class values in ways that reinforce the message they receive every day telling them they are less than others and that their dreams should be limited by secret rules. And that's been my life's work. That's why I am so disillusioned by Ruby Payne's success and by her promises to help teachers serve poor children by teaching them to act middle class.

But she is out there, pulling her medicine show from district to district, selling her elixir—the Framework for Understanding Poverty. And schools buy it. Why wouldn't they? Teachers are starving for ways to help struggling students. They know they don't understand the cultures and values of those they teach, and Payne promises a quick cure, reporting that schools following her program "in three years make AYP . . . sometimes in a year."

I quickly learned that being poor was an offense to those around me. In an interview on the website of one school where she works, Payne reports she became an expert on poverty through two experiences. First, during college, she spent a semester in Haiti studying poverty. And second, she married a man who grew up in "extreme" poverty. Payne goes on to explain one of the things she "teaches" teachers about poor people: "When you live in a survival environment, I don't care where you are in the world, one of the things you do . . . you physically fight. Because that's how you stay alive."

Now, I've never been in a fight in my life. Nor has anyone in my family. I remember no fights growing up in my neighborhood, no fights in any of my classrooms. And in all these years of working with people in poverty, I've broken up one fight—two middle school girls in 1975 fighting over a boy. But, I guess it never hurts to bolster stereotypes when you're hyping your wares.

The training, Payne explains, lasts two days—two days to understand and overcome poverty's effects on student learning. On the first day, she explains "the reality of what generational poverty is and how that makes you think." And poverty, she continues, "is not about what the system does. It is about how you think when you are at survival." So, there's nothing wrong with the system, there is only something wrong with the ways poor people think?

Exceptional Kids

I work at a tuition-free college that serves only students of limited means—students who exemplify the emptiness of Payne's framework. Payne sets teachers up to expect negative behaviors—like fighting—and, as we know, expectations tend to become self-fulfilling prophecies. My students have a remarkably deep well of personal power grown from the strengths of their cultures, among them resiliency, work ethic, and resourcefulness. They have overcome outrageous odds, not the least among them is the stereotypes designed to pigeonhole them as violent, unmotivated, and lazy. One might say these kids are the exceptions. I don't think so, but what if they are? If we want to help children in poverty, doesn't it make more sense to look at students who have overcome hardships based on strength than to perpetuate the same old ugliness we see in the framework?

Serious systemic issues limit too many children's opportunities and possibilities, not the least among them being the stereotypes perpetuated by some consultants.

Payne laments that critics love to hate her work. "Quite simply," she says, "the work breaks the rules of higher education." Those uppity academic researchers, she suggests, must publish in order to get tenure. That's why they criticize her. Well, I've got tenure, and I could hardly be characterized as playing by the rules of higher education. Even beyond the sweeping generalization of her response, her claim seriously mischaracterizes those who find her work objectionable. Many critics, like me, have long experience working for equity in schools. Many are teachers, former teachers, and school administrators who have devoted years to educating children in their schools and communities—not just a two-day pass-through. They feel compelled, as I do, to speak out. (See, for example, http://rubypayneiswrong.blogspot.com/.) Even *Teaching Tolerance*, a publication of the Southern Poverty Law Center, has refused to endorse Payne's work. But her work is research based, she reports. After all, she points out, it is "based upon a 32-year longitudinal study of living next to and in a poverty neighborhood." She thinks living next to a community of poverty counts as research? Feels more like voyeurism.

In response to her research claims, I could only scratch my head. Why is it, I wondered, that her "32-year longitudinal research" findings don't jive with my 65-year longitudinal research? I lived in a neighborhood where poor people live. I studied how to get out of poverty by pretending to be middle class, and I learned the terrible toll that strategy takes on personal identity. I didn't spend a semester in Haiti—there was no money for that privilege. And, really, I don't need to go to Haiti to study poverty. I saw it and lived it every day. But I've spent my entire professional life working with families in poverty. By Payne's standards, my research makes me an expert on poverty. And here is my expert opinion: For too long, we have blamed poor people for being poor when serious systemic issues limit too many children's opportunities and possibilities, not the least among them being the stereotypes supported in Payne's trainings. We can continue to buy the snake oil, potions, ointments, and elixirs hoping for the quick cure, or we can deal with the real ailment. I don't begrudge her the money she's made selling the Frameworks of Poverty. I really don't. What hurts so personally and deeply is the way her message distracts from real cures. And meanwhile, so many children are being urged to give up the richness of who they are in exchange for hollow promises.

Note

Reprinted with permission of Phi Delta Kappa International, www.pdkintl.org. All rights reserved. Starnes, B. A. (2011). On grifters, research, and poverty. *Phi Delta Kappan*, 93(3), 72–73.

10

THERE *REALLY IS* A CULTURE OF POVERTY
Notes on Black Working-Class Struggles for Equity and Education

Kristen L. Buras

Robert Charles, a Black man who was born and raised in Mississippi and later resided in New Orleans, Louisiana, shot 27 White people (including seven police officers) between Monday, July 23, and Friday, July 27, 1900. Seven died, eight were seriously wounded, and 12 had minor injuries. White newspapers described Charles as "an unreasoning brute," a "cocaine fiend," a "worthless, crapshooting negro," and a "ruthless black butcher" (Hair, 2008, p. 2). In a piece titled "The Making of a Monster," one reporter for the New Orleans *Times-Democrat* pondered,

> It is only natural that the deepest interest should attach to the personality of Robert Charles. What manner of a man was this fiend incarnate? What conditions developed him? Who were his preceptors? From what ancestral strain, if any, did he derive his ferocious hatred of the whites, his cunning, his brute courage, the apostolic zeal which he displayed in spreading the propaganda of African equality? These are the questions involving one of the most remarkable psychological problems of modern times. (Quoted in Wells-Barnett, 1900/2005, p. 45)

Was Robert Charles a "fiend incarnate," as this reporter and many others characterized him?

Without the need for any additional detail regarding Charles or what transpired during that week in turn-of-the-century New Orleans, many White people today might respond to this question without hesitation (and not so differently from those in 1900): Yes, he was fiend. The fact that Charles was Black and shot 27 Whites—killing seven of them—is presumably all one needs to know. The question is, *why* would such information be deemed sufficient?

The answer explains much more than the assertions White people made about Black men like Charles in 1900. Tragically, it explains why Trayvon Martin, an African American teenager who was strolling home with iced tea and candy, was shot dead on February 26, 2012, in Sanford, Florida, while the man who killed him initially continued to walk the streets without investigation or arrest (Alvarez & Cooper, 2012). A ready-made set of assumptions about African Americans, and poor folks of color more generally, is nearly instantaneously available for use and abuse; a ready-made set of assumptions also exists about White people, but they function with substantially different consequences. On the basis of an alleged *culture of poverty*, African Americans are believed to be lazy, drug-addicted, violent, and simply not invested in the hard work and dreams of upward mobility that propel so many White people to self-actualization; that is to say, Black people are responsible for their own impoverishment and demise. This brings us to the issue of why Martin's killer was believed by police to be the victim rather than the perpetrator, just as the White people killed by Charles in 1900 were presumed to be innocent. Put simply, White people are assumed to be motivated, intelligent, law abiding, and civilized—they, too, are responsible for their status, which more often than not is superior to that of people of color. While one group is considered culturally deficient, the other group "naturally" possesses cultural capital or the cultural, social, and economic assets required for mobility (Bourdieu, 1984).

Neoconservatives from Daniel Patrick Moynihan to E. D. Hirsch have regarded the so-called culture of poverty as a cause of educational failure, unemployment, and crime. They believe that poor students of color lack the dispositions and cultural assets necessary for educational pursuits. In this chapter, I shift the culture of poverty argument onto a new terrain, affirming that there *really is* a culture of poverty, but it certainly is not the one described by White people over a century ago or by neoconservatives today. Through a critical analysis of Black working-class struggles for equity and education, including the life history of Robert Charles and the lives of present-day students of color in New Orleans, I reveal that racially and economically oppressed communities command a host of assets typically overlooked by White people. I draw on critical race theory, specifically Tara Yosso's (2006) discussion of *community cultural wealth* or the accumulative resources and forms of knowledge that enable people of color to navigate and survive racism and poverty. In the process, I demonstrate that the culture of poverty is itself an impoverished understanding of the realities faced by people on the margins and, even more important, that the focus should instead be on a *culture of White supremacy* that relies on physical, cultural, and economic violence to sustain the privilege and structural power of Whites.

I should make clear that I focus in this chapter on communities of color, and specifically African Americans, because they are disproportionately represented among the poor. Moreover, although poor and working-class Whites may suffer economic inequities, their subordinate class position is not compounded by race; they possess Whiteness as a form of property, which bestows protections and benefits, even if mediated by class position (Harris, 1995). In addition, culture of poverty arguments target poor communities of color, even if they sometimes are presented as race-neutral critiques of lower-class culture (e.g., see Banfield, 1968).

"The Style of Life Is Squalid and Vicious"

Before turning to an examination of Charles's life history and what might be learned about cultural pathologies and assets from the events that transpired in New Orleans in 1900, it is important to consider the more recent past. In the 1960s, a number of commentators—all part of a newly emerging neoconservative movement bent on moderating demands for Black Power—expressed concerns about what they called the culture of poverty (Buras, 2008). Perhaps the most well-known statement came from Daniel Patrick Moynihan, who issued a report published by the U.S. Department of Labor titled "The Negro Family" in 1965. Moynihan argued that race and class inequity existed largely because "the Negro family in the urban ghettos is crumbling" (Moynihan, 1996, p. 24). It is the family, Moynihan emphasized, that shapes character and ability. According to him, the low-income Black family with its matriarchal structure is enmeshed in a "tangle of pathology" that threatens the future not only of poor Black children but also of middle-class youth unable to "escape from the cultural influences" of the "unstable half" of the community (p. 33). National policy, he reasoned, should focus on "strengthening the Negro family so as to enable it to raise and support its members as do other families" (p. 36). Apparently the culture of White supremacy that engendered racial and economic subordination was no longer to blame. "At this point," concluded Moynihan, "the present tangle of pathology is capable of perpetuating itself without assistance from the white world" (p. 36).

A few years later Edward Banfield published a tract titled *The Unheavenly City: The Nature and Future of Our Urban Crisis* (1968). While Moynihan had written about the tangle of pathology in urban ghettos in explicitly racial terms, Banfield directed his concerns to class culture (which I would argue he used as a proxy for race). "A slum is not simply a district of low-quality housing," contended Banfield, but rather a place where "the style of life is squalid and vicious" (p. 45). Drawing distinctions between upper-, middle-, working-, and lower-class cultures, Banfield argued that each group "displays distinctive attitudes toward . . . authority, self-improvement, risk, violence, and distinctive forms of social organization." Each group also was said to exhibit a particular "orientation toward the future," including the ability to imagine a future and the discipline to forego present satisfaction for future benefit (p. 47).

According to Banfield (1968), the upper-class individual believes that if he applies himself then he can "shape the future to accord with his purposes." He recognizes that "he would be cheating himself if he allowed gratification of his impulses (e.g., for sex or for violence) to interfere with his provision for the future" (p. 49). The middle-class individual, by comparison, is slightly less future-oriented. He is "less likely . . . to have means that he considers adequate to assure a satisfactory level of goal attainment" (p. 51). Banfield goes on to explain that the working-class individual "does not 'invest' as heavily in the future" as the middle-class one. He has a "stronger sense of being at the mercy of fate, a 'power structure,' and other uncontrollable forces," and thereby places greater importance on "luck" (p. 52). A member of this class culture supposedly lacks a desire for self-improvement. Finally, the lower-class individual "lives from moment to moment" and "impulse governs his behavior." What is worse,

> his bodily needs (especially for sex) and his taste for "action" take prec-edence over everything else—and certainly over any work routine. He works only as he must to stay alive, and drifts from one unskilled job to another. . . .
>
> He feels no attachment to community, neighbors, or friends, resents all authority (for example, that of policemen, social workers, teachers, landlords, employers), and is apt to think that he has been "railroaded" and to want to "get even.". . .
>
> The lower-class household is usually female-based. . . . In managing the children, the mother . . . is characteristically impulsive: once they have passed babyhood they are likely to be neglected or abused. . . .
>
> The stress on "action," risk-taking . . . [and] fighting . . . makes lower-class life extraordinarily violent. (pp. 53–54)

In other words, lower-class culture is "pathological" (to use Banfield's words once more).

The culture of poverty has remained a common point of reference in explain-ing race and class inequities. In the mid-1980s, neoconservatives such as James Q. Wilson (1996) continued to argue that the absence of "character" was fundamen-tally a public policy issue. From education and welfare to public finance and crime, Wilson urged policy makers to consider the moral dimensions of the educational and economic policies they adopted, lest they advocate reforms that strengthen rather than challenge the culture of poverty. In 1987, E. D. Hirsch published his best-selling book *Cultural Literacy: What Every American Needs to Know*, which delineated the knowledge that poor children of color should command to be upwardly mobile. Within two decades, Hirsch's effort to "compensate" for stu-dents' alleged cultural deficiencies had grown into a full-fledged movement around the Core Knowledge curriculum (Buras, 2008). In many ways, the most recent work of Ruby Payne, which specifies the "hidden rules" of poverty so that teachers can "fix" poor students and set them on a path to assimilation, is an adaptation of deficit thinking with quite a long history (for more on Payne, see Gorski, 2007).

From a critical race theory perspective, deficit thinking is deeply problem-atic. Tara Yosso (2006) has stressed that "a traditional view of cultural capital is narrowly defined by White, middle-class values" (see also Buras, 2008). Instead she shifts the focus to cultural knowledge that "is very valuable to students [of color] and their families but is not necessarily considered to carry any capital in the school context." In fact, Yosso asserts that the groups so often criticized as deficient actually possess *community cultural wealth* or "an array of knowledge, skills, abilities, and contacts . . . utilized by Communities of Color to survive and resist racism and other forms of oppression" (p. 175). Some of the cultural assets that Yosso mentions are as follows:

- *aspirational capital*—the ability to maintain hopes and dreams for the future, even in the face of structured inequality;
- *familial capital*—cultural knowledge nurtured through kinship that carries a sense of community history, memory, and cultural intuition;
- *social capital*—networks of people and community resources that provide instrumental and emotional support;
- *navigational capital*—skills of maneuvering through social institutions not created with communities of color in mind; and
- *resistant capital*—knowledge fostered through oppositional behavior that challenges inequality. (pp. 177–179)

From this vantage point, one may speak of cultures informed by experiential knowledge of poverty and racism but not cultures of poverty that are necessarily impoverished. Consider, for example, aspirational capital. The notion that the racially oppressed aspire to a future more ideal than present circumstances and have struggled individually and collectively for such transformation is strikingly different from, say, Banfield's assertion that poor people live by impulse alone and lack the desire for self-improvement. Needless to say, these are divergent understandings of subalternity.

The culture of poverty argument did not originate in the 1960s; it has much deeper historical roots. To illustrate this and to expose the culture of White supremacy, which should instead be the focus, I examine the life history of Robert Charles and the race riot that occurred in turn-of-the-century New Orleans. Along the way, I also highlight the cultural assets that have enabled Charles and those who followed him to survive and challenge inequality.

"What Manner of a Man Was This Fiend Incarnate?"

Ida B. Wells-Barnett (1900/2005), a well-known and outspoken antilynching advocate during the late 19th century, wrote the following about Robert Charles:

As usual, when dealing with a negro, he is assumed to be guilty because he is charged. . . . The minute the news flashed across the country that [Charles] had shot a white man it was at once declared that he was a fiend incarnate. . . . The reporters of the New Orleans papers, who were in the best position to trace this man's life, made every possible effort to find evidence to prove that he was a villain unhung. With all the resources at their command . . . these reporters signally failed to disclose a single indictment which charged Robert Charles with a crime. Because they failed to find any legal evidence that Charles was a law-breaker and desperado his accusers gave full license to their imagination and distorted the facts that they had obtained . . . to prove a course of criminality. (p. 43)

It was Wells-Barnett (1900/2005) and historian William Ivy Hair (2008)—not the reporters of the New Orleans papers—who traced Charles's life history with the hope of separating fiction from fact. What they learned in the process reveals that the Black poor are not the problem; the culture of White supremacy is.

Robert Charles was born in late 1865 in Copiah County, Mississippi, to Jasper and Mariah Charles. After Emancipation the family lived as sharecroppers on a cotton plantation. In 1880, when Charles was 14 years old, "the total annual value of the farm production of this family of eleven was listed as $375, of which half went to the landlord and probably most of the rest to pay off a merchant" (Hair, 2008, p. 12). The dire life circumstances under sharecropping illuminate two crucial points: White upper-class culture was itself sustained by Black labor, and exploited Black laborers survived only because of their own hard work and navigational capital.

Despite Emancipation and Reconstruction, Democrats in Mississippi had regained control by 1875 through paramilitary demonstrations, which were threatening exhibitions of White power. To control elections, in fact, Democrats developed the Mississippi Plan—the week before voting, private White military companies would parade into Black precincts with a thundering cannon. Despite this, a biracial alliance of Blacks and poor Whites existed in Copiah County and managed to elect a Republican majority of district supervisors (who assessed taxes, selected jurors, etc.) in the election of 1881. In 1883, the alliance presented another slate of candidates, which prompted what was known as "The Procession." Some 150 armed men on horseback would gallop, fire shots, and terrorize politically active Black families in the middle of the night. When the alliance's White leader went to cast his vote, he was murdered. Needless to say, Democratic candidates "won" the election (Hair, 2008). Charles was 17 years old when this travesty occurred, and it likely taught him a great deal about the character of White supremacy.

Charles worked at unskilled and semiskilled jobs throughout his life. In 1887, he left Copiah County to work in Vicksburg, Mississippi, where he laid pipe for the city's water system. While there he bought a pistol. Gun carrying was a common practice in the South, and there had been 334 lynchings in Mississippi between 1882 and 1903; thus Charles would have possessed the gun for defensive purposes. In light of later accusations of criminality, it should be noted that in 1892 Charles visited the Rolling Fork train depot with his brother to retrieve a pistol someone had taken. When he demanded the pistol, a shoot-out occurred, and the trainman who had the pistol pitched it from the departing train. Hair (2008) stressed, "Police reports from Mississippi would be sent to [New Orleans in 1900] saying that . . . [Charles] had brutally murdered a [train]man. . . . Actually [Charles] never killed a [train]man, or anyone else, in Mississippi" (p. 56). This fact would be ignored for fictionalized accounts of Charles's monstrous record of crime.

This incident prompted Charles to return to Copiah County. By this time another form of violence called *whitecapping* had developed in his birthplace. In this case, vigilantes (usually White farmers) would drive Black families from land they rented or owned. During his stay in Copiah, Charles was charged in court for "unlawful retailing," which amounted to selling whiskey in a dry county—a charge that pales in comparison to whitecapping. On this account Charles ultimately stood trial, and the jury found him not guilty (Hair, 2008).

By 1894 Charles had left Copiah County for New Orleans, where just a few years later he joined the International Migration Society and initiated payments for a voyage to Liberia: a demonstration of aspirational capital and the hope that equity could be realized elsewhere. If whitecapping in Copiah had menaced Blacks, living conditions in New Orleans were criminal:

> The problem of most blacks in the city was simply survival. With few exceptions their work was the lowest paying, their housing the flimsiest, their mortality rate the highest, their treatment by police the harshest, their education the most neglected, and public services for their residential areas the most inadequate. (Hair, 2008, p. 72)

The conservative New Orleans newspaper the *States* explained that the death rate of Blacks in New Orleans was attributable to their "vicious habits" (*vicious* was the same descriptor invoked by Banfield 70 years later). As Hair (2008) suggested, "The fact that black residents on the average had a worse water and sewage system pointed to a more logical explanation" (p. 89). Such explanations were never considered since "virtually all whites in the South, including New Orleans, were absolutely convinced that the mass of Negroes were innately inferior mentally and morally to most whites" (p. 89). In words that would foretell Charles's own fate, the founder and editor of the *States* published an editorial in 1900 titled "The Negro Problem and Its Final Solution." Here the word *extermination* was used in presenting a remedy (p. 91).

All of this provides context regarding the vicious nature of White supremacy in New Orleans and throughout the South. It certainly shaped Charles's increasing commitment to African migration. During his time in New Orleans, Charles worked a number of jobs for pay—at the docks, cleaning streets, stacking lumber—and sold *Voice of Missions*, a back-to-Africa magazine, without remuneration (Hair, 2008). After Charles's interactions with police, his roommate would report that he "often grumbled about the wrongs inflicted on the black race in America and said that emigration to Africa was the best solution" (p. 99). Prior to July 23, 1900, Charles was never involved in any wrongdoing in New Orleans.

On the evening of July 23, Charles and his roommate made plans to visit Charles's girlfriend, Virginia Banks, and one of her friends at a house on Dryades Street. Banks rented a room from a White woman named Ms. Cooley. Waiting for the appropriate time to visit after Cooley was asleep— she likely wouldn't welcome Black men into her home at night—Charles and his roommate sat on some steps down the block. It was there that three police officers approached the two men and demanded to know what they "were doing and how long they had been there" (Hair, 2008, p. 120). Charles explained they were "waiting for a friend" and "got up." At that moment, Officer Mora reported,

> I grabbed him. The negro pulled, but I held fast, and he finally pulled me into the street. *Here I began using my billet* [billy club] and the negro jerked from my grasp and ran. He then pulled a gun and fired. I pulled my gun and returned the fire, each of us firing about three shots.

Mora later admitted that he—*not* Charles—had drawn his pistol first and "a moment later Charles drew his weapon" (p. 120).

What mattered to the vast majority of Whites, however, was that Mora had been shot by Charles. Charles also had been shot by Mora, but he managed to escape and returned to his place to nurse his wound and retrieve his gun. Within hours police with guns came searching for Charles, which resulted in the shooting of two more officers. Charles managed to escape once more, and this set in motion the largest manhunt in New Orleans history. Finding *Voice of Missions* in Charles's abandoned room, the police superintendent claimed such materials "gave an insight into the *character* of the negro and [showed] that his intention in life was one of evil toward the white man" (Hair, 2008, p. 132; emphasis added). That the White man had historically shown evil toward the Black man apparently said little about the character of Whites.

Relying on social capital and networks of support, Charles sought cover from people he knew on nearby Saratoga Street—one of the residents had lived in Copiah County. Police received a tip that Charles might be there, and a crowd of Whites grew to 5,000 by Tuesday afternoon, July 24. Police arrested Black men who vocalized approval of Charles, and one White man was fined for merely suggesting that Charles "might simply have been defending himself and in any case he 'should be given a fair show'" (Hair, 2008, p. 143). On Wednesday, July 25, the acting mayor of New Orleans posted a $250 reward "for the capture and delivery, dead or alive, [of] the body of the negro murderer," with the state governor authorizing an additional $250 (p. 146). By Thursday, July 26, at least 70 Blacks had been seriously injured, shot, or killed by angry and impulsive White mobs.

Two policemen entered the house on Saratoga Street on Friday, July 27, and were shot by Charles. Assuming a position upstairs near windows, Charles began to shoot periodically into the yard below, where the crowd within one block had swelled to 20,000 Whites. It is estimated that 5,000 bullet holes penetrated the house over the course of several hours. Hair (2008) reflected,

> What Robert was actually thinking during the night of July 23 will never be known. Perhaps he regretted that he did not meekly submit to being hit over the head by Officer Mora; perhaps he looked back on his actions with exultant pride; very likely he alternated between these two conflicting emotions. But, once he had fired his gun at a New Orleans policeman, a sense of desperation unquestionably took possession of him. His lifetime in Mississippi and Louisiana had taught him that a black man who shoots a law officer would probably be better off dead than in custody, and that one who actually kills a policeman . . . was liable to die in some terrible fashion at the hands of a white mob. . . . That was a fate he was utterly determined would not be his. (pp. 135–136)

Armed with resistant capital, Charles defended himself to the end, but a fire was set to drive him out of the house. He was shot when he fled.

> For the white mob, his death was not enough. Hair describes repulsively violent behavior: Men ran up and dragged the body from the doorway into the muddy street. More shots were pumped into the corpse. . . . Those who possessed no guns cursed at or kicked the corpse, which soon became indistinguishable from the trodden mud of Saratoga Street. . . . Shouts of "burn him burn him!" began to grow louder. . . . When Charles's body [was thrown] on the [police] wagon it fell in such a position that the mutilated head hung over the end. As soon as the

wagon wheels began to turn, hun   lair,
2008, pp. 174–175)

An autopsy later revealed 34 bullet hol   and leg
wounds, a skull "almost beaten to a pul

But even this was not enough to red   of July
27—the same evening that Charles's mu   orgue—
Whites burned down Thomy Lafon sch   chool in
New Orleans (Hair, 2008).

In her book *Mob Rule in New Orleans*, Wells-Barnett (1900/2005) righ-
teously asserted,

> The only evidence that Charles was a desperate man lay in the fact that
> he had refused to be beaten over the head by Officer Mora for sitting on
> a step quietly conversing with a friend. Charles resisted an absolutely
> unlawful attack, and a gun fight followed. Both Mora and Charles were
> shot, but because Mora was white and Charles was black, Charles was
> at once declared to be a desperado, made an outlaw, and subsequently
> a price put upon his head and the mob authorized to shoot him like a
> dog, on sight. (p. 9)

Was Robert Charles the fiend incarnate? Or did White supremacists epitomize a
violent culture that had the force of law?

Who Am I?

There is a good deal of resonance between the struggles that defined Charles's
life in 1900 and those of Black students today in New Orleans. As part of a
writing program called Students at the Center (SAC)—the program is based in
several New Orleans public schools and has enabled students to write about
their lives and communities for almost 20 years—students published a collection
titled *Who Am I?* (SAC, 2011; see also Buras, Randels, ya Salaam, & Students
at the Center, 2010). The students, most of them from working-class African
American families, reflect on issues of culture and identity and make evident the
community cultural wealth that exists as part of their life histories. Not unlike
Charles, they continue to confront a culture of White supremacy that depicts
them as deficient and as products of a culture of poverty. Their lives defy such
simple characterization.

Shana O'Connor shared the story of how she came to have her last name.
Her great-grandfather Joseph (Joe) Roberts was a Black man who had relations

with a White woman in the 1800s. When asked about this, the woman said she had been raped. "This accusation spread around the town so quickly," explained Shana, "that every white person in Tennessee wanted to get their hands on Joe" (SAC, 2011, p. 441). Two White men discovered where Joe was hiding and made plans to kill him; in his defense, Joe killed the two men, fled to New Orleans, and changed his last name to O'Connor. It turns out that the same kind of navigational capital that brought Robert Charles to New Orleans (and led him to temporarily change his name to Curtis Robertson after the train depot confrontation) is also a part of Shana's history. Much like Charles, her great-grandfather Joe was presumed to be the aggressor.

In a piece titled "My Bloodlines," Terrioues White reflected, "It was not my choice to be born a black male from New Orleans. It feels like a punishment, mainly because secretly, to most people, I'm considered a potential threat to a person's safety" (SAC, 2011, p. 445). Drawing on resistant capital to challenge such narrow understandings of his personhood, White declared, "I'm going to take my freedom." Thus he rejects the mold cast upon him. Similarly, Ariel Estwick reported that during time she spent in Nebraska, she "was instantly judged by the stereotypes of 'New Orleans people.'" She recollected, "I was assumed to be a very violent, funny talkin' and party-loving Creole person of minimal intelligence. They treated me not as what I was but what they wanted to see in me" (p. 170). Ariel provides a critique of culture of poverty assumptions—one that resists Moynihan's and Banfield's negative depictions of Black and lower-class families:

> The lives of both races are portrayed by the media . . . to be polar opposites. A white child grows up in a middle class home with both parents. The child is bright and humble. There are no problems at home. There are no financial worries. A black child grows up in a lower class environment, maybe a ghetto. The child most likely has one parent and has a family member suffering from an addiction. They are wild and violent because of their high stress environment. (SAC, 2011, p. 171)

Ariel underscores that in reality Whites and Blacks evidence a range of lifestyles.

Perhaps the cultural capital of working-class communities would be evident "If the Streets Could Talk." This is Bruce Lightell's contention in a poem bearing that title (SAC, 2011). "They would probably tell you about the constant flow of drugs being sold/on almost every block," he pondered. At the same time, he asserted, "They would tell you about how a single mother rushes to catch the bus/at five in the morning to her second job so she can make ends meet." The poem concluded, "If the streets could talk, they would say that some of the smartest kids in school/come from the projects and how many poor people have the brain power" (p. 141). But the streets don't talk, which is why struggles for equity and education must push back. These young people remind us that there is a thriving culture of resistance to build on.

Many of the students write about the hardships faced by their families and often give special notice to their mothers. Despite the portrayal of female-headed households as deficient and abusive, Ivyanne London stressed, "My hero is my mother, putting people before herself. . . . She lends money or provides help to other family members and friends when they need it most, even though she needs assistance just as bad" (SAC, 2011, p. 75). Ivyanne knows that her mother struggles to take care of her and her siblings, and she recognizes the skill, hard work, and sacrifice this requires. She attested, "When I grow up, I want to have the determination like her to never give up even when there isn't a penny to my name. Her courage is to never give up on herself nor her family" (p. 75). Ivyanne's mother is part of the network of social capital that helps her own children and extended family to survive. Without "a penny" to her name, she endows her children with aspirational capital or the ability to maintain hope amid difficult and unjust circumstances.

Keva Carr, writing "Louisiana, My Home," acknowledged the complexities of growing up Black and working class. On the same city streets where Charles sold *Voice of Missions*, Keva has her own memories. "Seventeen years I lived in my neighborhood," she recalled, "and recently I lived through gunshots going off and my mother's tears of fear." Nonetheless, Keva said, "I love passing through that block just to see Ms. Harrison's beautiful flowers" (SAC, 2011, p. 202). There are all kinds of days in Keva's neighborhood, not just the ones that seem to affirm the most prevalent images of the city in crisis. A similar sense of history, or familial capital, inspired Jennifer Harden to tell the story of her grandmother's wedding ring, which her mother now wears. The ring "is modest and simple with so much value—not with monetary value but the memories it holds." It reminds Jennifer's mother of

> all the days she and her siblings caught whippings from doing something they had no business doing. . . . The times they ate together. The laughs. The story-telling. The tears shed. The sick moments. The happy moments. The tired moments. The weak days. The sunny days. The no gain without pain days. (SAC, 2011, p. 408)

Perhaps Alia Fleury put it best when she wrote "Brighter Days . . . Possibly, Maybe." In one poetic stanza, she addressed both the culture of White power ("them") and the culture of working-class African Americans ("my people") in the context of the struggle to rebuild communities after Hurricane Katrina, especially amid efforts to rid the city of the culture of poverty that was supposedly responsible for its troubles:

> *For them to think that we didn't have any sense,*
> *For them to kick my people out and surround their homes with a*
> *fence;*
> *For them to put up demolition notices saying our houses weren't struc-*
> *turally sound.*
> *For them to tear down our homes quicker than the police could load*
> *their guns with another round*
> *For my people coming back "cus' ain't no place like home,"*
> *For my people screaming "WHO DAT" in the super dome.*
> (SAC, 2011, p. 375)

Just as Charles defended his life, Alia affirms that the members of the community will continue to fight to the death for the home they love, even as many Whites see little value in their presence (see also Buras, 2011, forthcoming). Another student, Veronique Dorsey, paid tribute to her family's house on First Street, which was purchased in 1933, rented out, and "the money used to put members of the family through school" (SAC, 2011, p. 450). The city demolished the house after Katrina.

Teachers and education activists can learn from Charles's life history and from the stories of SAC students in New Orleans. First and foremost, these stories challenge educators to question the view that working-class youth of color are culturally deficient and to build instead on existing forms of community cultural wealth. SAC teacher Kalamu ya Salaam pushes fellow educators to recognize students' assets:

> A sure sign that many of us do not understand our students is our refusal to understand that even if students can't spell, they can reason, even if students can't pronounce multisyllabic words, they can express themselves. How well a person does on a standardized test is no indication of that person's character or desire to learn. (Buras et al., 2010, p. 71)

The oppositional knowledge demonstrated by SAC students and teachers, and Charles's last stand, illuminates a legacy of resilience: Educators should draw insight and inspiration from this and situate their work within this tradition. Finally, these stories remind teachers that the culture of White supremacy merits interrogation rather than singularly blaming poor students of color for their problems. Ultimately, educators cannot teach in transformative ways if they do not understand the root causes of inequity.

In *Mob Rule in New Orleans*, Wells-Barnett (1900/2005) documented the horrors of White depravity, destruction, and violence. Considering the profoundly morbid history of lynching, she concluded with a question that squarely challenges those who depict people of color as the problem, asking, "Men and women of America, are you proud of this record which the Anglo-Saxon race has made for itself?" (p. 54). It was a disruptive question then, and it remains so now. White news reporters in New Orleans focused on Robert Charles. But who were they? Perhaps even more relevant today, who are we?

References

Alvarez, L., & Cooper, M. (2012, April 11). Prosecutor files charge of 2nd-degree murder in shooting of Martin. *New York Times*. Retrieved April 20, 2012, from www.nytimes.com

Banfield, E. C. (1968). *The unheavenly city: The nature and future of our urban crisis*. Boston: Little, Brown.

Bourdieu, P. (1984). *Distinction*. Cambridge, MA: Harvard University Press.

Buras, K. L. (2008). *Rightist multiculturalism: Core lessons on neoconservative school reform*. New York: Routledge.

Buras, K. L. (2011). Race, charter schools, and conscious capitalism: On the spatial politics of whiteness as property (and the unconscionable assault on black New Orleans). *Harvard Educational Review, 81*(2), 296–330.

Buras, K. L. (forthcoming). *Charter schools, race, and urban space: Where the market meets grassroots resistance*. New York: Routledge.

Buras, K. L., Randels, J., ya Salaam, K., & Students at the Center. (2010). *Pedagogy, policy, and the privatized city: Stories of dispossession and defiance from New Orleans*. New York: Teachers College Press.

Gorski, P. (2007). Savage unrealities: Classism and racism abound in Ruby Payne's framework. *Rethinking Schools, 21*(2), 16–19.

Hair, W. I. (2008). *Carnival of fury: Robert Charles and the New Orleans race riot of 1900* (Updated ed.). Baton Rouge: Louisiana State University Press.

Harris, C. I. (1995). Whiteness as property. In K. Crenshaw, N. Gotanda, G. Peller, & K. Thomas (Eds.), *Critical race theory: Key writings that formed the movement* (pp. 276–291). New York: New Press.

Hirsch, E. D., Jr. (1987). *Cultural literacy: What every American needs to know*. New York: Vintage Books.

Moynihan, D. P. (1996). The negro family: The case for national action. In M. Gerson (Ed.), *The essential neoconservative reader* (pp. 23–37). New York: Addison-Wesley.

Students at the Center. (2011). *Who am I? Reflections on culture and identity*. New Orleans, LA: Author.

Wells-Barnett, I. B. (2005). *Mob rule in New Orleans. With- Southern horrors: Lynch law in all its phases*. Cirencester, UK: Echo Library. (Original work published 1900)

Wilson, J. Q. (1996). The rediscovery of character: Private virtue and public policy. In M. Gerson (Ed.), *The essential neoconservative reader* (pp. 291–304). New York: Addison-Wesley.

Yosso, T. J. (2006). Whose culture has capital? A critical race theory discussion of community cultural wealth. In A. D. Dixson & C. K. Rousseau (Eds.), *Critical race theory in education: All God's children got a song* (pp. 167–189). New York: Routledge.

11

WAY DOWN YONDER IN THE PAWPAW PATCH
Resiliency in Appalachian Poverty

Joy Cowdery

"What is that smell in your room?" The "college prep" English teacher had walked over from across the hall after my "general" English students had exited my classroom. I noticed for the first time the familiar, though not unpleasant, smell of smoked ham. It was the beginning of November, and the families of my students had begun to heat their homes with wood furnaces. The students carried with them through the school day, clinging to clothes and hair and emanating from the pores of their skin, the smell of smoke and sweat. This was also the time of year when my high school students, often in charge of stoking the fire several times during the night, would fall asleep in class or fight to stay awake in many classes that seemed irrelevant to their immediate concerns.

As a fifth-generation Appalachian growing up in and around poverty, I have experienced many such contradictions between the expectations of the education system and the reality of children in Appalachian poverty. It is easy for us to buy into the stereotypes reflected by the White, poor, ignorant images of Appalachians that are perpetuated by the media and the resulting misperceptions about people who live in the hills and hollows of the Appalachian Mountains. While Appalachians share common history, art, music, and language, they also are diverse in fundamental ways. Conversations about poor Appalachian families rarely acknowledge our common thread of shared resiliency in coping with poverty and systemic barriers in health care, education, and the legal system. Looking at our lives through a lens of strength rather than deficiency can provide insight into how to capitalize on, rather than repress, the resilient qualities that Appalachian children and their families bring to the community.

Living in Appalachian Ohio, on the border of West Virginia, the only state that is considered totally in Appalachia, I have seen firsthand the damage that stereotyping and misunderstanding have done to children. Schools often unknowingly perpetuate a view of failure by not valuing the strengths poor children bring to the classroom. For poor students in Appalachia, the most discouraging image may be the one promoted by the media, depicting them as backwoods, ignorant isolates. From comic strips that once depicted feuding moonshiners in *Li'l Abner* to the portrayals of ignorance among characters in the *Beverly Hillbillies* and the more disturbing portrayal of West Virginians as cannibals in the *Wrong Turn* movies, negative images of how people in this region live are burned into common perception. More recently, a disparagement on the popular television sitcom *Modern Family* demonstrated that while the show promotes acceptance of diverse families, it is still all right to laugh at Appalachians. In one scene, a gay couple, Cam and Mitchell, had agreed during a drunken tête-à-tête with Mitchell's sister, Claire, to allow her to donate her eggs to create a genetically related baby for the couple. Once sober, the couple had second thoughts. But, as a parting shot, Mitchell looked at Cam, nodded knowingly, and said, "Too Appalachian" (Levitan, Lloyd, Higginbotham, O'Shannon, & Spiller, 2012).

This oppressive humor directed at Appalachians extends beyond Hollywood. I once had a national accreditation board member assessor who was visiting our Appalachian college tell me that the only thing he knew about Appalachia was from the movie *Deliverance*. He felt this comment was humorous and appropriate. I found it offensive.

What We're Up Against

It is important in combating stereotypes to look at what in the political and economic systems have caused poor rural Appalachian people to react in ways that may appear different or unreasonable to outsiders. An examination of the political and economic systems affecting the daily lives of poor rural Appalachian people may explain some reasons for behaviors that are the basis of the stereotypes I would like to see eliminated. Appalachian rural poverty is marked by unique problems. Health concerns, for example, are exacerbated by a lack of medical personnel and a lack of access to the latest forms of treatment. A lack of reliable transportation to cities that might offer better medical treatment impedes access to the preventative measures that ensure a healthier life. In some Appalachian families, decades of coal mining or other work in which laborers are exposed to asbestos, lead, and mercury has left a generation of older people disabled and chronically ill. The cancer rate is particularly high in Appalachia (Wingo et al., 2008). Appalachians also experience a much higher rate of heart disease than people in all other areas of the United States (Appalachian Regional Commission [ARC], 2011).

As the economy tightens, children in Appalachia are the first to feel the pinch. The lack of close, convenient, or affordable child care can keep some young families from seeking stable employment and deny them access to safe child care. Traditionally, many families have shared the responsibility for free child care, but as women become the primary wage earners in minimum-wage jobs during this economic downturn, free care for children is disappearing. Unlike in more populous areas where public transportation is available, local schools in sparsely populated areas of Appalachia cannot offer after-school programs because families have no way to pick up children after school bus routes are finished. There are also no youth centers or Boys and Girls Clubs in most rural areas. Some local schools are in such financial distress that busing for high school students has been eliminated. The result is that many students are now, and not by choice, "home schooled" or forced to attend an online school. The success rate for students forced into an alternative route to high school completion is far below that of their peers in the traditional school setting or of those who willfully choose alternative routes (Rasey, 2010).

The obstacles, in other words, are many.

Culture and Resiliency in Appalachia

I remember my own childhood in rural southeastern Appalachian Ohio, West Virginia, and Kentucky. Commonly shared values among my family and friends included the love of land and a sense of place-belonging. There was and still is an attachment to nature among many Appalachians, to the hills, the creeks, the fields. We widely share a profound respect for the awesomeness of nature. The uncontrollable factors of nature in this part of the United States—floods, droughts, and snowstorms—make weather a constant topic. It affects everyday life in a way not experienced in other modern settings. Sometimes the lack of central heating, spotty electrical systems, the scarcity of air conditioning, quickly rising water, and the threat of crops being destroyed by early frost or lack of spring rains dominate the day-to-day lives of people who are geographically isolated from their nearest neighbors. One natural catastrophe can financially wipe out a family for many years. This is when resilience among poor people in Appalachia is most clearly observed.

A combination of self-sufficiency and a healthy suspicion of government programs increases the support Appalachian families provide one another. Many communities, while geographically dispersed, are very tightly knit emotionally. It is expected that neighbor will help neighbor. This independence from outside help leads many communities to recuperate from loss with little government assistance. Because of the history of exploitation of Appalachians by outsiders, there is a prevailing mood that only family and community can be counted on in times of trouble. Our collective memory holds the lack of government support at Matewan. It includes the use of government subsidies to mining corporations who defrauded families of their farms as they kept them in abject poverty and dangerous working conditions. It is no secret that the coal-mining companies with "company store" policies forced families into producing illegal moonshine for money, operations that federal agencies regularly shut down. We remember the unfulfilled promises during the Great Society and how our grandparents watched as the government took over huge sections of land to build hydroelectric dams. In our own lifetimes the land has been taken for nuclear reactors, national parks, and interstate highways. This abuse by both corporations and government entities has led to a mistrust of those who come to our communities professing a desire to help. Unfortunately, this same attitude also leads many families to avoid applying for government assistance in the form of food stamps and parents to frequently refuse to sign their children up for free lunch programs. Although free and reduced-price lunch programs are widely available, one recent study found that one in four children eligible for free meals (23%) was not enrolled in the free and reduced-price lunch program (Burghardt et al., 2004).

The reliance and loyalty to family is also why a phenomenon that is perplexing to many health, business, and education system professionals occurs. Often, when an Appalachian family member seeks health care at an emergency room, the whole extended family accompanies the patient. Generally skeptical of the medical profession because of the high doctor turnover in remote areas (Coyne, Demina-Popescu, & Friend, 2006), the patient's family members will miss work and school, sometimes for lengthy periods of time, to assist the ill kin. Many times family members are offended by negative repercussions brought about by these sorts of absences.

In Appalachia, it is always family first because family will be there in tough times even when government services are unresponsive. When institutions like schools fail to recognize this, many Appalachians will simply get out of the system. One example of this is when university professors who teach in, but are not from, Appalachia do not understand how simply applying the attendance policies of their courses might force first-generation college students to drop out of higher education. This is in part why rural poor people often grow to feel more and more disconnected from schools—not because they don't care about education but because they learn that they are invisible to the education system.

Despite the fact that some sociologists, and particularly those who have endorsed the "culture of poverty" mentality, have identified this traditionalism or familism as a deficiency (Lewis & Billings, 1997), most Appalachian families see it as a way to collectively protect themselves in response to social ills. Generally speaking, in my experience, Appalachians do not resist change, but we do resist relinquishing the value of family first.

A similar misunderstanding is the assumption that rural and Appalachian residents do not value education (ARC, 2012), as evidenced by their lower attainment of postsecondary degrees. In a survey conducted by Ohio University in 2009, most of the Appalachian high school students surveyed greatly overestimate the cost of attending postsecondary education (ARC, 2012). Furthermore, both parents and students indicated a lack of knowledge about financial opportunities and the process of applying for financial aid (ARC, 2012). This lack of information can prevent Appalachian families from even applying for college.

Also, sometimes families fear the prospect of higher education taking younger family members out of the community. When success is measured by the quality of life rather than the size of a paycheck, having family close by is important. When adult children move away to accept a job, they frequently return to the nuclear family. It is not uncommon for many young family members who move to a city a few hours away to come home every weekend to be with their family (Coyne et al., 2006; Lewis & Billings, 1997). Another stressor is unfamiliarity with navigating a system that contrasts with the experiences and, sometimes, values of Appalachians (Howley, 2006). In many cases, Appalachian parents who want the same happiness and fulfillment for their own children as all other parents want believe that higher education is out of reach financially for them and do not actively pursue that goal.

It is easy for anyone not living in poverty to be insulated from the realities of people in poverty. It is easy to misinterpret others' actions. I can remember reading in our local paper one winter that our town council had flooded the basketball court on the "wrong" side of town to make an ice skating rink. My husband grew up in that neighborhood. The local kids smashed the ice with cement blocks. The town was outraged by the "vandalism." I commented on it, and my husband looked at me in amazement. He said, "Those children don't have ice skates!" They did have basketballs. The idea that they were clearing off *their* court had not occurred to me. People in poverty are not unlike anyone else. They make choices based on what they think is in their own best interests. This is called resilience.

Growing Up Old in Appalachia

Often poor Appalachian children are expected to grow up and assume adult responsibilities at young ages. The pleasures of childhood can be short-lived. Their lives often are invaded by the sharp realities of navigating a larger world that often looks upon their circumstances with disapproval and disrespect. Systems and circumstances frequently create barriers to success and, in some cases, survival.

One of my students died from what my other students called a "weak" heart, found too late by doctors. A lack of transportation had delayed the family making a 30-mile trip to the doctor when the boy initially became tired and listless. By the time a doctor saw him and sent him to the big city hospital two hours away, it was too late. During his brief stay in the hospital, his classmates wrote him letters. I gathered them in a big envelope and sent them to his mother. I did not share with my students that he probably had died before the letters reached him. When several of his friends returned from his private funeral, I asked about his family. His best friend described his final good-bye with tears in his eyes: "We took him from the church and walked down the big hill by the Pawpaw Patch near his farm and buried him. I helped carry him, but I just couldn't shovel the dirt on his casket." Then he broke into sobs. "He's home now," he choked.

Knowing the common religious language of most Appalachians in the region, I wasn't sure if he was referring to his friend finally going to heaven, which many identify as their true "home," or saying that his friend was back from the stress of a big city and safely "home" in his own backyard. He probably meant both. It was one of those times I was proud to be an Appalachian. I admired so much the deep sense of responsibility felt by somebody so young to "take care of our own," to ensure that his friend was home again after others had failed to protect him. This is what happens when you grow up fast, a common phenomenon in Appalachia.

Many Appalachian children are expected to be independent early in their lives. It is an economic necessity for most families to stretch the parent paycheck as far as possible. Most Appalachian and rural children work as soon as they are able to do so. Children as young as 10 or 12 years old work on family farms, in family businesses, or in jobs that cannot be tracked by overseers of employment laws. I was babysitting for cash by age 10. Many of my friends spent summers earning less than a dollar an hour packing tomatoes for local farms. The first time I earned five dollars for babysitting was the last time my parents bought my school clothes. I have shopped for and purchased my own clothing since I was in fifth grade. By the time I was 16 and could legally work, I became self-sufficient.

This sort of self-reliance is common in poor Appalachia. Children are expected to take care of many of their own needs and certainly the needs of younger siblings. Parents teach children the necessity of contributing to the survival and success of the family. Parents frequently talk to their toddlers in much the same way as they speak to other adults. The expectation is that they will become contributing members of the family unit as soon as possible. All parts of the unit work together to help the unit as a whole. Children rarely question the expectations of their adult family members to shoulder the responsibility for "taking care of their own business" such as doing schoolwork, acquiring food when hungry, and entertaining themselves when bored.

Unfortunately, too many educators interpret this lack of adult involvement as a sign that the parents just don't care about school. As is the case in every economic bracket, some parents don't care, but most do. The lack of school involvement certainly does not reflect a lack of caring. In addition to the challenges that people in poverty face in becoming more involved with schools such as a lack of transportation, a lack of affordable child care, and long working hours, a lack of on-site involvement among some Appalachian families might reflect parents' views that school personnel are more qualified to be responsible for learning than they are. In addition, many parents have not had positive school experiences, so they might avoid interacting with teachers and administrators. Finally, the expectation that the child is responsible for his or her learning may influence the amount of parental involvement in the day-to-day involvement in school assignments.

In contrast, perhaps, to people from other cultures, Appalachians can experience praise for their accomplishments as a source of embarrassment. Calling attention to one's own accomplishments is fodder for ridicule. My friend often refers to this phenomenon as the "whack-a-mole" attitude. Just like the popular game at the county fair, when a child thinks he or she is superior enough to rise above the crowd, someone, including parents, might verbally whack him or her back down. Generally, Appalachians pride themselves on maintaining an egalitarian community. It is often seen as distasteful for someone to imply a hierarchy in which some people deserve better treatment than others. Respect is earned and mutual. Using "title" antecedents may imply superiority, so many Appalachians will not use them. So, it is no surprise when adults expect Appalachian children to "wait, obey, and be grateful for adult praise" that the children are confused. Teachers often perceive this resistance and self-reliance as being noncompliant. These same teachers could, by indicating trust in the child's judgment, find themselves teaching a loyal, hardworking, and pleasant student.

Appalachian parents do, at times, speak with pride about their children. Often it is in referring to the times they see their own children standing up for themselves or resisting bureaucracy. Appalachian pride tends to be focused on the admiration of strong individualism. This is the pride, for instance, that Appalachians feel in their own music and art. Appalachian art is generally created from something natural and familiar. Being able to create something new from what is available is a source of pride. It is the pride of resourcefulness and creativity.

The Challenge of School

School can be a challenge for any person in poverty. Frequently, the cultures of home and school collide. It is no different for Appalachian poor youth. One example would be the hygiene lessons taught in school. Schools teach the importance of being clean. It is very difficult for many people in rural poverty to meet the "clean" standards taught implicitly and explicitly in schools. Access to facilities that are taken for granted by most teachers often are not available to people in rural poverty. For example, poor families who must depend on their own water wells have to dole out measures of water for the week, and laundry often is not the top priority. Children may wear the same clothes for many days without washing them, not because they don't want their clothes to be clean but because the families can't afford to keep them clean. When I was growing up, I was not allowed to use the family's washing machine because of the fear of it breaking and the family not being able to afford repairs. Many times I went to school in clothes I wore multiple times before washing them.

It was at school, actually, that I was "outed" as poor by a substitute teacher. Like many rural poor students, my home life and the expectations of school were in direct contrast to each other, and I learned to lie and hide the ways that made me different from what schools taught I was supposed to be. When I was in seventh grade, a substitute teacher baited me by asking if I had put on clean clothes that day. I, of course, said yes, lying through my teeth. She called me on it, saying, "I know you are lying. You wore that shirt last week and the same spot is still on it." I was so ashamed. Caught between not being able to do anything and the lack of clothes I had to wear, my only recourse was to transform from being a child who had not missed a day of school in 7 years to being a child who missed school as frequently as I needed to in hopes that people would not notice my lack of wardrobe options.

As a teacher in Appalachia, I recognized that some of my students did not even have running water for parts of the year. Outside pipes would freeze during the winter, especially for families living in trailers. Many homes burned to the ground as residents tried to thaw the pipes with blowtorches or other open flame devices. A shower was not worth losing a home. Covering their own smell was a delicate tightrope many high school girls walked. Too much perfume was worse than the body odor. For students lucky enough to find a ride to school before the school day started, gym showers were available, but often they would have to put on dirty clothes over their clean bodies. Many students adopted my own philosophy and just stayed home. Sometimes missing out on an education is easier than being humiliated.

There were other times school taught me I was poor and unworthy. A program in my elementary years allowed poor students to work for their lunches. So, in sixth grade, while my classmates enjoyed an extended recess after lunch, I was eating alone and washing pans, scraping food off trays, and spraying boiling water onto dishes. Needless to say, the whole school could identify who was in poverty very quickly. We were identified, as well, in the lunch line through a sign-in process for those of us who qualified for free lunch. It has been many years since I was in elementary school, but this kind of process remains at many local schools. I also have seen office doors with publically posted lists of students still owing school fees. I am amazed to realize how little has changed.

Too often, schools, and those of us working in them, simply do not recognize how students in poverty must transverse the most difficult circumstances even to attend school. A fellow teacher told me about her student who was the oldest sibling of three younger brothers. Her mother was addicted to meth, and she, as a high school freshman, was trying to hold the family together. Every morning she would wake up her brothers and get them ready for school. She would walk them to a nearby elementary school. Her high school classes, of course, began an hour earlier than the elementary school day did. By the time she walked her brothers to the elementary school each morning, she was an hour late for the start of her own classes. Each day she would be given detention for coming late to school. That was the reward for her conscientiousness.

Similarly, I find that many schools, and far too many teachers, have lower expectations for children in poverty. In small towns in Appalachia, as in most communities, neighborhoods for the poorest of the poor are very well-known. A street address is a dead giveaway for children most likely to be in families struggling economically, with the least resources. My husband grew up in one of these neighborhoods. His home address often was enough to convince guidance counselors that he would be unsuccessful in school. Despite his outstanding math scores on standardized tests, he was placed in a remedial math class for the first few months of middle school. He ended up helping the teacher teach the class until she advocated for him to be moved to her advanced courses. This was too little, too late. He already had been denied a start in the "honor" track, which kept him out of the most advanced math classes until college.

As a teacher, I always have had to balance my desire to teach skills that would help my students be "successful" in the society outside the shelter of their Appalachian neighborhoods with my desire to acknowledge their realities and strengths. One incident clearly allowed me to see that even the most innocent request from a teacher might create serious obstacles for a child. One night, I stopped by a local discount store to pick up note cards. Two disheveled young men were in the school supply aisle. As I approached, I overheard part of their conversation. The older one of the pair was trying to explain to the younger one that he simply didn't have the money to purchase a five-subject notebook.

"But my teacher said I have to have a five-subject notebook," pleaded the younger boy as he eyed the name-brand, official-looking notebook.

"Look, I don't have the money for that, but we can buy five of these one-subject notebooks for 88 cents each. She won't care. You can put them together," the older boy patiently explained. There was no response from the younger boy.

In an attempt to find something cheaper, the two went up and down the aisle; however, the younger boy kept coming back to the five-subject notebook. I could only imagine what was going through his head as he picked up and put down the notebook. Would his teacher think that he just didn't care, that he didn't listen, or, worse, that he was being downright defiant? Would the substitution of cheaper notebooks color the teacher's perception of him? After all, who would imagine that this particular young man cared so much about what his teacher wanted? It was a big dilemma created by what the teacher surely imagined was a simple request.

After listening to the conversation, I offered to purchase the five-subject notebook along with my items, but my offer was met with suspicion. After explaining that I had overheard the conversation and, being a teacher, understood how important it was to have what was required for school, the boys agreed to let me buy the notebook. As we were walking to the checkout counter, I learned that the older of the two boys had dropped out of high school. It wasn't hard to imagine the same fate for the younger boy.

Pride

For Appalachians, surviving the disadvantages of poverty is difficult but not devastating. Most of the time food scarcity and lack of medical resources can be survived. It is the rejection and blame placed on children by people in the very systems that should support them that create invisible scars that last a lifetime. Poverty doesn't diminish the values of family, community, independence, and faith. While no one wishes to be denied basic needs, that is not the worst part of poverty. Navigating a system that places us in a powerless situation is the worst part of poverty. Being made to feel less by overt or subtle actions is what keeps many Appalachians resistant to "outsiders." I believe that Appalachian pride is a response to that degradation. It is worn like a shield to protect against the respect that is so often denied. It grows from a recognition that investing only in people who share the same values can give one self-worth.

Even today, I am sometimes caught by surprise by how much my roots influence my perceptions of situations. Not long ago, in response to a negative reaction to a child's behavior, I experienced Appalachian pride. It was an instinctive and primal reaction. I was standing in line at a family restaurant that kept crayons by the registration desk. Suddenly, a little two-year-old girl in ill-fitting clothes from a large family helped herself to the crayons and coloring page. The hostess raised her eyebrows and then frowned. My first thought was that the hostess was disrespectful. She obviously disapproved of the child's behavior. I knew that the child was not being rude. She was doing what she had always done. She was taking care of herself without the help or permission of adults. I smiled. I was proud of her. I was proud of our Appalachian independence and self-reliance.

References

Appalachian Regional Commission. (2011). *Data reports, socioeconomic data by county*. Retrieved January 1, 2012, from www.arc.gov.data.www.arc .gov

Appalachian Regional Commission. (2012). *Development and progress of Appalachian higher education*. Retrieved October 26, 2012, from www.arc .gov.data/DevelopmentandProgressofAHENetworkHistory/

Burghardt, J., Gleason, P., Sinclair, M., Cohen, R., Hulsey, L., & Milliner-Waddell, J. (2004). *Evaluation of the national school lunch program application/verification pilot projects: Volume I.* Retrieved November 5, 2012, from www.fns.usda.gov/oane/MENU/Published/CNP/FILES/NSLPPilotVol1.pdf

Coyne, C., Demina-Popescu, C., & Friend, D. (2006). Social and cultural factors influencing health in southern West Virginia: A qualitative study. *Preventing Chronic Disease, 3*(4), 124–132.

Howley, C. (2006). Purpose and place: Schooling and Appalachian residence. *Journal of Appalachian Studies, 12*(1), 58–78.

Levitan, S., Lloyd, C., Higginbotham, A., O'Shannon, D. (Writers), & Spiller, M. (Director). (2012). Aunt mommy [Television series episode]. In Levitan, S., Lloyd, C., et al. (Executive producers), *Modern Family.* New York, NY: ABC.

Lewis, R., & Billings, D. (1997). Appalachian culture and economic development. *Journal of Appalachian Studies, 3*(1), 43–69.

Rasey, M. (2010). *Ohio online school performance analysis and program information.* Retrieved December 2011, from http://michelle-rasey.suite101.com/ohio-online-school-performance-analysis-and-program-information-a320663#ixzz1qoKe0cpo

Wingo, P. A., Tucker, T. C., Jamison, P. M., Martin, H., McLaughlin, C., Bayakly, R., . . . Richards, T. B. (2008). Cancer in Appalachia, 2001–2003. *Cancer, 112*(1), 181–192.

12

MENDING AT THE SEAMS

The Working-Class Threads That Bind Us

Jaye Johnson Thiel

The edge to be bound should be held well within the center. (Singer Manufacturing Company, 1941, p. 37)

I sat at my dining room table, books beside me and computer in front of me. Peering out of the double panes of my dining room windows, I was mesmerized by the man from the auto glass repair shop as he replaced the windshield of my eldest son's car. Prying, scraping, pressing, aligning, the man worked diligently for an hour and 15 minutes in bitter 30-degree weather, glove-less so he could have better control of his fingers.

The work he did was precise work. Hard work. Intellectual work.

I must admit, I never had given much thought to the job of glass repair; never, that is, until I needed someone who could fix the cracked windshield of our beat-up 1988 Volvo. It's not easy, I found, finding somebody with the skills to fix the old import or even to find parts for such repairs. However, as luck would have it, we found a skilled craftsman and compatible parts.

As I watched him carefully align the glass, I contemplated all the skills some-body must possess in order to complete such work. I found myself less and less interested in my e-mail. I became distracted from my writing and disenchanted with the theoretical and philosophical reading I was doing. Instead, I became lost in memories I had ignored for quite some time; flashes of my mother slowly came back to me, visions of her bent over a sewing machine, shoulders curved, eyes squinting in pale light to thread needles and load bobbins, toiling over extraordinary handiworks with intricate details.

Sewing costumes for a church play and our dresses for Sunday school proved to be lucrative for my mother. Women noticed her work and wanted her to sew for their homes: decorative pieces from expensive fabrics that sometimes had to be special ordered. My mother agreed. No longer would she sew only for kin. Now she would sew for other people, a job that came with a little money and a lot of stress.

It was tedious work. Creative work. Intellectual work.

Her artistry was flawless, so word spread. Soon women living in well-to-do neighborhoods coveted her work. She was offered steady jobs that often kept her sitting up late at night in our doublewide trailer making drapes, cushions, and bedspreads to adorn the rooms of affluent homes. Because she knew her work was going to be showcased in these homes, nothing less than perfection was acceptable to her. If even one stitch seemed out of place, she would rip out the seam and start over. Never quite satisfied with her final product, she often asked for less than the money she was due for the time and effort she had expended.

Occasionally she took a break from sewing jobs to create beautiful garments for me. This was especially true at the start of a new school year or on the eve of a pressing event like a formal dance or Easter Sunday. I remember one dress especially, a pink semiformal she made for me for a Valentine's dance. Tea length with wide straps, the dress was made of a shiny cotton fabric. Antique lace, remnants from a bargain table, covered the entire dress. It had '50s vintage flair and was exquisite. All my friends commented on its beauty. To this day, despite the fact that it no longer fits me, it hangs in the back of my closet, a memento of years past.

Adjusting for Tension

The sound of the heat circulating in my house returns me to a sense of now, the moment at hand. Staring out the window, I watch as the glass repairman rubs his hands together to generate warmth and bends his fingers—open, closed, open, closed—in a movement I have seen my mother perform as she sewed. I sigh and think about the pink dress and, maybe for the first time, realize what it represents.

More than aging fabric, the dress holds in its bodice something profounder than the memories of a dance or a long-forgotten date. Woven into each stitch is the deep and remarkable care of my mother's hands and what they taught me growing up. It was from her that I learned what it means to cut on the bias, backstitch, and fill a bobbin. She introduced me to batting, casing, piping, presser foots, and interfacing. She is the expert who taught me how to hem, search for patterns, make my own handbag. She is the teacher who showed me how to straight stitch, apply fusible web, and take account of seam allowances before making the first cut.

These memories, like threads, are stitched into my being, and I can't help but wonder if the man outside has similar scraps of memories from his past. Does he have memories of learning about car repair or some other skill passed down from his folks? There is something there, in the seam allowance between his fabric and mine, that makes me feel as though we share a sort of solidarity.

Glass repair and sewing—both unravel separately and then tie back again, intertwined in my mind.

Two jobs.

Two people.

Two sets of hands.

I think about hands carrying the evidence of years of work, stained nails and calluses; I look around me and imagine the hands that crafted everything in the room.

A banana picked far away, delivered on a truck, stocked on a shelf.

A coffee mug molded from clay, painted and fired, sold at a local market.

A book written, printed, bound, shipped, shelved.

Hands all around me, easy to forget once the fruits of their labor have left their fingers.

Why do the workers behind the work become invisible? Why are they forgotten? Why do we often fail to see the craft as part of the person who crafted it? I look down at my own hands and I remember they are attached to a living body that is capable of action well beyond the work they do—just like my mother or the glass repairman. It occurs to me that the action of work cannot be untwined from the worker or the worker's life. They are always entangled. And, yet, in our educational traditions, these working-class lives often are unrecognized and underappreciated, absent from our teaching and learning.

I cannot remember a time when my working-class family was represented in the academic spaces I traversed. I don't know if my teachers and my principals saw the work my family did as less valuable or less intellectual than their work or the work of those women buying my mother's work. But I do know that in school, the work of electricians, of seamstresses, and of store clerks was never discussed. With the exceptions of the few stitches I brought with me from home and a home economics class, the threads of working-class labor were never sewn into the fabric of my school experiences.

I was taught to read the "classics" and write about them. I memorized theorems and learned to figure sines and cosines. I dissected animals in order to learn about the inner workings of living, breathing beings. I loved school. I loved my family. But the two were made from different cloths, always separate. At home, the work of a seamstress provided for me, clothed me, fed me, and loved me. At school, the work of a seamstress was seen as a joke, a home economics class that was, in essence, a filler on course schedules for the non-college-bound students; an easy A. As a teenager, sewing these two worlds together seemed almost impossible.

When one sews, there are two important things about which to be aware: (a) the tension of the threads in the machine and (b) seam allowances on the fabric. If the tension on the thread is set too tight, the threads will break or pull the cloth so taut that it won't lie flat. The seam allowance refers to how much fabric is left between the edge and the stitching. To put two pieces together, one has to leave room for the seam. If the fabric is cut too close to where the pieces should be stitched together, the garment will come out missized and misshaped.

When I look back on my school experiences, I realized that, like threads in a machine, there was often too much tension being pressed on the fabric of my identities. I lived one way but was expected to strive for another. I found myself haphazardly trying to make the two pieces—my working class-ness and my academic-ness—fit together. This left me always cutting away at the material of my own experiences in hopes of bringing school and home together. But no matter how much I tried to seamlessly sew these cloths into one, it could not be done.

School and home identities were so distinctly different in texture, so distinctly classed, that when one fabric would give, the other would ravel at the ends. So I kept cutting and scrapping very important aspects of my life. When I understood cross-pollination and genetics in science, I never told people it was because we grew and raised most of our food. When my teachers gave us writing assignments, I was ashamed to write about the Saturday mornings I spent helping my stepfather sell watermelons from the back of the truck to neighboring communities because we needed extra cash to pay for cheerleading outfits and cheer camp. Instead, I wrote tragic "Brontë-esque" stories with young female characters losing loved ones.

Even school relationships were not immune. When going out with friends, I would fret over someone picking me up at my trailer home—I never let that happen on a first date. First dates were always scheduled to meet at a rendezvous point: another friend's house or the local movie theater. Over time, it seemed the more I cut away, the less allowance I left for the seams, the space where school and home might join. As a result, who I had become no longer fit who I was. I pretended to be a middle-class, college-bound student, trying to blend in with the rest of the kids in my classes. But I wasn't. I was a fraud, and the fraudulent representation of myself was emotionally difficult to bear because "class hybridity does not sit easily with a sense of authenticity. Feelings of being an imposter are never far away" (Reay, 2001, p. 337). I felt missized, misshaped, and taut, like a garment that was sewn with little care.

Refilling the Bobbin

When somebody sews on a machine, there are two sources of thread that compose the stitching. One is the spool atop the machine, where the thread is threaded through the workings of the machine and into the needle. The other is hidden in a little compartment directly under the needle and presser foot, wrapped around a small flat spool called a bobbin. Many people don't know the bobbin is there. Novice sewers often forget the bobbin, failing to load it before starting to sew. But the bobbin is important, despite being hidden inside the machine. If the bobbin runs out, the stitches made by the top thread will not remain and cannot lock, joining the pieces of the fabric. The needle has to pick up thread from the bobbin to make the interlocked seam that holds it all together.

Sometimes I feel like my working-class past is like the bobbin: hidden, forgotten, but important, holding it all together.

It is only recently, as an adult, that I have realized how much I need both threads—the ones you can see *and* the ones you can't—because it is the thread on the bobbin, my working-class threads, that sews all of the fabric of my life together into one piece. Without it, the top stitch, everything else I encounter, would be just a loose thread, a needle constantly piercing the material without any staying power. Yet it is this very thread, the one on the bobbin, that so often has been ignored in public spaces.

The threads in the seam are delicate. When under pressure, they can split apart, ripping the two sides away from each other. I would bet the same could be said of glass in a windshield. It always appears to be weaker around the edges. School put too much pressure on my seams, and because I have the perfectionist qualities of my mother, I often was left feeling as though I needed to rip them out and start over. In other words, I was constantly trying to reinvent myself. I tried to find new ways to take the spotlight off my family life and redirect it onto my academic life. I held myself like my counterparts, often poking fun of the so-called redneck persona, when, in fact, that persona is where I came from—hard work, the kind that leaves dirt under the nails, comes with long hours, and barely gets a family through Thursdays. In history classes I focused on the conversations about the American Dream and agreed when teachers said that everyone has an opportunity to make it in America if they just work hard enough, were educated enough, were invested enough, never minding the role luck plays in so-called upward mobility. Never taking into consideration the countless people who work their bodies to physical exhaustion each week just to make ends meet—people like my family. I came to believe that working-class life was something to be ashamed of, that it was not enough.

I was wrong.

Eventually, it was the working-class thread I brought from home that was the strongest thread of all. It was the one that locked everything else into place. And in the end, it was the only thread that could mend my broken seams. Because it wasn't until I allowed myself to acknowledge that the other half of me was an asset and embodied potential, rather than see it as an absence of assets or as failure, that I finally felt free of shame and more dignified as a being in this world. This was a realization that I didn't embody until well into my college career, when I met a professor who wrote about, and encouraged me to read about, working-class lives in new ways, showing me, for the first time, that "purposeful theory and criticism are not divorced from the physicality of working-class lived experience" (Zandy, 2001, p. xv).

Cutting on the Bias

Nowadays, most days, I read, write, think. I own a sewing machine and boxes of fabric. Sadly, though, they seldom are brought out into the light and often are pushed aside for other work. But I still find comfort in knowing that they sit there, waiting in plastic bins for me to come back to them some day. Sometimes I find myself wondering how I can merge these two worlds—bring stories, and theory, and philosophy to life through my mother's craft. How do I allow for and mend the seams? How can I bring these two threads together? And then I realize that is exactly what I do when I work. Just as my mother sewed antique lace over shimmering pink cotton in order to create my Valentine's dress, I find ways to put two seemingly impossible fabrics together through writing.

I have always been cutting on the bias, creating pages of words that weave in and out of both my academic and working-class experiences, writing that differs from the traditional patterns of the academy. When I write for academic reasons, I choose to give my narrative voice a place in my theoretical and philosophical thinking. I give autonomy to my experiences of growing up working class. I allow myself to be vulnerable in these spaces in hopes that others won't have to feel so vulnerable. I work to bring dignity to pedagogical spaces by paying particular attention to the generative lives of the working class.

My writing is my work—productive, inventive, and intellectual.

I tell my stories, allowing my threads to show, even when it is difficult to do so. I refuse to let go of my working-class past because I know it is the thread that embodies my understitching and I would be nothing without it. Even as I write this, I bristle at speaking in the academic voices I so often read during my schooling. I have come to realize that the threads of my experience matter and have the potential to add to the academy in a way that nothing else can. Each story I write pieces remnants from my past to swatches of my present, surging a seam where a working-class life and an academic life merge. Something I was unable to do when I was younger.

I often wonder if it would have been different had teachers taken the time to consider working-class lives in their curricular and pedagogical choices. What if courses had taken a social-class-sensitive approach to pedagogy (Jones & Vagle, 2013)? What if history classes discussed unions and local work history or recognized social-classed systems as entities and conditions that continue to exist rather than mentioned them only in a brief blip during our study of the Great Depression? What if students created maps that included economic landscapes of their local communities and used them to discuss inequalities? What if elementary school libraries included working-class stories in their collections? What if high school reading materials included working-class perspectives, such as those penned by Dorothy Allison, Sherman Alexie, or bell hooks? What if students were encouraged to write narratives that explored autobiography bonds through *all* types of work or persuasive and opinion pieces examining living wages? What if summer vacation stories about running through the sprinkler were met with as many "oohs" and "aahs" as those about trips to beaches and Disney World? I believe that if we truly want to educate all children, we must take these sorts of questions into consideration when making pedagogical decisions. It would have made a difference for me, and I believe it has the potential to create a dignified space for all students, regardless of social class, in school.

Allowing for Seams

The man from the auto glass repair shop finished replacing the window in my son's car. As I paid him, I realized how thoughtless I had been not to offer him coffee or hot tea or cocoa—something to warm his body, something to warm his hands. As an attempt to make amends, I walk back to the computer and begin to write. Any doubts I had that morning about whether I belong in this academic space have faded. I do belong here, as does my story.

The fibers of the working class and working poor are tightly twisted. They are strong. They stretch. They resist chemicals and abrasion. And they make a variety of beautiful stitches. Yet in the academy we seem to allow ourselves to get tangled up, cutting these threads away from the educational fabric. Instead, let's take time to see the lives those threads are attached to and what those lives have to offer us. Stop telling working-class students that they must "adjust [their] language, [their] behavior, and perhaps [their] values, to get rid of all [the] working-class baggage, and travel light if [they] want to 'make it out'" (Zandy, 2001, p. 246). Better yet, don't think of the goal as "making it out" at all but rather set a collective goal for economic justice, dignity, and respect instead.

As educators, see *all* work as creative, *all* lives as meaningful. Embrace the lives children and families bring to the classroom, consider each child as a learning opportunity, an opportunity to change self rather than change others, turning what was once perceived problematic into possibilities. We must question our selves, become reflexive, when the lives of our students don't match the lives of our own. Perhaps, then, we will begin to realize that the threads of *all* lives have a place here in the fabric of academic spaces. We just have to remember to allow for the seams.

References

Jones, S., & Vagle, M. (2013). Living contradictions and working for change: Toward a theory of social class-sensitive pedagogy. *Educational Researcher, 42*(3), 129–141.

Reay, D. (2001). Finding or losing yourself? Working-class relationships to education. *Journal of Educational Policy, 16*(4), 333–346.

Singer Manufacturing Company. (1941). *Instructions for using Singer Portable Electric Sewing Machine 221–1: Lockstitch, for family use with foot control.* Form No. 19657. The Singer Manufacturing Company. Retrieved from www.ismacs.net/singer_sewing_machine_company/manuals/singer-sewing -machine-221-1-featherwight-manual.pdf

Zandy, J. (2001). *What we hold in common: An introduction to working-class studies.* New York: Feminist Press at the City University of New York.

13

"STUDENT TEACHERS"

What I Learned From Students in a High-Poverty Urban High School

Lori D. Ungemah

After 11 years of teaching in Title I schools in Brooklyn, New York, I left my high school with great heaviness in my heart to teach at a community college. Throughout my career the job had gotten increasingly harder. A struggling school, we were victim to a bevy of new reform measures; each year we scraped to make Adequate Yearly Progress for No Child Left Behind until eventually we were put into a transformation model for Race to the Top money. Because of these stresses, the administration and teaching staff constantly shifted, and this hurt the student body, which was becoming increasingly poor and lower skilled (in regard to what was measured by the high-stakes tests). My teacher friends, some of whom had taught with me but left our school for one less "high needs," would ask passively insulting questions like "Why are you still *there*?" or "Why don't you go teach at a *real* school?" I never knew how to answer their questions at the moment, but I do know this: I walked into that building one person and left a different, better one.

My school was attended almost exclusively by students of color, and by the time I left our student population included more than 80% living in poverty. We had all the problems that are portrayed in Hollywood movies about inner-city schools, but, to me, we were rich in the beauty and complexity of what makes us all human.

So why did I stay there? I *chose* to stay at my school for 10 years because teaching there allowed me to engage in social justice work every day. It allowed me to be on the ground, knee-deep in the muck of life and its challenges in low-income communities, and to grow with the students. My work was not solely about teaching students many of my teacher colleagues would not dare to teach but about the learning that made me a better, more compassionate, more understanding citizen of this world.

As much as I enjoy teaching, I might enjoy learning from the students even more. My students taught *me* during my career. They were the student teachers, and they gave me an education I could not have gotten anywhere else. No, they didn't walk in with a Learning Objective that matched the Common Core

Standards for College and Career Readiness, complete with a Do Now, a lesson with multiple entry points for differentiated learning, a structured format for me to share out my findings, and an informal assessment at the end of the period to gauge whether I had grasped the material of their lives. The beauty of the students teaching the teacher (and the rest of the class) was that these lessons were organic and spontaneous. There were many moments in my classes when I found myself at a crossroad: Either I could move on with the lesson plan or I could pause, step aside, and give the students the floor. It wasn't until the middle of my second year of teaching that I began to recognize what, exactly, was happening in those moments, but after that first lesson from my students (one I will never forget on the code of the streets), I embraced the moments when their ideas supplemented mine. This open exchange of knowledge made us an authentic community of learners.

Recently I attended a colleague's wedding, and she seated me at a table of teachers who all worked at one of the most respected high schools in Chicago. After a few minutes of polite dinner conversation, the man next to me, a fellow English teacher, came to the quick conclusion that our student populations and teaching experiences were starkly different. He was correct. But then he asked me, earnestly, "After your years in the classroom, what conclusions did you take away about that student population?" (Of course, I took issue with his use of the word *that*, but, as we were at a wedding, I politely ignored the term. Plus, he seemed honestly curious.) Great question, I thought. As I navigate this transition in my professional life from high school teacher to community college professor, I find myself asking, What did I learn after almost a dozen years in a low-income urban classroom, surrounded by students defined as "at risk" because of their poverty and race? What did I learn about my students? What did I learn about myself?

We all are and we all aren't our stereotypes. During my first years teaching, I was continuously perplexed by how easily my students and I constructed and categorized each other along stereotypical racial lines. They saw me as a typical White girl, and I saw them as typical urban kids. We were flat characters in each other's eyes.

"What? I don't sound like *that*!" I'd exclaim when I heard them mocking my voice; they made me sound like a Valley girl from the movie *Clueless* each time they parroted my directions or lectures in class. As much as they mocked me, they were equally curious. I blatantly and shyly was asked questions about White people. Why do White people eat so much salad? Why do White people dance badly? Why are White people all rich? Why are White people racist? At first I was slightly frustrated with their questions, but eventually I began to realize I *was* a lot of those stereotypes, and I began to see myself as White. Yes, it might sound ridiculous, but I never had to think deeply about what it meant to be White before I became a teacher at age 26. And yes, I *do* sound like a stereo-typical White girl when I talk, and I *do* eat a lot of salad.

But my lived experiences are what define me beyond these stereotypes. I have a sister who twice was a teenage mom, I have biracial nieces and a nephew, I have a crack dealer in my family, my dad died of diabetes complications when I was a young adult, and I was adopted as a baby because I was accidently created by two curious high school seniors. The realities of my life transcend my stereotype, and the students slowly understood that yes, although I am a White girl, I am also a complex person with a twisted, layered life who is a lot more than she might initially seem. We learned that about each other.

I had the same perception of my students. On the facade, many were every stereotype of the urban "at-risk" student that I had heard of, and that was what struck me first. From their saggy or too-tight clothes to their constant cursing, from their tattoos for friends killed by gang violence to their open allegiance to gangs, they too were the stereotypes I had heard about. But when they talked, wrote, and discussed the complexities of their lives, their choices, and their behaviors, when they schooled me on what it was like to grow up as them, I realized they were so much more than the tough urban student veneer they projected to the world. When I got to know them as people, as individuals, instead of a nameless, faceless group, they became real to me.

Again, that must sound ridiculous, but racism and classism are just that: ridiculous. The most hardened student had a beautiful and deep story full of choices, thoughts, and emotions, and once that story was told—*bam!*—the stereotype of who I thought she or he was split open like a chrysalis revealing the beautiful complex person inside. Amazing. My students, especially because we differed in race and class, taught me to see that in the classroom and beyond. What a gift.

Every student has a story to tell, and often those stories are difficult to hear. Teaching English has to be one of the best and most difficult jobs available, because even within the most stringent test-driven scripted curricula, we can allow students to write about their lives in class. I do a lot of free write exercises in class; it builds writing stamina. Students should connect what they read to their lives through writing; the text-to-self connection is a tenet of literacy. Even the best argument-based paper has an element of narrative in it. There are many opportunities for students to find the power of their voices and their personal stories within an English class, and with pedagogy and curriculum on my side, I encouraged them to write about their lives.

Their words helped me get to know them as individuals, and with that knowledge I was able to be a better teacher. However, I learned over and over that when I gave my students the freedom to write about their own lives, the stories I read often left me breathless. Teachers need to respond to these stories both as teachers and as human beings, and that might be hard for those of us who never experienced such hardships or who have never come to terms with our own hardships. I found myself in the second category; I was 26 years old and only beginning to reflect on the roller coaster of my own life. But even when I did not know how to respond, I responded to let the students know I heard them. Year after year I realized that my students had harder lives than I could ever imagine.

Many, if not most, of my students lived lives I doubt I could survive. Their resilience amazed me. Truly. How does a 16-year-old boy come to school the day after his sister was shot and participate in a Socratic Seminar? How does a freshman girl, living in a homeless shelter in the Bronx, commute to Brooklyn and get to school on time, every morning, although her clothes haven't been washed and she hasn't eaten? How does a 15-year-old boy show up for English class with a black eye and a split lip and then write about being jumped out of a gang during the class free write?

My students wrote about these obstacles, and in the beginning of my career, I was not sure how to respond. Of course the traditional comments on grammar, spelling, organization, and idea development wouldn't suffice. I did my job as their English teacher, but I also wrote notes back to the students about their personal stories. I acknowledged their pain and how hard their circumstances were, and I told them I was proud of them and respected them for living through it and coming to school. I told them they were brave. I celebrated their resilience. I offered a variety of resources, from books to cookies to counseling. But the most important thing is that I told them I heard them and that I would be there if they ever wanted to talk.

But sometimes written or verbal feedback didn't feel like enough. Take, for instance, the homeless student I mentioned earlier, whom I will call Denise. She lived in a shelter in Brooklyn that became overcrowded. The city's solution was to relocate her family to a shelter deep in the Bronx that was less crowded. The high school near her new shelter was notoriously violent, so Denise chose to commute via three subway trains for two hours back to Brooklyn to continue her education at our school, the only stable home base she had. She came to school every day, on time. Free breakfast closed at our school as first period started. She missed breakfast at the shelter because she left before it was served. Neither institution made their meal times flexible so that Denise, who was trying to get to school, could get breakfast. But still she showed up and engaged every day.

It took time for Denise to reveal this complicated story to me; it came in pieces through her writing notebook during class free writes. Suddenly I understood why she often put her head down and claimed dizziness in class and why her weight was dropping. Her one reliable meal each day was the free school lunch. I began to pack her whatever I could grab on my way out the door in the morning. A granola bar, a piece of fruit—she was not picky—and I let her eat it in class. Of course, then I had to let the other students eat breakfast during first period too, which was against school rules. I didn't care. Often her friends would share their bacon, egg, and cheese sandwiches with her, and she would come alive for the next half hour of class, her academic productivity increasing because she had food in her stomach.

Students who live in poverty, however resilient, face obstacles that are layered, like matryoshka dolls, and once one issue is somewhat rectified, another one might reveal itself. These multilayered issues do not make an education or a successful life impossible, but they certainly provide more than a healthy dose of challenges for young people like Denise. This is why I stayed at my "failing" school, with poor students, for years. I could not change the larger circumstances of their lives, but I could do small things within my classroom to ameliorate their situations.

All students are capable of learning. Regardless of their circumstances and regardless of what policy folks say, all students are capable of learning at any age and in any subject. I truly believe this. And I feel it is most evident with high-poverty students who often have had subpar educational experiences due to either the schools zoned for the poor neighborhoods where they live or the circumstances that disrupted their schooling trajectories. The students know that school is a sacred space; they constantly demonstrated this to me. From our regular conversations on school violence during which students repeated that they "keep the street on the street and school in school" to the almost perfect attendance after 9/11, after the election of President Barack Obama, or after the winter or spring breaks, the students demonstrated they wanted to be at our school. And this is good, because they are all capable of learning. But the catch is that they have to be ready to take that leap, to be vulnerable to failure, and to make a go of it. And that can be hard.

I constantly think of one student, Ivan, who came to my class every day, on time, and did nothing. Nothing. I could not get him to put pen to paper. He was congenial and participated in class discussions, but he would not read or write for anything. After a month, I mentioned him to a coworker in passing, a special education teacher in her 30th year of teaching. "I don't get it," I said. "He comes every day, on time, and he doesn't ever sleep, act rude or crazy, or distract others, but he does no work. What is going on?" My colleague replied with a gentle, "Send him to me." This woman was a soothsayer of all issues related to literacy and numeracy, and after one brief meeting she reported back to me, "He can't read. At all." He was in 11th grade. Judy, my coworker, took him out of my class every day and brought him to her office where she brought magnetic ABCs, stuck them on her file cabinet, and taught him how to read. It was not easy, and he resisted at times, but Ivan eventually passed the English Regents (and all of his Regents) and graduated from high school. He wanted to learn, he was capable of learning, but that first step of getting help was too much for him to initiate.

What if that had been you? What if, somehow, you slipped through the cracks for years and found yourself in high school unable to read? Impossible, you say, but it is possible. We all like to think that we would self-advocate if our parents and teachers were not stepping up for us, but I am not sure I would have. In fact, I know at that age I would have hidden my academic difficulties at all costs. It would have been too embarrassing, too humiliating; it would have revealed too much about my life outside of school. No way. But, as evidenced with Ivan, students want to learn and are capable of learning at any age. They just need someone to give them a push toward thinking of themselves as a learner, and they need to be pushed again and again and again until they believe it for themselves. That is the real work of teaching in any setting, but it is a task equal in importance to teaching skills when working with low-income students.

Teaching is a career that has no end. I resist hurting people (with words or physical violence) when they snarkily mention how easy it is to be a teacher, with our many breaks and summers off. Anyone who teaches knows that is a lie because teaching has no end. No. End. This is both a curse and a blessing. It is a curse because my mind is always in teacher mode. When I read a book, I think of how I might teach it. When I see an article in the newspaper, I assess its reading level for my students. I lesson plan in the shower.

But on the flip side is a blessing. Once you are a student's teacher, you are his or her teacher forever. In my experience this lifelong relationship is even more pronounced when I teach students from low-income backgrounds, because although teachers are not rich, we might be a student's connection to the middle class. I receive several Facebook messages each month from prior students asking about jobs, college, and graduate schools. They ask for references, for feedback on an admissions essay, and for career guidance.

Just last week I attended my daughter's elementary school's First Friday event. During First Friday parents are allowed in the classroom from 8:30 to 9:00 a.m. to read to their kids and see their children's work. As I sat and read to Alexandra, a young woman caught my eye. We smiled at each other, and my brain flipped through the card catalog of my life as I tried to determine how I knew her. Then she asked, "Are you Ms. Ungemah? You were my English teacher!"

Cassie had been in my English class in the spring of 2002, my first year teaching high school. Our daughters were in the same kindergarten class! We caught up quickly because the groundwork of a relationship was already there. She told me about her kids, her dad's recent passing, her job, and her desire to go to graduate school. I listened, offered my condolences, offered to read her graduate school essay if she wanted me to do so, and suggested the schools in New York City I thought were best for what she wanted to do. I advised her on moving toward a job in elementary education instead of early childhood education because of its stability as a union job, its prospect for greater pay over time, and the benefits of health insurance and a pension as a city employee. We slid back into the teacher–student relationship 10 years after she left my classroom, and we were able to talk honestly and openly about jobs, income, benefits, and life with kids on a budget with little preamble. Explicit conversations like this help demystify class and one's ability to move between the classes, and I feel they are, again, an essential part of the job of teaching in low-income schools.

My students have shown me, through years of accidental and purposeful reconnecting, that not only can I continue to mentor and teach them, but they also can continue to mentor and teach me. One of my former students, Willia, is presently in the Peace Corps in Cambodia, and she messages me about her experiences and travels in a part of the world I have never seen. Another former student, Shana, is a high school English teacher in downtown Brooklyn. We trade teaching resources and classroom management strategies. Many of my former students are now parents (Rudy! Heeba!), and we talk about the challenges of raising our children. My students, who were so different from me on so many levels, became my community in our classroom, and that community lives beyond the time and space of high school.

I now teach community college. I felt drawn to community college because of the overlap between the students I taught in high school and the students who attend community college. I felt my teaching philosophy could remain the same, but I could put my doctorate to use and try my hand at being a professor. Although I taught in a high school that was all students of color and majority poor, it was the small percentage of students from the burgeoning to solid middle-class families that attended four-year universities upon graduation—about 10 from of our graduating class (of 100+) each year. Most of the students from the school who attended college went to community college. The students here at community college are amazing, and the work we are doing in class is strong, but there is a nagging heaviness in my heart. Why? This is a veritable utopia compared to teaching at my high school; it was such a drastic shift that I literally wept from shock after my first day of teaching Freshman Composition. The facility with which I taught for two straight hours was nothing like the struggle of getting through a 43-minute period at my former high school; it was so easy that it reduced me to tears.

But sadly, the shift from high school to college teaching has only magnified for me that a large number of the students I taught in high school *never* make it to college. The homeless students, the very poor, the largely disenfranchised— where are they now? They are not here at community college. Or very few are here. I think about this as I work with my new students, and it bothers me deeply.

Working in high-poverty secondary schools for over a dozen years woke me up to the educational injustices that are forged by economic injustice and how those injustices trickle up and out of high school and into college. My students taught me to see them as complex individuals who all wanted an education, and having learned these lessons from my students, I can't close my eyes to the fact that many of them do not attend college—something that is taken for granted by many of their even slightly wealthier peers. Thanks to my years of teaching in low-income schools, and thanks to my student teachers, my eyes are wide open to this disparity.

I am gathering my strength and planning my agenda for the next chapter in my career: Get those truly left behind ready and into college. I have 20+ more years of work until retirement. Wish me luck. Or join me.

14

THE POOR ARE NOT THE PROBLEM
Class Inequality and the Blame Game

Nicholas Daniel Hartlep

When we consider why "poor" people in our society continue to be stuck in a rut of poverty, some of us turn to pat, easy answers: Economic recession. Character deficits. A lack of morals. A poor work ethic by lazy freeloaders. Cultural background. Just plain bad luck. These clichés, which ignore the complex realities of classism, allow the more privileged people among us to dismiss the problem while maintaining another popular myth: that the United States is a country of unbiased opportunity, a level playing field where everybody has equal access to the American Dream, where fortunes can be made by people who are willing to work hard.

This notion, that hard work and a good education inevitably will pay off, is occasionally challenged by people's experiences, as in stories about individuals who have to use welfare despite holding PhDs (e.g., see Patton, 2012) or in videos of Yale and Brown University alums who are homeless.[1]

Far more often, though, the stories we see in the mainstream media reinforce popular conceptions of equal access and reward. We are regaled with heartwarming accounts of people overcoming brutal personal and economic situations to gain admission to Harvard or to earn degrees from Ivy League institutions (Bermudez, 2009; Hibbard, 2012; Keneally, 2012; Kuo, 2012; Murray, 2011).

However, the narrative of meritocracy has a dark side. It implies that a person who does not succeed must lack ambition and, conversely, that anyone who is successful must have gotten there solely on her or his own. When we assume we have a healthy meritocracy, we overlook the ways in which mainstream institutions marginalize poor people and make them much more likely than their wealthier counterparts to fail. This is unfortunate because the poor are ultimately blamed for their own failures, both for their perceived unwillingness to play by the rules and for their inability to cash in on the American Dream.

Adherents to meritocracy—people who are convinced that great achievement in our society is solely a result of individual effort—have to overlook certain types of individuals in order to justify their view. What about people who did not work hard or do particularly well in school but who nevertheless were admitted to Harvard or Yale as "legacies," inheriting institutional advantages because of who their ancestors are? This particular quandary of legacies is addressed by Golden (2007) in his book *The Price of Admission: How America's Ruling Class Buys Its Way Into Elite Colleges—and Who Gets Left Outside the Gates,* where he explains how wealthy elites pay exorbitantly high prices and rely on informal personal networks in order to send their children to Ivy League institutions.

In fact, even middle-class families have an advantage in this area, noted Lui, Robles, Leondar-Wright, Brewer, and Adamson (2006), since even they have economic avenues unavailable to poor people. So, although class inequity is commonly understood at the individual level rather than the systemic level, it is built right into the structures we point to as being "the great equalizers" such as school. Does that sound like meritocracy to you?

Purpose of the Chapter

Although anecdotes and other qualitative "data" often are not considered by privileged people and organizations to hold the argumentative weight of statistical data, I believe we need more counternarratives to gain deeper insights into injustice and how it affects people in their everyday lives. We need stories that illustrate the ideas borne out by poverty research, anecdotes that counteract popular stereotypes about poor people, people of color, and other disenfranchised communities. Counterstories are worthwhile since we know that "people are more likely to notice and remember information that confirms an applicable stereotype than information that disconfirms it" (Gorman, 2005, p. 704). In effect, counternarratives *disconfirm* stereotypes.

With a commitment to counternarratives in mind, I intend to share in this chapter some of my experiences with family members. They could be described as everyday citizens; they are representative of many people in our society who are convinced that disadvantaged people have only themselves to blame. My observations of and discussions with them—I call them Frances and Peter to protect their identities—are illustrative of how cultural narratives and classism can warp even a relatively benign person's understanding of poor people.

Frances's and Peter's Misunderstandings

Frances and Peter, like so many of their middle-class peers in the small Midwestern city where they live, believe in the myth of the "culture of poverty" (Gorski, 2008). This belief, reinforced by socialization, can lead individuals like Frances and Peter—members of the dominant mainstream society—to blame (often unconsciously) poor people for their poverty (Ahlquist, Gorski, & Montaño, 2011; Gorski, 2006, 2008, 2012).

Conditioned by biased media, including television "reality shows" like *Cops* and "news" sifted through the filter of Fox Broadcasting, Frances believes that the few African American males who move to her community are drug dealers out to make a quick buck. Having had little firsthand experience with African Americans, and not a single African American friend, her judgments are based mostly on the classed stereotypes that she acquires from a narrow range of popular print and television sources. Both the local newspaper that she reads before work and the nightly news program that she watches before bed portray African Americans as not valuing education, as substance abusers, and as linguistically deficient (for an explanation of four commonly held stereotypes of poor people, see Gorski, 2012). On more than one occasion, Frances has informed me that most of the African Americans she sees in town have come from Chicago to sell drugs. She assumes none of them go to college and that they therefore see selling drugs as a way out of poverty. Sadly, Frances's convictions on this matter are seldom questioned by her peers and are validated by similarly misguided family members.

Fᴏʀ instance, Frances's son, whom I will call Joe, is a police officer in the same community. Joe, who is married and the father of two young boys, expresses many comparable class-biased and racialized beliefs about African Americans. On more than one occasion, I have heard him talk negatively about apprehended African American suspects in front of Frances, even though it is obviously unprofessional for him to do so.

Not only Frances's neighbors and coworkers but also her own son, who holds a position of authority in the community, reinforce these judgmental views. Consequently, her perspective is rarely, if ever, challenged by counter-factual evidence, such as the fact that wealthy people have been found to have the most problems with substance abuse (Humensky, 2010). This counterstory makes sense. Rich students have more resources, more disposable income, than their poorer classmates. Also, under intense pressure to succeed, college students who attend topflight colleges may find drugs such as cocaine or Adderall attractive because of the drugs' supposed abilities to enhance concentration and focus, allowing them to study for longer periods of time (Schwarz, 2012). Frances's lack of awareness is unfortunate, because her perspective is rooted in mainstream "sedimented perceptions."

According to Kincheloe, Slattery, and Steinberg (2000), *sedimented perceptions* are "a sort of natural subconscious reflex or reaction that nevertheless manages to perpetuate an ideology of injustice or stereotyping" (p. 94). The following is their textbook example of sedimented perception in action: A White man, who considered himself to be an antiracist, was new to his mostly White neighborhood. One day he noticed an African American cutting grass a few houses down from his own. The White man approached the African American man, struck up a conversation, and eventually got around to asking how much he charged to mow a lawn. The White man was rightfully embarrassed when he learned that the African American was not "hired" help but was, in fact, the owner of the property.

Although Frances almost certainly does not consider herself to be classist or racist, she clearly holds sedimented perceptions of African Americans when she blithely assumes they all must come from poor uneducated urban environments intent on spreading their gang territories and expanding their drug trade. This is one reason individuals move from the city to the suburbs; parents believe that suburban schools will protect their children from "those children." However, in their analysis of the National Longitudinal Study of Adolescent Health, Greene and Forster (2004) found that suburban public high school students have sex, drink, smoke, use illegal drugs, and engage in delinquent behavior as often as (and at times more than) urban public high school students. Certainly middle-class students in Frances's community suffer from drug addiction and engage in delinquent behavior, even if Frances projects these sorts of things only onto poor, urban people.

Frances's skewed assumptions are reinforced further by her husband, Peter. Whenever I visit them, I am a reluctant witness to their misconstructions of poor people and people of color. One day, while returning home from visiting Peter and Frances, I expressed to my wife my exasperation with their lack of empathy, their woeful misconceptions of class inequality and racism. My wife reassured me that they meant me no harm, reminding me that their limited perspective is caused, in large part, by their social setting.

This sort of bias—that wealthier individuals are perceived differently, and with greater levels of respect, than their lower-income counterparts—can have adverse ramifications for poor families in a variety of contexts. In schools, for example, low-income students are more likely than wealthier students to be "tracked" into lower-level classes (Hochschild, 2003; Oakes, 1985). Consequently, wealthier students are deemed to be *college* material, whereas poorer students are perceived as incapable of succeeding in college. In their study of fourth-, sixth-, and eighth-grade classrooms, Woods, Kurtz-Costes, and Rowley (2005) found that even the students themselves stereotyped wealthy peers as more academically competent than poor students.

The complexities of class-based perceptions are observed in the social scientific research of Ray Rist (1970) and Jonathan Kozol (1991). Rist (1970) provided a detailed example of how a kindergarten teacher assessed and organized students along lines of socioeconomic class, such as by how they dressed, smelled, and talked. Rist's well-known observational study found that low-income children were treated inequitably when compared with their higher-income peers. This kindergarten teacher's class-based treatment transcended race, since all of her students were African Americans.

Another example comes from Kozol's (1991) research on urban public schools in the United States. He noted countless situations in which U.S. schools are built for middle- to upper-class children but not for children in poverty. According to a principal he interviewed in Washington, DC, if you are rich you try to send your kids to private school. Meanwhile, middle-class families try to place their children in particular public schools that have resources that are unavailable to their neighborhood schools. Last, the principal noted that poorer families have no choice but to attend their neighborhood schools. Kozol documented many narratives like this that illustrate the injustices poor students face in schools that neither have their best interests at heart nor deliver them adequate education.

Perhaps predictably, isolated incidents often are treated as catchalls that pigeonhole people who are poor. Like many middle-class people, Frances and Peter talk ambivalently about people who are different from them. Unfortunately, their comments often reflect stereotypes.

Who Is the Problem?

Peter and I were talking one day. A series of declarations he made illustrates how easy it is to blame poor people for being poor. Peter targeted a complaint against his newest neighbors: The family seemed to never work. This family, who moved into a duplex near his house, was a large intergenerational family that appeared to be poor. According to Peter, his neighbors, like the African Americans Frances targeted earlier, were uneducated and unable to control their urges to have children. He seemed to be playing on the stereotype that poor people have a lot of children so that they can receive welfare benefits. He did not understand why they never worked and how they could afford to live in such a nice duplex. He was also annoyed that some members of the family drove loud motorcycles through the neighborhood, disrupting his peace and quiet. He repeatedly expressed his bewilderment over how the family qualified for low-income Section 8 housing, especially when they had nice Harleys.

Although Peter and his neighbors are both White, it was their supposed socioeconomic differences that were highlighted. Why? People who are "different"—in this case people who are perceived to be "poor"—are deemed irresponsible and are criticized when they do not exhibit the class-based stereo-typical behaviors expected of them. For instance, Peter's neighbors violated his perception of the poor because they owned expensive bikes and lived in a nice subdivision. During his soliloquy I thought to myself, How does Peter really know that nobody in that house works? Maybe they work nights. Maybe they work from home. How does he know they are unemployed? Maybe they are on disability and cannot work. Maybe they are retired. Gorski (2012) pointed out that stereotypes lead people to selectively ignore, omit, and suppress factors that contradict the stereotypes. Peter, for some reason, latched onto the belief that his neighbors were willfully poor, failing to consider how *he* might be misperceiving the situation based on his own ideological biases. And if the family was *not* poor, then it should not be eligible to live in the Section 8 housing. If this were the case, then they would be "milking" the system, something Peter loathes.

How do these anecdotes testify to Peter's and Frances's misunderstandings? A good deal of literature in social psychology confirms that people who are deemed "different" in most any context are treated as "others" or outsiders (Branscombe, Wann, Noel, & Coleman, 1993; Tajfel, 1982). Peter thinks of his low-income neighbors, who he *assumes* do not work, as different from himself, assuming they are not hard workers. As a result, he can blame "those people" for their poverty by pointing to a clear distinction between them and him.

The "Blame Game"

Although race often is used to blame people for inequality—consider the popular perception that the "achievement gap" will narrow only when *uninvolved* parents of color begin to care about their children's education—people like Peter and Frances also attribute low socioeconomic status to a deficit in values or discipline. Even though they might feel some sympathy when they observe someone in poverty, they often simultaneously cast judgment. For instance, they might quip, "If they are so poor, then why do they buy $100 sneakers for their children?" Perhaps this tendency to blame the victim serves to assuage feelings of guilt that might otherwise attend one's sense of privilege. Instead of reflecting, "There but for the grace of God (or luck) go I," the privileged person can proudly assert, "I would never allow myself to be so low." I call this unfair judgment of poor people by more economically privileged people the "blame game."

As Gorski and Landsman indicated in this book's introduction, "the poor" are not the problem; inequality and misunderstanding are the problem. Handler and Hasenfeld (2007) addressed similar concerns in their book *Blame Welfare, Ignore Poverty and Inequality*. The authors pointed out how poor people are blamed for their poverty even while we ignore how inequality functions at the structural level. Attempting to bridge this gap, David Berliner (2006) in "Our Impoverished View of Educational Research" alerted readers to the impact that poverty has on teachers' work and students' learning. He asserted that teachers and schools are unequipped to ameliorate poverty. He explained, "In my estimation we will get better public schools by requiring of each other participation in *building a more economically equitable society*" (p. 988; emphasis added).

Jean Anyon (1997) echoed Berliner's point: "Attempting to fix inner city schools without fixing the city in which they are embedded is like trying to clean the air on one side of a screen door" (p. 168). The grip that poverty has on education (teaching and learning) is profound. Therefore, understanding the impact socioeconomic inequality has on individuals in society is vital to reducing it.

The Poor Are Not the Problem, and the Blame Game

Kincheloe et al. (2000) pointed out, "When one lives in the mainstream, one is less likely to notice the ways outsiders are silenced" (p. 100). I have had several discussions with Peter and Frances about how institutionalized structures impact poor individuals in ways that make their lives even more difficult than they already are. It is discouraging that, despite these conversations, Peter and Frances continue to assume that the problems faced by poor people are self-induced. This should not be surprising given that their sedimented perceptions and stereotypes shape the way they interpret socioeconomic positioning (Kincheloe et al., 2000; Steele, 2010).

So what can we, as a community of educators, do to avoid falling into this cognitive trap? We can begin by being cognizant of the population of students we teach, vigilantly avoiding the "blame the victim" mentality. We can challenge ourselves constantly to avoid holding lower expectations of students who are poor.

In her study of five fifth-grade elementary schools, Anyon (1980) found that the socioeconomic and professional statuses of children's parents were highly correlated with the type of educational instruction that they received. In what Anyon described as "working-class" schools, students were subject to rote pedagogies and required to memorize material, whereas students in "middle-class" schools were many times simply expected to regurgitate the *correct* answers. The teachers in these schools held lower expectations and required lower levels of thinking, apparently because of their students' working- and middle-class backgrounds. Meanwhile, students who attended what Anyon identified as "affluent professional" schools received instruction that encouraged creativity, independence, and expressiveness. Last, students who attended an "executive elite" school had much more autonomy over their learning, stemming from the ways in which their teachers cultivated their intellectual ability while simultaneously developing their analytical skills. We must challenge ourselves not to become part of this pedagogical inequity; all students deserve to be held to high educational expectations and experience a rigorous curriculum irrespective of their socioeconomic class.

Concluding Thoughts

The personal interactions with Frances and Peter that I have shared here will, I hope, help illustrate how largely unconscious assumptions can shape the biases of people in the economic and racial mainstreams. My conversations with them confirm research (e.g., Chamberlin, 1999; Edelman, 2012; Gorski, 2012; Katz, 1989) showing that economically privileged people tend to overlook the sources of their own privilege, engaging instead in the blame game, pointing the finger at economically disadvantaged people and those who are racially and culturally different from themselves.

Asymmetrical reporting by the media bolsters public misunderstandings by infrequently reporting situations in which once-advantaged people become disadvantaged while frequently reporting on "success" stories, such as when poor and homeless people graduate from Harvard or Yale. This lopsided reporting reinforces citizens' faith in the perception that the United States is a meritocracy—a mainstream sedimented perception (Kincheloe et al., 2000). Unwitting players of the blame game are let off the hook; in failing to take an honest, dispassionate look at themselves and at society's structural inequalities, they fail to recognize a basic truth that "the poor" are not "the problem."

It is incumbent upon us to ensure that we do not contribute to the blame game. We accomplish this by teaching and leading in ways that make the familiar *unfamiliar* and the unknown *known* for students and staff. In other words, problematizing the *bon sens* on which many practicing teachers and leaders rely is an important place to begin. Holding high expectations for all students, poor or not, is critical, too. Recognition that low-income people are in fact victims of economic injustice is a meaningful part of this process. Let's carve out more space for counterstories that reject the credibility of the "culture of poverty myth" (Gorski, 2008) and the stereotypes, misunderstandings, and victim blaming on which the myth is constructed.

Note

1. See www.youtube.com/watch?v=BDGhE3MQ7d0&feature=related.

References

Ahlquist, R., Gorski, P., & Montaño, T. (Eds.). (2011). *Assault on kids: How hyper-accountability, corporatization, deficit ideology, and Ruby Payne are destroying our schools*. New York: Peter Lang.

Anyon, J. (1980). Social class and the hidden curriculum of work. *Journal of Education, 162*(1), 67–92.

Anyon, J. (1997). *Ghetto schooling: A political economy of urban school reform*. New York: Teachers College Press.

Berliner, D. C. (2006). Our impoverished view of educational research. *Teachers College Record, 108*(6), 949–995.

Bermudez, E. (2009, June 20). She finally has a home: Harvard. *Los Angeles Times*. Retrieved August 29, 2012, from http://articles.latimes.com/2009/jun/ 20/local/me-harvard20

Branscombe, N. R., Wann, D. L., Noel, J. G., & Coleman, J. (1993). In-group or out-group extemity: Importance of the threatened social identity. *Personality and Social Psychology Bulletin, 19*, 381–388.

Chamberlin, J. G. (1999). *Upon who we depend: The American poverty system*. New York: Peter Lang.

Edelman, P. (2012). *So rich, so poor: Why it's so hard to end poverty in the United States*. New York: New Press.

Golden, D. (2007). *The price of admission: How America's ruling class buys its way into elite colleges—and who gets left outside the gates*. New York: Three Rivers Press.

Gorman, E. H. (2005). Gender stereotypes, same-gender preferences, and organizational variation in the hiring of women: Evidence from law firms. *American Sociological Review, 70*(4), 702–728.

Gorski, P. (2006, February 9). The classist underpinnings of Ruby Payne's framework. *Teachers College Record*. Retrieved August 29, 2012, from www.tcrecord.org

Gorski, P. (2008). The myth of the "culture of poverty." *Educational Leadership, 65*(7), 32–36.

Gorski, P. C. (2012). Perceiving the problems of poverty and schooling: Deconstructing the class stereotypes that mis-shape education practice and policy. *Equity and Excellence in Education, 45*(2), 302–319.

Greene, J. P., & Forster, G. (2004, January). *Sex, drugs, and delinquency in urban and suburban public schools*. New York: Center for Civic Innovation. Retrieved November 1, 2012, from www.manhattan-institute.org/pdf/ewp_04.pdf

Handler, J. F., & Hasenfeld, Y. (2007). *Blame welfare, ignore poverty and inequality*. Cambridge, MA: Cambridge University Press.

Hibbard, L. (2012, June 4). Dawn Loggins, student, heading to Harvard after being homeless, abandoned by parents. *Huffington Post*. Retrieved August 29, 2012, from www.huffingtonpost.com/2012/05/04/dawn-loggins -harvard-homeless-abandoned_n_1478895.html

Hochschild, J. L. (2003). Social class in public schools. *Journal of Social Issues, 59*(4), 821–840.

Humensky, J. L. (2010). Are adolescents with high socioeconomic status more likely to engage in alcohol and illicit use in early adulthood? *Substance Abuse Treatment, Prevention and Policy, 5*, 19–28.

Katz, M. (1989). *The undeserving poor: From the war on poverty to the war on welfare.* New York: Pantheon Books.

Keneally, M. (2012, May 9). Janitor at Columbia to graduate with an honors degree from the university after 19 years of taking classes. *Mail Online.* Retrieved August 29, 2012, from www.dailymail.co.uk/news/article-2142114/Janitor-Columbia-graduate-honors-degree-university-19-YEARS-taking-classes.html

Kincheloe, J. L., Slattery, P., & Steinberg, S. (2000). *Contextualizing teaching: Introduction to education and educational foundations.* New York: Longman.

Kozol, J. (1991). *Savage inequalities: Children in America's schools.* New York: HarperPerennial.

Kuo, V. (2012, June 8). From scrubbing floors to Ivy League: Homeless student to go to dream college. *CNN.* Retrieved August 29, 2012, from www.cnn.com/2012/06/07/us/from-janitor-to-harvard/index.html

Lui, M., Robles, B., Leondar-Wright, B., Brewer, R., & Adamson, R. (2006). *The color of wealth: The story behind the U.S. racial wealth divide.* New York: New Press.

Murray, L. (2011, January 15). From homeless to Harvard: How the daughter of drug addicts turned her life around. *Mail Online.* Retrieved August 29, 2012, from www.dailymail.co.uk/home/you/article-1346184/From-homelessness-Harvard-University-How-Liz-Murray-turned-life-around.html

Oakes, J. (1985). *Keeping track: How schools structure inequality.* New Haven, CT: Yale University Press.

Patton, S. (2012, May 6). The PhD now comes with food stamps. *The Chronicle of Higher Education.* Retrieved August 29, 2012, from http://chronicle.com/article/From-Graduate-School-to/131795/

Rist, R. (1970). Student social class and teacher expectations: The self-fulfilling prophecy in ghetto education. *Harvard Educational Review, 40*(3), 411–451.

Schwarz, A. (2012, October 9). Attention disorder or not, pills to help in school. *New York Times.* Retrieved November 5, 2012, from www.nytimes.com/2012/10/09/health/attention-disorder-or-not-children-prescribed-pills-to-help-in-school.html?pagewanted=all&_r=0

Steele, C. (2010). *Whistling Vivaldi: And other clues to how stereotypes affect us.* New York: W. W. Norton.

Tajfel, H. (1982). Social psychology of intergroup relations. *Annual Review of Psychology, 33,* 1–39.

Woods, T. A., Kurtz-Costes, B., & Rowley, S. J. (2005). The development of stereotypes about the rich and poor: Age, race, and family income differences in beliefs. *Journal of Youth and Adolescence, 34*(5), 437–445.

PART THREE

Making Class Inequity Visible

15

blissful abyss or how to look good while ignoring poverty

Tricia Gallagher-Geurtsen

in the classroom
my student with leukemia
lived in a car
with her brother
with her mother, who sold her body to feed her children

in the classroom
my undergraduate with a computer
shopped online
during a break
during my class, on teaching for social justice

in the classroom
my colleagues with papers
read their research
in a nice hotel
in a conference, all about justice

in the classroom
my teachers with kindergarteners
told me about their students
who knew no couch
who knew no zebra, not even one.

16

THE GREAT EQUALIZER?
Poverty, Reproduction, and How Schools Structure Inequality

Taharee A. Jackson

Horace Mann was on to something. When he witnessed an angry street riot in New England, his conviction that "the educated, the wealthy, the intelligent" had gone morally astray by abandoning the public was fortified (Johnson, 2002, p. 79). Mann chided the economic elite for shirking obligations to their fellow man by favoring private education over common schools. He conceptualized public education as "the great equalizer," or the most powerful mechanism for abating class-based "prejudice and hatred," and, most important, the only means by which those without economic privilege or generational wealth could experience any hope of equal footing.

Whether inspired by Mann's plea to elevate the masses to higher moral and financial ground via schooling, or other notions of social justice, even now Europeans refer to publicly funded education as "the social elevator" (Lopez-Fogues, 2011). As Mann originally conceived the function of public education, there was overt recognition that something in society was amiss, and that "something" could be effectively redressed by offering public education to all—not just some. The same "something" that Mann was acutely aware of and deeply troubled by was and is the gross and *growing* disparities among the social classes. We continue to need methods for shrinking overwhelming and widening class divides. Many of us choose to address the equity gap by struggling to supply universal access to high-quality, free, and appropriate public education. Nearly two centuries later, "the great equalizer" cannot equalize soon enough.

"Twelve Years of Free Schooling: It's There for the Taking"

I have been teaching teachers for over a decade, primarily in teacher education programs designed to prepare urban educators and *always* guided by a social justice framework. For years I have been floored by the number of candidates who believe not only that public education is the great equalizer but also that children and families who remain poor are to blame for not exploiting such a freely available opportunity to improve their lots. My students struggle to comprehend why young learners and groups who have been traditionally under-served by public schools continue to be challenged in education and life. These teachers of tomorrow are particularly concerned that even after all students have been offered "12 years of free schooling," they are unable to "lift themselves" out of poverty. In short, they genuinely wonder how such dismal outcomes for poor children could persist when the great equalizer undoubtedly works and a poverty-ending solution is clearly at hand. Year after year, I continue to observe that as a result of this flawed, deficit thinking, both pre- and in-service teachers have come to develop and staunchly cling to their disgust at what they perceive to be squandered opportunities. Poor children fail in schools because they are not taking advantage. Poor people exist because they wasted a good, free educa-tion. The poor themselves are the problem.

What scores of students—well-meaning educators, all—fail to realize is that public education does not serve its intended function as the great equal-izer. Quite contrarily, schools actually *structure* inequality (gasp!) in insidiously subtle ways. To introduce countless future teachers to this "radical" notion, I devised a plan to combat pernicious thinking about poor students, the educa-tional "failures" of poor students, and the "self-inflicted" demise of the poor.

Why Are People Poor? An Introduction to Reproduction

My new tradition is to begin each foundational course in my program by con-textualizing and historicizing public education. To assist me, I use the diagram shown in Figure 16.1. The topics I address and the stories I tell within each rung of the ladder of structured inequality are candid, personal, and decidedly pointed in order to stimulate discussion.

When I begin discussions about poverty and achievement in public schools, my students often ask, "Why do poor students perform poorly?" The question is not about poor students and why they underperform in a system purportedly designed to elevate their opportunities and outcomes. The question is, "Why are people poor?" I insist that we begin with the lowest "rung" on the diagram because there we unpack the existence of a class of "poor people" who seem not to be living up to their potential in a presumably benevolent public education system that was designed—at least in the spirit of Horace Mann—specifically with them in mind.

Any serious discussion about the inception of poverty in this country must begin by recognizing that class is highly racialized (even globally), and vice versa. The origins of poverty among people of color—specifically descendants of African slaves—are rooted in several centuries of colorized, chattel slavery with no economic reparation after its formal or informal "end." The majority of poor people in the United States are White, but the majority of people of color

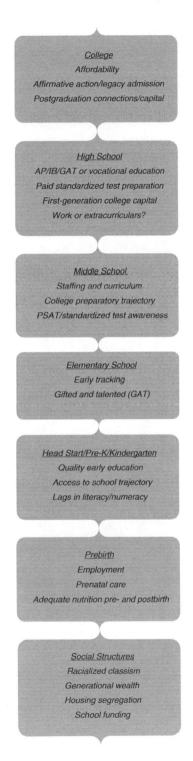

Figure 16.1   How Schools Structure Inequality.

are poor. Racial minorities (better phrased, "global majorities") are disproportionately represented in poverty. Therefore, an inordinate and overwhelmingly
fewer number of people of color have access to generational wealth based on
their recognition as only three-fifths of a human being and the subsequent denial
of property ownership as a direct result of *being property* themselves. Masses
of people of color who have been denied personhood, rights to stolen lands,
citizenship, and any number of basic human freedoms based solely on race have
also been denied generational access to wealth in the form of inherited property
and assets.

The surest way to build wealth—as indicated by the *real* in real estate—
is to own a home. Both Katznelson (2005) and Wise (2005) mapped, in bril-
liantly unconsidered ways, how "affirmative action" in the United States has
always benefited Whites and most significantly in the building of White wealth.
From establishing the country's earliest legislation restricting the landed gen-
try to White males, to offering mortgage loans to Whites only via the Federal
Housing Authority and the GI Bill, to *excluding* Blacks and people of color from
home loans and subdivisions by way of redlining and restrictive covenants, both
scholars illuminate the long-standing and state-sponsored wealth gaps (ravines)
between Whites and all others.

On the basis of the inability of far too many people of color, as well as a vast
number of Whites—neither of whom inherited wealth from their forebears—to
purchase homes or, more important, to purchase homes *in a "good school district,"* housing segregation continues to plague the educational and social outcomes of multiple members of the underclass. And on the basis of the method
by which we have chosen to fund public schools in this country (relying heavily
on the values of the surrounding properties), "demography is destiny" in that
"students' test scores are highly correlated with the amount of money their
parents make and the zip codes where they live" (Atkins, 2010, p. xi). It should
be no secret, then, that people who lack access to generational or inherited
wealth—and were legally barred from purchasing homes as the best prospect
for building wealth—end up in subpar school districts that are funded by subpar tax revenue. It should also be no wonder that the *children* of poor people
attend poorly performing schools in poorly funded districts with disproportionate concentrations of poor classmates. And yes, students in these circumstances
are more likely to perform poorly.

Why are people poor? Most notably, why do the *same* groups of people tend
to endure poverty from generation to generation? And ultimately, why do children of the poor predictably perform poorly in public schools? As noted earlier,
a historicized and contextualized view points to several factors, including the
by-products of imperialism, colonialism, capitalism, and racism. Bourdieu's cultural and social reproduction theories, alongside the Marxist "correspondence
principle," just to name a few critical tools, help provide answers to our queries.

Historically and contemporarily, U.S. public schools illustrate the simplicity of reproduction—that is, the indelible relationship between current and eventual class membership—by way of replicating class status in the superior educational opportunities of those with more money. If you can—by way of inheritance, real estate, or accumulated class capital and wealth—afford a better home in a better school district, you will therefore receive a predictably better education (McGrew, 2011). Likewise, the correspondence principle refers to the perpetuation of social class stratification by sifting the same *types* of individuals into various labor classes by design, over time, and in full collusion with the public education system in a capitalist society (Au, 2006). Whereas Bourdieu was concerned with the transmission of cultural values, norms, and capital writ large, Marx specifically described the überimportant role of *schooling* in accomplishing the deliberate sorting and generational reinforcement of the classes. Why are people poor? Because our historical and social structures mean them to be.

Woes in the Womb: Prebirth Effects on Educational Outcomes

When I first constructed the ladder to describe how schools structure inequality, I struggled with where to begin. My training as an early childhood educator, experience as a child care provider, education in developmental psychology, and specialization in human development told me to start in the womb. What are the factors that affect poor children before they are even born? First, women and children are overrepresented in poverty (Gollnick & Chinn, 2009). Part-time employment is the only sphere in which women outearn men. Their pay on full-time jobs continues to lag, with women earning a mere 81 cents to the dollar when compared to men with equal or fewer credentials (Mundy, 2012). I often share with students that my sister's employer worked her 39 hours per week *for years* to avoid providing health insurance. She had no access to pap smears, annual "well woman" breast exams, birth control, or a regular physician when she took ill. My mother recently ended a one-year stint at Walmart, where she was daily promised full-time employment. She is 63 years old, takes 11 prescription medications, and suffers from a number of health conditions that require frequent doctor visits. She was consistently worked just shy of 40 hours—again, the employer avoiding having to provide full-time benefits. During her final week on the job, she worked 39.5 hours.

Lack of access to health care and, more specifically, to *prenatal* health care plagues far too many women in poverty and, consequently, their children and future public school students. Inadequate nutrition, undiagnosed difficulties prior to childbirth, and treatable in vitro illnesses all contribute to the poorer health of these future scholars. And because so many poor neighborhoods are veritable "food deserts" where fresh produce, meats, and healthy items are elusive, children gestated then reared in poverty enter the world with unspoken disadvantages, many of which are totally preventable, medically remedial, and unnecessarily difficult to overcome.

A Head Start for Whom? How Many Years Behind Am I?

Thankfully, poor children may have access to the federally funded Head Start program, but children of the wealthy have a different kind of head start. My sister recently sent me a copy of one of our favorite films, *Baby Boom* (Meyers & Shyer, 1987). In it, the corporate mogul lead character inherits a toddler, about whom she is immediately rebuffed for needing to "catch up." One fellow, a wealthy Upper East Side New Yorker, becomes fiercely inquisitive about which "preschool entrance exam preparation institute" she would be attending and for which "Ivy League preschools" the child was wait-listed. When the flabbergasted new mother indicated that her child was not on any wait-lists, that she had not listed her prebirth, and that she had no idea how the preschool preparation track worked, the nosy neighbor walked away in utter incredulity.

The neighbor's point was an excellent one. Access to quality child care, early learning, preschool, and even kindergarten (which is not mandatory in all states) is key. Investments in quality early childhood education not only has one of the highest yields—for every $1 spent on early education and care, $8 is saved on crime, public assistance, supplemental schooling, and so on—but is also one of the most important stages at which a child's educational trajectory is shaped (Nisbett, 2009). The question we must ask of children reared in poverty is, When they set foot in kindergarten, how many years "behind" are they in learning opportunities, literacy and numeracy development, reading and writing "behaviors," and the many benefits of quality early care? Although the nosy neighbor in our favorite film highlighted the disgustingly expensive extremes to which the wealthy will go to start their children's educational careers off right, the notion of needing to start *every* child's education with the highest quality experiences is spot on.

On Kittens and Puppies: Starting Off on the Wrong Paw

Tracking is never innocent. In my supervision of student teachers in classrooms across multiple cities, "ability grouping" and its more perilous effects are the order of the day. In any grade, but particularly the early grades, all too often students are sorted according not to their demonstrated ability but to the teacher's assessment of their behavior, likability, or academic *potential* (Smith, Polloway, Patton, & Dowdy, 2004). In classrooms where I have observed as a university professor, children continue to be sorted for any number of reasons: reading, writing, the ability to assist others, mastery of the material, and so on. They are often given names like kittens and puppies, bees and bears, and I most recently heard (and enjoyed) butterflies and worms.

This form of early tracking, or dividing children into labeled groups based on the teacher's designation of their skill level, seems innocent. What we know, however, based on mounds of research—most notably among them Rist's (1970/2000) study of same-raced children of various social classes—is that teacher and peer expectations for academic achievement (and their subsequent treatment of students) are based largely on low and negative perceptions of the poor, regardless of their actual ability. We know that disproportionate numbers of poor children are far more likely to be identified as less academically adept or even as having special needs. The early tracking and labeling of children reared in poverty is cumulative and devastating. It not only hampers students' self-esteem and cripples their *own* expectations of themselves but also, as Rist (1970/2000) discovered, becomes a self fulfilling prophecy for what too often becomes a trajectory of underachievement.

When I ask my students if they have tracking programs at schools they have attended or where they completed their student teaching, many of them routinely answer "no." When I inquire about gifted and talented (GAT or TAG) programs, many of them instinctively begin to describe, in detail, the differentiated curriculum, enrichment opportunities, and vastly different experiences each program entails. Children of color, boys, and students from economically exploited backgrounds are consistently excluded and underrepresented in such programs (Callahan, 2005). Gifted programs are not the enemy, but the muddled definition of what constitutes "giftedness" is, and it overwhelmingly excludes poor and minority children. Programs like these represent early forms of tracking. They simply provide opportunities for class elitism and socioeconomic exclusion on the opposite end of the spectrum. Being labeled "gifted" or "talented" versus "regular" or "normal" or to be labeled a "kitten" or "puppy" is psychologically and educationally significant. And, too often, class-biased and deeply enduring.

Middle School: College Preparation Starts Here

In one of our famously interactive (and highly spirited!) discussions about how schools *structure*, rather than promote, equity, I ask my students the following: If you're going to make it to statistics, discrete math, or advanced placement calculus BC as a high school senior, when would you need to begin taking algebra? If you were to take physics or organic chemistry in your senior year, what are the benchmark years for completing biology, chemistry, and the prerequisite sciences? If you are to become fluent in a second language, or at least take an advanced placement exam for that language, when would you need to begin learning that language? When do students in the best schools take the PSAT (Preliminary Scholastic Aptitude Test)? What are the consequences of doing well on the test? What is a National Merit Scholarship, and when do you begin to be considered for one? The answer? Middle school.

The middle grades are where the rubber meets the road. This is where college-bound freshmen and all the rest are separated like oil and water. Here, the issue of school funding and the deleterious effects of how we fund public education in this country becomes an obvious barrier to students' academic success and their ability to move upward in the social classes. "A college education is the most reliable step for moving from a low-income to a middle-class and higher status" (Gollnick & Chinn, 2009, p. 86). Contrary to popular belief, preparation for college, and therefore the surest promise of social mobility, does not occur in high school. Rather, it is a function of the staffing, teacher quality, curricular offerings, standardized testing capacity, counseling wisdom, and resources at the *middle school level*. Indeed.

Children reared in poverty disproportionately attend schools with the least-prepared, least-experienced, least-qualified teachers (Irvine, 2003). Staffing and course offerings are crucial in middle school because students who hope to attend college must engage in specific prerequisite courses *prior* to entering high school if they are to have any chance of competing for admission to top-tiered or even average-quality four-year universities. For instance, my high school offered advanced placement and college-level courses that would grant students "jump-start" credits once admitted to an institution that recognized such credits (which many do). I attended Harvard as an undergraduate and was therefore eligible to forgo an entire semester of courses if I received a score of 4 or 5 on four advanced placement exams. Given that my tuition and fees easily exceeded $50,000 that first year, not having to pay for a full semester's worth of college credit would have benefited my family tremendously. But no one told me about the course sequence in middle school. That's when I would have had to enroll in my first algebra and Spanish classes and the appropriate high-level science courses. To reach discrete math, Spanish VII, and physics, I would have had to begin taking those courses in the sixth grade. My school did not offer those. I missed out, and the effect was costly. Over $25,000 to be precise.

Luckily, I did take the PSAT, or the precursor for one of the most popular college entrance exams, as part of my GAT program in the seventh grade. We were told that this was a very important test that would prepare us for another very important test, and if we scored well enough, we could skip a grade. Taking the PSAT early and being aware of the SAT, ACT, and standardized testing requirements for college entry were *vital* pieces of class capital that neither of my parents could offer. Like so many other children in first-generation college families, I would never have taken the PSAT, or had my name entered in a database to begin receiving information directly from colleges, or been aware of the National Merit Scholarship—something I could look forward to in high school if I practiced the PSAT enough in my gifted program—if the opportunity had been absent in middle school. Lucky me?

Does *every* middle school have the capacity to facilitate PSAT testing for its students in the lower grades? Does *every* middle school in economically blighted districts have highly qualified teachers who can teach college preparatory courses? Does *every* middle school employ counselors who can set each student on a trajectory toward college? No. Even less so in schools that serve poor children. This is how schools limit college admission for poor students and, in turn, mass social mobility much earlier than we realize. This is how schools structure inequality.

"Borrow Money If You Have to From Your Parents": The Wealthy on Becoming Wealthy

In the throes of his 2012 election-year bid for president, and deeply steeped in his own wealth, Mitt Romney issued a word of advice for young people about what it might take to be successful and wealthy. To contextualize his contribution, he first offered the example of Jimmy John Liautaud, who borrowed a whopping $20,000 from his parents to begin his sandwich franchise, Jimmy John's. Romney then told students at Otterbein University that such opportunities were afforded to them too. He encouraged—admonished—them: "Take a shot. Go for it. Take a risk. Get the education. Borrow money if you have to from your parents. Start a business." Just like that.

By the time students—especially *poor* students—enter high school, one of the most crucial forms of cultural capital they will need is the ability to pay for a college education. On the basis of the lack of access to generational wealth, inexperienced parents who often have not attended college, and the pangs that stem from being a first-generation college goer, high school becomes a critical juncture at which students are either aware, prepared, and savvy about college admissions or woefully behind in their ability to navigate the application process.

Romney's assertion that one should simply "Get the education. Borrow money if you have to from your parents" is indicative of his and many people's inability to understand poverty or any class status other than their own. Romney's assumption is that education is there for the taking. All one needs to do is reach out and grab it. In addition, he is making a bold assertion about your parents' financial holdings. *Of course* they have money you can borrow. Lots of liquid assets. Just ask for them. Just like that. In his naive, ridiculous, and class-ignorant "advice," Romney demonstrated a profound lack of understanding for how education, particularly at the high school level, can be a daunting and dangerous time for students who, unlike himself, are *not* wealthy. For instance, if a student does not attend a high-quality school in a wealthier, better-funded district, programs such as the International Baccalaureate (IB), advanced placement, and other college credit programs that often facilitate the matriculation of students into postsecondary settings are not likely to exist. Furthermore, if the school is located in an economically exploited area characterized by racial diversity, as is the case in the lowest-income wards in New Orleans and the most highly populated Latina and Latino schools in Houston, high schools may even have a more vocational, trade-based, law enforcement, or strictly military focus (Buras, Randels, ya Salaam, & Students at the Center, 2010). They are designed to steer poor students into trades, vocations, and jobs, not professions and high-paying careers. On purpose.

My sister, who is half Chinese, one-quarter Thai, and one-quarter Southeast Asian Indian, attended a historically Black college. Not by choice but by lack of cultural capital. As the eldest child in our family, she was the first to brave the collegiate admission process. Her high school counselor never called her in for counseling, "noticed her potential," or placed her in contact with various colleges and admissions offices around the country. Those consultations happened frequently for her White counterparts. She had no idea when applications were due, what they entailed, what fee waivers were, or when to take standardized tests. She dreamed of attending James Madison University. She ended up at Norfolk State University because it was the only college to accept her application late. She dropped out before the midpoint of her first semester.

In addition to the sheer volume of cultural capital students dwelling in poverty need just to take command of the college application process, other class issues are at play: Do I have to work instead of participate in résumé-boosting and community-building extracurricular activities? Will my family need my services as a caregiver or contributor while I am away? Most important, can I afford costly, for-profit test preparation programs such as Kaplan or Princeton Review to score better on the SAT or ACT and strengthen my candidacy? And if I am accepted to a college, can I afford to go?

Unfortunately—and this may be news to Mitt Romney—the ultimate question is the most problematic for far too many. Not everyone has parents or family members with access to magic money that students can borrow to "get the education." Rather, high school represents a sad and all too common divergence in the road for the "haves" and an excessive number of "have-nots." There are those who have better-resourced schools, advanced curricula, funds for test preparation, and the counseling and wherewithal to successfully master the college process. They will likely attend college and maintain or even improve their class status. And there are those who *have not* a clue as to how one might go about "getting the education" in the absence of disposable money, only available to some. The poor are not the problem. Ignorance about widespread poverty and how it functions, however, is.

A Trail of Tears: Debts, Tokens, Jobs, and Knowing No One

When a student who is poor makes it to college, it is unlikely that he or she is a "legacy admit." These are applicants whose parents or relatives have attended, have contributed to, or are in some way affiliated with the university. As a Harvard alumna and admissions interviewer, I can verify that the application includes an inquiry about any person you are related to who went to Harvard. And there is consideration for that.

Even *after* poor students enter college, there is often an imposed sense of not feeling entitled to their own admission. Minorities of any kind are positioned as "affirmative action babies" or "token [fill in the blank]." Legacy admits, however, are rarely if ever questioned. Gurin et al. (2004) candidly put forth that the only time admissions standards are drastically lowered or foregone in order to accommodate an unqualified candidate is in the instance of legacy admission. In other words, it is only when applicants are affiliated with a significant donor or "major money" that their candidacy is strongly considered and too often accepted below standard. Not the other way around. That is, we are not admitting disproportionate numbers of poor and minority candidates who hail from humble backgrounds. Rather, we are filling our collegiate campuses with a mix of legacy admits who would *never* have been accepted but for their connection to financial resources.

In addition to dealing with any number of indignities as a result of being perceived as somehow undeserving of their admission slots, poor college students must also face dilemmas that the moneyed do not. Students from low socioeconomic backgrounds suffer not only the damaging comments and class-based assumptions from peers and professors but also the social isolations that stem from the frequent predicament of not having college-experienced family members or friends with whom to relate. Expensive opportunities may elude them: Can I afford to study abroad and gain more global citizenship skills, or must I work one or several jobs to pay my tuition? Once paid, whom will I need to financially support back home? Moreover, it is often difficult to prepare for graduate or professional schools if none or few around you have advanced degrees. I learned what PhD stood for during the fourth year of my doctoral program. My father finished seventh grade, and my mother is an immigrant from Bangkok, Thailand.

At the baccalaureate service during one of my final days at Harvard, the speaker made what he believed to be a joke. He said, "Remember, graduates: It's not who you know. It's *whom*." Everyone got the joke immediately and laughed uproariously. As a grammar freak, I could appreciate the sly lesson in mechanics. What I found incredibly scary, however—at a time when people were falling off the pews of Memorial Church in stitches—was that he was right. And dead serious. If I had any hope of being as successful as my well-connected peers, many of whom outclassed me, I would need to *know* some people. Someone to set up my internships in the summers, my job interviews for the 90% of positions that are never advertised, my "foot in the door" or "let me see who I can talk to" opportunity that only insiders can get you. I didn't know anyone. I was from a poor family. None of my relatives owned businesses or knew anyone. We didn't have physicians, or attorneys, or engineers in our family because we were deliberately kept out of those spaces. There was no legacy. No one to open the door, leave it cracked, and let us in. I looked around, and people were dying laughing. I was dying. I cried.

At long last, even after first-generation and poor students like me surmount class-based difficulties in college, the debt looms for decades. Although a college education is "the most reliable step" for upward social mobility, the debt that poor college students incur and retain for years keeps them at a handsome distance below their more well-off contemporaries in building net worth and wealth (Gollnick & Chinn, 2009). Therefore, matriculating and even graduating from college does not remedy wealth gaps in as "clean" a manner as we might hope. Moreover, the cultural capital that one brings to the collegiate table and then builds while there is often more valuable than the degree itself. The Posse Foundation, which sends traditionally underadmitted students to college in teams, has found a way to combat at least the social isolation and class-based hostilities that poor students often face, as well as to preserve the community cultural capital of the underrepresented group itself. In this way, groups or "posses" of students who tend not to fare well in college can surround themselves with familiarity, solidarity, and the potential to build connections together. They may not have as many nepotistic or wealth-based connections as their peers, but at least they have their posse (Rosenberg, 2012).

Insisting on Class Equity: What's Really at Stake

When my students and I conclude our discussions about the ways in which schools *structure*, not ameliorate, inequality, I am faced with questions about what to do and why we should do anything at all. Public education is the largest mechanism for socialization in any society (Spring, 2008). It is also the bedrock of a participatory democracy where citizens can pursue self-actualization without hindrance and with full right. If we truly believe that "the potential for brilliance is sprinkled evenly across all ethnic groups" and all social classes, then we will make decisions that dismantle structural barriers to quality public education for all, and we will govern ourselves accordingly (Bennett, 2007). At the time of this writing, Horace Mann may not have gotten his wish of using public education to promote and, indeed, to remediate the ills of a highly stratified society. But brilliance can come from anywhere. If we insist on class equity in schools, it will come from *everywhere*.

References

Atkins, N. (2010). Foreword. In D. Lemov (Ed.), *Teach like a champion: 49 techniques that put students on the path to college (pp. xi–xiii)*. San Francisco: Jossey-Bass.

Au, W. (2006). Against economic determinism: Revisiting the roots of neo-marxism in critical educational theory. *Journal for Critical Education Policy Studies*, 4(2). Retrieved March 1, 2006, from www.jceps.com/index.php?pageID=article&articleID=66

Bennett, C. I. (2007). *Comprehensive multicultural education: Theory and practice* (6th ed.). Boston: Pearson.

Buras, K. L., Randels, J., ya Salaam, K., & Students at the Center. (2010). *Pedagogy, policy, and the privatized city: Stories of dispossession and defiance from New Orleans*. New York: Teachers College Press.

Callahan, C. M. (2005). Identifying gifted students from underrepresented populations. *Theory Into Practice*, 44(2), 98–104.

Gollnick, D. M., & Chinn, P. C. (2009). *Multicultural education in a pluralistic society* (8th ed.). Upper Saddle River, NJ: Pearson Prentice Hall.

Gurin, P., Lehman, J. S., Lewis, F., Dey, E. L., Hurtado, S., & Gurin, G. (2004). *Defending diversity: Affirmative action at the University of Michigan*. Ann Arbor: University of Michigan Press.

Irvine, J. J. (2003). *Educating teachers for diversity: Seeing with a cultural eye*. New York: Teachers College Press.

Johnson, T. W. (Ed.). (2002). *Historical documents in American education*. Boston: Allyn and Bacon.

Katznelson, I. (2005). *When affirmative action was White: An untold history of racial inequality in twentieth-century America*. New York: W. W. Norton.

Lopez-Fogues, A. (2011, September). *Voices from vocational education and training (VET): A capability based case study of disadvantage as vulnerability in Spain*. Paper presented at the meeting of the European Educational Research Association, Berlin, Germany.

McGrew, K. (2011). A review of class-based theories of student resistance in education: Mapping the origins and influence of *Learning to Labor* by Paul Willis. *Review of Educational Research*, 81(2), 234–266.

Meyers, N. (Producer), & Shyer, C. (Director). (1987). *Baby boom* [Motion picture]. United States: Metro-Golwyn-Mayer Studios.

Mundy, L. (2012, March 26). Women, money, and power. *Time, 179*(12), 28–34.

Nisbett, R. E. (2009, February 7). Education is all in your mind. *New York Times.* Retrieved February 18, 2009, from www.nytimes.com/2009/02/08/opinion/08nisbett.html?pagewanted=1

Rist, R. C. (2000). Student social class and teacher expectations: The self-fulfilling prophecy of ghetto education. *Harvard Educational Review, 70*(3), 257–301. (Original work published 1970)

Rosenberg, T. (2012, February 15). Beyond SATs, finding success in numbers. *New York Times.* Retrieved February 16, 2012, from http://opinionator.blogs.nytimes.com/2012/02/15/beyond-sats-finding-success-in-numbers/

Smith, T. E. C., Polloway, E. A., Patton, J. R., & Dowdy, C. A. (2004). *Teaching students with special needs in inclusive settings* (4th ed.). Boston: Pearson.

Spring, J. (2008). *American education* (13th ed.). New York: McGraw-Hill.

Wise, T. J. (2005). *Affirmative action: Racial preference in black and white.* New York: Routledge.

17

A PEDAGOGY OF OPENNESS
Queer Theory as a Tool for Class Equity

Whitney Gecker

The predominant feeling I associate with my junior and senior high school years is underestimation. Teachers and other students never seemed to understand my actions or ideas. Perhaps the problem was that I made sense of things more through metaphors and visuals than memorization and repetition or that I approached the world from a decidedly queer and fat-bodied perspective. For these and many other reasons, it was common for others to underestimate me.

Furthermore, whenever I questioned the status quo or expressed a passion for social justice, I encountered unpleasant reactions: shock and awe, laughter and mockery, disregard and impatience. Being so young and vulnerable, I was disturbed to the core by these reactions. I responded by sealing up the more sensitive sides of myself, which—in retrospect I can see—only validated the narrow identity space into which the school system had pigeonholed me. It was in realizing that I have *multiple* sides, interests, and passions that I came to develop the institutional critique of public schooling that you are about to read. The fundamental lesson I learned from being an outsider in the school system was that all students have multiple sides. And if these sides are forbidden to enter the process of schooling, many students will remain chronically underestimated, as I was.

I'd like to use queer theory to help educators better understand their students. Queer theory emerged when some pioneering scholars began to recognize and identify the inherent class and racial bias within lesbian and gay studies. This recognition pushed them to reassess how scholars had defined such basic categories as sex, gender, and sexuality. Though social theory can seem abstract and irrelevant for practical application, it is also true that ideas are often the catalyst for change. I want educators to understand why I felt so isolated and underestimated throughout my schooling experience; I believe there is a common thread between my experiences and the schooling experiences of students who are poor, working class, and of color.

What Can Queer Theory Do for Education?

Class issues in educational settings can often be invisible, covertly expressed in tiny details such as assumptions about students' family backgrounds or their stock of cultural knowledge. These small details may seem insignificant, but they in fact constantly reinforce that there is a norm—a hidden standard that students are pressured to live up to. Compounding the isolation I felt as a White, queer, fat-bodied high school student was the fact that I was raised by a working-class single mother in a very affluent suburban area. Many of my identities were kept well hidden all throughout high school: I wasn't "out," and teachers never asked about my home life. Furthermore, my mother always purchased, using credit cards, new clothing and school supplies for me, which shielded me from outright ridicule. But every student knows the "smelly" kid, the "dirty" kid, or the classmate who comes to school in wrinkled clothes and hand-me-down shoes. Every kid knows who's an outcast, who's gay or at least "flamboyant," who's butch or a tomboy, or who's just weird because she or he doesn't fit into "mainstream" styles or norms.

Norms often materialize to create comfort and stability, but for whom? In the school system, educational norms simplify the institution's already complex web of goals and obligations. Certainly, some standard educational practices, even including testing and measurements of intelligence, can help evaluate a school's progress toward educating all students. But whether intentionally or not, the educational system also produces and regulates norms of conduct and practice, such as classroom etiquette, language, and other kinds of cultural cues, all of which covertly define people who follow the norms as intelligent and capable and those who do not as deficient. For example, students who slouch in their seats and remain silent throughout class: They've not said anything but, somehow, because of their presentation and silence, we assign "deficient" to them.

Queer theory calls into question the very basis of these labels and identities. What even makes a person poor rather than middle-class? What makes a person male? *Queer* is a term that is intentionally vague: It exists specifically to call attention to the not-so-fixed nature of many precious, taken-for-granted categories. For example, sexuality is often seen as fixed—"born this way," as Lady Gaga would put it—but queer theory disagrees.

When we recognize, as queer theory encourages us to do, the *fluidity* of sexual categories such as "gay" and "straight"—that is, recognize that the world of sexual tastes and practices is far too complicated to be adequately captured by such simplistic labels—it is easier to understand other kinds of categories (such as gender, class, and race) in the same way. We can also more easily see how all of our identities are blurred together much like physical boundaries between ocean and land. For example, women who are poor (a class category) often are presumed to be sexually promiscuous (a sexual distinction); likewise, Black men (a racial category) are often assumed to be less articulate (a class distinction) than White men. In this way, our many identities are mixed together in how we perform them, as well as in how they are perceived by others.

Because queer theory always questions the fixedness of our categories, it is a useful tool for critiquing social structures and institutional processes. This is because large institutions often rely on and reinforce such categories in the course of their formal and informal administrative practices. Consider, for instance, the enforcement of dress codes (which can be subjectively administered) and the reliance on measuring achievement through standardized tests. Furthermore, social norms within schools pressure disenfranchised students, such as low-income students, to conform to mainstream values through style trends, behavioral expectations, and language use. These students must announce or defend themselves; poor students might face the tough choice of having to either continually rebut accusations of being dirty or "low class" or work hard to gain the approval of their classmates by giving up friends in their own communities or conforming to a certain style of dress.

Using a queer perspective to rewire our institutional practices won't fully erase these pressures, but it would, at the very least, push us to think more about the problems that result from the categories we often inadvertently assign to our students. The stifling norms within our schools are borne out of the invisibility of class issues in the school system and the assumption that class has a fixed meaning. A student's ability to "buy" into the trending norms of dress and behavior does not erase the complexity of her or his story, but it does increase the chances that the student has a whole life and identity that is hidden, which requires spending energy hiding that could go toward learning.

Queer theory is a start. It presents an opportunity to focus students and teachers away from standards and instead get people to embrace multiple styles and paths to success. When we allow institutions and gatekeepers—inherent biases and all—to mark people who are intelligent and worthy of material success, to distinguish them from those who are not, we give our consent to the classism, not to mention the racism, sexism, and homophobia, that continues to ruin the educational experiences of so many students. Students like me, who find ourselves hiding in one way or another, not only lose motivation to learn and participate in the classroom but also shy away from mentors, advisors, and the like. Trust is lost, and with trust we lose opportunity and access. In high school I skipped as much school as possible. I actually had a system of coming in late and leaving early in order to be there just enough to be counted as present for the day. My senior year I skipped over 20 days of school in addition to coming in late and leaving early, not because I was a bad kid and not because I didn't think education was important but because school had become hostile. Students start to feel access to an institution when they trust the institution, and I did not feel welcome. Queering education might have helped. It is about a conviction toward openness; it is about allowing all students, and their many ways of expressing their identities, their many sides, access—*true* access—to classrooms and schools.

In this spirit, I offer the following ideas for putting queer pedagogy into practice in the service of class equity and, in fact, equity in general:

- Try to "mix up" the language you use. If you find yourself saying "mom and dad" or "at your house" a lot, consider saying "family," "guardians," "where you live," or "at home or at a family member's house." Students notice little assumptions in teachers' language, so using vague language or simply being mindful of what you might convey through language opens the classroom to greater possibility and greater inclusivity.
- If it feels safe to do so, share parts of your story with your students. Share experiences of times when you didn't fully succeed, when you learned something about yourself, or when you discovered that an assumption you were making was false. Students want to see teachers as human, so you won't lose their respect by doing this. In fact, you might gain it. It's helpful to hear from people who are older and in positions of power—to hear that they don't know everything.
- Whenever possible, allow students their individual styles. Even in a math class, some students would do better with headphones on, figuring the work out on their own, perhaps with occasional check-ins from the teacher, while other students need more interactive or directive lessons.

Obviously these suggestions are not a silver bullet; nothing is. But they're a start, and they would have made a big difference in my schooling.

18

FIRST FAINT LINES

Sherrie Fernandez-Williams

Before Fifth Grade, Before Ms. Chase

It started with a headache—not my headache, but Ms. Hirschman's. My teacher was not much taller than her eight-year-old students. She had light brown hippie hair and wore dashikis with blue jeans and espadrille shoes. I believed she had a headache that morning because I watched her pop two aspirin and wash them down with a sip of her Tab soda.

She handed out sheets of yellow paper that looked like they might have been sliced into halves with a paper cutter. She placed the remaining sheets on her desk. In large letters, she wrote the word "COMPOSITION" on the board and told us that we would be writing about anything we wanted to write about until it was time for lunch. If we needed more paper, we should feel free to come up to get more.

I struggled with the first "faint line," noticing, perhaps for the first time, how frightening freedom can be, but eventually I came up with something. Soon, I found that my hand was moving eagerly across the page. I was up for more paper after filling the front and back of the first sheet. The bell rang, and it was time for lunch, followed by recess. I begged my teacher to let me stay in class because I wasn't even close to finished. She looked down at me with indecision, as if she was determining whether it would be more important to make the skinny child eat or to let the silent child speak. After all, it was the first time in the child's life she'd discovered that she had something to say.

Ms. Hirschman chose the latter and instructed me to come to the lunchroom when I was done. But I was not done by the time lunch was over. When all the children ran screaming into the yard for recess, I still was not done. When the children returned from recess and stood at the long line for gulps of water from our classroom's water fountain, sweating and panting from playing hard, I still was not done. My teacher told me that it was time to move on, collecting my scattered sheets.

What came next startled me. At the end of the day, my teacher decided that she wanted to read my composition to the rest of the class. The class appeared entertained. They laughed when I said something funny, though I never knew

I could be funny. Then, Ms. Hirschman walked over to me, rested her hand on my shoulder, and said, very quietly, "Excellent job."

Disbelief overtakes me even now when I recall that day and the first time those words were spoken to me. I haven't a clue what I was writing about when I was eight, but I would not be surprised if it resembled what I have written about as an adult dabbling in fictional characters who possess what I lack.

Fifth Grade and Meeting Ms. Chase

First-day jitters were hard to contain, as usual. Back in first grade, my neighbor, Anthony Mojicha, had been the kind soul who patted the empty mat next to him, inviting me to sit by him during story time. As long as I live, I will never forget his kindness. However, by fifth grade, our classroom was full of kids I had known for years. Most of us lived right across the street from school, in Farragut Projects located near downtown Brooklyn, which housed low-income Black and Latino families. A handful of students were bussed in from other areas, like the lovely brownstones of Clinton Hills. Because Dr. Daniel Hale Williams was designated a MES (more effective school) and was provided with additional funding to increase reading and math scores, the school was attractive to some middle-income families of color who lived outside of the projects. It was observable to me that bussed-in students were often higher achieving than those of us from the neighborhood.

In the '70s and '80s, our teachers were primarily White and, more specifically, Jewish. There were exactly five Black women on the teaching staff, including Ms. Chase. She dressed sharply in skirt suits just at the knee and thin high heels the color of plums—never wedges or flats for her dignified feet. She carried her slightly bent hands at her sides while taking small, quick steps on the tips of her toes across the white ceramic tile glossy enough to see her own reflection on those first days of school. Ms. Chase owned the chalk between her fingers the way a judge owns her gavel, the way a pitcher owns her ball, the way a rider owns her whip.

I have wondered what women like Ms. Chase and her sister-colleagues, Ms. Loe, Ms. Wilson, Ms. Mann, and Ms. Poindexter, had to stomach to become the professionals they were. They would have come of age at a time when discriminatory practices in education and in every other sector of society were acceptable codes of conduct. Were they affected by the New York City teachers' strikes that pitted the Black and Jewish communities against one another? Black communities fought for greater involvement on their district school boards and inevitably fought for cultural representation in public schools. Jewish teachers felt like they were being displaced. They argued in favor of hiring tools such as civil service examinations, exams found to be racially biased by the Black community, who felt that the largely Jewish teachers' union was, essentially, fighting against affirmative action.

In the epic fights of 1968, the teachers' union won, while the community members, mostly parents of the student body, lost. The turbulence occurred before my parents' divorce, and two years before my birth. My parents were raising seven children together in the New York City housing project. When they first moved in, Farragut was a slice of paradise, as my father called it, with well-maintained lawns and clean streets. There was plenty of housing staff responsible for the upkeep of 17 acres of government property. However, Farragut became paradise lost when enormous cuts were made to public housing. The maintenance staff was greatly reduced, and the housing police were eliminated just as heavy narcotics began to infiltrate the neighborhood. Our home collapsed, as did my parents' marriage. Soon, my mother was raising eight children in the projects with no chance of working her way out of poverty. Not only was she a poor mother of a large pile of children, she had a sixth-grade education and significant cognitive delays. She turned to welfare as a means of survival.

Ms. Chase and her coworkers pursued higher education and became teachers in a highly competitive market at a time when Black women had limited options as to what they could be. I do know that there has always been such a thing in this country as the Black middle class, and I also know that, regardless of what class our folks might have been in, there were always people who treated us as though we did not belong. For seven hours each day, these women shared the same space with students who were children of color and mostly of the same racial heritage as the teachers. However, by fifth grade, I could sense that, in spite of what we had in common, we still lived worlds apart. Their worlds included bank accounts, motor vehicles, and college degrees.

In all of my years prior to having Ms. Chase, my socioeconomic status held little relevance for me. The federal government classified my family as living below the poverty line. In fact, the government supported my family with a monthly check, food stamps, subsidized housing, and medical benefits. Still, until fifth grade, I did not claim "poor" as part of my personal identity. I saw those commercials about starving children with skeletal frames and stomachs bloated with hunger. When I was in the fourth grade, Ms. Steinberg placed an orange UNICEF collection box on her desk and asked that we drop loose change into the box as we were able. My mother gave me dimes, nickels, and pennies to help end hunger.

I defined myself by my individualities. I was a quiet daydreamer who loved playing with imaginary friends who joined forces with me to save the day against imaginary antagonists. I loved things with wheels, particularly my roller skates and skateboard. I could cartwheel my way across a field of grass without dizzying. I was a sensitive little sister who could easily be made to cry by someone calling me something other than my name: four eyes or turkey neck or, sometimes, idiot or dumb-dumb. Television was a great escape from random insults from an older brother, and I particularly loved watching *Happy Days* and *Laverne & Shirley* on Tuesday nights on ABC. What did it mean to say that I was poor when I ate three times a day, had a place to lay my head at night, and had the luxury of watching mindless television before going to bed at a decent hour?

Although fifth grade was a time of strange turning points, life under the fluorescent lighting felt familiar at first. Ms. Chase was new to me, but because I had the tendency to go with the flow the second that I was outside the safety of my mother's presence, I expected life as usual. I had the same group of friends for years. My grades were above satisfactory, if less than exceptional. Overall, I was good. I never fought in school, nor had I been disciplined for disrupting class in any way.

Fifth grade started with us kids sitting in rows. That was nothing new. In previous years our configuration started one way but soon was redesigned. After a week of sitting in rows, we ended up in a large rectangle so that our teachers could see each of our faces and we could not hide behind the heads of other children. I always thought that our teachers did not place us in our permanent seating right away because they wanted to get a sense of where the behavior problems might come from and seat us accordingly.

As in previous years, the first two hours of school were devoted to reading and comprehension. Part of the two hours was spent reading, after which we responded to the questions listed in the back of the chapter we had read. Finally, we would discuss the text as a class. Although I tended to be introverted, I did participate. Some stories I enjoyed more than others, and in those cases I raised my hand more often.

After the first few weeks of school, our classroom was restructured again. Our desks were not lined up in front of the four walls of our classroom, the way to which I had become accustomed. Instead our tables were pushed together in clusters of six. Instead of worrying only about the one person on the left and the one person on the right of me, hoping that neither was one of the class bullies, I now was clustered with five other children, each in close enough proximity to cause me harm if they wanted to do so.

We each stood at the perimeter of the room as she called our names and pointed to where we would be sitting. From my new seat, I was able to see that my best friends were clear on the other side of the room. Brand-new reading texts fresh out of boxes were placed on our tables. Most were burgundy. However, at my table, Ms. Chase put six blue textbooks for the six students who were assigned to sit there. We were asked to take one apiece and write our names in it.

It did not take me long to notice that I was in the higher reading group. I was sitting at the table with the smart kids, including three bussed-in kids, Connie and Evelyn, who wore Buster Brown shoes, and Ashante, who came to school each day in sweater vests and button-up shirts. Also at my table were Tony and Rolando, who lived in the projects, but not for long. They would stay just long enough for their fathers to purchase houses in Queens. They were Little League baseball players who were nice-looking and well put together in designer jeans and clean, white sneakers. I was the disheveled kid who always grew taller before anyone could afford to replace my shrinking clothes and who wore oddly shaped tortoise shell glasses, readily identified as "welfare glasses," a marker of poverty. I was placed in the group with the well-groomed high achievers who always scored years ahead of their peers on standardized reading and math tests.

We were given the more complicated text because of our "demonstrated ability." As we sat in our clusters waiting for further instruction, lanky Connie with the Buster Brown shoes said to me, "I don't know what you are doing in this group. You are too stupid to be sitting here." I knew that Connie was right. There must have been some mistake. I wasn't one of the *smart* kids. They knew it, and I knew it.

Before this, I was the student who did my best, who put forth effort, who was well liked by my teachers because, generally, I was compliant and did what I was told.

Our teacher worked with the larger class before coming to the blue book table. For the first time, my school days began in a state of panic. My group peers always completed the daily chapter way ahead of me. They would be done answering the comprehension question when I was just beginning to read it. Luckily, I usually had time to catch up while Ms. Chase worked with the rest of the students with the burgundy text. Most of the time, I could finish before it was our turn. However, on occasion, I would skip a question if I were uncertain in order to complete as many of them as I could.

I had unlucky days in Ms. Chase's classroom. When she called my name, my body tightened and my heart quickened. I was asked to share my answer for question number seven. Of course, it was the question I had skipped. Still, I nervously flipped through the pages of my text, hoping to land upon the answer.

Ms. Chase had a way of letting her students know that her patience was running thin. Pursed lips and narrowing eyes gave her away.

"Tell Sherrie which page she should turn to." Of course the rest of the kids knew. Tony reached over and turned to the page and pointed to the passage that held the answer.

"Read, Sherrie."

I obeyed my teacher's instruction and read the passage quietly. I then was asked to read the question again and answer it. I read the question again but was still unsure of the answer.

Ms. Chase glared as she began to talk through her teeth. "Girl, if you do not get your behind out of this classroom this very instant, so help me." She didn't shout, but she spoke loudly enough for the entire class to hear her.

"Get out, and I don't want to see your face until you can answer the question. Do you understand?"

Her directions were clear. I grabbed my book and left the classroom. I had never been asked to leave a classroom before. I had never been sent to the principal's office. I had no idea where to go or what to do, so I ran down the hall to the girl's bathroom. I don't remember if I cried. I remember feeling dread. I locked myself in a stall and read the passage over again. I'm sure that I asked God to help me.

"Sherrie." Natasha whispered my name. "Sherrie, it's me."

I was embarrassed to show my face, but it was Natasha, my best friend who never judged me. Natasha, who was not in my reading group, was holding a bathroom pass even though she really did not need to go. She just wanted to see if she could help me. I gave her a shot. I showed her the passage where Tony said that the answer was supposed to be. However, it was hidden from Natasha as well.

"I'm sorry, Sherrie."

"It's okay."

"I don't know why she had to send you out of the classroom. She is such a bitch. Don't let her bother you," Natasha offered as a word of encouragement. Natasha left, and I stayed in the bathroom not sure what to do next.

Ms. Chase discovered what the other teachers before me either were unable to detect or were too kind to share. I was a very stupid little girl. It began to feel like I was selected to be on my teacher's shit list. Ms. Chase would get so frustrated with me. She would yank one of my ponytails or push the hard nail of her index finger against my temple as she scolded me for being an idiot.

Quickly I was moved out of the "brainy" group, and instead of being in the burgundy reading group with the rest of my fifth-grade class, I joined Ms. Poindexter's fourth-grade class for reading. Throughout all of my elementary school years, I've always tested at reading level, but I wasn't going to protest. Each morning, I took my new fourth-grade textbook and went next door. Ms. Poindexter was still as laid back as I remembered her to be when I was in second grade. Corporal punishment had been outlawed by then, although Ms. Chase still found a way to poke, yank, and grab her students when she wanted to make a point. My time with Ms. Poindexter was completely without stress. The book was easy, and I flew through the questions with little effort. My mornings were completely void of the sound of terror pounding against my eardrums.

Ms. Poindexter was convinced that fourth-grade reading was not a challenge and that I needed to go back to Ms. Chase. Ms. Chase was reluctant to take me back, but she did so anyway. Of course, I would not go back to the blue text with the bused-in kids but instead joined the mass of average students with whom I belonged. They were students like me, students from the projects who did not play organized sports or speak "standard English" and who were despised by our teacher.

All of the students in my class were people of color. However, differences existed between how those of us who were poor were treated and how those of us who appeared not to be poor were treated. Those who were poor were treated as nuisances who would never amount to anything. Those who seemed to have come from financially stable families were academic all-stars and treated with respect. They did not have to fend off daily abuse from the teacher. I could not hide in the crowd. Although I had rejoined the masses, I was still not removed from Ms. Chase's gaze. There was a bulls-eye on my psyche, and my teacher had incredible aim.

One day I found a biography on Phillis Wheatley in our school library. The fragile slave girl in poor health became my first heroine. As with all of the other book reports and compositions I wrote for Ms. Chase, she marked the word "POOR" in large red writing on my report about this book. Whatever flames my previous teachers were able to spark in me were doused during my time with Ms. Chase, who was Black like me and who I assumed would know me best because of it. My dumb ass was doing nothing but taking up space and my teacher's precious time.

Sixth Grade: Ms. Chase Versus Mr. Gappleburg

At the end of the year, I still managed to test at grade level on my standardized exams, which meant that I would be promoted to sixth grade. I wanted to praise God for allowing me to survive my year with Ms. Chase. But then rumors started that one of the sixth-grade teachers was leaving our school and, in the reshuffling process, Ms. Chase would be moving to sixth grade along with the students.

"God in heaven. Please say that it isn't so!" When I heard that it was true, I experienced one of those moments in my life when I seriously questioned God's existence. I was beginning to believe that I was being forsaken.

I continued to frustrate Ms. Chase, and she continued to exasperate me. I remained compliant, but I found other ways to rebel. My attendance declined. I missed a lot of school with one ailment or another. Once I convinced my mother that I might have the mumps even though she knew darn well that I had been vaccinated.

Sleeping became difficult. Often I stayed awake most of the night. At 3 a.m. I would turn on the small black-and-white television in my room, left behind by my older sister, and watch *Ben Casey*. If only I could get so sick that I had to be hospitalized like one of Dr. Casey's patients, I thought, I would never have to see Ms. Chase ever again. In the dead of winter, I opened my windows and shivered in my bed. If I could give myself the sniffles, or better yet, pneumonia, then I would escape the hell that was sixth grade. On occasion, I would make myself throw up in the bathroom and then show Ma the evidence that I was not well enough to go to school. I already had been a finicky eater and was thin because of it. Now, my eating was worse than it had ever been. Often my knees would give out, and I would find myself on the floor in a blink. My mother took me to the doctor, who scolded her for neglect.

"She is malnourished. Don't you feed her?" the doctor in the white coat asked accusingly of my poor mother, who used every tactic imaginable to try to get me to consume food.

"She won't eat!" My mother tried to explain.

I wasn't starving myself on purpose. My already small appetite had gotten smaller, and I continued to make myself vomit to prove that I was sick. Later, I heard terms like *anorexia* and *bulimia* and learned about young girls who were dying to be thin.

I didn't want to be thin. I wanted to be home. I wanted to be safe.

Relief came in the form of jury duty. Ms. Chase was gone for at least two weeks. Instead of getting a substitute, our class was distributed among the other sixth-grade classes. For two weeks I sat in Mr. Gappleburg's classroom. Mr. Gappleburg's classes were known for putting on fantastic plays written or adapted by Mr. Gappleburg himself. My favorite was *Oliver and Olivia Twist*. He gave Oliver a twin sister because he wanted a boy and a girl to share the lead.

During my time with Mr. Gappleburg, we wrote a lot of essays and shared current events. We always had to answer the five Ws: Who? What? Where? When? Why? He pinned my work on the bulletin board with gold stars. His approval confused me, but I delighted in it.

When Ms. Chase returned, long and unpleasant days persisted. I suffered one made-up or self-inflicted illness after another. I remember telling Ms. Chase one day that I would not be in school the next day because I had to go to "Face to Face" with my mother. It sounded official. My mother had official business, and I needed to go with her. I did not realize that "Face to Face" was actually the welfare office in downtown Brooklyn. Ms. Chase gave me that look she normally gave me when I answered a question incorrectly or said something she considered asinine. Then came that look of disgust.

Years later I have wondered what her biggest problem with me was. Was it that I was on welfare or that I did not have the good sense to hide it?

I'm not sure what my attendance record was in the sixth grade, but I am certain that I was absent for as many days as I was present. I knew it was over—my life, I mean—the day Mr. Gappleburg came to our classroom to ask Ms. Chase to select students from her class to write reflections about their time at our elementary school. These narratives would be compiled and provided as gifts to all of the graduates leaving our school to face the horrifying halls of junior high. Though

Mr. Gappleburg spoke softly near the door during his impromptu teacher-to-teacher conference, I knew that he was speaking about me. All of this happened in slow-moving frames, which is why I can still see the details that I have played in my head multiple times for years. Mr. Gappleburg gave me several quick glances out of the corner of his eye as he spoke to my teacher. I remember the gold stars he gave me. How could I not? He was definitely there for me.

I stared at the back of Ms. Chase's head and tried to will her face to turn to me. "Please see me for once." And then, I saw it: The back of her head, the two-inch Afro turning, her pursed lips and critical gaze caught my look of desperation. "Say, yes," I begged with my eyes. "Please." I was afraid to smile, but I couldn't help but smile in that moment because for once she was going to see that I might be more than a dumb ass. I might actually have something to say. However, her look of consideration faded into something closer to "no fucking way."

As she turned back to Mr. Gappleburg, I watched her shake her head, no. "No one here," she said.

Liberty in Seventh Grade Thanks to Frank

At the end of sixth grade, I still scored at grade level on my reading and math standardized exams. This meant that I would be promoted to junior high school. Those of us from Farragut Projects walked the extended block along the defunct Brooklyn Navy Yard to reach McKinney Junior High, the school just outside of Fort Green Housing. My passive nature worried folks who cared about me. It was predicted that I would lose my life at McKinney. Some punk-eating ruffian from Fort Green would swallow me whole.

The disorder I encountered in Mr. Martinez's homeroom was expected. I was placed in 7–3, which meant that I was in the third of four tracks. 7–1 was supposed to be the most capable students. 7–2 was considered average. 7–3 was less than average, and 7–4 was considered least capable.

I remember walking past 7–1 and noticing the order of the classroom. No balled-up sheets of paper were being thrown from one side of the room to the other. The room was clean and quiet. There was no shouting and cussing and kids talking about somebody else's ugly, fat, or stupid momma. I figured that the kids in 7–1 were on a path different from that of the kids in 7–3. The students in 7–1 were on their way to college and good-paying jobs. If lucky, the students in 7–2 would one day be hired by the students in 7–1. I imagined that those of us in 7–3 would never make it to college and would cope with life as minimum-wage earners. What did that mean for 7–4? Welfare or jail?

We all knew what the numbers 1, 2, 3, and 4 signified. I was 7–3, which meant that Ms. Chase was right about me. I would not amount to much and would likely be poor for the rest of my life.

Up until seventh grade, I had been tracked by New York City Public Schools as an average student with average ability; in other words, a number 2. After my 2 years with Ms. Chase, I was considered "less than." This is what it meant to be number 3 at McKinney Junior High.

For the rest of my life, I will always remember Mr. Fracarro. Now that I am an adult, I refer to him as Frank although I have not seen or talked to my seventh-grade English teacher since I left junior high school.

When Frank returned one of my first assignments, he asked me a question that would alter my life's path forever: "Do you know that you are very good at expressing yourself on paper?"

I remember the question. I do not remember my answer or whether I answered him at all. Knowing the girl that I was back then, I probably said nothing.

Mr. Fracarro told his students about an annual contest that he facilitated with all of the seventh graders. Each class would be represented by four of its students. To be a class representative, we first had to compete against our classmates. Our class was broken into newscast teams, just like you might find on the nightly news. Each team member was asked to write about something newsworthy and pertinent to our lives as junior high school students. We then would sit at a long table in front of the rest of the class and deliver our story. There were categories: Two students wrote about current events, one person covered sports, and I decided to take commentary, which meant that I was allowed to provide my opinion on anything that I viewed to be an issue at our school. Winners from each category would compete with the other seventh-grade English classes. If your team won, the entire class would miss a day of classes for a movie and a pizza party.

The judges were the principal, the assistant principal, the school librarian, and District Thirteen's superintendent. My only goal was to not embarrass myself in front of these important people. I tried different topics and decided to go with school vandalism. I realize now that I played it safe. I hadn't even considered the deeper angst I felt as a young person growing into a woman's body and being propositioned to give some guy with droopy eyes a blow job for money. If I knew what I know now, I would have used the platform to speak out against the boys who groped my ass in the lunch line or the one who hurled basketballs at me in gym class because I was uneasy around him and he took that to mean that I was stuck up.

Nope, it was going to be vandalism. Still, I gave my safe topic all that I could, given the limitations that I felt speaking in front of the entire seventh grade, other teachers, and some folks I had never seen before. After my teammates delivered their stories, I delivered my commentary against school vandalism with as much gusto as I could. After all of the teams were done, we sat and waited for the results. The announcement came from our school principal, Ms. Mosely.

"In first place . . . Class 7–1!" Cheers erupted from the students in the top class as they found themselves, yet again, at the top. While the 7–1 students continued to rejoice in their victory, it was announced that Class 7–3 took second place. Second wasn't bad. I was very accustomed to being a number 2, and it sort of felt right.

As my teammates and I congratulated each other on doing better than what was expected of us, Mr. Fracarro summoned me to the judges table.

Ms. Mosely extended her hand to me as the other judges offered approving smiles.

"We want you to know, Sherrie, that on the individual scores, you were the only person to get a perfect score from each of the judges. You've done a wonderful job."

Who knew that seventh grade would be a time of magic? I never could have predicted things to turn out the way they had. The next day Mr. Fracarro told me that I deserved to be celebrated as much as anyone, so he invited me to attend the movie and pizza party with the winning class.

"Would you like to invite a friend from your class to join you?"

I was relieved because I did not have any friends in 7–1. Although it had rained early that morning, it turned out to be a gorgeous day when Tina Patterson and I met the kids from the winning class outside of the school building as Mr. Fracarro completed his head count. We were all there and ready to go.

Not surprisingly, Mr. Fracarro had become my favorite teacher and English my favorite subject. However, my grades improved in every subject, and I made honor roll each quarter. In some ways, I had developed obsessive study habits, and some might say that this period of my life was the start of my perfectionistic tendencies. I didn't think about any of that at the time. I enjoyed the results of my work. My reading scores increased two years during the seventh grade, and by the next academic year, I was placed in 8–1. In 8–1, my reading scores increased another two years. In 9–1, my reading score went up another two years, and I knew without a doubt at that point that I was college bound. I wanted to have a bank account, a motor vehicle, and a college degree, like my teacher, Frank, who seemed to think that it was possible for me. I wanted to encourage young people to believe in themselves so they too can succeed in life.

All the while, I never forgot my two years with Ms. Chase. Every exam taken and every paper written began with an attempt to scrape her words from my psyche. Even now she sticks to my memory like burned cheese. She is forever fixed to my 10-year-old self, who never had the opportunity to have the adult conversation I am capable of having now. If I could hear her story, would that change my view of her?

What about Ms. Chase? During the time she came of age, was a career pursuit in education a viable path to the middle class? Is that why she became a teacher? Was it disdain she felt for her low-income students? Did I remind her of what her life could have been? Or did she believe that if she was stern with me, I would snap out of my daydreaminess and become more alert and tough-minded like a soldier in enemy territory? Would I have responded to Mr. Fracarro's approval and encouragement in the same way if I hadn't experienced what felt like the intense disapproval of Ms. Chase? Water tastes best when we are thirsty. By the time I met Mr. Fracarro, I was brittle and crumbling in small pieces from lack of moisture.

I am a person who has lived multiple lives in higher education. Currently, I work at a small private college as a career educator. If my only purpose on earth was to see, listen to, and experience the person in front of me and to have that person know that he or she is seen, then I have lived a deeply meaningful life.

Still, even with fulfilling work and 42 years of life lessons, I must admit that every day I exert significant energy trying to combat self-doubt. I catch myself reliving my time with Ms. Chase in present situations, remembering how humiliation felt in my 10-year-old body when I was sent out of her room because I was not good enough to be there. Often I am given some reprieve from the fight. Life provides me with moments when I am surrounded by people who are to me now what Frank was to me at age 12. My mystical teachers, in and out of the classroom; my friends, colleagues, family; my loving partner, all lift my face from the cracked earth and nourish me with living water until I am soaked.

As somebody who experienced poverty and lived to share what I have learned, I offer these recommendations to teachers:

- We should try not to label students or have preconceived notions about our students' abilities. Tracking often does not allow students the opportunity to realize their full potential.
- We should try not to view students through the limited lens of class. All people are more complex than their social status.
- We should notice that every individual person was born with particular gifts. Let us search for these gifts in each of our students and share with them what we see in them. Teachers should also notice that children growing up in poverty have developed particular skills such as resiliency, creative problem solving, and the ability to adapt in the midst of chaos.
- We should recognize our own biases. Our students will sense them and internalize our negative feelings about them.
- We should recognize that even teachers who are teaching students with racial and class backgrounds that are different from their own can be effective at doing so when their eyes are willing to see and their hearts are open to the magnificence in every person.

19

"WHO ARE YOU TO JUDGE ME?"
What We Can Learn From Low-Income, Rural Early School Leavers

Janet Kesterson Isbell

Each spring, young people who have completed high school observe a rite of passage to adulthood, receiving a high school diploma. The cap and gown portrait, the formality of graduation ceremonies, and the lengthy conferring of diplomas by roll call all herald the importance that communities and families place on this ritual. But not everyone who experiences high school is privileged to take part in graduation ceremonies. Every year in the United States more than half a million high school students withdraw from school without completing the requirements for a diploma (Stillwell, 2010), and being poor increases the likelihood of early withdrawal (Chapman, Laird, Ifill, & KewalRamani, 2011; Suh & Suh, 2007).

The voices of business and political leaders are demanding more rigor in the high school curriculum (Balfanz, 2009), and the voices of federal and state policymakers are pushing schools to improve graduation rates. In response, scholars and educators have turned their attention to long lists of risk factors for identifying early school leavers, resulting in finger pointing at poor families rather than in more intensive attempts to attend to the economic policies that lead to inequities in schools. Even the word *dropout* assigns blame and a label to the student, regardless of her or his circumstances.

If we really want to understand why low-income youth withdraw from school, we should start by listening to what they say is happening in the hallways and in the classrooms of those schools. Furthermore, in order to understand *how* and *why* many low-income students are not completing school, it is important that we look at the contexts of students' experiences (Christenson & Thurlow, 2004).

Among low-income students one group whose experiences have received particularly little attention in national conversations about poverty and schooling, and the group on which I focus in this chapter, is low-income youth living and attending schools in rural areas. Although they share many of the same challenges as their low-income urban and suburban counterparts, they also experience unique challenges specific to rural geographical contexts (Khattri, Riley, & Kane, 1997; Tilleczek & Cudney, 2008). For example, rural schools usually are smaller and more isolated than suburban or urban schools. Rural teachers tend to be paid less, have fewer resources, and drive longer distances to and from work. They are expected to take on after-school duties and are asked to teach courses outside their areas of expertise more often than their urban and suburban counterparts. As a result, rural schools have more difficulty than larger schools recruiting and retaining the most effective, experienced teachers (DeYoung, 1989; Mathis, 2003). In this sense, low-income youth in rural schools are victims of inadequate funding and policies that fail to address inequities in access to high-quality schooling.

In 1991, Michelle Fine asked a question about early withdrawal from school that, more than 20 years later, is still pertinent: "What if public schools were constructed around the needs of the student" (p. 221)? Listening to the voices of low-income youth from rural schools, and particularly students who withdrew from school before earning a diploma, can help us understand those needs. Their voices can guide us in our search for ways to help them complete that rite of passage, high school graduation, by making schools more equitable and just.

It is in that spirit that I share what I learned when I interviewed a variety of early school leavers from Appalachian communities in Tennessee about their school experiences. Their wonderfully candid responses form the basis for the recommendations I offer in this chapter about creating more equitable school experiences for students like them.

"I Slept Through Every Class"

In classrooms across the United States, in communities of all shapes and sizes, effective teachers help students succeed academically. But some communities, particularly low-income rural communities, find it more difficult than others to find and hold onto effective teachers. It should come as little surprise, then, that low-income youth who have withdrawn from school have a lot to say about teaching and learning, or the lack thereof, in their classrooms.

Effective teachers make content interesting and involve students in their own learning. Without this sort of engagement, students become bored and disinterested. Charles, who attended school in the same rural district for 12 years, was one of those disinterested students. "School bored me," he told me. And when he lost interest, he crossed his arms and put his head down on his desk: "I did that. I slept through every class. There was even one time that the teacher . . . didn't wake me up when the bell went off. They just let me sleep just to see if I would. And I ended up sleeping . . . through that whole class and half the other class."

In many rural high schools in Tennessee, classes are 90 minutes long. According to students like Charles, unless teachers engage and involve students, those 90 minutes can be difficult, particularly when students must sit at a desk for the entire class period. Justin, who withdrew after four years in a rural high school, said 90-minute classes were most difficult when the teacher did all the talking: "Lecture, lecture, lecture! I mean, like, I could be wide awake, sitting there watching, and the next thing I know, I'm waking up." Matt, who left his rural high school when he turned 18, said the monotony of a 90-minute English class was excruciating. He struggled to stay awake in classes that were irrelevant and boring: "Just classwork and the same stuff every day, knowing what you're going to do for seven hours—same ol' same ol'."

The experiences of these students illustrate how students in poor, rural schools are marginalized when inequities in school funding limit and restrict rural schools' hiring practices. Teaching that is boring, rote, and unengaging is more prevalent in low-income schools, regardless of size, than in wealthier districts where teachers are better paid, better trained, and better equipped to make learning interesting, interactive, and creative. The problem is compounded in areas that are both rural and poor because rural schools "often lose their most experienced employees to higher-paying districts in nearby suburban and urban areas" (Alliance for Excellent Education, 2009, p. 4), forcing them to staff their classrooms with less qualified teachers.

Andrea's high school was among those that needed more qualified teachers. "A lot of the teachers there don't really seem like they're supposed to be teachers. That's not really being rude, but a lot of them don't seem like they really know what they're doing." Her experiences in a low-income, rural high school in Tennessee illustrate how students are shortchanged in classrooms staffed by unlicensed teachers or teachers teaching outside their licensure areas, which is more common in rural schools. Andrea described a core content class:

> Usually, everybody would just be standing around talking, and then finally the teacher would get mad and yell at everybody and they'd sit down. And she would try to explain the lesson or whatever, but either [the teacher] didn't know how to explain it or everybody wasn't listening, so even after you started working on it there's all these—just people that have no idea what's going on. They're trying to copy off of you or trying to take your paper. They're not really even paying attention [to what's] going on.

Andrea also shared that her teachers relied heavily on textbooks, and students had to make sense of the material on their own because teachers did not know how to explain it. "Some of them don't have . . . a teaching degree," she explained, "and they're teaching classes they're not certified to be teaching."

The limited resources of low-income, rural schools, like the one Andrea attended, often prohibit districts from hiring qualified teachers for every subject area. Even when schools can hire, they may not have the resources to fund a search for the best candidates. Consequently, schools sometimes staff class-rooms with less qualified candidates or, while the search is under way for a suitable teacher, by uncertified staff such as teaching assistants or substitute teachers. It is important to understand that the issue is not one of commitment or bad intentions among assistants or subs who are taking on regular teaching duties—they, too, are being put into unfair situations.

Effective teachers know how to support and scaffold learning for all students, including struggling students like Eddie, who fell behind during high school. Some teachers, he said, were willing to help him. "Then there's oth-ers that, they'll just sit and won't do a thing." When teachers were unwilling to help him, Eddie slept or cheated. "I thought, if the teacher wasn't going to help, I just wasn't going to do anything. So I was just basically a rebel. I mean, I really didn't try 'cause there really wasn't no reason to." When teachers set high expectations and create a caring environment, where students' own interests and experiences are recognized and valued, students are likely to respond posi-tively and experience success; in contrast, when teachers undervalue students' abilities and demonstrate a lack of interest in their lives, students are more likely to respond negatively, as Eddie did, and may internalize feelings of inadequacy and inferiority. Again, poor rural students often are at a greater risk of this because they are most likely to have multiple unlicensed teachers.

Another challenge for low-income, rural students was illustrated by Matt, who believed teachers at his low-income rural school undervalued his own goals and attempted to push him toward a path that conflicted with his own plans. While in high school, Matt worked nights to help his mother pay bills and vol-unteered as a local firefighter. He planned to continue to live, work, and serve in his community, and he believed the content of his English and biology classes was irrelevant to those aspirations. When he raised this issue with teachers and administrators, they told him he should be preparing for college, in effect invali-dating Matt's own thinking. But Matt was certain: "College ain't for me." Matt quit school when he turned 18, leaving behind English and biology to work full time while continuing to serve as a local community volunteer.

Today's efforts to standardize learning and make college the only worthy goal for secondary students fail to take into consideration the realities of school-ing in low-income, rural communities. Some students prefer to work from within their communities to build a better world but, like Matt, are told that their aspi-rations are imprudent and shortsighted. Schools in low-income, rural communi-ties are uniquely positioned to connect learning to students' own experiences. Small businesses, fire halls, rescue squads, libraries, medical facilities, local governments, and senior centers are resources that could be tapped by schools in order to make learning relevant to students' lives while also strengthening their communities. When schools ignore the people and places where students live, students may begin to feel that their lives and their communities have no real value; when students' communities become part of their learning, students develop pride in their communities and a sense of purpose in their own lives.

Out of Step

Schools in the United States expect students to move toward graduation in a lockstep manner. For the most part, we all start school at the same age, move with our peers from grade to grade, study similar core content, and hope for grades high enough to earn high school diplomas, which we all receive at the same time. Students who struggle academically or experience disruptions to their school lives often have a hard time meeting the requirements for a diploma, and sometimes they just give up.

Samantha fell out of the step because her family often moved, forcing her to change schools on a regular basis. In her fourth year of high school, her family moved to a rural Tennessee community, where she enrolled in the local high school. Samantha made good grades and hoped to become the first person in her immediate family to earn a diploma. She tried multiple times to request confirmation from the guidance counselor that her transcript was in order, but Samantha felt as though the counselor was avoiding her:

> She would tell me that she would call me down and we'd go over credits and everything, and she never would. And I would come to her office and I would wait and, you know, sometimes she wouldn't be there, and sometimes she would get there and I would talk to her and she would say, 'Oh, just go to class, you know, and I'll call you in whenever I get everything together.' It never happened.

Samantha speculated that, because the rural school offered fewer course options than the bigger schools she had attended, her transfer credits were difficult to reconcile and the guidance counselor "just didn't want to mess with it."

As too often happens with youth who are made to feel invisible, Samantha eventually gave up. She could see no alternative but to walk away from high school and take control of her own life, so she quit the day she turned 18. One moment of acknowledgment from that school counselor might have been all Samantha needed to avoid this ending to her school experience.

Sometimes, of course, rural schools do provide alternatives for students who are considered "at-risk" for leaving school. But alternatives that help students who live in suburban or urban communities may not work as well for poor, rural students. The distance to and from alternative programs requires students to spend more time on the road and more money on fuel, and inclement weather in rural areas, such as flooding, ice, or snow, often makes rural roads impassable and results in school and alternative program cancellations. If students who leave school also have children, they may find it difficult to locate and pay for child care.

Eddie had fallen behind in school after the death of his father, and court orders and social service decisions moved him around to six rural high schools. By the time his peers became seniors, Eddie was lacking the credits he needed to graduate. His teachers advised him to enroll in an alternative degree program where he could work at his own pace and make up for lost time. He remembered his best friend begging him not to make the switch, but adults convinced Eddie that the alternative program was his "best bet" for a high school diploma. In the alternative program, Eddie tried to work through the textbook chapters in order to catch up to his peers. But he continued to struggle with content and was isolated from his peers. Students learn best in learning communities where they explore and share ideas, guided by a knowledgeable teacher who knows students' strengths and weaknesses and who recognizes that textbooks are not paramount. In Eddie's alternative program, there was no such learning community, and Eddie drifted in and out of the "best bet" program for nearly 3 years.

Low-income youth need more flexible and high-quality degree options to complete school when life's circumstances get in the way, and high schools and alternative programs need qualified teachers who recognize and can accommodate the needs of struggling students.

The trouble, again, is that many rural schools already struggle with limited funds and resources; where will they find money to support such programs and teachers? Until all schools are provided with adequate funding to meet the needs of all students, low-income youth who fall behind in high school may continue to be left out or shuffled into ineffective programs.

No One Cares

Students are more likely to quit school when they are at odds with their teachers (Tilleczek & Cudney, 2008); likewise, students are more likely to stay in school if they have good relationships with their teachers (Lee & Burkam, 2003). When Samantha moved to a rural Tennessee school, she needed a caring teacher. She hoped the small school environment would enable her to make new friends and find such teachers. Instead, she felt ignored by students and teachers, and she became despondent. She remembered a single act of kindness from one teacher:

> I was in the library one day sitting by myself and [a teacher] came in and she kind of just asked me what was going on in my life, and I explained

it to her, and she was the only one that actually really paid any attention, that actually took time out and was like, "Hey, I'm going to, you know, go talk to her." She was the only one.

Samantha said the encounter in the library was the first and last time the teacher showed any interest in her.

Eventually Samantha abandoned her desire to finish high school. "It had been building up that nobody really cared, you know, this whole time, and I was just like, you know, I just—I can't do it anymore! And that's when I decided, *I'm not going back*." She was surprised by school officials' angry responses. They complained that her decision would reflect poorly on the school. She remembered seeing the high school principal, who had never spoken to her, and feeling his disdain when he looked at her. "And I just thought, *You know, first of all, you don't know my story; you don't know me. . . . You've never talked to me, so who are you to judge me?*"

In considering why low-income youth withdraw from rural schools, we have to look at the schools, themselves, which "exert important organizational effects on students' decisions to drop out or stay in school, above and beyond their individual behaviors and backgrounds" (Lee & Burkam, 2003, p. 384). Teachers, counselors, and administrators should be trained not only to recognize early risk factors but also to respond appropriately to students' diverse needs. And schools and communities, recognizing the inequities in funding, must join forces to make the most of local resources, care for the students in their charge, and fight for change at the state and federal level.

Conclusions

The difficulties that follow early school withdrawal affect generations of students, their families, and their communities. Children of early school leavers are more likely to quit school and more likely to be in poor-performing schools, "creating powerful intergenerational social problems" (Orfield, 2004, p. 2). Early school leavers earn less and pay less in taxes (Alliance for Excellence in Education, 2009). Political rhetoric sometimes suggests that early school leavers are the "problem," that they are shortchanging the community, the state, and the nation, and that we "can no longer afford" (Alliance for Excellent Education, 2009, p. 4) the dropout problem. They use these claims to justify hyper-accountability, high-stakes testing, and more programs to fix the problem. The concern rarely seems to be about what is best for poor, rural students.

Will policies designed to increase accountability in the nation's schools work in poor, rural communities already struggling due to inequities in funding? Will we give the same attention to making coursework relevant to low-income rural students' lives as we give to standardizing the curriculum? Will we give the same attention to teacher pay and training in low-income rural schools as we give to measuring rural students' outcomes on high-stakes tests?

When we listen to the voices of the low-income rural youth who are at the heart of the dropout debate, they tell us powerful stories about what happens in the hallways and classrooms of their schools. And from those stories, we recognize that the "problem" is not disinterested youth, but instead the ways that they and their rural schools continue to be marginalized by funding, instructional, and other disparities—that often what we call a "dropout" is better described as a "pushout."

References

Alliance for Excellent Education. (2009, August). *The high cost of high school dropouts: What the nation pays for inadequate high schools* [Issue brief]. Washington, DC: Author. Retrieved from www.all4ed.org/files/HighCost

Alliance for Excellent Education. (2010). *Current challenges and opportunities in preparing rural high school students for success in college and careers: What federal policymakers need to know.* Washington, DC: Author. Retrieved from www.all4ed.org/publication_material/RuralSchools

Balfanz, R. (2009). Can the American high school become an avenue of advancement for all? *The Future of Children, 19*(1), 17–36.

Chapman, C., Laird, J., Ifill, N., & KewalRamani, A. (2011). *Trends in high school dropout and completion rates in the United States: 1972–2009* (NCES Publication No. 2012-006). National Center for Educational Statistics, U.S. Department of Education. Retrieved from http://nces.ed.gov

Christenson, S. L., & Thurlow, M. L. (2004). School dropouts: Prevention considerations, interventions, and challenges. *Current Directions in Psychological Science, 13*(1), 36–39.

DeYoung, A. J. (with Huffman, K., & Turner, M. E.). (1989). Dropout issues and problems in rural America, with a case study of one central Appalachian school district. In L. Weis, E. Farrar, & H. G. Petrie (Eds.), *Dropouts from school: Issues, dilemmas, and solutions* (pp. 55–77). Albany: State University of New York Press.

Fine, M. (1991). *Framing dropouts: Notes on the politics of an urban public high school.* New York: State University of New York Press.

Khattri, N., Riley, K. W., & Kane, M. B. (1997). Students at risk in poor, rural areas: A review of the research. *Journal of Research in Rural Education, 13*(2), 79–100.

Lee, V. E., & Burkam, D. T. (2003). Dropping out of high school: The role of school organization and structure. *American Educational Research Journal*, 40(2), 353–393.

Mathis, W. J. (2003). Financial challenge, adequacy, and equity in rural schools and communities. *Journal of Education Finance*, 29(2), 119–136.

Orfield, G. (Ed.). (2004). *Dropouts in America: Confronting the graduation rate crisis*. (Introduction). Cambridge, MA: Harvard Education Press.

Stillwell, R. (2010). *Public school graduates and dropouts from the Common Core of Data: School year 2007–08* (NCES Publication No. 2010–341). National Center for Education Statistics, Institute of Education Sciences, U.S. Department of Education. Retrieved from http://nces.ed.gov

Suh, S., & Suh, J. (2007). Risk factors and levels of risk for high school dropouts. *Professional School Counseling*, 10(3), 298–306.

Tilleczek, K., & Cudney, D. (2008). Rural youth and school cultures: Rethinking "place" and school disengagement. In K. Tilleczek (Ed.), *Why do students drop out of high school? Narrative studies and social critique* (pp. 143–158). Lewiston, NY: Edwin Mellen Press.

20

LOOKING PAST THE SCHOOL DOOR
Children and Economic Injustice

Steve Grineski and Ok-Hee Lee

Attempting to fix inner city schools without fixing the city in which they are embedded is like trying to clean the air on one side of a screen door. (Anyon, 1997, p. 168)

Among industrialized nations, the United States has the highest child poverty rate, at 23% (Darling-Hammond, 2010). That's 31.9 million children younger than the age of 18 years living in poverty (Addy & Wight, 2012). It is more than twice the rate in most European countries and higher than the 15% U.S. poverty rate in the early 1970s, following the implementation of the many programs that composed the War on Poverty (DeNavas-Walt, Proctor, & Lee, 2006; U.S. Census Bureau, 2006). The high poverty rate in the United States makes us wonder why one of the richest countries in the world is trailing other industrialized nations in providing supports and resources for poor children's well-being, particularly their education.

It is our intention to address this concern and suggest an approach toward realizing equitable education for all youth. To that end, we begin by discussing the concept, the "culture of poverty," because we view the pervasive stereotype held by most Americans that poor people have a universal culture of poverty as one of the biggest obstacles to eliminating insidious class inequities. We debunk the concept as a fallacy based on harmful stereotypes about poor families and their children. Then we pinpoint the lack of access to basic necessities and services, rather than a mythical culture of poverty, as the real reason behind the challenges poor families and their children face. Next, we discuss the ways in which current schooling denies poor children access to equal educational opportunity and how the strong belief in meritocracy leads us to place blame for poor academic performance on poor children and their families. Finally, on the basis of the reasoning that schools alone cannot eliminate poverty since children "don't live at school" (Berliner, 2012, para. 6), we suggest an approach to holistic reform that includes both humanistic *inside-of-school reforms* at classroom, school, and system levels and comprehensive *outside-of-school reforms* that target the sources of economic injustice.

A Misguided Myth: The Culture of Poverty

Most people in the United States believe that poor people are poor because of their own deficiencies rather than because of inequalities in opportunities and access (Gorski, 2008). This belief, which in fact is untrue, is so pervasive as to influence—even *shape* in some cases—not only our individual perceptions about poor people but also our policymaking and schooling practices. It can be easy for even the most well intentioned of us to inadvertently perpetuate stereotypes about poor people by implementing educational policies and school reforms that suggest we must "fix" them instead of eliminating the inequities they endure. To disrupt this unsettling reality, we need to examine the notion of the "culture of poverty" for what it is: a corrupting and limiting myth (Gorski, 2008).

The culture of poverty concept is based on the notion that poor people share a universal set of beliefs, behaviors, and values. It is based on a series of existing stereotypes: Poor people are inherently lazy, they don't care about education, they have no desire to work for a living, they are alcoholics and drug abusers. It is sad that if teachers operate with these assumptions, it becomes easy to assume, for instance, that the cause of gaps in school performance between low-income students and wealthy students is poor people's indolence or a lack of parental support (Gorski, 2008). Contrary to common beliefs about poor people, however, numerous empirical studies that have tested the culture of poverty concept, while differing in some of their conclusions about poverty, collectively have shown that there is no culture of poverty (e.g., Billings, 1974; Carmon, 1985; Jones & Luo, 1999). Differences in beliefs and behaviors among poor people differ as widely as they do among affluent people.

Although it is true that many poor children struggle in school, the cause of their struggle is not a culture of poverty but rather an "opportunity gap" characterized by unequal access to basic necessities such as food, safe housing, health care, high-quality early childhood programs, and well-funded schools. As described by the Urban Institute (2005),

> The vast majority of low-income parents today are working, but still struggling to make ends meet. . . . These families have much in common with other American families as they seek to balance work and family life, yet parents and children in low-income families are more financially vulnerable than those in higher-income families. (para. 1)

The median U.S. hourly wage is $9.00/hour, making the median annual salary $17,280 for primary wage earners in low-income families. These low wages make poor families vulnerable in a variety of ways. For example, compared with their wealthier counterparts, they are

- less likely to have health insurance and more likely to experience health problems;
- less likely to have jobs that offer paid vacation days, sick leave, and flexible work schedules;
- more likely to experience food insecurity;
- more likely to struggle to secure permanent, affordable, safe, and stable housing; and
- more likely to rely on a nonparent for child care, for longer periods of time per week. (Urban Institute, 2005, para. 1)

As the most vulnerable and dependent citizens of our society, 31.9 million children younger than the age of 18 years bear the brunt of grinding poverty and its associated economic injustices (Addy & Wight, 2012). All children unconditionally deserve lives shaped by economic and social justice, as eloquently captured in the United Nation's 1959 *The Declaration of the Rights of the Child*, which reminded us that adequate education, food, housing, and medical services are absolute rights of all children. Disturbingly, 46 years later the United States and Somalia are the only two nations that have not signed a 2005 UNICEF report acknowledging these same human rights.

The Educational Opportunity Gap for Poor Children

The educational costs of economic injustice are considerable. Too many poor children begin school behind their middle- and upper-class peers and fail to graduate, not because of their lack of curiosity or motivation to learn but because of the insurmountable challenges they and their families face (Gorski, 2007). A negative effect of these adversities is evident through the well-documented income-based educational opportunity gap between low- and high-income students and the racially based educational opportunity gap between many students of color and White students (Berliner, 2006).

For example, poor children are more likely than their wealthier peers to attend run-down, overcrowded, and underfunded schools that are inadequately staffed and under-resourced. Because of chronic underfunding, these schools, in contrast to well-funded schools, might struggle to recruit and retain the best teachers (although we celebrate the experienced teachers who choose to teach in low-income schools as some of their colleagues leave) or offer a variety of advanced placement courses, before- and after-school enrichment programs, summer school programming, and much in the way of intra- and extramural activities (Duncan & Murname, 2011; Kozol, 2005). In other words, many of these schools simply cannot fund the kinds of educational opportunities needed for their students to succeed while in school, to graduate, and to go on to postsecondary education or satisfying employment. They are cheated out of equitable schooling, as explained by Linda Darling-Hammond: "The opportunity to learn—the necessary resources, the curriculum opportunities, the quality teachers—that affluent students have, is what determines what people can do in life" (as quoted in Coutts & LaFleur, 2011, para. 8).

For a localized example, according to a report titled *A Rotting Apple: Education Redlining in New York City* (Schott Foundation, 2012), students who are poor and African American or Hispanic in the lowest income areas of New York City are denied an equitable opportunity to learn. They are enrolled in the city's poorest high schools, have fewer experienced teachers, and do not have access to gifted and talented programs. Three high school students' accounts of their accessibility to computers in school, in a different study, provide similar stories on the abysmally poor condition of their urban schools compared with well-funded suburban schools:

> Nikki reported that in her small urban high school, there were only three working computers and "[*the school*] won't let us use them." Jody and Crystal, on the other hand, told the team that their suburban school had three computer labs as well as portable laptop carts for classrooms. (Taines, 2011, p. 424; emphasis added)

We wonder what conclusion these students would draw about the alleged U.S. value of fairness.

Student success and graduation rates are directly related to school funding levels. In well-funded schools typically serving high-income and White students, academic performance and graduation rates are strong. Unfortunately, the opposite is true in underfunded schools typically serving low-income youth and youth of color (Duncan & Murname, 2011).

The Myth: Meritocracy as a Reality

Despite the educational opportunity gaps poor children face, too many educators still blame them, on the basis of the nation's meritocracy ideology, for their poor performance. According to this ideology, people achieve what they do based solely on merit. McNamee and Miller (2004) described it as follows:

> Getting ahead is ostensibly based on individual merit, which is generally viewed as a combination of factors including innate abilities, working hard, having the right attitude, and having high moral character and integrity. (para. 1)

If low-income students with asthma miss school for an extended period of time because of a lack of access to health care, their school performance likely will suffer regardless of how hard they work. The matter might be exacerbated if they do not have the necessary resources at home to complete their homework. In these instances their grades are not a true reflection of their merit; rather they reflect the opportunity gap stemming from the structural and economic inequity with which low-income youth and their families struggle. Simply, meritocracy is not the reality for many poor students. If we continue to blame them and their families for the symptoms of inequalities over which they have no control, we disenfranchise them even further.

To eliminate the inequities that oppress poor children and their families, we as educators must abandon our reliance on the fictitious culture of poverty and reject the meritocracy myth. Let us, instead, tackle the real cause of the struggles that poor youth and their families endure: the *opportunity* gap.

To do so, we suggest implementing holistic, comprehensive, and trans-formative initiatives. We must begin by acknowledging that making small shifts in school practices, although an important step, will not necessarily lead to meaningful change for poor students because the cause of educational injustice is located largely outside of schools. "Outside-the-school-door" reforms must address the existing economic and political conditions that make life in poor communities very difficult outside of schools, as well as the unequal educational opportunities inside schools (Berliner, 2006). Without understanding what these outside-school-walls reforms should look like, we as teachers might make uninformed inside-school reform efforts that fail to produce greater justice for low-income youth.

Outside-the-School-Door Reforms

We propose three reforms that, we believe, need to happen alongside trans-formative changes to school practice if our goal is to create more equitable educational and life opportunities for low-income students and their families.

First, all children should have access to comprehensive health care cover-age, including dental and vision care. When children have health problems, not only do their school attendance and performance diminish but their ability to concentrate on learning does as well. Low-income children, on account of the harsh social and economic conditions in which they live, are more susceptible to health problems such as asthma, which is *the* crisis disease for them and the leading cause of school absence. Thus, ensuring comprehensive universal health care coverage for all children is a critical step toward realizing equal educational opportunity for poor youth.

This universal health coverage for all children is not something schools by themselves can—or can be expected to—make happen; it obviously requires reforms at the state and federal levels outside schools. However, this doesn't mean that schools have no role to play in ensuring health care for all children, because children's health care needs outside school do not disappear once they step inside the school door. What can schools do? Collins, Goodman, and Moulton (2008), after reviewing school laws and policies concerning child and adolescent health, suggested integrating public health and education services so that children can receive more comprehensive preventive care and treatment without seeking isolated, disjointed health services from different agencies. If we adopt their recommendations, schools can play an integral role in shaping the health services children receive through collaboration with public health agencies and professionals.

Second, to reduce income inequality, which is the most direct source of economic injustice for poor children and their families, we must implement essential measures such as raising the minimum wage, protecting collective bargaining rights, establishing regulations forcing employers to offer full-time employment with paid sick leave and benefits (rather than avoiding doing so by hiring more people part-time), and expanding the earned-income tax credit. Without economic stability, children's access to food, safe housing, and a healthy environment free of toxins, which are directly correlated to equal educational opportunities in school, is jeopardized, which also puts at risk equal educational opportunities. Taking food insecurity and its relationship to children's education as an example, experts say there exists no "safe" level of inadequate nutrition for growing children (Adepoju, 1996; Esu, 2000). Even nutritional deficiencies that span a relatively short amount of time—one missed meal or inadequate breakfast—impair children's abilities to function and learn in school (Berliner, 2009). Therefore, efforts to reduce, if not eliminate, stark income disparities should be a top priority in realizing economic justice and educational equity for all children.

Third, all children deserve access to quality early childhood education. We see this as a *right* rather than a privilege granted exclusively to people who can afford it. A growing body of research suggests that the extent of access to early learning experiences, before children enter formal schooling, is a substantial predictor of their entire life paths. For example, access to high-quality early childhood education programs like the Perry Preschool Project, which enrolls low-income children free of charge, reduces the probability of students being retained a grade, needing special education, dropping out of school, being unemployed, and being incarcerated (Copple & Bredekamp, 2010; Reynolds & Temple, 2006). Thus, universal early childhood education, through expanding existing federal programs like Head Start, can be a starting point to provide poor children access to quality early childhood education and to prevent costly remediation later on (Reynolds & Temple, 2006). In this reform *all* children, not just a fraction of children, as with current Head Start programs, will have access to quality early childhood programs. This, therefore, in conjunction with other outside-school reform efforts mentioned previously, would help eliminate, rather than simply mitigate, inequities poor children face.

Inside-the-School-Door Reforms

Although the root cause of educational inequity is located outside school walls, reform efforts need to be implemented inside schools as well because economic inequality is manifested inside schools. We suggest approaches to inside-school reform at the system, school, and classroom levels.

At the system level, policymakers must devise ways to equitably distribute resources to schools so the economic status of individual communities does not dictate the amount and quality of resources schools receive. All children deserve the education that currently only the wealthiest families can afford. If we truly believe in fair and equal schooling, working to ensure poor students' access to excellent teachers, gifted and talented programs, computers and the Internet, advanced placement courses, and special education programs when they best meet children's real needs should be our priority (Coutts & LaFleur, 2011; Gorski, 2007).

At the building level, full-service or community schools offer great promise (Dryfoos, 2002). For example, the Children's Aid Society (CAS) currently operates 21 community schools in New York City. These community schools are the result of partnerships between CAS, the New York City Board of Education, the school district, and community-based partners. Their aim is to develop a model of public schools that combines teaching and learning with the delivery of an array of social, health, and child and youth development services, while also meeting the unique needs and strengths of individual communities. A recent study confirmed the effectiveness of 20 of the nation's full-service schools. Some of the positive outcomes included enhancements to student attendance, learning, and behavior; increases in parent and family participation; improved community-school safety and security; and a heightened sense of pride in both school and community (Coalition for Community Schools, n.d.).

An engaging curriculum is another important element in creating equitable opportunities for low-income students. Although difficult in the current climate of No Child Left Behind and Race to the Top, all students should have access to curricula embedded with higher-level thinking skills, problem-solving skills, and discovery learning. In fact, we believe that students should learn about issues related to class and poverty, helping them become citizens who actively confront the inequities that exist in society and their own communities. Unfortunately, lower-level-thinking curricula, often coupled with teacher-directed instruction, are far more common in underfunded schools typically serving low-income and minority students than in well-funded schools typically serving high-income White students (Kozol, 2005). If we want all students to be successful regardless of their families' income levels, we must offer all students high-quality curricula; a lack of intellectual stimulation should not be the price poor children pay to attend school.

To ensure high-quality curricula for all students, schools serving low-income students must be able to recruit excellent, dedicated teachers who teach critical thinking and other higher-order skills and adopt engaging pedagogies. One possible way to level the recruitment and retention playing field would be to improve working conditions in low-income schools by reducing class sizes, making sufficient materials available, establishing common planning times, and utilizing teacher mentoring programs. Of course, this cannot happen without equitable, adequate funding.

Inside classrooms we all should reject the concept of a culture of poverty and the meritocracy myth and then constantly reflect on our assumptions and beliefs so that our teaching and interactions with poor children and their families are fair and relevant. None of us as human beings, including those of us who are well intentioned and well informed on equity issues, is completely free from biases. If we are willing to accept this as a fact, reflecting on our own biases and the ways in which our prejudices often inform, and sometimes even shape, our practice as educators seems to be a critical step. In the meantime, educating ourselves by seizing professional development opportunities that help us examine our biases and what role stereotypes play in the education milieu can be helpful. Although it can be difficult at times, we might need to respond to colleagues and students when they stereotype poor students or parents and encourage open dialogue about the harmful effects of socioeconomic stereotypes.

Our attitudes and perceptions are reflected daily in our words and actions; students and parents perceive them quickly and accurately. This is why it is so important to confront our stereotypes. For example, how might we judge low-income students when they don't turn in homework assignments? Do we immediately slip into the stereotype that they are lazy? Or do we instead look deeper into why they might have struggled to complete an assignment? Perhaps they were caring for younger siblings or didn't have access to computers or the Internet or couldn't afford the materials they needed to finish the homework.

Finally, we suggest building strong relationships not only with parents who are actively involved in school activities but also with parents who are less engaged in schools, without assuming we know why. It is challenging to build strong connections with parents when they don't attend parent-teacher conferences or other school activities, but we can still explore other ways to reach out to them even when they seem unresponsive. We acknowledge that finding creative ways to connect with parents requires time and extra effort, and it becomes more challenging when we have limited resources. Still, we might be able to arrange meetings outside of the regular meeting hours, do home visits if that is the only way to see families, seek interpreters for nonnative-English-speaking parents, or advocate for transportation or on-site child care services for parents who need them in order to participate in school-based activities.

Conclusion

Paul Gorski (2008) in "The Myth of the Culture of Poverty" powerfully captured the message of "looking past the school door" and showed why a holistic and comprehensive approach is the only way to reduce the life-limiting effects of economic injustice on poor children:

> The socioeconomic opportunity gap can be eliminated only when we stop trying to "fix" poor students and start addressing the ways in which our schools perpetuate classism. This includes destroying . . . inequities . . . as well as abolishing such practices as tracking and ability grouping, segregated redistricting, and the privatization of public schools. We must demand the best possible education for all students—higher-order pedagogies, innovative learning materials, and holistic teaching and learning. But first, we must demand basic human rights for all people: adequate housing and healthcare, living-wage jobs, and so on. (p. 34)

We know children do not live in school 24 hours a day, which is why solely focusing on within-school reform measures by themselves do not work. It is time to tackle the root causes of economic injustice so the quality of children's lives can be elevated inside and outside the school's walls.

References

Addy, S., & Wight, V. (2012). *Basic facts about low-income children, 2010: Children under age 18.* Retrieved from www.nccp.org/publications/pub_1049.html

Adepoju, A. A. (1996). Sex difference, home background, and pupils' performance in English and mathematics. In S. Adejole (Ed.), *Education in the service of humanity* (2nd ed.). Ibadan, Nigeria: Educational Research and Study Group.

Anyon, J. (1997). *Ghetto schooling: A political economy of urban school reform*. New York: Teachers College Press.

Berliner, D. (2006). Our impoverished view of educational research. *Teachers College Record, 108*(6), 949–995.

Berliner, D. (2009). Are teachers responsible for low achievement by poor students? *Kappa Delta Pi Record, 46*(1), 18–21.

Berliner, D. (2012). *Fixing schools isn't everything*. National Education Association. Retrieved from www.nea.org/bare/print.html?content=bare/12206.htm

Billings, D. (1974). Culture and poverty in Appalachia: A theoretical discussion and empirical analysis. *Social Forces, 53*(2), 315–323.

Carmon, N. (1985). Poverty and culture. *Sociological Perspectives, 28*(4), 403–418.

Coalition for Community Schools. (n.d.). *Frequently asked questions about community schools*. Retrieved from www.commuinityschools.org/aboutschools/faqs.aspx

Collins, J., Goodman, R., & Moulton, A. (2008, February). A CDC review of school laws and policies concerning child and adolescent health. *Journal of School Health, 72*(2), 69–128.

Copple, C., & Bredekamp, S. (2010). *Developmentally appropriate practice: Educational practice for children birth through age eight*. Washington, DC: NAEYC.

Coutts, S., & LaFleur, J. (2011). Some states still leave low-income students behind; others make surprising gains. *Propublica*. Retrieved from www.propublica.org/article/opportunity-gap-schools-data

Darling-Hammond, L. (2010). *The flat world and education: How America's commitment to equity will determine our future*. New York: Teachers College Press.

DeNavas-Walt, C., Proctor, B., & Lee, C. H. (2006). *Income, poverty, and health insurance coverage in the United States: 2005. Current population reports*. Washington, DC: U.S. Department of Commerce.

Dryfoos, J. (2002). Full-service community schools: Creating new institutions. *Phi Delta Kappan, 83*(5), 393–399.

Duncan, G., & Murname, R. (2011). *Whither opportunity? Rising inequality, schools, and children's life chances*. New York: Russell Sage Foundation.

Esu, A. E. O. (2000). Parental care and control in child development. *Journal of Early Childhood Education, 2*, 22–25.

Gorski, P. (2007). The question of class. *Teaching Tolerance*. Retrieved from www.tolerance.org/magazine/number-31-spring-2007/feature/question-class

Gorski, P. (2008). The myth of the culture of poverty. *Educational Leadership*, 65(7), 32–36.

Jones, R. K., & Luo, Y. (1999). The culture of poverty and African-American culture: An empirical assessment. *Sociological Perspectives, 42*(3), 439–458.

Kozol, J. (2005). *The shame of a nation: The restoration of apartheid schooling in America.* New York: Crown.

McNamee, S. J., & Miller, R. K., Jr. (2004). The meritocracy myth. *Sociation Today,* 2(1). Retrieved from www.ncsociology.org/sociationtoday/v21/merit.htm

Reynolds, A., & Temple, J. (2006). Economic returns of investments in preschool education. In E. Zigler, W. S. Gilliam, & S. M. Jones (Eds.), *A vision for universal preschool education* (pp. 37–68). New York: Cambridge University Press.

Schott Foundation. (2012). *A rotting apple: Education redlining in New York City.* Retrieved from www.schottfoundation.org/publications-reports/education-redlining

Taines, C. (2011). "What the real world in schools is like": Urban youth in dialogue about educational inequality. *The Urban Review, 43,* 414–435. doi:10.1007/$11256-010-0169-3

United Nations. (1959). *The declaration of the rights of the child.* Retrieved from www.unicef.org/Legal/global/General/declaration_child1959.pdf

Urban Institute. (2005). *Low-income working families: Facts and figures.* Retrieved from www.urban.org/publications/900832.html

U.S. Bureau of Census. (2006). *Poverty status of people, by age, race, and Hispanic origin: 1959–2006.* Washington, DC: U.S. Department of Commerce.

PART FOUR

Insisting on Equity
Students, Parents, and Communities Fight for Justice

21

RECKONING

Paul C. Gorski

A time comes when you can no longer say: my God.—*Carlos Drummond de Andrade (from "Your Shoulders Hold Up the World")*

A time comes
when we no longer can say
Change
      takes
          time.
A time for reckoning.

Tears are not enough.
Even if we collect them
in buckets
they are no mitigation
for hunger, no cure
for asthma.

Nor the half-crooked grins
of good intentions:
what are they against
the cold? Who wins when
we wear them like badges,
wave them like banners
in half-hearted protest
or when we say
Change
      takes
          time?

A time comes
when slow and steady
means
when *I'm* ready,
when peace vigil therapy
for the shame-ridden soul

folds into itself
and emerges polite
inaction inaction inaction.

A time comes for urgency,
for measurement
against the metrics
of history.

22

TRAVERSING THE ABYSS
Addressing the Opportunity Gap

John N. Korsmo

something peculiar happened the other day while reviewing my research with first-generation, low-income college students: I cried. It was unexpected, as I have been engaged in emotionally charged work for many years and have become accustomed to keeping my emotions in check. My professional experiences include human service and education roles in both rural and urban settings, predominantly with people living in poverty. I have worked with homeless youth and families, gang-affiliated and incarcerated youth, drug-addicted youth and adults, people nearing death due to complications from HIV/AIDS, victims of domestic violence and sexual abuse, and other vulnerable populations.

As might be expected, when I began this work with people in crises, I came across all sorts of heart-wrenching experiences. What I did not anticipate, however, was how frequent and powerful the positive and inspiring experiences would be. For years I was trained to work through both "good" and "bad" experiences without becoming "too attached." So I was surprised when I was brought to tears by stories and insights from low-income, first-generation college students. In this chapter I share snippets of those stories, drawing parallels to my own experiences, while offering simple suggestions for how to support low-income students.[1]

Evoking the Past

My emotional reaction happened while reading transcripts of an interview I conducted with Steven,[2] who was only two weeks away from becoming the first person in his family to graduate from college. He shared parts of his story through occasional tears and nervous laughter, and although many of his experiences were similar to others I have heard, some details were unnervingly familiar to me:

> I applied [to college] almost on a whim, and with no one's help. Amazingly I got in. I broke the news to my family, and Dad got pissed. Mom seemed proud, but Dad was a different story, and he basically refused to

[accept it]. . . . I packed all my crap when it was time and finally talked
my mom into coming to campus with me for freshmen orientation. We
drove through the night from the other side of the state, took forever
to figure out where we were supposed to go, and finally found a place
to park. The whole trip seemed to take forever. Campus was huge and
confusing. We walked toward [the main] square, where we could hear
all the people but ended up leaving right away . . . we felt like a freak
show . . . and were totally out of place. . . . My mom doesn't even have
teeth, and she was uncomfortable with that. . . . We left right away, and
I almost didn't even come back. My mom hasn't been back since, and I
just hope she comes for graduation.

Perhaps it was his description of his dad being upset, or that he felt so out of
place in college, or the detail of his mom not having teeth, or that neither of his
parents ever came to visit during his four years on campus. Maybe it was the
combination of all of these things, but Steven's story took me back to my own
experience of leaving home for college. Memories spanning many years kept
interrupting my train of thought.

Steven's dad's response to his admission into college reminded me of the
fight that ensued between my father and me the night before I left for college.
I was contacted by the local tavern to come down and extract him from his
bar stool, as he was causing angst among the more faint-of-heart clientele. My
80-year-old neighbor received the call and walked over to let me know, as my
family did not have a phone. It was rarely a good omen when the tavern called
my neighbor to track me down. Generally a very loving man, my father had
a flash temper that was not to be provoked. He was fired up by whatever alter-
cations were brewing at the bar, and his mood was soured even before I arrived
to bring him home. Thus, I had no intention of broaching the subject of my
leaving for college. Unfortunately, he mentioned needing me to do something
the next afternoon, so I had to remind him that I was leaving in the morning.
He recycled some of his favorite arguments for why I should not go off to
university, including how much they needed me at home and how I was going
away only because I thought I was better than him and the rest of the family.
His diatribe spiraled into his landing what would end up being the final blow
I would ever allow him to strike.

The image of my mom's sunken cheeks clinging to her toothless gums then
flashed in my mind as Steven described his mother. This memory caused me to
feel ashamed of the times I was embarrassed as a teenager when someone I knew
saw us together. Similarly, Steven's feeling out of place on campus led me to consider my own sense of not fitting in and my self-consciousness. A feeling of being
entirely out of place was a major factor in my dropping out of college after my

first year. Many years later, I still occasionally feel out of place on campus, even in my privileged position as a professor.

After I had been worn down emotionally by reviewing hundreds of stories about poverty and struggle, charity and humiliation, and heroic efforts to persevere and succeed, Steven's story provoked in me a flood of memories, from grade school in the mid-1970s through graduate school in the mid-2000s:

> It's three days before the rest of the fifth graders will be leaving on an epic field trip, flying from central Michigan to the nation's capital. The principal pulls me out of class and informs me that I will be able to go on the trip after all, as my best friend's mom has paid the fees and bought me two new outfits for the occasion.
>
> It's my first day at a new middle school—my fifth school in 7 years—and I am matched up with a "school buddy," Earl, whom I am told I will "hit it off with." He resembles me a bit with his blackened teeth and ragged clothes. Functionally illiterate, he is a couple years away from dropping out of school.
>
> It's Christmas my junior year, and I answer the knock at the door, only to receive a well-intended donation box—delivered by none other than the girl of my 17-year-old dreams, as part of her church's annual giving campaign.
>
> I'm days away from starting college and am excited to cash the first scholarship check I ever received. I schedule a dental appointment, and with the money I pay to have them perform a root canal and replace a front tooth that had rotted out years prior, because having front teeth for my first year of college seems more prudent than buying schoolbooks.
>
> My doctoral advisor is squeezing my hand while the commencement speaker shares parts of my experience as a "pull yourself up by the bootstraps" story, in front of thousands of people at graduation. I am sitting in my gown and wishing I had not allowed my story to be used.

The challenges my family faced, and the degree to which my parents, and their parents before them, fought and sacrificed to provide for their families merged with the struggles of others. The stories of past and current hardships got to me. I can imagine many of my previous supervisors in various human services and mental health roles suggesting I had gotten "too close" to Steven and the other interviewees. However, I challenge that perspective and believe we fall short of understanding low-income students when we don't get close enough. The reality of their struggles ought to bring all of us to tears or minimally to a point of empathic understanding. Although each story I've heard from low-income college students is unique to their upbringing and interpretations of their life experiences, there are two overarching themes I consistently hear. They need positive relationships with others (school personnel, as well as peers and family) and a high degree of self-efficacy.

CONFIDENCE

Class Matters

A relational approach or a general sense of being "related to" is imperative. This is not to say that a teacher needs to be his or her student's buddy. The students, however, need to know they are valued and that their teachers believe in their abilities to learn and succeed. The relationships students have with school personnel, and with each other, are principal predictors of whether they will remain actively engaged throughout their educational journeys, from early childhood education through postsecondary schooling. In addition, the individual student must have intrinsic motivation, the ability to persevere, and an optimistic sense of self to succeed. In other words, having a mentor or some other adult who encourages the child is necessary but not sufficient. The individual is her or his own primary motivator, and thus we must aspire to build strong self-efficacy within all children.

There is much discussion of the differences between how higher education is experienced for first-generation college goers and those who have parents with college degrees. However, it is not merely the notion of being the first in one's family to go to college that explains the difference in experiences, so much as their socioeconomic status (SES). Eighty percent of the very low-level SES students in one of my recent studies reported that they were "very dissatisfied with the support they received" from their family to go to college, compared to only 17% for low-level SES students and 0% for students in the medium- to high-level SES groups.

When students shared stories related to their families' support, however, the results were more evenly divided, with many of the students discussing constant encouragement from parents and family members. One student, Monique, explained, "For me, college has always been expected . . . and there really was no alternative, or even a need to discuss an alternative. College can't just be a hope—it needs to be an expectation." Other students shared similar stories, pointing to the importance of high expectations, together with a sense of being loved and supported by family, regardless of how dire their circumstances might be. Other students indicated that family members were more neutral on the subject. One student, Tim, stated, "My family never talked about higher education. I never felt it was an option, because I didn't even know about it. College was something that people with money pursued." In cases such as Tim's, although his family did not necessarily empower his educational pursuits, at least their more benign level of engagement did not actively work against him, as was the case for some others.

In consideration of what it was like when they got to college, a majority of the very low-level SES participants stated they "frequently felt as though they did *not* fit in with their peers during their first year of college" compared with only 8% of mid- to high-level SES students. Perhaps more startling, 20% of very low-level SES students stated that they "always felt as though they did *not* fit in." When we consider these feelings together with the frequent sense of not being supported to pursue college in the first place, there is little wonder that so many low-income first-generation students second-guess their college enrollment and are considerably more likely to drop out after their first year (Chen, 2005; Ishitani, 2006; McKay & Estrella, 2008).

Some of the people I interviewed pointed to more blatant roadblocks and disapproval from family members, as in Steven's quote at the beginning of the chapter. This, of course, contradicts the common view that everyone is encouraged by their parents to focus on school and pursue higher education. It may be difficult for some readers to imagine parents not being excited about, or even supportive of, their children's education, but this is a reality for many of our children, for many different reasons. One common explanation was a belief that their families felt as though they would "lose" their children if they pursued college. This loss includes literal separation due to geographic location, the realistic potential that their children may not live near home after completing college, and a general sense of cultural or identity loss. This is particularly the case for families in more rural environments. In such locations the concept of "brain drain," or the flight of human capital, wherein highly educated individuals move to more favorable geographic, economic, social, or professional environments is easily discernible (Carr & Kefalas, 2009; Sherman & Sage, 2011).

There is risk of loss whenever someone leaves home, regardless of SES. People change as they experience new things and learn more about themselves, about others, and about life overall. This happens whether someone enters college, military service, the workforce, or any other life experience that takes her or him away from familiar surroundings. What differentiates college-related separation from these other kinds of separation, however, is the potential for change in personal identity, including elements related to class and culture (Barnett & Coate, 2005; Dall'Alba & Barnacle, 2007; hooks, 2000; Luckett & Luckett, 2009). Families often fear this change the most. A family may not literally lose its son or daughter to college, but rather the student may change so much as an individual through the educational experience that his or her family members feel as though their connections to the person they knew are compromised. Stories of relational and emotional separation or loss were commonly reported from students I interviewed, with significant variation based on SES. For instance, when students were asked if their education "separated them from family relationally," 68% of students from the very low and low SES groups strongly agreed. In comparison, only 20% of students in the middle and upper-middle SES category strongly agreed. The following segment of an interview with Kasey reflects a common sentiment of students who after attending university felt a sense of decline in their ability to relate with family members:

> My parents expected me to attend a technical college, but I chose a university environment, much to the consternation of my parents. As I matured into my education, my beliefs and values changed along with me, and my relationship with my parents grew more distant. Though we remain close, we have very little in common beyond family relationships.

Seeking Guidance

Another problem is that first-generation college students with lower SES reported receiving less support to pursue college from high school personnel such as guidance counselors and teachers. A full 80% of very low-level SES students indicated being "very dissatisfied with the support" they received compared with 29% of the low-level SES students and 21% of students in the medium- to high-level SES groups. For many of these students, the pursuit of education is a challenge they must bear alone, without supports from home or school. It's important to clarify here that parents may be unsupportive of their child's higher education pursuits and still be loving and effective parents. Their roles as parents are well beyond supporting academic achievements, particularly considering that not all children want to go to college. To the contrary, however, the paramount duty of school personnel is to ensure academic and educational opportunities and supports for all students. Therefore, when a teacher or school counselor drops the ball, it is a matter not just of subjective opinion (such as a reader having the opinion that parents should encourage their child to aspire for higher education, which is subjective and value-laden) but rather of professional dereliction.

The students I interviewed expressed frustrations with ineffective guidance counselors in particular. Some elaborated in detail the degree to which they were "shut down" or "turned away" by their counselors. These kinds of disempowering interactions with school personnel take a toll on students and can leave a lasting impression. More than 25 years after a 15-minute meeting with my high school counselor, I remember vividly his response when I turned down the Marine Corps brochure with a tepid pronouncement that I wanted to go to college. He told me, "You know you might want to get some work experience first," not knowing I had been working for several years on farms, in food processing plants, and on a variety of construction-related sites, among other jobs. My workweeks ranged from 10 to 30 hours during the school year and frequently were more than 100 hours per week during the busy summer months. But, of course, he had no idea. Although there were only 88 students in my graduating class, he had no clue *who* I was; however, he had an opinion of *what* I was, and college material was not it. He dismissively ended our brief meeting by telling me that I needed to understand that college would require a lot of work. I was in the National Honor Society, took all of the advanced placement classes the school offered, graduated as a three-sport letterman with eight varsity letters, and tended to family responsibilities in addition to the previously mentioned work schedule. Being responsible solely for college would feel like a holiday.

What he knew of me was limited by what was visible. I was no doubt unkempt; dirty and sometimes pungent from farm work, a lack of proper hygienic supplies, no shower, and frequently no hot water. I had several broken, blackened, and missing teeth and was adorned with unflattering, mightily used secondhand and thirdhand clothes and a do-it-yourself haircut. From his observations he easily extrapolated further conclusions about me. I would like to give him the benefit of the doubt here, as very few of my peers expressed an interest in postsecondary education, and he certainly did not expect anything different from me.

Although none of my close friends went to college, I wonder if some would have done so if provided some genuine counsel from someone who connected with and cared about them. For some, such an opportunity might have set the course of their lives on a distinctly more positive trajectory. This is not to say that college is the cure-all we are looking for to lead people to the mythical utopia of middle-class life. In fact, a four-year degree is not for everyone. However, educational attainment is a significant contributor to opportunities for personal and professional development, including increased lifetime satisfaction and earning potential (Cheung & Chan, 2009; Davis & Friedrich, 2004; Wilkinson & Pickett, 2010). It is an option everyone deserves.

Thankfully, my counselor does not reflect all counselors. There are countless amazing school personnel around the country who are making connections and positive differences in students' lives. It is common for students coming from a low SES background to remark on the significance of the support they received from teachers, coaches, and guidance counselors, as well as ancillary staff who often are overlooked, such as playground aides, bus drivers, cafeteria staff, and others. Many of the people I interviewed recounted simple supportive statements such as "You are so smart," "You are really good at that," and other seemingly insignificant remarks as reinforcement that they remembered many years after hearing them. The simplest of things sometimes make a world of difference, and students who otherwise may not receive affirming feedback about their intellectual capacities often cherish such positive comments.

Conversely, much also might be said about the potential harm caused by people in students' lives who are *not* supportive. Inattentive and non-relational school personnel create roadblocks for students even without intending to do so. Sometimes the roadblocks come in the form of misinformation, the abuse of "knowledge power" simply by not sharing cogent and useful information, or comments or nonverbal behavior and body language that chip away at a student's self-esteem. I doubt that my counselor had any idea of the degree to which our brief chat set me back in my thinking. His was yet another burden of doubt for me to endure at a time when even minimal support could have meant a great deal.

My counselor had no idea how nervous I was to even schedule the appointment, let alone to say out loud that I wanted to go to college. I would like to think of myself as having been self-confident enough to shrug off the naysayers, but the truth is that there was a perpetual internal struggle between my personal motivations for success and my insecurities. Substantial amounts of scholarship articulate the importance of self-efficacy, the many ways a person's esteem is built or broken, and the consequences of this construction or destruction. In my case, as a high school student, I was unsure about what I wanted, insecure about what I might be able to pursue, and, frankly, intimidated even by talking about going to college. This is not the case with everyone, of course, but we need to consider the many students today who lack the confidence, independence, or bravery that it takes to stand up to common public perception. It should not be their burden to bear alone.

Leveling the Playing Field

Despite the mythology of equality, we do not have equal educational opportunity in the United States. This is a goal for which to strive, but until we get there, we need to acknowledge and respond to the fact that some people have a tougher trail to blaze than others. Even when done well, providing equal opportunity to everyone at any single point in time does not take into account the inequitable barriers with which some have been contending. That is why even if a school implements a well-planned and executed education policy or philosophy that provides equal opportunity, it will miss the mark unless it takes into account the historical imbalances that have occurred. Children of color, students with limited English-language proficiency, and youth coming from low SES backgrounds, for instance, have had the cards stacked against them and their families, perhaps for generations. With each additional generation of learners who are marginalized and not supported in their educational experiences, the gaps in opportunity expand. For decades we have been discussing the supposed "achievement gap" in this country, referring to the disparity in educational outcomes between different subgroups of students, usually based on categories of race. Recently this has more accurately been referred to as the "opportunity gap" in order to avoid insinuating that people at the lower end of the opportunity scale are responsible for their own plights and to recognize the difference as related to limited opportunities rather than capabilities (DeShano da Silva, Huguley, Kakli, & Rao, 2007). Unfortunately, this gap is rapidly evolving into an abyss. And whereas gaps can generally be overlooked, an abyss can swallow you whole before you even know it exists.

Like so many others, my counselor never seemed to consider me as anything other than what my appearance confirmed in his mind: I was *poor* in all biased senses of the word. His doubts of my abilities to succeed because of my family's social pedigree did not create observable roadblocks; however, they certainly did not empower me. I am reminded here of a statement by Martin Luther King, Jr.: "True peace is not merely the absence of tension; it is the presence of justice" (as cited in Oats, 1982). In this case, true equity in education is not merely the absence of obvious obstructions but rather the presence of opportunities. It is not enough for us only to minimize barriers, but we must also take on the difficult task of addressing the voids.

Cross-Class Connections

The topics of class and SES remain taboo in the United States and its schools. This was my experience when I worked in poor urban schools in the '90s and in the numerous rural schools I attended in the '70s and '80s. It seems as though we may have benefited from broaching the subject in my high school, at least, considering it was a farm town of only 500, where everyone literally did know everyone, and the gap between the "haves" and the "have-nots" was as obvious as the town's lone gas station. By not intentionally thinking, talking, and teaching about socioeconomic privilege and the consequences of class inequality, we undermine our abilities to make significant progress connecting with and supporting families who are withstanding the worst of the wealth disparity burden. On the other hand, we serve each other well when we initiate and sustain interdisciplinary and "cross-class" communication. When we ask and respond to questions of class distinctions and address the variance in opportunities and challenges, a critically important dialogue can ensue. This is particularly salient in recent times, as there is both a growing trend in higher education aspiration for low-income high school students and an unfortunate increase in people living in poverty. When the degree of affluence of students decreases, so too does their sense of belonging in institutions of higher education. Considering that upward of 80% of the students I interviewed who self-identified as very low SES frequently felt as though they did not belong in college and that those same students have a much higher likelihood of dropping out, more should be done to address cross-class barriers.

We have a shared responsibility to level the playing field for our schoolchildren and to eliminate unethical gaps in opportunity. Until then, it is our paramount duty to see to it that *all* of our children are supported in traversing the educational opportunity abyss. As identified by those first-generation students referenced in this chapter, two primary ways to do this include fostering an increased sense of inclusion or connectedness and increased self-efficacy. These two concepts are profoundly related (Bandura, 1994; Margolis & McCabe, 2006) and may be achieved in part through a relational approach between school personnel and students (Bingham & Sidorkin, 2004; Erickson, 1987; Rogers, 1983). A relational approach places a primary focus on the development of trusting and supportive relationships between the students and their teachers. The students I spoke with were aware of the challenges faced by teachers to build such relationships with all students given the number of pupils in each class and the lack of time for personal interaction. They spoke of very practical means for advancing a sense of personal connection, such as displaying appropriate physical contact (e.g., high fives, handshakes, and even hugs), being aware of some of their interests, referring to them by name in positive ways, and taking a moment to inquire about their day. One student, Sarah, put it this way:

> The way she simply knew who I was and that I was in band sort of told me she was paying attention. And then as she joked around with me sometimes and told me a little bit about her, like that she has a black Lab and simple stuff, and when we one day talked about being cranky if we don't get enough sleep, I felt like she was human. She wasn't a robot like some of the other teachers, and she even cared about me. That was a relationship, but we weren't friends. How many teachers do you know who have a real conversation with the kids? It seems stupid, but I can tell you not many. They are too busy to do anything but their class plan. But it doesn't take much to say hi to me and bump fists or something. Make me know you understand that I am alive.

Although there is a need for some complex systemic changes in our approach to equitable education, supporting and empowering students needn't be that complicated. Even simple and subtle adjustments to how we interact with and relate to students make profound differences in their school experience and consequently in their life.

Because I have experienced unstable housing, untreated medical and dental needs, multiple school transfers, and other challenges associated with poverty, people often seek from me an "insider's" opinion on how best to serve and support "the poor." Frankly, I wish I had a more profound answer to provide than to suggest something as simple as caring about them and using a relational approach, but that is where my response often leads. Having beaten the odds to become a university professor, I frequently am asked about my past, as it can be viewed as a veritable success story. The trouble is that *my* experiences breaking through generational poverty and under-education are just that: *mine*. We need to seek the multiple stories of the young people who are experiencing poverty today and offer a platform for marginalized youth to be heard. That is not to say that the stories of people who have succeeded in breaking out of poverty should not be solicited. On the contrary, it can be helpful for people to know that *success* (however one might define that term for himself or herself) is possible.

After years of working with people in poverty, I can see that they certainly are not the problem. In fact, I believe them to be the solution, if only we treat them and their experiences as the invaluable assets they are. In fact, the next time you find yourself passing negative judgment on "poor" students, please, for a moment, picture them as a future business leaders, doctors, teachers, or professors. Better yet, treat them, if only for a moment, with the respect, admiration, and courtesy with which you would treat your own children. Because in many ways, they are.

Notes

1. The stories and insights from first-generation college goers are part of a research project, "Pathways to Success: First-Generation College Goers' Challenges and Successes," sponsored in part by Western Washington University's Office of Research and Special Programs.
2. All names, including those of people and places, have been changed to protect confidentiality.

References

Bandura, A. (1994). Self-efficacy. In V. S. Ramachaudran (Ed.), *Encyclopedia of human behavior* (Vol. 4, pp. 71–81). New York: Academic Press.

Barnett, R., & Coate, K. (2005). *Engaging the curriculum*. Maidenhead, UK: Society for Research Into Higher Education and Open University Press.

Bingham, C., & Sidorkin, A. (Eds.). (2004). *No education without relation*. New York: Peter Lang.

Carr, P., & Kefalas, M. (2009). *Hollowing out the middle: The rural brain drain and what it means for America*. Boston: Beacon Press.

Chen, X. (2005). *First generation students in postsecondary education: A look at their college transcripts* (NCES 2005–171; U.S. Department of

Education, National Center for Education Statistics). Washington, DC: U.S. Government Printing Office.

Cheung, H., & Chan, A. (2009). The effect of education on life satisfaction across countries. *Alberta Journal of Educational Research*, *55*(1), 124–136.

Dall'Alba, G., & Barnacle, R. (2007). An ontological turn for higher education. *Studies in Higher Education*, *32*, 679–691.

Davis, N. C., & Friedrich, D. (2004). Knowledge of aging and life satisfaction among older adults. *International Journal of Aging and Human Development*, *59*(1), 43–61.

DeShano da Silva, C., Huguley, J., Kakli, Z., & Rao, R. (Eds.). (2007). *The opportunity gap: Achievement and equality in education*. Cambridge: Harvard Education Press.

Erickson, F. (1987). Transformation and school success: The politics and culture of educational achievement. *Anthropology and Education Quarterly*, *18*(4), 335–336.

hooks, b. (2000). *Where we stand: Class matters*. New York: Routledge.

Ishitani, T. (2006). Studying attrition and degree completion behavior among first-generation college students in the United States. *Journal of Higher Education*, *77*(5), 861–886.

Luckett, K., & Luckett, T. (2009). The development of agency in first generation learners in higher education: A social realist analysis. *Teaching in Higher Education*, *14*(5), 469–481.

Margolis, H., & McCabe, P. (2006). Improving self-efficacy and motivation: What to do, what to say. *Intervention in School and Clinic*, *41*(4), 218–227.

McKay, V., & Estrella, J. (2008). First-generation student success: The role of faculty interaction in service learning courses. *Communication Education*, *57*(3), 356–372.

Oats, S. (1982). *Let the trumpet sound: A life of Martin Luther King Jr.* New York: HarperCollins.

Rogers, C. (1983). *Freedom to learn for the 80's*. Columbus, OH: Merrill.

Sherman, J., & Sage, R. (2011). Sending off all your good treasures: Rural schools, brain-drain, and community survival in the wake of economic collapse. *Journal of Research in Rural Education*, *26*(11). Retrieved from http://jrre.psu.edu/articles/26-11.pdf

Wilkinson, R., & Pickett, K. (2010). *The spirit level: Why greater equality makes societies stronger*. New York: Bloomsbury Press.

23

FOSTERING WIDEAWAKENESS
Third-Grade Community Activists

Lenny Sánchez

[Teaching] is a question of thinking what one is doing—achieving a wide-awakeness with respect to one's own life situation. (Greene, 1973, p. 189)

I grew up in a poor, working-class, rural family. It was not until entering school that I felt a private shame for having to paint my shoes to hide their long-lived scuffs, stand in the designated free- and reduced-meal line to receive my lunch food, and walk roadsides to collect recycling items to help pay the bills as familiar passersby looked the other way. I grew up watching my mother tend devotedly to our family's garden to ensure we would have food on our table and watched my native-Spanish-speaking father work multiple jobs while learning English and pursuing college degrees to provide us with financial security. Although I was taught to appreciate what I had, my social class status was clear to me in the form of the judging stares and chatter that filled my school years.

I look back to these memories and wonder why no one in school helped me develop a critical consciousness about my experiences—why no one helped me to realize I was not to blame. Why didn't the adults recognize my burden or acknowledge my experiences as real? Why did the very place that made me conscious of my differences also make me feel ashamed?

These questions remain with me now as a teacher and teacher educator. Fortunately I have had the opportunity to be part of caring school communities that have worked tirelessly to bridge ties between children's life experiences and the social fabric of their schools. Despite their limits for combating systemic issues such as poverty or racism, these schools are not deterred from their commitments to invest in the personal welfare of the individuals, adults, and children who are part of their communities. In fact, when schools create a space in which each member is recognized as a public intellectual (Campano & Sánchez, 2010), they more easily can make the very issues that concern their communities central to the work of the classroom. Children and adults can work in tandem to pose complex questions, interrogate assumptions, and find ways to contest the conditions that impact their lives.

In this chapter I share my experience in a third-grade classroom as the children did just that, conducting community research projects that targeted issues affecting their neighborhood and school. These issues included White flight, assistance for displaced residents, school safety, and the deterioration of the schools' playground and parking lot. Through these projects, the class of eight- and nine-year-olds shed light on how various social issues impacted their lives. They also demonstrated that being in a nonprivileged position did not mean they could not take action to challenge structural constraints. Over the course of several months, the children generated photographs, interviews, questionnaires, flyers, movies, and other resources as they documented and researched in-school and out-of-school community members' experiences related to their selected issues. By making the community a text of study in the classroom, the third graders prevented school from ignoring or denying the challenges they carried with them into the building. As a result, they made it possible for themselves to be more actively rooted in their community.

It is my hope the stories shared in this chapter will remind us that as schools confront challenges such as class inequity, efforts must be made to include children's perspectives and insights. When we do this, we ensure students develop a true sense of agency and a real belief that they can contribute to the well-being of their community.

Creating a Community of Wideawakeness

From 2006 to 2010 I served as a liaison between a large Midwestern university and an all-boys public elementary school located approximately four hours away in Lake City (pseudonym). Largely an urban African American community (97%), Lake City is considered the state's largest city populated primarily by people of color. Similar to other large urban centers where economic stress is closely linked to racial segregation, the social status and economic infrastructures of Lake City were strained by a mass exodus of businesses that began around the mid-1960s and continue today. In fact, the city lost ownership of its most prosperous property, Martinsville, less than a decade ago. Martinsville was incorporated into a development contract with a neighboring township that also used to be part of the city. Now this property boasts the wealthiest business enterprises of the township with nothing to gain for Lake City's economy. As one can imagine, the politically and racially motivated maneuvers that brought this change about were detrimental to residents' social mobility. As a result, the fiscal rebuilding of

Lake City grew distressed as the housing market, tax base, land use opportunities, and commerce capacities were constrained. The closing manufacturing bases and loss of commercial businesses eliminated financial stability from many hundreds of families. As in other urban communities across the country that suffered similar fates, these municipal practices placed severe burdens on the school district as it strove to educate students who were forced to endure significant distress.

In my four years working at the all-boys school, I witnessed teachers, staff, administrators, and volunteers express their feelings of responsibility for offsetting the effects of unjust policies and conditions shaping their city. A part of this process involved acknowledging that the children were cognizant of these social crises and that it was important to build and sustain community in these struggles. Opportunities for students to examine these types of injustices regularly occurred at school and class levels through carefully orchestrated initiatives, curricular projects, and school celebrations. It was not uncommon, for example, to hear event speakers discuss issues of poverty, criminal justice reforms, and unemployment during schoolwide ceremonies and speeches or for teachers to address these topics in class lessons or hallway conversations with children.

Even though the adults in the boys school understood that the school, alone, could not overcome the consequences of economic disadvantage, they channeled their frustration into opportunities for student learning with respect for each child's life situation. For this reason, they felt it was crucial to foster *wideawakeness* (Greene, 1995) in their relationships with children. The encouragement of this state of mind involved instilling a concern for one another, building an imagination for action, and renewing a consciousness of possibility to help each child feel affirmed in his or her role in enacting personal and social change. In the following sections, I share three moments from the third graders' inquiries to illuminate aspects of wideawakeness and suggest how this type of undertaking can lead to children's fuller participation in society.

"They're Not Just Doing It for Themselves, but Doing It for Others"

As the third graders researched various class concerns, a group of five children formed a research team, calling themselves "The Park Fixers." They were frustrated with having insufficient and unsafe equipment for students to play on during recess at school. They also felt concern for the children who lived in the neighboring housing projects who, according to one team member, "also have no place to go to and play." This worry came from the fact that the school's playground operated as the neighborhood park in the evenings. Students'

Figure 23.1 Broken bridge.

Figure 23.2 Missing swings.

concern for this situation led to several team meetings where they discussed the destruction of the park: missing basketball hoops, missing swings, missing ropes, burned slides, broken walking bridges, and graffiti-covered equipment (See Figures 23.1 and 23.2). They also wanted to know who was responsible for fixing the park and how to protect any newly purchased playground equipment. These conversations aided the team in forming a shared vision for alleviating these problems. They also understood how success in achieving their goals could happen only through community action and collaboration.

On the first day the students met, The Park Fixers used classroom video cameras and digital photo cameras to document the playground's conditions. As they began to reenter the building, two fourth graders approached the third graders and the following conversation ensued:

(Cortez and Tyler are fourth graders. T.J. is a Park Fixer team member. Brackets indicate overlapping speech. Dashes indicate a complete break in talk.)

Cortez:	What'cha all doing?
T.J.:	We are researching about we need new parks and everything.
Cortez:	Yeah, we really do [need new parks].
Tyler:	[Yeah, we do need new parks.]
Cortez:	We need new swings, new court, new—
Tyler and Cortez:	playground.
Tyler:	We need the whole thing though.
T.J.:	We need new [slides].
Cortez:	We need [new everything].
T.J.:	[We want everything.] because every time we slide,
Cortez:	[There's a hole right there.]
T.J.:	[Every time we slide] down that thing, there's a hole right there and [we get our feet stuck.]
Cortez:	[And it hurts.]
T.J.:	And it hurt real bad.
Tyler:	We get injured.
Cortez:	And we do want to have some fun, so—
T.J.:	And every time we got to stay inside the building, and I don't like that. *(referring to indoor recess time)*
Cortez:	And there ain't really nothing to do out there no more. It used to be real fun.

In this conversation, T.J. did not hesitate to respond to Cortez's initial question, "What'cha all doing?" Upon hearing T.J.'s response, Cortez and Tyler instantly began sharing their concerns about the playground. T.J. jumped into the conversation as he, Cortez, and Tyler came to the same conclusions about their experiences, talking about how they sometimes got hurt on the slides and needed new swings and a basketball court. They explained how "it used to be real fun" and discussed how "there ain't really nothing to do out there no more."

In this exchange, all three children recognized their right for a better environment and were troubled by how existing structures affected their social and physical participation in school. Rather than feeling that the park's poor conditions were their fault, they saw this situation as an opportunity to examine their circumstances and their desire for a facility where they could safely enjoy physical play outside. This 40-second conversation also captured how the fourth graders engaged in "wideawakeness" alongside the third graders as they mutually validated one another's experiences. By respecting each other's need for a better built-in environment, the children were able to genuinely connect to one another around an issue that mattered to them.

If we look more closely at the conversation, we see that T.J., Cortez, and Tyler used the word *we* 14 times, indicating a sense of sharing and a need to work together as equals—as members of a community. Keep in mind Cortez and Tyler were not asked to share their opinions about the park, but they freely chose to disclose personal stories when they learned of The Park Fixers's topic. They, too, felt a right to question how things were and had a desire to try to change them.

During my role as observer, facilitator, and member of the third-grade research teams, I witnessed many other instances of how The Park Fixers and their counterparts built trust and common understandings with a reach extending beyond their individual teams. Toward the end of The Park Fixers project, for example, the children created surveys, letters, and a movie to share with teachers, staff, parents, and members of the park's neighborhood. They also recruited the classroom teacher's grandson to draw several blueprints for a new park after learning about his art and design skills. The Park Fixers produced these items not only to make their concerns public but also to invite others from the community to join with them on creating and sustaining changes to the park. In fact, the first question the children listed on their neighborhood survey was, "How can you help us fix and clean the park?" They hoped community members would help in tearing down old equipment, purchasing new equipment, and setting up a monitoring system to protect the playground.

Throughout their project, The Park Fixers designed their inquiries to elicit community participation because they recognized it would take community support to make a new playground possible. They valued their audiences as necessary allies and resources that could help mobilize the changes they hoped to see. They discussed the dangers of new equipment becoming damaged if the neighborhood was not involved in the vision and maintenance of a newly developed playground. They decided together on the rules and commitments they would propose to community members as they anticipated their involvement and approval.

At the end of the project, a fellow class member not involved on The Park Fixers team astutely commented about their work: "When they are fixing the park, they're not just doing it for themselves, but doing it for others." This student, like his classmates, recognized that even though the children understood the impact of the park's conditions on own their lives, meaningful change occurs when a whole community is involved.

Believing We Are Worthy: Finding Courage in Our Fears

As the third graders built relationships with people within and outside their research teams, they often faced points in their research when they had to make decisions about revealing stories and emotions that were private to them. Yet, even though telling personal stories may be risky business, the third graders accepted it as a necessary part of inquiring into matters close to their hearts. As demonstrated in the following stories, the third graders acknowledged the importance of discussing their deeply rooted fears and dreams in order to bond with their teammates and help others understand their experiences. These "heart sharings" became a way for the children to recognize they are not alone in the world. By committing large amounts of time together on a project they valued, they were able to have their personal concerns become a collective struggle that deserved public attention.

A Story of Home Displacement

One research team decided to study the role of homeless shelters in the community and the variety and extent of the services they provided. Street living was common in the neighborhood and affected a large number of residents. The boys school experienced continuous changes in its student population as families were forced to follow provisional jobs in and out of the city. It had become increasingly difficult for low-income families to find permanent housing accommodations. For instance, after my last year there, plans were announced to demolish the housing projects located directly behind the school, coercing generations of families who lived together to disband. As one teacher told me, "It was a class of people: grandma, mother, and then daughter. It's always been a generation, and in that generation they stayed in the same area, the same housing. . . . They lived together." These families were involuntarily uprooted from their homes and forced to desperately find alternative living spaces.

After several discussions, this particular research team of third graders focused their efforts on investigating shelters. They decided to do this as a way to determine how they might help displaced families. They contacted city hall to talk to the mayor's office, spoke with and visited several local shelters, and interviewed family and community members about their concerns for individuals experiencing homelessness. When preparing for the phone interviews, the students created scripts that consisted of introducing themselves, explaining the purpose of their call and project, and asking questions. They also decided to videotape themselves making the phone interviews so they could watch and reflect on them as they arranged future calls. One of the students mentioned at his team's end-of-year project presentation that, in spite of "being

Figure 23.3 Students hanging up a shelter flyer in school.

scared and nervous," he and his teammates "didn't hear from anyone that, 'Aren't you too little to be calling or calling on phones?' So, we figured kids could call shelters and other places too." This confidence beamed from the students' faces when they hung up the telephone after their first interviews. Their smiles were wide and unforgettable. In fact, teachers and students who walked into the teachers' lounge during these first phone calls congratulated the boys when they realized what the third graders were doing. One teacher even offered additional shelter names she thought the boys might be interested in calling.

About 10 days into this multimonth project, one of the team members, Ryan, decided to disclose to the group that he, too, used to live in a few of the city's shelters. Very quietly, and rather tentatively, he interrupted his group's conversation about their recent phone call to the mayor's office to tell his peers of his mother's decision to move him and his siblings into a referral-based shelter location until they were able to move in with extended family. After Ryan finished sharing these experiences, his teammates revealed their own familiarities with shelters. Although no other group members had lived in shelters, they had memories of dropping off donations of clothes at these facilities. They discussed the many times they walked past homeless centers en route to friends' houses and described people they knew who resided in shelters. One student even shared a story about how he invited a homeless man to his house for a sandwich. Not one child communicated a word of judgment against his teammate who bravely exposed what was a very sensitive part of his life; instead, the group treated his story and their own as a call to care about an issue they knew impacted individuals in a personal way.

Because of Ryan's willingness to divulge his personal experience of being homeless—a topic often treated as unmentionable in schools—his teammates spoke about their own personal interactions with shelters. These recollections are what inspired the group to eventually reach out to the shelters and research the temporary solutions they offered for disadvantaged families. One of their goals involved producing and distributing flyers and self-made videos about the specializations and needs of each shelter (See Figure 23.3 for a photograph of students hanging up a flyer in school). Although frustrated about the underresourced and insufficient number of shelters in the area, the children were gratified to learn about the programs and operations that did exist.

A Story of School Displacement

Another example of how the third-grade researchers kept their work personally grounded occurred seconds after The Park Fixers returned to the room to browse the digital pictures they had taken just moments before of the dilapidated playground equipment. Two team members had begun to review their photos when another member, Tony, dashed through the door and ripped a sentence strip from the front chalkboard where it had been posted for many weeks (See Figure 23.4). He turned the sentence strip around to show it to his group as he read aloud the words printed on it: "What is your fear?"

Pacing around the room with the sentence strip in hand, Tony went on to say, "My fear is that this school will be no more. *Gone! Out of the blue! That's* my fear. And *my* fear is that I'll lose family members or teachers. I'll really be upset. . . . This is a school I have been [at] for a long time. I have memories *in* this school, *from* this school, and, um, we have memories about other teachers that used to work here. And this school holds all these memories." Then, without pause, one of his teammates who had been looking at the camera he

Figure 23.4   Tony tearing a sentence strip from board.

held in his hand during Tony's short oration raised his head and shouted out, "That's right!"

Seconds earlier, Tony and his teammates had documented the many ways they had been denied opportunities to play on the playground because of its deterioration. Tony, like his classmates, was well aware of what it meant to grow up in a place of abandonment. He knew he existed in a school community that faced the stark realities of school closure. He had heard teachers and parents complain about the constant restrictions placed on the school because of decreasing high-stakes test scores. He witnessed other schools in the area shutting down each year and even experienced the reconstitution of his own school when he was a kindergartner. It is not difficult to imagine how he was able to connect these stories of school uncertainty with the pictures he and his team had taken out on the playground.

He also shared grave concerns for the relational losses he would experience if the school, in addition to the park, were taken from him. Perhaps his fears stemmed from the years of losses he already experienced as teachers were forced to leave the school because of enrollment shifts. He valued these teachers and family members as important contributors to his school community. In many ways, his story of fear was a passionate plea for preserving these relationships. From his perspective it was clear his future rested on the hope that he be allowed to continue being a part of this school and the families who belonged to its community.

Like Ryan's confession, Tony's declaration helped his team connect their research topic to the everyday life politics affecting their experiences and those of people they knew. Tony's teammate's response with "That's right!" was more than a polite gesture indicating he heard what Tony had to say. It was an act of affirmation of the gravity of the issue and the necessity to confront it. Although it did not initiate a series of stories from his classmates as Ryan's story did, Tony's expression of his deep-seated fears of historical erasure through school closure opened up a possibility for his group, and for me as a bystander, to empathize with him about the emptiness that terrified him. In both examples, the third-grade teams exhibited a desire to know, above all else, that their concerns mattered and were worthy of attention.

Resetting the Ground Rules

When it comes to discussing community conflict in schools, we must find tools that allow children to engage with their world (Campano & Sánchez, 2010). The adults in the boys school encouraged a culture that nurtured personal storytelling and confronting truths about economic, social, and political (dis)advantage. They took the time to make it happen in spite of standardized testing mandates. For the third-grade inquiry projects, the teacher and I created alternative spaces that would allow the community to become a text of study for the children.

Across months the teacher and I devoted time two to three days a week for the students to work on their classwide inquiries. The work was grounded in rigorous interdisciplinary instruction. Students generated research notebooks in which they included meeting notes, classwide discussion notes (e.g., What makes a good question?), reading responses, paper documents (e.g., flyers, announcements, letters), reflections, and anything else they might have crafted or collected. Students participated in practice sessions in which they rehearsed conducting interviews. They constructed interview questions. They also made photo movies and used cameras and recorders to document how they performed these skills on their own. Most important, a genuine climate of intellectual respect and shared decision making underpinned the entire project. This climate guaranteed that all of us—children, teacher, and researcher—could remain wide awake to class equity matters and related concerns. Although the children selected the community issues to explore, they never felt they independently "owned" the problems or responsibility for solving them. Instead, they understood the need to mobilize their relationships with their peers and with adults in their school and home communities to bring about a more socially just future.

As schools support children to link their personal testimonies to the larger struggles of their communities, every single person in these schools must be mindful to remove all shame children might feel about the issues they keep tucked away in the privacy of their hearts. In building a community of support around these issues, schools can restore a sense of dignity to students who are often silenced by the education establishment.

As I spent time participating in the third-grade classroom at the boys school, I was inspired to see how willing the children were to discard the stigmas attached to their own poverty. Through examining topics and stories of great concern to them, they shaped their classroom work to address personal and collective needs. They saw the study of their community as a necessary means for improving the welfare of all who lived there. I cannot help but wonder what would have happened if I had been given the opportunity as a young child to explore the burdens I felt in school. How might I have understood the world and myself differently if my dreams and fears had been embraced by my teachers and peers? Schools such as the boys school give me hope for what possibilities exist for children when their teachers teach from a caring, socially just perspective. Everyone learns, then, what it means to be wide awake.

References

Campano, G., & Sánchez, L. (2010). Embodying socially just policy in practice. In S. J. Miller & D. Kirkland (Eds.), *Change matters: Qualitative research perspectives for moving social justice theory to policy* (pp. 205–212). New York: Peter Lang.

Greene, M. (1973). The matter of justice. *Teachers College Record, 75*(2), 181–191.

Greene, M. (1995). *Releasing the imagination: Essays on education, the arts, and social change.* San Francisco: Jossey-Bass.

24

PARENTS, ORGANIZED

Creating Conditions for Low-Income Immigrant Parent Engagement in Public Schools

Russell Carlock

Stray clouds float along the receding edge of a front that has scattered leaves over the puddled streets of the Mystic Public Housing Project in greater Boston. The sun is warm as I pass narrow, beige towers of apartment blocks connected by wide annexes of brick. A young boy yells in glee, chasing another child into a playground of blue metal swings and climbing apparatuses. On the edge of the playground, two girls with light brown skin dressed in blue jeans and bright blouses trade stickers from shiny books. Families stroll the sidewalks and converse in Creole, Spanish, Portuguese, and English.

The metal door creaks as I enter the Mystic Activity Room to teach an adult English class for immigrants called "Helping Your Children in School." The class is sponsored by a small nonprofit called the Welcome Project with a mission to "build the collective power of Somerville immigrants to participate in and shape community decisions." At around 9:00 in the morning, the parents begin entering, some pushing baby strollers, others chatting with friends. Judith, a grandmother from Brazil with short white hair, sits beside me. She punches me lightly on the arm and asks, "You have a good weekend?" Two young women in black hijabs converse in Arabic. By 9:15, 16 of us crowd around the plastic folding tables pushed together in a square. We represent 12 countries, 7 languages, and 5 continents. We discuss their children's progress in school and ideas for how to improve public education.

The parents I taught from 2010 to 2012 in my adult English class sponsored by the Welcome Project represented a significant and growing proportion of public school parents in the United States. They came to the United States in a period of immigration unparalleled in magnitude since the Industrial Revolution. They encountered an economy increasingly stratified between rich and poor, and like many other immigrant families, they lived in a low-income community with public schools that struggled to connect with them across divisions of language and class. As the numbers of children in low-income immigrant families increase, the question of how schools and families can partner across divisions of language and class to advance student learning becomes more important to ensure educational justice for immigrant families. In this chapter I address this question by connecting research on parent engagement to questions about power relationships in schools and describe three imperatives for strengthening the participation of low-income immigrant families in their children's education. I base my recommendations on what I learned from the low-income immigrants with whom I had an opportunity to work for two years as an adult English teacher. At the end of the chapter, I provide a list of action items schools may adopt to build partnerships with immigrant parents across language and class.

Across the country, many schools struggle to engage low-income immigrant parents. Research shows that low-income and immigrant parents are less likely to be involved in school-based activities than their native-born, wealthier peers (Kao & Tienda, 1995; Lareau & Horvat, 1999; Shuang & Koblinsky, 2009; Soomin & Wang, 2006; Stevenson & Baker, 1987), reflecting stereotypes that low-income immigrants are less engaged in their children's education. These stereotypes, however, overlook the fact that low-income immigrant parents are more likely to be involved in children's education at home (Huntsinger & Jose, 2009; Ingram, Wolfe, & Lieberman, 2007) and often have higher educational aspirations for children than their native-English-speaking peers (Kao & Tienda, 1995; Schaller, Rocha, & Barshinger, 2007). Unfortunately, studies of parent involvement in schools rarely examine the types of relationships between school personnel and parents that lead to family engagement or disengagement in school activities. Because one in four children in the United States is the child of an immigrant and many of these children live in poor communities (Passel, 2011; Walters & Trevelyan, 2011), it is imperative that we strengthen collaboration between schools and low-income immigrant parents if we hope to achieve equity in education.

It can happen. My students from the Mystic Public Housing Project taught me that schools, families, and communities *can* collaborate across differences of class, ethnicity, and language to improve education for all students. Most of my students were single mothers struggling as both primary caregivers and wage earners for their families. When I began teaching our English class, they often did not participate in activities at their children's school, though it was only a few hundred meters from their homes. Some people outside of the community referred to Mystic parents as an "absent voice" from the discussions that took place among teachers and other parents at the school. Many, including myself, assumed the parents from the housing project did not participate in school activities because of barriers of time, education, child care, resources, and English fluency.

But I learned that power relationships can be just as important as these other factors in determining parents' engagement in school. Though my students were "poor" by U.S. standards of living, they did not consider themselves poor, especially relative to what they had experienced in their countries of origin.

They were strong, focused, and determined. They had clear ideas for what they believed was best for their children. But they experienced discrimination in the community, making many of them question their roles in their new country. They felt disempowered and separated from their community. They had little control over institutions of law enforcement, schools, and the city council, even as they struggled with crime, failing schools, and reduced access to public services. In their native countries, they had experienced military dictatorships where critical participation in public institutions was often dangerous, so they were reluctant to voice dissent to public officials. In short, despite their talents and strengths, they had few opportunities to channel these resources into solving community problems. To engage these parents in school and bring educational justice to their community, we need to change their power relationships among themselves and with their children's school, which is just as important as their overcoming their community's lack of material resources.

Upon meeting other parents with similar challenges, the parents in my class developed a mutual support network and became active in their children's school. They attended school events in groups, bolstered by solidarity with one another. They demanded high-quality interpretation and translation services so they could share ideas with school personnel and other parents. Their collective participation led to a shift in power: Teachers and administrators began to collaborate with Mystic parents to make decisions about their children's education. They worked together to incorporate the strengths of the Mystic community into their children's school to improve education for all children. A change in parents' relationships with one another, coupled with responsiveness on the part of the school, led to a more democratic representation of parents in the neighborhood school.

As the most ubiquitous of public institutions, the public school can be a nexus of community action to challenge inequity in and out of school. Changing the way that schools and parents interact across language and class can be difficult, because it often requires administrators and teachers to put forth greater effort to reach out to parents and to relinquish some of their power in school. Educators must make significant changes to how they interact with parents to build new relationships that facilitate communication and shared decision making. In this chapter, I argue that, at the very least, we must (a) ensure language justice for all parents, (b) acknowledge the strengths of parents' communities, and (c) foster parent participation in school decision making.

Ensure Language Justice for All Parents

Lupe Ojeda immigrated to the United States in the '90s. She had been laid off from a factory job in Mexico after it was taken over by a U.S. company. Her neighbor, Maryann Vo, came to the United States as a refugee from the Vietnam War. Her father fought for the south and then was jailed after the fall of Saigon. Before knowing each other, they felt disempowered in their children's school because no interpretation services were available to them and no other parents from their community attended. On the rare occasions when they attended events at school, they felt isolated and frustrated by the language barriers they encountered.

In their community, however, they developed a friendship that transcended language, sharing recipes and cooking for each other's families. They began to attend school events together and advocated for interpretation and translation in the community's languages so that other parents would attend as well. Their participation stemmed from their solidarity and allowed them to improve interpretation and translation at their children's school. As a result of their advocacy, increased access to multilingual communication spawned growing participation by many other immigrant parents from the public housing community.

Parent engagement and disengagement often result from the social environments parents encounter at school. School personnel often believe that poor and immigrant parents do not attend school events because they don't care about education, because they are uneducated, or because barriers in their lives prevent them from attending. Less often do they consider how school communications and events can make parents feel unwelcome. United States schools often privilege English as the language of dominance for parent participation in school. Only rarely are school forms sent home to parents in their native language, and even if they are, the translations are of such poor quality or use language at such a formal register that parents find them difficult to understand. Districts often do not provide teachers and parents a clear system for requesting trained, impartial interpreters to facilitate communication for regular conferences or emergency communication needs. Back-to-school nights, PTA meetings, and other events for parents tend to occur in English only, with no plan for interpreting for and welcoming parents from other language backgrounds. Because of the difficulty of communicating with parents who do not speak English, monolingual English-speaking school personnel may be less likely to engage these parents in decision making about their children's education. Language and power go hand in hand. If a person's language is not connected to the decision-making apparatus of a community, that person is effectively disempowered. This lack of language justice disproportionately impacts low-income immigrant parents' ability to advocate for their children and contribute to their school's improvement, because these parents have fewer opportunities to learn English because of longer work hours and jobs that do not provide paid leave or professional development. Nearly all immigrants to the United States *want* to learn English, but this process can take up to seven years even with dedicated study. Low-income immigrants are more likely to live in linguistically and ethnically segregated communities with less access to quality adult education and thus are more likely to feel linguistically isolated in English-only environments.

Parents attend school events when they know they will not be isolated because of their language. They attend when they feel confident they will share the space with other parents who live in their neighborhood, whose children are in the same programs, and who attend the same community events. They participate in school events in solidarity with others to build relationships that will support their children. If parents cannot participate in this social aspect of school engagement, then they are not likely to be aware of or able to support school initiatives to advance student learning. So, as a very basic starting point, we must examine school events that ostensibly are organized to encourage parent involvement to ensure they are equally welcoming to all parents.

The first step to improving parent engagement across language and class is to ensure language justice by adopting systems of interpretation and translation that allow parents to participate in the language that is most comfortable for them. Lupe, Maryann, and other parents in my class collaborated with the Welcome Project to bring simultaneous interpretation to community forums with school personnel. The Welcome Project provided fairly inexpensive radio transmitters with headsets to enable these events to be accessible across multiple languages simultaneously. Bilingual community youth provided simultaneous interpretation so that school principals, elected officials, teachers, and parents could converse across languages in the Mystic community. For parent-teacher conferences, the school offered greater access to professional interpreters. This improved communication created a positive feedback loop: More parents attended school events because they knew their voices would be heard, and their greater participation, in turn, drove the school to continue improving its multilingual communication systems.

Many politicians and school personnel do not see interpretation and translation as budget items of primary importance, even as some of them disparage parents for not attending school events, do not strive to become multilingual themselves, and do not advocate for improved labor conditions or high-quality adult education that would allow parents working in low-wage jobs to study English. This misunderstanding of the challenges facing low-income immigrant parents who strive to provide the best education they can for their children blinds us to the immense benefits of a truly multilingual community in public education. Multilingual communication facilitates improved understanding among educators of students and creates a public space for parent solidarity that is a stepping-stone to shifting ossified school structures that contribute to educational inequity. An active parent community is vital for holding schools accountable for student learning and for ensuring that local community knowledge is available to help solve the problems facing educators struggling to meet the needs of all students.

In addition to providing simultaneous interpretation so that parents and school officials can hold discussions in which each participant can use the language in which he or she feels most comfortable, schools can use other strategies to change the dynamics of language dominance in a school's community. School personnel can visit low-income immigrant communities where English is not the dominant language and seek to become multilingual themselves or to provide their own interpreters so that they can participate in events in these communities. They can collaborate with immigrant organizations to invite large groups of parents to schools to share their concerns with school personnel. In these events, interpreters would primarily serve the monolingual school staff so that they could understand and respond to parent concerns.

As educators we must shift our implicit beliefs about language dominance. This begins by realizing that interpretation and translation are necessary, not only because an immigrant parent might not speak English but also because school personnel do not speak parents' languages. In this sense, interpretation and translation are services not solely for immigrant parents but for all parties who need to understand one another in order to embark on a common endeavor. In the case of schools, interpretation and translation is the first step toward creating a multilingual community that can collaborate across language and class to provide engaging learning opportunities for all students and confront larger community problems that contribute to educational inequity.

Focus on Community Strength

The Immigration and Customs Enforcement (ICE) detention center in Boston is composed of a series of towering brown concrete edifices rising from beside the interstate that passes along the edge of the city's high rises. A 5-foot-thick, 25-foot-high wall surrounds much of the complex and stretches along its corrugated concrete exterior. On a cold spring day, members of my English class and more than 50 others gathered along the sidewalk outside the prison to protest the detentions of the more than 200 undocumented workers awaiting their deportation hearings inside. Among the prisoners was the spouse of one of the members of our class. When her community discovered what had happened, members rallied around her family, donating food and clothing and offering advice about immigration law. They watched her children, cooked for her family, provided transportation, and helped her family by doing household chores. Their strength sustained her family through its crisis.

My students taught me a valuable lesson about the incredible strength present in their community. When I began teaching my course, I first viewed my students and their community as people who needed help. I saw through a prism of deficit and sought to get them involved in their children's school before understanding their goals for themselves. Like many service providers, I created a plan to help the community without first considering the wide diversity of strengths and experiences of its members or the "funds of knowledge" already in use to solve their problems (Vélez-Ibañez & Greenberg, 1992). These funds were the myriad strategies the parents already used to improve their lives and the lives of their children.

I learned to step back and follow the parents' interests. I respected their strengths and sought to collaborate *with them* rather than dictate *to them*. I retreated from my focus on outcomes and strived to *listen* rather than *lead*. This helped create a classroom community of parents who shared their strengths with one another and improved their community. Those with more child-rearing experience helped those just beginning as parents, those with jobs helped those looking for work, and those with more time in the United States helped newcomers. They shared child care, rides, and advice about navigating their children's school.

This mutual support was evidence against a myth of cultural deficiency among poor communities. Many educators and others in positions of power tend to stereotype low-income immigrant communities as I did: as needing help and being deficient in capacity to assist in their children's education. These communities are not deprived of assets, however, so much as they are deprived of opportunities to share these assets with the larger community and opportunities to have their strengths recognized by people in positions of power.

Teachers often think of poor, immigrant parents as lacking the tools necessary to effectively engage with their children's education. These perspectives reinforce power inequalities and the prominent idea that poor communities are in need of *intervention*—a term from the health field that connotes sickness. But poor communities are not sick. A society of extreme inequality is sick. Effective interventions to address social inequality must target *the sickness that plagues all of society* rather than only poor people. Many programs that try to engage these parents attempt to fill what they perceive as holes in these communities as compared with middle-class, native-English-speaking communities. For example, family literacy programs often attempt to teach immigrant parents to speak and read to their children in English rather than focus on their ability to teach their native language, despite the metacognitive benefits of multilingualism, the importance of language in a child's relationship with his or her caregivers, and copious research showing that native-language literacy in early childhood does not interfere with second-language acquisition and is the most important factor in developing literacy in any language, including English. Similarly, school personnel might lament that poor immigrant children come to school speaking little English but do not realize that monolingual English-speaking children are often even more lacking in multilingual ability than their poor immigrant peers.

To shift dynamics of inequality in schools, educators must focus on the strengths of parents and incorporate these into school pedagogy. Rather than assuming, for example, that a mother from rural El Salvador who does not speak English and has low levels of Spanish literacy has nothing to contribute, a teacher could learn on a home visit that such a mother has a thriving garden she uses to treat common illnesses among neighbors. The teacher could invite the mother to help children create their own herb garden and teach about the healing properties of common plants.

Instead of believing that speaking a language other than English is a deficit that must be overcome, teachers could recognize an opportunity for monolingual English-speaking children to learn the languages of their peers and their peers' parents. A dual- or multilanguage curriculum could honor the native languages of the community's members and foster multilingualism and academic achievement for all. In a dual-language program, all children are language learners, and their achievement is defined by their ability to shift across multiple languages rather than by their mastery of a dominant language spoken in the homes of only some students. Such a program builds on the strengths of the community to offer all students the academic and social benefits of becoming multilingual.

By recognizing the strengths of parents, rather than casting their differences as deficits, schools can build authentic community partnerships that benefit all children. Power does not have to be zero-sum, such that recognizing the benefits of other languages reduces the academic successes of English-speaking children. Rather, hierarchical power relationships can be recast as reciprocal, and formerly segregated communities can come together to achieve higher goals. If school personnel improve their relationships with low-income immigrant communities, they may discover the vast social and cultural resources that exist in these communities and the values of sharing and mutual support that characterize many of their relationships. These values and resources can become part of the school's culture as well through opportunities for parent volunteering in the classroom and connections among curriculum, pedagogy, and the day-to-day lives of students who come from these communities. Schools that integrate the strengths of all parents become communities that honor the diversity of immigration and break down disparities across social class and language that perpetuate injustice and inequality in education.

Embrace Democracy in Parent Engagement

On a cool New England evening, four women from my English class attended a district school committee meeting in the neighborhood school library to advocate for the improvement of interpretation and translation at all district schools. They wanted schools to recognize the value of the diversity of the community that represented more than 50 languages and teach children about this cultural resource. They had knocked on the doors of their neighbors in a letter-writing campaign and sent over 100 letters to school committee members to share their ideas. They now waited eagerly to hear whether their letters had the intended impact.

In response to the parents' campaign, the district enforced a policy requiring interpretation in Haitian Creole, Portuguese, and Spanish at all PTA meetings and parent-teacher conferences. When the meeting concluded, the mothers celebrated months of relationship building, planning, writing, and deliberating to improve their community and their children's school.

The parents' participation in the decision making regarding their children's school was a small example of the kind of political participation that is necessary for bringing equity to education. Since the early days of the U.S. republic, democratic theorists have explained democracy's strength by its ability to engage people who are most affected by social problems in the resolution of those problems (Addams, 1902; De Tocqueville, 1835; Gaventa, 2006; Manor, 2004). There was a time when "democracy" was a privilege reserved for White, propertied men. Through organizing among excluded groups, however, democracy is slowly becoming more democratic. Hallmarks of a successful democracy include deliberation, collaboration, and action. Unfortunately, public schools rarely engage poor or immigrant parents in the resolution of educational problems, even though their families are most harshly affected by educational inequities. Making matters worse, children in poor communities attend schools that are less likely than the schools attended by their wealthier peers to provide opportunities to participate in school decision making (Hess & Leal, 2001). This disparity is even more glaring for poor immigrant communities, in which many members cannot vote or run for office in local elections and are separated from decision-making bodies not only by class but also by language. Democratic theory predicts that such a system will lead to a disparity in efficiency and quality between public education for wealthy, native-English-speaking students and that for students from poor immigrant communities (Ackerman, 2004; Dorner, 2010; Fung & Wright, 2001; Skocpol, 2003). Such is the system we presently have.

Historically, inequalities in power have been ameliorated through community organizing, and schools have been sites of these struggles. Both the civil rights and chicana/chicano movements used the basic principles of community organizing to transform public education. They built new partnerships among people and channeled relationships into activism to shift inequities in power (Ganz, 2002). Schools marked by inequity across divisions of race, ethnicity, language, and class can learn from this organizing and apply it to help all students succeed (Warren & Mapp, 2011). The challenges facing parents who wish to participate in schools to help their children are challenges to democracy.

Educators and parents must work together to overcome these challenges and ensure participation in school decision making by all parents, regardless of their language, ethnicity, or class.

Teachers and administrators can begin the process of democratizing schools by transforming school-based parent events into opportunities for authentic deliberation toward a vision for children's education. Most back-to-school nights, PTA meetings, and parent-teacher conferences reinforce hierarchy, placing school personnel in the role of expert and parents in the role of passive recipient of a public service. These events might, instead, become opportunities to hear parents' goals and expectations for children's learning and to begin equitable partnerships to attain these goals. Schools can invite community organizations run by immigrants to participate in the planning and implementation of parent events. School systems can invite community-led organizations to conduct independent "equity audits" of parent participation, with suggestions for how to change structures that prevent parents from participating. These investments in engaging parents across language and class will pay dividends by creating a better-connected school community with greater capacity to advance the learning of all students. When parents participate in forming and implementing school policy for the benefit of their own children, the policies are more likely to produce equitable outcomes.

The challenges facing low-income immigrant communities are many and great: unfair labor practices, a broken immigration system, linguistic and ethnic discrimination, growing economic inequality, and diminished access to quality public services and democratic institutions. Public schools, however, can be sites for mitigating these challenges. With authentic collaboration between educators and families, schools can become models of a multilingual democracy that embraces the strengths of the entire community to protect and develop its most important asset: its children. One of my students told me, "La union hace la fuerza." Union makes strength. If schools do not strive to unite their communities across all that divides them, how will they have the strength to ensure that all students achieve to their utmost potential regardless of where their parents live, how much money they have, or what languages they speak? Schools serving communities divided by class and language must begin the work of bridging these divides to realize the democratic vision of the public school as a foundation for equal opportunity.

I end by offering the following suggestions, not as a proscriptive guide but as a point of departure toward this kind of unification between schools and low-income immigrant families:

- Ensure language justice by offering high-quality interpretation and translation services in all parent communication.
- Provide opportunities for all parents to share their strengths in efforts to improve their children's school.

- Facilitate parent organizing by building relationships with and among parents during school-based events.
- Collaborate with immigrant community organizations on initiatives to make schools more welcoming.
- Work in solidarity with parents to overcome the causes of socioeconomic and linguistic inequity.
- Democratize parent engagement by responding to parent voices and ensuring authentic representation of all parents in school decision making.

References

Ackerman, J. (2004). Co-governance for accountability: Beyond "exit" and "voice." *World Development, 32*(3), 447–463.

Addams, J. (1902). *Democracy and social ethics.* New York: Macmillan.

De Tocqueville, A. (1835). *Democracy in America.* New York: The Library of America.

Dorner, L. (2010). Contested communities in a debate over dual-language education: The import of "public" values on public policies. *Educational Policy, 25*(4), 577–613.

Fung, A., & Wright, E. (2001). Deepening democracy: Innovations in empowered participatory governance. *Politics and Society, 29*(5), 5–39.

Ganz, M. (2002, Fall). What is organizing? *Social Policy, 33*(1), 16–17.

Gaventa, J. (2006). *Triumph, deficit or contestation? Deepening the "deepening democracy" debate.* Brighton, UK: Institute of Development Studies.

Hess, F., & Leal, D. (2001). The opportunity to engage: How race, class, and institutions structure access to educational deliberation. *Educational Policy, 15*(3), 474–490.

Huntsinger, C., & Jose, P. (2009). Parental involvement in children's schooling: Different meanings in different cultures. *Early Childhood Research Quarterly, 24,* 398–410.

Ingram, M., Wolfe, R., & Lieberman, J. (2007). The role of parents in high-achieving schools serving low-income, at-risk populations. *Education and Urban Society, 39*(4), 479–497.

Kao, G., & Tienda, M. (1995). Optimism and achievement: The educational performance of immigrant youth. *Social Science Quarterly, 76*(1), 1–19.

Lareau, A., & Horvat, E. (1999). Moments of social inclusion and exclusion: Race, class, and cultural capital in family-school relationships. *Sociology of Education, 72*(1), 37–53.

Manor, J. (2004). Democratisation with inclusion: Political reforms and people's empowerment at the grassroots. *Journal of Human Development, 5*(1), 5–29.

Passel, J. S. (2011). Demography of immigrant youth: Past, present, and future. *Future Child, 21*(1), 19–41.

Schaller, A., Rocha, L., & Barshinger, D. (2007). Maternal attitudes and parent education: How immigrant mothers support their child's education despite their own levels of education. *Early Childhood Education Journal, 34*(5), 351–356.

Shuang, C., & Koblinsky, S. (2009). Parent involvement in children's education: An exploratory study of urban, Chinese immigrant families. *Urban Education, 44*(6), 687–709.

Skocpol, T. (2003). *Diminished democracy: From membership to management in American civic life*. Norman: University of Oklahoma Press.

Soomin, S., & Wang, C. (2006). Immigrant parents' involvement in American schools: Perspectives from Korean mothers. *Early Childhood Education Journal, 34*(2), 125–132.

Stevenson, D., & Baker, D. (1987). The family-school relation and the child's school performance. *Child Development, 58*(5), 1348–1357.

Vélez-Ibañez, C., & Greenberg, J. (1992). Formation and transformation of funds of knowledge among U.S.-Mexican households. *Anthropology and Education Quarterly, 23*, 313–335.

Walters, N., & Trevelyan, E. (2011). *The newly arrived foreign-born population of the United States: 2010* (American Community Survey Briefs). Washington, DC: U.S. Census Bureau.

Warren, M., & Mapp, K. (2011). *A match on dry grass: Community organizing as a catalyst for school reform*. Oxford: Oxford University Press.

25

CHALLENGING CLASS-BASED ASSUMPTIONS
Low-Income Families' Perceptions of Family Involvement

Lisa Hoffman

"Because I'm not there doesn't mean I don't care."
"I wish I had more fluid communication with the teachers."
"Sometimes school feels like a competition my kids will never win."

When parents are asked to talk with educators about their experiences with their children's schools, what perceptions do they choose to share? From their perspective as the experts about their own children and communities, what might parents want to teach teachers about communicating and connecting with families? How might listening to families from less privileged socioeconomic backgrounds affect popular assumptions about parent involvement in schools?

Although educators and parents both work on behalf of students, relations between schools and families can be distant for a variety of reasons. As educators, we often fail to think of all parents as sources of valuable knowledge. I believe that one reason we fail to recognize the contributions and expertise of all parents is because we are socialized with and surrounded by prejudices based on socioeconomic status. These prejudices inform class bias, which involves deeply ingrained assumptions about poor and working-class families.

This chapter represents my attempt, with my colleagues, to invert the typical education hierarchy and challenge classist assumptions by inviting parents and custodial grandparents from "working-poor" backgrounds to teach educators in a university school of education about family involvement in schools. The perceptions of these parents provide the framework for this chapter.

Examining Assumptions

Listening to how parents perceive their involvement in schools has challenged my interpretation and understanding of my prior experiences with parent involvement. To evaluate my own beliefs, I found that I needed to examine my assumptions about the intersections of education and poverty.

I think the difficulty of critical self-reflection and self-examination is partly an indication of how widespread and deeply ingrained social class prejudices are. For example, in the past I found it disturbingly easy to point to parents' apparent lack of interest in their children's education as a reason for low school achievement among students living in poverty. This unintentional blaming of parents is common among educators and even some popular authors and speakers, such as Ruby Payne (2005), whose work focuses on poverty and schooling. At the same time it is challenged by years of research showing that parents' dedication to their children's academic development is constant across social class (Haberman, 1995; Heath, 2012; Kozol, 1992; Lareau, 2000). That is why the tacit blaming of poor families and communities for inequalities in school performance is a characteristic of "deficit ideology," which leads educators to focus on deficits or shortcomings of individual children rather than recognize and seek to understand the systemic inequities facing these children and their families (Flores, 2007; Gorski, 2008; Ladson-Billings, 2006).

This tendency is a symptom of class bias, as described by Lea (2011): "Classism associates deficits with poor people or people from low-income backgrounds. It constitutes unequal socio-economic, political, cultural and educational relations, and justifies hierarchy" (p. 135). Class-based prejudice is such a part of U.S. culture that classist labels often are considered humorous vernacular. For example, someone who would not use epithets overtly based on race might nonetheless use classist labels such as *redneck*, *hick*, *cracker*, or *trailer trash*, either as insults or as ostensibly neutral descriptive terms for social class identity.

In my experience, the vast majority of educators demonstrate care and concern for all of their students. Educators also tend to be well aware of the inequality some students face, starting with the beginning of their educational careers, because of the physical, emotional, and cognitive effects of poverty (Books, 2004; Kozol, 1992; Lee & Burkam, 2002). However, the assumptions of deficit ideology—and the rhetoric of our corporatized, test-oriented educational culture—too often lead us to focus on individual students' or communities' "achievement gaps" rather than on the "opportunity gap" (Flores, 2007) or "education debt" (Ladson-Billings, 2006) experienced by children of poor and working-poor families. Most educators express a commitment to help "every child succeed," but how many do so while still espousing the common "culture of poverty" myth that all poor people share certain traits that cause them to be fundamentally "at risk" in school (Haberman, 1995; Lea, 2011; Osei-Kofi, 2005; Rogalsky, 2009)?

In the area of family involvement in schools, specifically, deficit ideology often translates into prioritizing convenience for middle-class families or assuming that all parents should adopt the type of family involvement preferred by those from the middle class (Brantlinger, 2003). Teachers' attitudes about parents affect family involvement in schools (Epstein, 2001), yet many teachers have no training or modeling in ways to create connections between parents and schools (Lawrence-Lightfoot, 2003), especially across lines of social class or culture (Hoover-Dempsey et al., 2005).

I share this challenge. When my colleagues and I considered inviting parents to be visitors to "my territory," at the university where I teach, I asked myself how dedicated I really was to the more substantive and systemic changes that would help facilitate increased equity and participation from families from socioeconomically disenfranchised families. I challenge other educators to join me by listening to parents and examining our own assumptions about social class and inequities in schooling and society.

Communicating Across Class

One of the ironies of U.S. culture is that although social class structures affect so many aspects of society, the supposedly egalitarianism of the United States renders social class difficult to label or define. I use the broad term *working poor* (Shipler, 2004) for the families whose voices provide the framework for this chapter. This term includes families whose household income might fall above the federal government's official poverty line but whose income is low enough that they are not always able to meet their families' basic needs (Ehrenreich, 2001; Keown-Bomar & Pattee, 2011). After all, even though low-wage employees might work long hours at multiple jobs, "more people than those officially designated as 'poor' are, in fact, weighed down with the troubles associated with poverty" (Shipler, 2004, pp. x–xi).

I should mention, as well, that some of the parents whose voices you will hear in this chapter are also recent immigrants to the United States. Some may be undocumented immigrants. Undocumented status renders families vulnerable to additional forms of repression, as if they are part of a caste whose members often try to remain invisible out of fear of deportation. Although we might assume that culturally and linguistically diverse children struggle primarily because of their cultural and linguistic differences from dominant school culture, the struggles of children from immigrant families often are closely tied to poverty and social class status (Keown-Bomar & Pattee, 2011).

At the university where I work, parents and custodial grandparents are invited to be guest speakers to audiences of college students studying to be teachers, current teachers enrolled in our graduate programs, and teacher educators. In these venues, we ask parents to share their perceptions of family involvement and their experiences interacting with their children's schools. We ask them to "teach teachers" about communication between schools and families (Herdoíza-Estévez, 2011). You will notice that not all parents mentioned in this chapter shared the same opinions and responses. One parent's comment cannot be representative of every working-poor parent—as if lower socioeconomic status comprised a monolithic group or a single culture of poverty. In particular, we must consider that all parents quoted here volunteered to speak to educators on a university campus; this choice of how to spend scarce time and resources may not be shared by every parent, regardless of social class background!

Parents' Perceptions of Family Involvement in Schools

Next I present experiences shared by low-income parents and guardians on five themes related to family involvement in schools: (a) building respect and trust, (b) communicating with teachers, (c) being present at the school, (d) keeping up with schoolwork, and (e) speaking about struggles. You will notice that I chose not to use parents' names in this chapter, and in some cases I paraphrase direct quotes to avoid identifying particular speakers. Although I value parent voices and wish they could be recognized for their contributions, the anonymity is intended to protect their privacy and, and in some cases, an attempt to be cautious about immigration-related legal concerns.

The Importance of Respect and Trust Between Parents and School Personnel

"Each year I explain our situation to the teachers," explained one parent. "Some of the teachers have been understanding and supportive. But some of them have treated me like I was—well, like I was White trash. It's like they thought if I really cared about my kids, I would have found a way to provide better for them."

When parenting practices don't match teachers' expectations, parents can feel that their parenting skills, competence, and even love for their children are being questioned. "We want our children to grow up successful," commented one parent. "We know education is an important part of that. No one who really knew us could question how much we value education. We may not show that in the same way as the schools expect. But I will do anything to protect and provide for my children. We love our children just as much as you love yours."

"We are trying to be involved," a custodial grandmother stated. "We are doing the best we can. Things happen. People struggle. But parents love their children."

I am struck that parents or grandparents would feel that they must make a case that they love their own children. Part of my middle-class privilege as a parent is that I am always treated with respect and trust in schools. I have never felt that my love for my own children was being questioned. These stories from low-income parents indicate that at least some working-poor families do not share this benefit. This points to another symptom of deficit ideology: our failure to give all parents the benefit of the doubt that they are competent, caring, and concerned about their children and their children's education.

Respect for families should be extended to *all* parents. A legal guardian commented that when the child's biological mother comes to school events, teachers eye her suspiciously. "It looks like they're thinking, 'How awful must you be to have had your children taken away. How can you not care enough about your kids that someone else has to take care of them.' I want to tell them, 'She's here. She walked into this school building, knowing people were going to look at her like she's terrible, but she came anyway. She's here for her children. She is trying to be involved.'"

Reflecting on this anecdote as an educator, I am reminded that I must be aware that families struggling with poverty are more susceptible to depression and stress-related challenges while also lacking the resources for physical and mental health care (Weiss et al., 2003). Reflecting on this anecdote as a middle-class parent, I realize that if I were unable to care for my children because of catastrophic illness, drug rehabilitation, or another debilitating condition, I would have social and economic resources that are unavailable to the mother in this story. A network of relatives and friends in financially stable households could potentially allow me to manage a crisis situation without requiring the intervention of child protective services and exposure to community shame and judgment. My health insurance might cover outpatient treatment to allow me to stay with my children. My community assets and benefits provide a safety net that is absent for many working-poor families. Realizing these sorts of disparities is one step toward respecting families' struggles.

Parent-Teacher Communication

The most common statement made by parents serving as guest speakers at the university is this: "We would like to know what we need to do to help our kids." Teacher participants are sometimes surprised to hear that parents would prefer more parent-teacher conferences throughout the year and more consistent communication with their children's teachers.

In some cases, the work restrictions and limited resources of working-poor parents can complicate conversation between parents and teachers (Heymann & Earle, 2000). Several parents have mentioned difficulty contacting a child's teacher when the parent is not able, or allowed, to receive returned telephone calls at work. "I'd like to know the teachers, but it's hard to reach them," one mother explained. "I call during the school day because that is when I can use a phone privately, but I need to leave a message because they are busy teaching. But when my work break is over, I am not available for them to call me back until after school hours. But I'd like to hear something. If it's bad, if it's good—I need someone to tell me."

The technology gap and the delivery of school announcements can combine to form another obstacle for working-poor parents. Although official school communications might be sent home in children's backpacks, other school-affiliated information such as PTA invitations and classroom directories often are distributed through e-mail. These electronic communications are inaccessible to parents without sufficient computer skills or access (Eamon, 2004; Ridout, 2009).

Parent Presence at the School

Parents also often share their experiences regarding their presence at school events. In terms of coming to their children's schools, researchers have documented various reasons parents may not be present at school (McCarthey, 2000). One parent mentioned that announcements about school events, including end-of-year recognition, are sometimes sent home only one week prior to the event. Many families need several weeks' notice in order to alter work schedules. Economically disadvantaged parents are particularly likely to be working in jobs in which they lack input and flexibility regarding their working hours (Ehrenreich, 2001); such jobs also rarely offer paid leave.

Defying classist assumptions about working-poor parents belonging to a single culture of poverty, a variety of parent responses regarding presence in schools demonstrate that varied influences affect expectations about school-parent interaction (Valdes, 1996). "Parent involvement was much higher in our home countries, but in different ways," commented one recently immigrated mother. "Parents in Central America help take care of classroom supplies and come into classrooms regularly to help the teacher. Schools in the U.S. have a closed-door policy. I'd like to help. It's hard to know how to approach the school and what you can do." In contrast, several other low-income Latina and Latino parents noted different cultural expectations such as *not* asking questions and "letting schools take care of education" because teachers are experts who deserve unquestioning respect (Mount-Cors, n.d.).

Perceived pressure to give money at school events or during fund-raising drives can leave parents with negative perceptions of school involvement. One parent shared, "I hate telling the kids no, but I can't keep up with how often the school asks for money." Some parents mentioned schoolwide assemblies held to award prizes to children who sell the most items or raise the most money during a fund-raising campaign. Other times, fund-raising can be more subtle but equally uncomfortable to the point of being coercive to parents. Some schools sponsor a Lunch Guest Day, inviting family members to eat lunch with students; however, the event includes a parent-child visit to the school library for a book sale. The book fair is promoted heavily to students beforehand, so children expect their lunch guests to purchase books.

Such situations can be avoided by building respectful and trusting relationships between parents and school personnel. We can plan and implement family involvement events and (separate) fund-raising drives with sensitivity to working-poor families. Regarding funding, we should also advocate for adequate funding for public schools so that students are not pushed into consumerism and pressured to raise their own funds so that a public school can afford to teach them.

Difficulties Keeping Up With Schoolwork

Homework and projects requiring extra resources are a common frustration for working-poor families, especially when assignments are due in a relatively short period of time or when families don't have access to reliable transportation to purchase necessary materials. "When I brought it up, the teacher said it should be no problem because I can just get the materials at the dollar store," said one mother. "But it's not that easy."

"My kids' projects will never look as good as some of the others," another parent lamented. Assignments and projects requiring parent involvement can be unfeasible for a parent working two jobs, which is commonly the case for working-poor parents. Assigning projects requiring posters, trifold boards, photographs, photocopies, or cutouts from magazines assumes parents have access to transportation to a store on short notice, a printer and ink, or money for extra supplies.

"I want them to learn good computer skills. But we can't keep up with that at home," a parent explained. Parents often refer to computer-based assignments and projects including logging a certain number of minutes on an online remedial math program, typing assignments, or creating PowerPoint presentations as challenging. If a family has a computer, which obviously is less likely for a working-poor family than wealthier families, a child might be alternating computer time with other siblings. In some cases, students without computers at home are expected to go to the public library after school or use the school computer lab during recess. However, parents working long hours cannot necessarily transport a child to a public library while it's open.

As educators, I believe we should reconceptualize homework so that it is assigned only if it can be completed by every child without assistance from adults or computers. As one example, a "backward" method of undertaking projects allows children to conduct research at home (given photocopied materials, if necessary) and then to complete the actual project at school. Along similar lines, although many educators advocate moving toward a "flipped" classroom—in which students view lectures at home on their computers and practice "homework" in class—we must always consider whether students without consistent computer access at home would have full access to all necessary materials.

An instance of my own interaction with a teacher of one of my children made me think about how class-based assumptions can relate to keeping up with schoolwork. On a few occasions, my child didn't complete the week's reading log by the assigned day, or we left a homework packet on the kitchen table the morning it was due. As the parent of a primary school student, I bear responsibility for monitoring homework completion and delivery. When I apologized to the teacher, she responded, "It's okay. I know you're really busy." I appreciated the understanding response and my child not being penalized. When I hear other teachers in other schools complain about parents whose children don't complete their homework, I wonder how many of those parents don't have strong communication rapport with the teachers, for whatever reason. As educators, we must ask ourselves—giving families the benefit of the doubt—Aren't those parents likely to be just as busy as I am?

We must challenge ourselves to consider that many working-poor parents are highly involved in their children's education, but this involvement may take forms we don't expect. For example, one mother explained why she brings her children to work on weekends and during school breaks: "I clean houses. I bring the children with me because it's good for them to work. Also, while we're working it is a good chance to talk about school things." Our assumptions about parents who may be less "involved" in traditional school-based ways relates to building respect and trust with families—and can thereby counter classism and deficit ideology.

The Importance of Speaking About Struggles

When parents speak to teachers in public venues, I notice that many do not discuss their economic struggles. Because I might not feel comfortable disclosing my own struggles in front of groups of strangers, I find it all the more notable when a parent in a public gathering says, "It can be hard for my kids to focus on school when there is so much struggle in their lives. It's like the poor just get poorer."

When respect and trust have been established, teachers can better understand the struggles students face. "When the kids were visiting their mom," said one legal guardian, "I visited and the air [conditioning] wasn't working. It's 90 degrees. What little girls can think about their homework when they're all huddled into the coolest room, sleeping on the floor?" When families are comfortable revealing struggles, we can better understand student needs and, as necessary, make modifications within the classroom and connect families with school- and community-based resources outside of the classroom. Parents' willingness to speak about struggles can lead teachers and other school personnel to advocate on behalf of their students in situations where they may not otherwise have been aware of problems. For example, a grandparent shared her pressing concern:

> I don't want those kids drinking water at home. I get hysterical. The house is infested with lead. They all are, every house in this town that rents to low-income people. The renters have to sign a disclosure saying

they understand there's lead in the pipes and the paint. And you know where it's written? On the third line from the bottom on the back page of the rental agreement. No one reads that.

In this example, a family member is referencing one of the hidden but dire effects of poverty and housing inequity. When families and school personnel are "on the same team" advocating on behalf of the students, schools can become a key site for community organizing and activism against these sorts of systemic class inequities.

Turning Reflection Into Action

Reconsidering family involvement in more equitable ways will require all educators, from K–12 teachers to administrators to teacher educators in universities, to recognize prejudicial assumptions about social class, value parents' roles and expertise regardless of their class status, and concentrate on building respect and trust with students' families. As a teacher educator, I believe educators need to understand social class and economic prejudice and inequality in order to be truly culturally proficient (Van Galen, 2004). Therefore, I need to critically examine my own practice. For example, inviting parents to serve as guest speakers in education classes has an impact on my students, yet it does not lead to any actual institutional shifts that will help those parents or their children. If listening to parents is the extent of my move toward equitable and anticlassist education, then perhaps I am unwittingly operating under a deficit ideology myself—praising my simple, feel-good actions without critically examining what changes in our educational system would help these families in a more substantive way. I am challenged to become more involved in social justice action within my community. I also must use my own educational privilege to advocate for more equitable education policies within the school, the district, and the state.

Educators at every level must undertake the challenges of reflecting on our own assumptions based on social class prejudice, building respect and trust with parents, and advocating for students' well-being. With dedication to challenging classism in our culture around us, our schools can be more equitable and welcoming places for all families.

References

Books, S. (2004). *Poverty and schooling in the U.S.: Contexts and consequences.* Mahwah, NJ: Lawrence Erlbaum.

Brantlinger, E. (2003). *Dividing classes: How the middle class negotiates and rationalizes school advantage.* New York: Routledge Falmer.

Eamon, M. K. (2004). Digital divide in computer access and use between poor and non-poor youth. *Journal of Sociology and Social Welfare, 31*(2), 91–112.

Ehrenreich, B. (2001). *Nickel and dimed: On (not) getting by in America.* New York: Henry Holt.

Epstein, J. (2001). *School, family, and community partnerships: Preparing education and improving schools.* Boulder, CO: Westview.

Flores, A. (2007). Examining disparities in mathematics education: Achievement gap or opportunity gap? *The High School Journal, 91*(1), 29–42.

Gorski, P. C. (2008). The myth of the "culture of poverty." *Educational Leadership, 6*(7), 32–36.

Haberman, M. (1995). *Star teachers of children in poverty.* West Lafayette, IN: Kappa Delta Pi.

Heath, S. B. (2012). *Words at work and play.* New York: Cambridge University Press.

Herdoíza-Estévez, M. (2011, April). *Welcoming new neighbors: A holistic approach to improving ESL/ENL education in local schools.* Paper presented at the annual meeting of the National Conference on Family Literacy, Louisville, KY.

Heymann, S. J., & Earle, A. (2000). Low-income parents: How do working conditions affect their opportunity to help school-age children at risk? *American Educational Research Journal, 37*(4), 833–848.

Hoover Dempsey, K. V., Walker, J. M. T., Sandler, H. M., Whetsel, D., Green, C. L., Wilkins, A. S., & Closson, K. (2005). Why do parents become involved? Research findings and implications. *The Elementary School Journal, 106*(2), 105–130.

Keown-Bomar, J., & Pattee, D. (2011). What's class got to do with it? A pedagogical response to a deficit perspective. In R. Ahlquist, P. C. Gorski, & T. Montaño (Eds.), *Assault on kids: How hyper-accountability, corporatization, deficit ideologies, and Ruby Payne are destroying our schools* (pp. 214–236). New York: Peter Lang.

Kozol, J. (1992). *Savage inequalities: Children in America's schools.* New York: HarperCollins.

Ladson-Billings, G. (2006). From the achievement gap to the education debt: Understanding achievement in U.S. schools. *Educational Researcher, 35*(7), 3–12.

Lareau, A. (2000). *Home advantage: Social class and parental intervention in elementary education* (2nd ed.). Lanham, MD: Rowman & Littlefield.

Lawrence-Lightfoot, S. (2003). *The essential conversation: What parents and teachers can learn from each other.* New York: Random House.

Lea, V. (2011). Why aren't we more enraged? In R. Ahlquist, P. C. Gorski, & T. Montaño (Eds.), *Assault on kids: How hyper-accountability, corporatization, deficit ideologies, and Ruby Payne are destroying our schools* (pp. 131–151). New York: Peter Lang.

Lee, V. E., & Burkam, D. T. (2002). *Inequality at the starting gate: Social background differences in achievement as children begin school.* Washington, DC: Economic Policy Institute.

McCarthey, S. J. (2000). Home-school connections: A review of the literature. *Journal of Educational Research, 93*(3), 145–153.

Mount-Cors, M. F. (n.d.). *Bridging the differences: Cultural background of Mexican students entering U.S. schools.* Retrieved from www.learnnc.org/lp/pages/4486

Osei-Kofi, N. (2005). Pathologizing the poor: A framework for understanding Ruby Payne's work. *Equity and Excellence in Education, 38*(4), 367–375.

Payne, R. (2005). *A framework for understanding poverty.* Highlands, TX: aha! Process.

Ridout, S. R. (2009, March). *Information parents/caregivers desire from school-based personnel.* Paper presented at the annual research symposium of the Indiana State Reading Association, Indianapolis, IN.

Rogalsky, J. (2009). "Mythbusters": Dispelling the culture of poverty myth in the urban classroom. *Journal of Geography, 108*(4–5), 198–209.

Shipler, D. (2004). *The working poor: Invisible in America.* New York: Knopf.

Valdes, G. (1996). *Con respeto: Bridging the differences between culturally diverse families and schools.* New York: Teachers College Press.

Van Galen, J. A. (2004). Seeing classes: Toward a broadened research agenda for critical qualitative researchers. *International Journal of Qualitative Studies in Education, 17*(5), 663–684.

Weiss, H. B., Mayer, E., Kreider, H., Vaughan, M., Dearing, E., Hencke, R., & Pinto, K. (2003). Making it work: Low-income working mothers' involvement in their children's education. *American Educational Research Journal, 40*(4), 879–901.

PART FIVE

Teaching for Class Equity and Economic Justice

26

V

Elizabeth E. Vaughn

The poor are poor because poverty is a choice
They could work and polish my new Rolls-Royce
If they're hungry they should get something to eat
If they're cold they should turn up the heat
So their floors are dirt or they live on the street
These Jimmy Choo shoes look nice on my feet
If they're sick they should just get well
If they have blood they have something to sell
If they were clean there would be no head lice
Buy me that fur coat no matter the price
The poor just want things that are free free free
I love my yacht on the open sea
How foolish to freeze to death in the cold
My new watch band is purest gold
How foolish to die in a house that's too hot
Would you look at this perfect diamond I got?
They could help themselves if they simply would
And I would help them if I only could.

27

COMING CLEAN

Carolyn L. Holbrook

My youngest daughter inherited something from me that I'm not particularly proud of. She is always late—for everything! In the mid-1990s, when she was in high school, I had to drive her to school more often than I care to admit in order to sign tardy passes. On one of those mornings during her sophomore year, the assistant principal asked me to come into her office. I braced myself, expecting to be warned about possible consequences for Ebony's habitual tardiness. Or, I thought, shuddering, that she may have wanted to talk about the protest my child recently led against her science teacher whose teaching methods she and her classmates thought were incompetent. Instead Ms. Rudel shared that she had been observing my relationship with my daughter. There were a lot of other African American girls at South High who could benefit from having a mother figure like me in their lives, she said, and then asked if I would consider taking one or two of them under my wing.

Relieved and surprised, I was pleased that the way I relate to my children had caught Ms. Rudel's scrutinizing eye. But she didn't know that Ebony was just beginning to recover from a struggle that had begun two years before when her sister left for college. The two girls are very close; in some ways Tania had become the mother figure to Ebony that Ms. Rudel hoped I could be to the young women she had in mind. You see, when my older children were growing up, I worked at home doing secretarial services and spent a few hours each week managing a creative writing program in our neighborhood community center. But when Ebony entered middle school, I took a full-time job directing programs at our local literary arts center. Since Tania and Ebony were the last of my five kids still at home by then, they spent a lot of time together after school.

Everyone in the family was proud of Tania and very excited for her. But her good fortune was devastating to Ebony. All of her older siblings had left home. I was now working outside of the home, and the sister to whom she was closest was 1,000 miles away. For the first time in her life, she would be alone for several hours every day after school. Her feelings of loss and abandonment were compounded over those two years by a series of incidents that neither she nor I could have predicted. I needed to keep her close, needed to protect her. No way I could consider disrupting her any further by bringing a strange girl into our lives. Nevertheless, I felt honored by Ms. Rudel's observation and wanted to find a way to honor her request.

There were plenty of options for ways to get involved. South High is known for its exemplary academic, fine arts, and world languages programs. It is also known for providing great resources to help troubled teens stay in school. After some thought I offered to teach a creative writing class in the school's program for teen parents. Ms. Rudel and the teacher who ran the program agreed, and within a matter of weeks I had developed a 10-week course, thanks to expert coaching from my friend, the writer and master teacher Julie Landsman.

The first few weeks were tougher than I had anticipated. Those students' daily lives were full of chaos, and creative writing was the furthest thing from their minds. I tried to connect with them using prompts Julie suggested from her work at an alternative school. I also thought of several prompts on my own based on things I'd heard students say to each other or items I saw in the classroom: colorful posters of famous people or nature scenes with inspirational quotes set in large letters across the bottom, pictures of smiling babies and celebrated elders, and baby items that were lying randomly around the room. But nothing worked. I could not interest them.

One day one of the girls said, "Ms. Holbrook, you're nice, but this is boring! No disrespect, but you don't know nothin' about us. Why you think you can help us by making us write about things that don't mean nothin' to us?" Heads nodded in agreement around the table, and I suddenly realized that in my efforts to be professional and avoid disappointing Ms. Rudel, I had denied these young women and men the very thing they wanted from adults who worked with them—to just be real.

I made a split-second decision to drop the plan I had developed and, instead, to come clean with them, show them that I knew more about them than they thought, that I wanted to work with them because, essentially, I was one of them. Their eyes popped open when I shared that I too had been a teen mom. I was 17 when I had my oldest son back in 1962. His father was a gangbanger from the projects on the north side of town, and I found him utterly intoxicating: the way he talked, the way he moved, the energy he exuded—so different from the south-side boys with whom I grew up. I was willing to follow him anywhere. Before long we were arrested when he robbed a small gas station and I sat behind the wheel of the getaway car. He had taught me to drive his old two-tone Buick. I was sentenced to the girls' home school in Sauk Centre, a small town about 100 miles north of the Twin Cities.

My students stared in amazement, mouths agape, as I explained that a heart condition with which I was born caused the doctor at Sauk to request that the juvenile authorities transfer me back to Minneapolis to the University of Minnesota hospital. He had discovered that I was three months pregnant. I spent the remaining six months of my sentence and my pregnancy incarcerated on the maternity ward, watching a steady stream of women in labor come in and leave with their newborns. One woman with whom I briefly shared a room had a serious heart condition and died in childbirth a couple months before my son was due to arrive in late April. I grieved heavily for Dorothy and spent many a sleepless night in fear that the same thing might happen to me.

Tongues clucked and grunts gurgled from the young parents' throats when I related that I was forced to place my baby in foster care for the first 14 months of his life and was allowed to see him only once a week for an hour. I think I understand my parents' reasoning now, but I certainly didn't back then. My mother and stepfather were very afraid of my son's father. They believed they would not be safe if little Stevie and I were in the home and he had ready access to us. The students were sympathetic when I explained that my simultaneous love for my son and bitterness toward my parents motivated me to fight hard for custody. I got my son back on my 18th birthday, but I didn't have a clue how to be a parent. Back then we teen parents were pretty much left to our own devices. We didn't have programs like the one from which this group benefited in the Minneapolis Public Schools system, a program that encouraged them to stay in school and taught them parenting skills. I already had dropped out of school and, with less than a high school education, struggled to keep a roof over our heads cleaning rooms with a motel housekeeping service to supplement my monthly welfare check. Trying to manage my frustrations was hard. There was so much I didn't understand about babies. Besides, Stevie didn't know me because of our separation.

When Stevie was three years old, I packed up our few belongings and with only $18 in my pocket took a Greyhound bus to Springfield, Massachusetts, to be with my father for a while. Once I was on my feet, I moved to Boston to find work and get involved in the arts. When Stevie was seven, I married a man I met in an arts program there.

The students listened in silence as I told them the next part of my story. My child and I experienced unbelievable violence at that man's hands. If you read Ntozake Shange's choreopoem "For Colored Girls Who Have Considered Suicide When the Rainbow Is Enuf" or saw Tyler Perry's film adaptation, you no doubt cringed and maybe gasped, screamed, or cried when the Lady in Red's boyfriend, Beau Willie, hung her children out the window by their ankles and then dropped them, killing them. But as horrifying as it was, you probably thought it couldn't be real, that it was just a scene in a play. I'm here to tell you that such scenes are very real and probably occur more often than anyone knows. The man I was married to hung my son from a sixth floor window by his ankles to strengthen a point he wanted to make after having beaten me bloody. And that was just one incident.

It took years for me to find my way out of that marriage. We moved from Boston to New York City and finally to his hometown of Greensboro, North Carolina. The beatings continued throughout that time, and I gave birth to three more of my children. With each new birth I felt more trapped.

A surprising event would eventually show me the way out. One Sunday morning our small church's pianist was sick and couldn't make it to the service. Remembering my childhood piano lessons, I tried to play the songs—disastrously, I must say. Some of the elderly congregants gave me much encouragement, so I started practicing and occasionally relieved the pianist as my skills improved. This gave me confidence, and after a while I decided to go back to school and earn a GED, boosting my self-esteem even more. Scary as it was, I then made a decision to strike out on my own. Now I was a single mother with a new struggle: four kids and my fifth child, Ebony, who would arrive a year later after I ran into an old love whose love I mistakenly thought would soothe my aching soul.

Back in the classroom, I definitely had the young parents' attention. Questions flowed one after another. Most centered around how my relationship with Stevie's father ended, why I stayed in the abusive marriage for nearly 10 years, how I dug myself out of poverty, and how I got to where I am now.

I answered all of their questions candidly, thrilled especially to tell them about Miss Johnson, my eighth-grade English teacher, who played a major role in my eventual return to education. She saw more in me than just a girl who was always in trouble. To her, I was much more than just a rebellious teenager who frequently provided teachers with reasons to send me to the principal's office or to simply ignore me, making me feel invisible. While those teachers made me feel invisible, Miss Johnson made me feel visible, accepted. She always had a smile for me when I entered her classroom and loved the poems I wrote in her class, so much so that she encouraged me to keep writing. Miss Johnson's belief in me stayed in the back of my mind throughout my years of struggle. She is the reason I continued with my education, eventually earning a PhD. And she is the reason why, to this day, I look for the light in the students with whom I work at the private university and community college where I teach. Because of Miss Johnson, I know how important it is to focus on that light even though it may be shining only dimly when the students first enter my classroom. I know firsthand that an ignited spark can someday catch fire. I also know that, like Miss Johnson, I may never be the one to witness the flame I ignited.

After I shared my story, the mood in the classroom perked up, and the students responded energetically to my writing prompts, producing a lot of interesting work. We had many more conversations about our lives and other topics that were on their minds on any given day.

One young father named Andy, a quiet, rather surly kid, never wrote or participated in our discussions. But he never missed a class. Andy seemed more sullen than usual the day after Speaker of the House Newt Gingrich announced the Republican Right's so-called Contract With America, which, among other things, suggested that the nation could reduce welfare rolls by placing the children of welfare mothers in orphanages. The goal was to prohibit states from paying welfare benefits to children whose paternity was not established and those born out of wedlock to women younger than age 18. The savings, according to this proposal, would be used to establish and operate orphanages and group homes for unwed mothers.

The morning he read about this proposal, Andy sat planted in his seat with his legs crossed, his arms folded tightly across his chest, his thick blonde eyebrows furled in a deep frown, making him look much older than his 17 years. His lips were glued together in an angry scowl. Then, in the middle of a writing exercise in which he hadn't participated, he suddenly blurted out, "I'm tired of the way people like Newt Gingrich and doctors and social workers treat us. I wanna write a letter to the editor!"

A brief silence ensued after which other students echoed Andy's comment. They also had experienced offensive treatment by doctors, social workers, and even some teachers. Their teacher, Sue, joined in, confirming that she could tell by a student's demeanor if she or he had come to class from an appointment or a different class that hadn't gone well. And now Newt Gingrich and his "Moral Majority" were insulting them by promoting a plan that could exacerbate the nearly unbearable restrictions under which teen parents already were living.

Moved by their passion, I tossed out my plans for the final few weeks of the class. I didn't have a clue how to teach anyone how to write a letter to the editor, but I knew somebody who did. The previous summer, I had served as interim editor of my neighborhood newspaper, *The Whittier Globe*. As such, I put together a series of community journalism workshops taught by seasoned feature writers, sports writers, and others. One of the journalists was Eric Ringham, then commentary editor at the *Minneapolis Star Tribune*. I called Ringham and was happily surprised by his response. I'd hoped he would give me a few pointers, but instead he offered to visit the class the following week, saying that what the kids really needed was instruction on how to write commentary—how to write an effective opinion piece. When he came to visit, he went even further. He gave the students a deadline and promised to publish all of the commentaries that were completed by then and to pay each student whose work he published $100. I would work with them in the weeks after his visit, helping them revise their work to prepare each commentary for publication.

As Ringham explained his work at the *Star Tribune* to the kids and his expectations for their commentaries, and even during the writing exercises he gave them, he couldn't help noticing the young woman who kept laying her head on her desk. He called her on her behavior, thinking that she must have been bored or just plain rude. She replied that neither was true. She was tired. The journalist in him took over. He became curious. He wanted to hear her story.

"Why are you so tired?" he asked.

"I overslept and missed my bus, so I walked to school," she replied with a yawn.

No big deal, I'm sure he thought to himself. But he asked the next question anyway.

"How far do you live from school?"

"Twenty blocks," she replied.

Now Ringham was even more curious. "Why didn't you catch the city bus or just stay home?"

"I didn't have any money and I need to get my education."

He stared at the young woman for a moment, dumbfounded, then asked when her baby was due.

"Next month," she replied and placed her head back on her desk.

Later, Ringham would tell me that those youth, especially the young mom who wanted her education so badly that she had walked twenty blocks to school in her eighth month of pregnancy, changed his view of teen parents. Until then, like so many others, he had bought into the myth that teenagers like them were lazy and promiscuous, uninterested in educating themselves. The intelligence and determination he witnessed that day caught him completely by surprise.

The students spent the next few weeks eagerly revising their stories. Andy, thrilled that he had been taken seriously, participated fully, basically taking ownership of the project, sharing feedback on his classmates' work and prodding them through the sometimes grueling revision process.

The article "Kids With Kids: Teenage Parents Find Power in the Pen," was published in the *Minneapolis Star Tribune* on Sunday, September 17, 1995, and a few days later we celebrated. The teacher bought treats, and the youth showed up with their $100 checks in hand, along with a few choice words for negative letters to the editor that followed the publication. Most of the letters were positive, but I guess we had to expect that some would slam the paper for "encouraging those awful little slackers by giving them (gasp!) money to buy expensive sneakers." The teacher and I both drew the students' attention to the letters that praised their determination and those that showed that some readers were inspired and indeed enlightened by their words.

Working with that amazing group of teens taught me several important lessons about teaching:

• *No matter how tough, defensive, strong, or even innocent or intelligent students appear to be when they enter your classroom, they all have a story to tell.* Some of their experiences can affect their ability to learn. My first major writing assignment, both at the community college and at the private college where I teach as an adjunct professor, is always a personal essay. Under the guise of a literacy narrative, I ask students to focus on something that has to do with how they have experienced education, particularly reading and writing. They can choose the topic.

The students usually begin their narratives reluctantly, with a story they think I want to hear. Over two or three class periods, during which I give them in-class writing exercises, they become more comfortable writing more truthfully, and the writing often serves as a much-needed catharsis. This allows them to focus on their studies, having purged something that could have held them back. One of them was a young man who, for the first time, was able to grieve the loss of his father who passed away in an ATV accident 10 years earlier. His family told him he now had to be the "man of the family," so he compartmentalized his grief until the day I assigned a writing prompt that evoked a flood of tears and relief for the safe place I provided.

- *Be yourself*. Kids know the minute they walk into your classroom whether you like them. Even more, they can sense if they can be themselves with you. Who knows? You might end up being the person my eighth-grade English teacher, Miss Johnson, was for me: a teacher whose honesty and caring still inspire me to be the best teacher I can be.

- *Remember that all students want to learn!* Last year, a student at my community college surprised me when she said she had to quit school when she became pregnant with her son, now 12 years old. She was so grateful to finally get back to school. As teachers, we should never buy into the idea that students' mistakes are life sentences. We should always be willing to explore options with them and help them think things through to give them a broader vision or different perspective. It would have been hard for her to complete her education when she became pregnant, but with guidance she might not have had to wait 12 years to continue school.

- *If your plan isn't working, be willing to throw it out!* Education should not be a one-stop shop. Our students are individuals with different learning styles, interests, and histories. We should be willing to tap into our own innate creativity to give them positive and memorable learning experiences.

28

INSISTING ON CLASS(ROOM) EQUALITY IN SCHOOLS

Curt Dudley-Marling

There is a greater tragedy than being labeled as a slow learner, and that is being treated as one. (Rist, 1970, p. 448)

Deficit thinking situates school failure in the minds, bodies, language, culture, and communities of poor children and their families. The deficit stance simultaneously blames poor students for school failure while deflecting attention from systemic explanations for disproportionately high levels of failure in high-poverty schools. However, as suggested in the previous Rist (1970) quote, it isn't the deficit perspective per se that harms poor children as much as what comes from this stance. There is an abundance of evidence that students living in poverty are likely to be offered a circumscribed curriculum that severely limits their educational and vocational attainments. Whereas students in affluent, high-achieving schools experience rich, challenging, and engaging curricula, students in high-poverty schools tend to be subjected to tedious, low-level curricula that focus on basic skill instruction (e.g., Anyon, 1980; Kozol, 2005; Oakes, 2008), what Haberman (1991) referred to as a "pedagogy of poverty." For instance, early reading instruction in affluent schools tends to focus on teaching the skills of reading within a context of rich and engaging literature. Early reading instruction in high-poverty schools, on the other hand, more often focuses on reading skills to the exclusion of literature (Allington, 2005). Arguably, such disparities in curricula account for the widespread finding that, as they pass through the grades, "children living in high-poverty areas tend to fall further behind, regardless of their initial . . . skill level" (Snow, Burns, & Griffin, 1998, p. 98).

There are, however, numerous examples of successful efforts to provide students in high-poverty schools with the rich, engaging "high-expectation" curriculum that is common in affluent, high-achieving schools and classrooms (e.g., Dudley-Marling & Michaels, 2012; Oakes, 2005). High-expectation curricula succeed, in part, because they are based on the assumption that all students are competent, regardless of their linguistic, cultural, or socioeconomic backgrounds. More important, high-expectation curricula provide students with access to the content, knowledge, and skills needed to achieve high levels of academic and vocational success.

In this chapter I present several examples illustrating the power of high-expectation curricula to engage and challenge students in high-poverty schools to achieve high levels of academic success, focusing particularly on research Sarah Michaels and I conducted on literature discussions in a South Bronx elementary school.

Challenging Curricula in High-Poverty Schools

Challenging low-achieving students in high-poverty schools with engaging, high-expectation curricula requires us to dismantle structures of schooling that sort students by perceived ability. These structures tend to offer rich, engaging curriculum to students in higher academic tracks or ability groupings and vocational or basic skill instruction to students in lower ability groups (Oakes, 2005). The differentiated instruction instantiated by tracking ensures that many students, particularly underachieving students in high-poverty schools, will continue to underachieve relative to their more privileged peers. Slavin (1990) observed, "Study after study . . . finds no positive effect of ability grouping in any subject or at any grade level, even for the high achievers most widely assumed to benefit from grouping" (p. 491).

Oakes (2005) argued that instead of offering differentiated instruction based on perceived differences in ability, all students should be offered a common curriculum "comprised largely of the high-status knowledge now primarily reserved for students in high tracks" (p. 206). Villegas (1997) was more specific:

> All students . . . need a fast paced curriculum that actively engages their attention. This curriculum must challenge students to develop higher-order knowledge and skills. The instructional goal should be to enrich students' experiences, not to correct deficiencies. (p. 284)

A substantial body of literature supports the efficacy of heterogeneous, detracked classrooms (Oakes, 2008; Thompson, 2001). For instance, Burris, Wiley, Welner, and Murphy (2008) examined patterns of student achievement in a school district that gradually detracked its middle and high school curricula by offering all students a rich, challenging mathematics curriculum in mixed ability classrooms. When all middle school students were offered the accelerated math curriculum previously reserved for the school's highest achievers in heterogeneously grouped classes, more than 90% of students entered high school having passed the first (New York) regents mathematics exam. Moreover, the percentage of Black and Latino students passing this exam more than tripled (from 23% to 75%). At the high school level, being a member of a detracked cohort substantially increased the odds of students attaining a regents diploma, increased by 70% the odds of students attaining an International Baccalaureate Diploma, and resulted in a decrease in school dropouts. Gains in these areas were particularly strong for Black and Latino students.

The Preuss School is another example of a successful detracked school. The Preuss School is a single-track, college-preparatory public charter high school on the University of California, San Diego (UCSD), campus that provides a rigorous curriculum to low-income students whose parents or guardians have not graduated from a four-year college or university (Mehan, 2012). The school selects through a lottery low-income students with high potential but underdeveloped skills. Seventy-five percent of Preuss students are Black or Hispanic. The school's curriculum, which emphasizes project-based learning and a portfolio of assessments, fulfills or exceeds the entry requirements of the University of California and California State University systems. In addition to its rigorous curriculum, the school also seeks to create a college-going culture reinforced by its location on the UCSD campus. An average of 84% of the graduates of the first classes at Preuss (2004–2009) attended four-year colleges. Preuss was also among the highest ranked high schools in the district in 2009, 2010, and 2011, outpacing many schools with a much lower proportion of students living in poverty. In 2009 Preuss was named by *Newsweek* as its "Top Transformative High School" ("The *Newsweek* Top 100," 2011).

Boaler and Staples (2008) offered another example of the effectiveness of high-expectation curricula in detracked schools. They reported on a five-year longitudinal study of approximately 700 students in three high schools: Hilltop High School, a rural school where approximately half the students are Latino and half are White; Greendale High School, situated in a coastal community with little ethnic or cultural diversity; and Railside High School, a diverse, urban high school whose students come from a variety of ethnic and cultural backgrounds and where "lessons are frequently interrupted by the noise of trains passing just feet away from the classrooms" (p. 614). The teachers at Railside created a challenging, problem-oriented mathematics program drawing on reform curricula such as the "College Preparatory Mathematics Curriculum," whereas the teachers at the other two high schools relied on more traditional math curricula. In addition, students at Railside were organized into heterogeneous (detracked) classes compared to tracked classes a Hilltop and Greendale. At the beginning of Year 1, students at Railside were achieving at significantly lower levels in mathematics than students at the other two high schools. At the end of Year 1, however, students at Railside were achieving at roughly the same level as students in the other high schools on a test of algebra, and at the end of Year 2,

Railside students significantly outperformed students at Hilltop and Greendale on a test of algebra and geometry.

Project Challenge (Chapin & O'Connor, 2012) offers additional support for the power of high-expectation curriculum in high-poverty schools. Chapin and O'Connor argued that mathematics instruction in urban schools is characterized by a pattern in which teachers present new content followed by student repetition of rule and algorithms. Students are then expected to engage in some sort of independent practice often in the form of worksheets. Moreover, instruction in these schools tends to focus on lower-level skills. Project Challenge, situated in an urban school district ranked in the bottom 20% on state assessments, engages students in the kind of high-level mathematical reasoning and problem solving often found in schools with high socioeconomic status. An example from the sixth-grade curriculum illustrates the demands of the Project Challenge curriculum: "What digit is in the ones place in 9^{25}? Look for patterns in easy powers of 9. Explain your reasoning" (p. 117).

This problem "requires students to apply their knowledge of exponents, multiplication facts and procedures, and to use induction to generalize to find an answer" (p. 117). Project Challenge requires students to go beyond simple computation, however. Students are also challenged to explain their thinking, to explain to other students how problems are set up or solved, and to explain how ideas are related to other ideas.

After two years students in Project Challenge were scoring better than 87% of students in the norming sample for the California Achievement Test of Mathematics. In addition, at the end of sixth grade, over three fourths (82%) of each Project Challenge class scored "advanced" or "proficient" on the math portion of the Massachusetts state achievement test, significantly better than students in Massachusetts as a whole, at 38%.

Special education is also a form of tracking that, arguably, limits students' academic and vocational opportunities by offering students with disabilities a curriculum focused on low-level skills and abilities aimed at remediating student *deficits* (Dudley-Marling & Paugh, 2005). There have, however, been efforts to bring rich, engaging high-expectation curriculum to students with disabilities. For example, the Optimal Learning Environment (OLE) project (Ruiz & Figueroa, 1995) brings pedagogy typically associated with gifted classrooms to bilingual special education settings in urban and rural schools in California (Ruiz, 2012). OLE classrooms feature holistic practices like "interactive journals and literature study, along with other instructional strategies such as writers' workshop, shared reading and writing, guided reading and writing, and the development of [students'] phonemic awareness and phonics through meaningful activities" (Ruiz, Vargas, & Beltrán, 2002, p. 304), which connect students' background knowledge and experience in literacy lessons and promote higher levels of interaction (oral language, reading, and writing) between students and teachers. A body of research indicates that such practices significantly affect bilingual special education students' performance in reading and writing (Ruiz, 2012; Ruiz & Figueroa, 1995; Ruiz, Vargas, & Beltrán, 2002).

Each of these examples documents the power of providing students typically assigned to lower academic tracks the sort of rich, engaging curriculum usually found in affluent schools and high-achieving classrooms. I now draw on my own research and offer a more detailed example of a high-expectation curricular practice.

High-Expectation Curriculum in Lexington Elementary

Lexington Elementary is a high-poverty school in the South Bronx, and until recently it was just another urban school with low test scores and a scripted basic skills curriculum. We were drawn to Lexington Elementary after learning about dramatic improvements in reading test scores at the school following the introduction of a practice called Shared Inquiry (Great Books Foundation, www.greatbooks.org). In Shared Inquiry students participate in evidence-based discussions of challenging texts in which they learn how to build, explicate, and weigh academic arguments—a hallmark of academic discourse. Shared Inquiry is part of a recurring set of tasks, usually lasting an hour each day over the course of a five-day cycle. In the first three days of the cycle, students have the text read and reread to them and are given opportunities to read (and reread) the text themselves. Students also have opportunities to ask questions about the text and discuss words, idioms, and concepts that may be unfamiliar to them. The purpose of this preparation is to ensure that all students have access to the text prior to the Shared Inquiry discussion. A separate day is dedicated to an activity called "Directed Notes" in which students get practice making claims and citing textual evidence. Day 4 is devoted to Shared Inquiry. To prepare for Shared Inquiry discussions, teachers select challenging texts that have some ambiguity and then prepare an interpretive question that has more than one possible answer and can be answered on the basis of textual evidence. The assumption here is that real interactive discussions require a degree of textual ambiguity. Questions that lead to a single correct answer provide little opportunity for meaningful discussion. It is crucial that the teacher draw on a set of talk-powerful moves (e.g., providing wait time, revoicing, asking for evidence) to orchestrate discussion (Michaels & O'Connor, 2011). Teachers are discouraged from doing any sort of evaluation during Shared Inquiry on the assumption that evaluation limits discussions to students pleasing teachers by coming up with correct answers. On Day 5 students translate the Shared Inquiry discussion into a piece of persuasive writing.

Arguably, Shared Inquiry is the sort of rich, engaging, and challenging activity that is common in high-achieving schools and classrooms but less so in high-poverty schools and low-achieving classrooms. The implicit assumption is that only the highest achievers have the skill and motivation for practices like Shared Inquiry. There is, however, a body of research indicating that Shared Inquiry is a practice that positively affects the reading achievement of students in urban schools (e.g., Criscuola, 1994; Hait, 2011; Heinl, 1988). Similarly, following the implementation of Shared Inquiry at Lexington Elementary, students made dramatic gains on the district reading assessments. In particular, in the year following the introduction of Shared Inquiry, fewer than 25% of Lexington students achieved the levels of "meets" or "exceeds" standards. However, after the implementation of Shared Inquiry, 50% of Lexington students reached these levels of achievement.

Data gathered from observations and video recording Shared Inquiry discussions in two fourth-grade classrooms at Lexington Elementary indicate that Shared Inquiry led to deep learning engagement with challenging texts by transforming the nature of teacher-student interactions during discussions. The default pattern of talk in many classrooms is recitation or initiation-response-evaluation (I-R-E) in which teachers ask questions, students respond (briefly), and the teacher then evaluates the correctness of the response (Cazden, 2001; Michaels & O'Connor, 2011). In this context, teachers do a significant proportion of the talking, and the form and function of students' language is highly circumscribed (Cazden, 2001). This pattern was reversed during Shared Inquiry discussions at Lexington Elementary. The analysis of a typical discussion in one of the fourth-grade classrooms, for example, indicated that, on average, students took more turns (268 versus 182) and longer turns (18 words/turn versus 15 words/turn) relative to their teacher. Overall, students did nearly two thirds of the talking in these discussions, a complete reversal of the pattern found in typical classroom discussions (Cazden, 2001). In addition, Shared Inquiry discussions at Lexington Elementary averaged nearly one hour, contradicting the myth that poor, low-achieving students in urban schools are incapable of sustained engagement in high-level activities.

Qualitative analyses of the data we collected at Lexington Elementary give further support for the possibilities of high-expectation curriculum like Shared Inquiry. In the following excerpt, students are discussing a story called "Cedric" (Jansson, 1962) about a boy named Sniff who gives away his stuffed animal Cedric but soon regrets it "to desperation." There is a story within a story here about a woman who thinks she's dying and gives away all of her possessions in anonymous parcels to different people. She doesn't die, but as she gives away her things, she's changed (she's nicer) and now has friends and finally goes off to travel the world. Eventually, Sniff finds Cedric abandoned and dirty, left out in the rain. Cedric's topaz eyes have been removed and the moonstone on the collar has been lost. But, as the story says, Sniff loves Cedric "all the same" but now "only for love's sake" (p. 161). The teacher frames the discussion by asking the following question: Why at the end of the story does Sniff love Cedric "only for love's sake"? Consider the following excerpt from this discussion, a segment we call "Derrick's Challenge."

Teacher	I see three, four, or five hands up. . . . Megan begin.
Megan	I think that Sniff only at the end loves Cedric for love's sake because now that he have no moonstone, so he thought that he should love him for who he was, now that he don't have the moonstone.
Teacher	Why did he think that he should love him, now just, even though he doesn't have the moonstone? You're saying he—you say that he thinks. [*several seconds of silence*]
Derrick	I have a question for you [*to Megan*]. Would he still love him if he still had the moonstone?
Megan	Yeah of course.
Derrick	So then why did you say that he loves him now that he didn't have the moonstone? And did that make any difference?
Student	It's just a moonstone.
Teacher	Clarify your question. She doesn't understand your question.
Derrick	It doesn't make any difference whether he has the moonstone or not. He still loved Cedric.
Teacher	So Megan, do you understand his question? [*Megan nods.*] So then, what's your answer to him?
Megan	It said in the story that he loved him, he loved him for the moonstone.
Teacher	Where did it say that?
Megan	[*Looks at page.*] Let me see.
Teacher	Hold on, honey, hold on. . . . [*Kids talking.*] Hold on. Go ahead. Do you need help Megan? [*Megan nods.*] OK. Go ahead, Jazmin, where?
Jazmin	On page 80.
Teacher	What does it say on page 80?
Jazmin	It says, it's in the first paragraph, it says, "An expression that no other dog could ever have. Possibly the jewels were more important to Sniff than the expressions."
Teacher	So . . . Derrick?
Derrick	So then he wouldn't love Cedric if it was because of the moonstone, would he?
Jason	But he loves Cedric. He—he say he loves Cedric for love's sake.

Derrick	I know but (not) what she's saying, it's because of the moonstone. [*two seconds of silence*]
Jazmin	At the end he realized that it doesn't matter if he don't have . . . jewelry on.
Teacher	How did he realize that? What makes you think he realized it?
Jazmin	[*Looks in book.*] I think that he realized that because he found him inside the rain, when he found him inside the rain, and . . . and he didn't have no jewelry on [*Teacher: Uh huh.*], and it says that he loved him ALL THE SAME, that he loved him the same way he loved him with the jewelry on.
Teacher	You guys heard that in the back? . . . Um Diara, what do you have to add to that?
Diara	I understand what Jazmin was saying, that he ended up loving him in the end because the time . . . he found him . . . finally he realized how much he really love Cedric, even though . . . he lacked so many jewels.
Derrick	So let me get this straight. You're saying that she loves him with or without the jewelry? I mean he loves Cedric with or without the jewelry?
Jason	Yes. He does.
Derrick	Then why would she say that she loved him, I mean he loved Cedric because of the moonstones?
Jason	The moonstones is jewels, right?
Teacher	Yes.
Jason	All right. She said for both, even without it. She says he loves him with the moonstones and without the moonstones.
Derrick	So then why would she say that now, I mean, so why would she say he loved him because of the moonstones?
Eric	It doesn't say that.
Jason	All right, but she said both of them. So that can be for both reasons.
Teacher	What do you think, Derrick?
Derrick	I think it's because, for love's sake . . . cause . . .
Teacher	Which means what? What does "love's sake" mean?
Student	Why would she love him?
Derrick	He actually loves him, like it doesn't matter if he has jewelry or not.
Tatyana	That's what Megan said. And Diara. So you agree with her.
Derrick	No, she said, she said because of the moonstones.
Jason	Diara didn't say that. She said loved him for both of them. Without or with.

This five-minute excerpt of a 54-minute discussion of "Cedric" includes 44 turns, only 13 by the teacher. For their part, students make claims, cite evidence in support of their claims, explain how their evidence supports their claims, agree and disagree, and build on one another's claims as they work together to answer the question posed by their teacher (and Derrick). The teacher orchestrates this discussion by calling on students and requesting evidence, explanations, and clarification.

As this excerpt illustrates, a group of students, many of whom are second-language learners or students with special education labels, working collaboratively with the support of their teacher in a high-poverty, underperforming school actively participated in a rigorous, evidence-based discussion of a challenging text, a practice highly valued in academic settings. The shape of this discussion closely resembles the discussions I aim for in my graduate courses at Boston College. Put differently, given the opportunities afforded by a rich curricular practice and strategic moves by their teachers, these fourth-grade students at Lexington Elementary demonstrate that, like all students, they are highly competent learners.

Conclusion

There are two essential points I've tried to make in this chapter. First, the practice of providing low-level, skills-based curriculum to students who are presumed to be "deficient" in ability and experience, including disproportionately high numbers of students in urban schools, severely limits these students' academic and vocational possibilities. Second, students in urban schools thrive when challenged by the sort of rich, engaging curriculum students in affluent schools take for granted. Equitable education for students in high-poverty schools, many of whom have fallen far behind their peers in suburban schools, likely requires more than equal curricular practices, however. To catch up, these students will require more frequent, intensive, and individualized instruction than their peers in more affluent schools. Allington (2005) argued that for students who have fallen behind academically to catch up, they will need to achieve accelerated growth at a pace faster than students in higher achieving schools and classrooms. If we want these students to catch up in reading, for example, they will not only need richer curriculum but also more of it (i.e., significantly more time devoted to reading instruction).

It is important to note, however, that implementing a high-expectation curriculum will not, by itself, be sufficient to overcome neglect, underfunded schools, or the debilitating effects of poverty. Students now living in poverty are entitled to high-expectation curriculum, but they're also entitled to adequately funded schools, high-quality teachers, and good health and nutrition. Attending to the needs of children living in poverty will require a broad approach that focuses on education, health, nutrition, and safety. We should do this not just because it will "work" but also because it is just.↲

References

Allington, R. L. (2005). *What really matters for struggling readers: Designing research-based programs* (2nd ed.). Boston: Allyn & Bacon.

Anyon, J. (1980). Social class and the hidden curriculum of work. *Journal of Education, 162,* 67–92.

Boaler, J., & Staples, M. (2008). Creating mathematical futures through an equitable teaching approach: The case of Railside School. *Teachers College Record, 110*(3), 608–645.

Burris, C. B., Wiley, E., Welner, K., & Murphy, J. (2008). Accountability, rigor, and detracking: Achievement effects of embracing a challenging curriculum as a universal good for all students. *Teachers College Record, 110*(3), 571–607.

Cazden, C. (2001). *Classroom discourse: The language of teaching and learning* (2nd ed.). Portsmouth, NH: Heineman.

Chapin, S. H., & O'Connor, C. (2012). Project Challenge: Using challenging curriculum and mathematical discourse to help all students learn. In C. Dudley-Marling & S. Michaels (Eds.), *High expectation curricula: Helping all students succeed with powerful learning* (pp. 113–127). New York: Teachers College Press.

Criscuola, M. M. (1994). Read, discuss, reread: Insights from the Junior Great Books program. *Educational Leadership, 51*(5), 58–61.

Dudley-Marling, C., & Michaels, S. (Eds.). (2012). *High expectation curriculum: Helping all students succeed with powerful learning.* New York: Teachers College Press.

Dudley-Marling, C., & Paugh, P. (2005). The rich get richer, the poor get direct instruction. In B. Altwerger (Ed.), *Reading for profit* (pp. 156–171). Portsmouth, NH: Heinemann.

Haberman, M. (1991). The pedagogy of poverty versus good teaching. *Phi Delta Kappan, 73,* 290–294.

Hait, N. A. (2011). *Learning to do shared inquiry in a fourth grade classroom* (Unpublished dissertation). Boston College, Chestnut Hill, MA.

Heinl, A. M. (1988, December). *The effects of the Junior Great Books program on literal and inferential comprehension.* Paper presented at the annual meeting of the National Reading Conference, Tucson, AZ.

Jansson, T. (1962). *Tales from Moominvalley* (T. Warburton, Trans.). New York: Farrar, Strauss and Giroux.

Kozol, J. (2005). *The shame of the nation: The restoration of apartheid schooling in America*. New York: Crown.

Mehan, H. (2012). Detracking: Re-forming schools to provide students with equitable access to college and career. In C. Dudley-Marling & S. Michaels (Eds.), *High expectation curricula: Helping all students succeed with powerful learning* (pp. 15–27). New York: Teachers College Press.

Michaels, S., & O'Connor, C. (2011). *Promoting academically productive talk across the curriculum: A high-leverage practice* (Unpublished paper).

The *Newsweek* top 100. (2011, June 27). *Newsweek, 157*(26), 60.

Oakes, J. (2005). *Keeping track: How schools structure inequality* (2nd ed.). New Haven, CT: Yale University Press.

Oakes, J. (2008). Keeping track: Structuring equality and inequality in an era of accountability. *Teachers College Record, 110,* 700–712.

Rist, R. C. (1970). Student social class and teacher expectations: The self-fulfilling prophecy in ghetto education. *Harvard Educational Review, 40,* 411–451.

Ruiz, N. (2012). It's different with second language learners: Learning from 40 years of research. In C. Dudley-Marling & S. Michaels (Eds.), *High expectation curricula: Helping all students succeed with powerful learning* (pp. 145–161). New York: Teachers College Press.

Ruiz, N., & Figueroa, R. (1995). Learning-handicapped classrooms with Latino students: The Optimal Learning Environment (OLE) project. *Education and Urban Society, 27,* 463–483.

Ruiz, N., Vargas, E., & Beltrán, A. (2002). Becoming a reader and writer in a bilingual special education classroom. *Language Arts, 79,* 297–309.

Slavin, R. E. (1990). Achievement effects of ability grouping in secondary schools: A best evidence synthesis. *Review of Educational Research, 60,* 471–499.

Snow, C. E., Burns, M. S., & Griffin, P. (1998). *Preventing reading difficulties in young children*. Washington, DC: National Research Council.

Thompson, S. (2001). The authentic standards movement and its evil twin. *Phi Delta Kappan, 82*(5), 358–362.

Villegas, A. M. (1997). Increasing the racial and ethnic diversity of the U.S. teaching force. In B. J. Biddle, T. L. Good, & I. F. Goodson (Eds.), *International handbook of teachers and teaching* (pp. 267–302). Amsterdam, the Netherlands: Kluwer.

29

CULTIVATING ECONOMIC LITERACY AND SOCIAL WELL-BEING

An Equity Perspective

Susan Santone and Shari Saunders

Our decisions to view students in poverty through an equity lens or a deficit one can have a considerable impact on their futures. Deficit models, grounded in individualism, elitism, hierarchy, and competition, explain poverty as personal failures in students and their families. In contrast, an equity perspective examines structural factors that contribute to poverty. The tension between the equity and deficit perspectives manifests itself in, among other places, curriculum content and the associated assumptions about what constitutes "expert" knowledge (Anyon, 1981; Apple & Beane, 2007; Pearl, 1997).

In this chapter, we explore contrasting perspectives on K–12 economics instruction and its implications for students in poverty. We begin by comparing two economic paradigms, neoliberalism and sustainability, describing their respective parallels to deficit and equity perspectives on poverty. We then describe how teaching from each perspective can affect opportunities for students to acquire and apply economic literacy in ways that support individual and community well-being. By focusing at the level of the classroom and curriculum, we demonstrate how specific elements of mainstream economics instruction marginalize students in poverty by dismissing their experiences and cultural knowledge. In contrast, we highlight how an equity perspective can help students acquire economic literacy; strengthen skills such as resilience, resourcefulness, and problem solving; and create economics opportunities at the individual and community levels.

It is important to state upfront that we are not *against* economics or business. We believe economic and financial literacy is essential for youths' success in civic, academic, and career roles. But economic systems are embedded in ecological and social systems, and we believe that the economy must serve the goal of "sustainable prosperity," the long-term well-being of the natural and social systems on which the economy ultimately depends (Daly & Farley, 2007; Porter & Mykleby, 2011). Likewise, we believe that economics educators have an obligation to support the development of informed, active citizens and an equitable society.

Economics Standards

In the United States, the most influential economics education organizations are the Council for Economic Education (CEE) and the Foundation for Teaching Economics (FTE). The National Council for the Social Studies is another important organization for social studies in general, but we focus in this chapter on the CEE and FTE given their focus on economics.

The CEE is a private nonprofit organization that "advocate[s] for better and greater school-based economic and personal finance education at the K–12 level" (CEE, 2010). The CEE offers voluntary economics standards that states may use as the basis of their own economics standards.[1] The CEE's funders include private donors and corporate foundations. The FTE is focused on "introduc[ing] young individuals . . . to an economic way of thinking . . . and to helping teachers of economics become more effective educators" (FTE, 2012). The FTE is also funded by donors and foundations.

The Dominant Economic Paradigm: Neoliberalism

In his influential book *The Structure of Scientific Revolutions*, Thomas Kuhn (1962) described a *paradigm* as an accepted set of models, patterns, beliefs, and assumptions about how the world operates. An economic paradigm, then, is a worldview about how the economy operates and is rooted in basic assumptions about human nature. Is greed natural? Is personal reward the only factor in economic decisions? The varying answers to such questions reflect the broad spectrum of economic theories (Santone, 2012).

We will refer to the dominant economic paradigm using a number of terms: *neoliberalism, conventional or mainstream economics,* or *free-market capitalism* (Barber, 2004; Keen, 2002; Maier & Nelson, 2007). The neoliberal paradigm is generally defined by themes of individualism, private ownership of wealth and capital, competitive markets, and limited governmental intervention. Grounded in the belief that unlimited growth is both desirable and possible, this paradigm measures success by increases in the gross domestic product, profits, and other quantitative indicators. Environmental and social impacts are often discounted as "externalities" (Daly & Farley, 2007).

Neoliberalism is further based on particular assumptions about human motivation. The logic of the system depends on the predictable behavior of its main actor, *homo economicus* (Daly & Cobb, 1989), an imagined species with unlimited wants that seeks to maximize profit and personal gain. For this economic creature, rewards such as higher wages or lower prices are the ultimate motivators, and maximizing self-interest is the ultimate expression of rationality

(Friedman & Friedman, 1962; Machan, 1987). Moreover, the profit motive offers moral rewards because it encourages hard work and diligence. In this view, capitalism provides *homo economicus* both the freedom of choice and the virtue of self-reliance.

These beliefs about freedom, choice, and individualism further depend on particular assumptions about the interactions between individuals, communities, the economy, and the environment. Consider, for example, the relationship between the economy and the environment. The conventional paradigm largely separates the two. Any economics textbook contains a model of the macroeconomy that frames the environment as one of three factors of production: land, labor, and capital. This model does not capture the value of life-sustaining services provided by ecosystems (Costanza et al., 1997). Environmental and social impacts are dismissed as externalities or market failures (Daly, 1980; Daly & Farley, 2007). Neoliberalism depends on a view of social relationships that is based on individualism and a belief in humanity's fundamental drive to compete. In this paradigm, *freedom* is defined as autonomy from social constraints (Daly & Cobb, 1989).

The concept of competitive individualism not only defines capitalism but also inextricably binds it to a deficit perspective of poverty. In this perspective, individuals are solely responsible for their fate, and those in poverty have internal deficiencies in virtue or character (Ryan, 1976). These flaws, located within the person or their "culture," prevent the individual from making rational choices. Markets are free and fair—the law of supply and demand tells us so. Poverty is thus the fault of individuals who lack the motivation or character to freely better themselves.

Neoliberalism: The Dominant Paradigm in K–12 Economics Curriculum

In an analysis of K–12 economic instruction in the United States, Maier and Nelson (2007) highlighted neoliberalism as the dominant paradigm entrenched in curricula and standards. The curricula from the FTE, and its interpretation of the CEE standards, reflect an especially dogmatic perspective typically associated with libertarian beliefs.

Choices and Freedom

The assumptions about choices and rational behavior are reflected in CEE Standard 4, "Role of Incentives." "People respond predictably to positive and negative incentives," the standard notes, then lists "choice" and "incentive" as related concepts (CEE, 2010). The FTE explores this standard in an extended lesson (or unit) titled *Is Capitalism Good for the Poor?* Consider the information provided for Lesson 5, "Character Values and Capitalism" (bullets added):

- By assuming the autonomy of the individual, capitalism grants dignity to the poor. By affirming people's right to their own labor, regardless of their position on the economic ladder, capitalism offers the poor the means to improve their own well-being.
- When individuals have the right to the output of their labor, they have a strong incentive to increase that output through effort and ingenuity.
- On the other hand, workers may voluntarily use their labor in the productive efforts directed by others. In the absence of slavery or other coercion, this voluntary exchange of labor takes place only when workers are rewarded.
- By providing strong incentives for individuals to become entrepreneurs, capitalism encourages diligence, initiative, and hard work. (FTE, 2012)

To emphasize its benefits for people in poverty, the same lesson also includes this quote from Professor P. J. Hill of Wheaton College:

Capitalism advantages the poor because, for the first time in history, it takes the dignity and the worth of individuals seriously and gives all people, especially the powerless and dispossessed, a sphere of action that is immune from the control of others. (FTE, 2012)

On the surface, and without a more critical analysis, this might sound logical—even appealing. But the framing skips several key realities. First, one's labor is not immune to the control of others; ask anyone who's been laid off. Moreover, labor alone has little value if someone does not also have access to jobs, credit, or capital. But the FTE's presentation omits these issues and instead places the burden for economic success wholly on the individual. The rhetoric of choices and freedom also ignores the element of coercion inherent in capitalism. In today's society, the means to survival is mainly accessed through the cash economy, and gaining access to basic needs requires that people enter into markets (Wood, 2002). As more and more elements of a society become monetized, economic relationships increasingly determine—or replace or degrade—social relationships (Daly & Cobb, 1989).

These complexities are nowhere to be found in CEE Standard 5, "Gain From Trade." As the standard explains, "Voluntary exchange occurs only when all participating parties expect to gain. This is true for trade among individuals or organizations within a nation, and among individuals or organizations in different nations" (CEE, 2010). "Beneficiaries of Competition" (Lesson 3 of *Is Capitalism Good for the Poor?*), further explains the win-win nature of "voluntary exchange":

> Market transactions are entered into freely, by both buyer and seller. Because exchange in markets is voluntary, every completed transaction indicates that, in the absence of fraud, deception or human error, both the seller and the buyer are better off. . . .
>
> Throughout history and continuing to the present day, competitive market economies have the best record of reducing poverty . . . by conferring benefits on the poor as consumers. A high level of competition among sellers leads to improvements in the well-being of the poor by making more goods and services available at lower prices.

These assertions ignore the reality that, in many communities, markets do not offer opportunities to make real choices. In "food deserts" (communities with little access to fresh foods), the only place to access food might be at a gas station, where unhealthy options abound. The opportunity to invest and build wealth does not really exist in communities where pawnshops and predatory loan services are the primary financial institutions. Simply stated, healthy competition implies that choices are available (Daly & Cobb, 1989). This basic principle, echoed in the writings of capitalism's "grandfather" Adam Smith (1776/2003), challenges the premise that everyone benefits from trade. But instead of helping students analyze these issues, the FTE lesson reassures us that competition serves as a safeguard against exploitation:

> Sellers compete with other sellers by offering lower prices, higher quality, or better service—whatever it takes to get buyers to purchase from them rather than from other sellers. Although sellers want to get the highest price they can get, competition from other sellers prevents them from selling at any price or "taking advantage" of the poor. (FTE, 2012)

Of course, capitalism has brought benefits to some people and regions. (The FTE offers many graphs showing the correlation—but not causation—of capitalism and poverty.) But who has really benefited, and what have been the impacts on "other" people and regions? What forms of social progress (e.g., civil rights) are attributable to democracy and civic action? These questions aren't important in an economic paradigm that dismisses the need for social relationships and instead reduces human interactions to market transactions (Barber, 2004).

Students as Consumers

Conventional economics emphasizes the concepts of consumers and producers with money as the primary means of exchange. This is reflected in CEE Standard 7, "Markets"; Standard 8, "The Role of Price in Market Systems"; and Standard 11, "Role of Money" (CEE, 2010). The centrality of money dismisses other exchanges and currencies that may be more prominent in the lives of low-income students: barter, repair, and nonmonetized networks of exchange such as car sharing, community gardening, and community caretaking. Moreover, labeling people as *consumers* or *producers* recasts students as economic actors rather than citizens (Barber, 2004).

We recognize the need for students to understand and function in the dominant economy as a springboard for agency and change. Yet the one-sided nature of the economics standards not only is ideological but also marginalizes students in poverty. It is time for a new paradigm of economics education.

The New Paradigm: Sustainability

Economics comes from the Greek *oikonomia*, which means "household management." The sustainability paradigm is based on a conception of household that includes ecological and social systems. Unlike neoliberalism, which measures success mainly through material growth, sustainability gauges success through real improvements in the health and well-being of the entire household, including people, communities, and the ecological systems they depend on (Daly & Cobb, 1989).

Sustainability also depends on healthy relationships among the members of the household with interdependence, not hierarchy and dominance, as the operating principle. That said, sustainability does not disavow competition. All species (human and nonhuman) compete for food, habitat, and mates to ensure survival and reproduction. But healthy competition does not result in an elimination of other species (Quinn, 1992). Likewise, in a geopolitical context, competing countries need not be adversaries, based on the mind-set that "a winner does not demand a loser" (Porter & Mykleby, 2011, p. 5).

The sustainability paradigm also challenges the idea that self-interest and profit are innate human drives. In his classic *The Great Transformation*, Karl Polyani (1944) identified the profit motive as an economic concept specific to modern capitalism. He noted that in earlier societies, economic relationships were formed to serve social, community, and family ends. The fields of

	Old Paradigm: Neoliberalism	New Paradigm: Sustainability
Measures of success	Progress is based on growth in material output and profits.	Progress is based on increases in well-being, health, and social stability.
Explanations of poverty	Capitalism helps the poor by providing choices, dignity, and the "right to one's own labor." Poverty reflects an individual's lack of virtue and ability to make good choices.	Poverty is impacted by structural factors (Royce, 2009). Structural inequalities in society replicate socioeconomic inequalities in schools (Anyon, 1981; Rothstein, 2004).
Competition	Relationships are hierarchical and negotiated through competitive individualism.	Competition can serve consumers when it is based on high road values.
Trade, markets, and competition	Trade is by definition fair because people enter into market relationships voluntarily. Competitive individualism is innate.	Coercion, monopolies, and lack of access to economic assets can skew markets in ways that limit choices or push people into involuntary exchanges.

TABLE 29.1
The Old and New Paradigms

Source: Creative Change Educational Solutions. (2008). *Community sustainability inventory*. Retrieved from www.creativechange.net

psychology and evolutionary biology also indicate that empathy and cooperation are innate drives that ensure human survival through caretaking and the provision of community needs (Carr, Iacoboni, Dubeau, Mazziotta, & Lenzi, 2003; Hoffman, 2001; Krebs, 1982).

Table 29.1 compares the principles and assumptions of neoliberalism and sustainability.

Teaching From the New Paradigm

Sustainability's focus on interdependence links it to the equity perspective on poverty. Just as the new paradigm locates the economy within social and ecological systems, an equity perspective addresses poverty within broader social contexts. Teaching from this perspective requires educators to reframe content and pedagogy in ways that help learners

- understand and critique the current economic paradigm as they see it operating in their own lives,
- recognize the range of resources they have (self, family, community),

- broaden their perspective on what counts as valuable work,
- develop the types of capital needed to thrive in the existing economic system as they work toward transforming the economic conditions that have a negative impact on their lives, and
- engage with communities around problems that are meaningful and relevant.

In the following section, we explore the equity perspective that teachers must cultivate and outline an approach to instructional design that supports this endeavor.

Valuing Knowledge, Skills, and Multiple Forms of Capital

Families and community members in underserved areas have funds of knowledge and skills that can be valuable for students. These skills might include gardening, carpentry, painting, house maintenance, child care, appliance repairs, cooking, and folk cures (Moll, Amanti, Neff, & Gonzalez, 1992). As funds of knowledge, they can meet individual and community needs and represent useful skills for future citizens, regardless of career. In addition to funds of knowledge, students possess various forms of capital including aspirational, linguistic, social, and familial (Yosso, 2005). Aspirational capital focuses on being resilient and remaining hopeful about possibilities beyond families' and students' current situations, even in the face of obstacles (Yosso, 2005). Duncan-Andrade (2009) described this as *critical hope* and noted that educators can foster it by "connect[ing] . . . young people to actions that relieve the undeserved suffering in their communities" (p. 182). Accessing students' funds of knowledge and capital and facilitating the development of critical hope are essential elements of teaching from the equity perspective. Sound instructional design is one way to achieve this.

Inquiry as Narrative: When Students Shape the Story

A sustainability perspective on economics requires transdisciplinary learning in which students construct and integrate knowledge across disciplines and apply it to address real community problems (Beane, 1997, p. xi). Framing inquiry as an extended story (i.e., a narrative) can support this. In this approach to instructional design, learning unfolds as a story driven by questions that emerge as students investigate issues in their communities. In the narrative, students (and other stakeholders) are the characters, communities are the settings, and sustainability challenges form interconnecting plot lines. Students live and shape the story in a four-stage process of engagement, deep inquiry, decision making, and positive action (Creative Change Educational Solutions [CCES], 2011).

Next we describe a sample middle school economics unit based on this framework, which also address CEE standards, but from a sustainability paradigm.

Stage 1: The story begins. The opening of the story introduces the main plot by situating economics within students' lives and communities. A good entry point is CEE Standard 1, "Scarcity." This standard addresses needs and wants, core concepts that span both neoliberal and sustainability paradigms. A typical conventional lesson asks learners to identify needs and wants, emphasizing the idea that individuals (i.e., *homo economicus*) have unlimited wants and that scarcity requires making choices.

Needs and wants are relevant to sustainability as well, but this paradigm extends the thinking beyond material goods by asking, "What do we need for a fulfilling life?" (CCES, 2003a) or, for younger children, "What do we need to be happy and healthy?" (CCES, 2011). These questions invite students to consider a definition of needs and wants that includes elements such as love, family, friends, health, education, fun, faith, and clean water and air. The sustainability paradigm thus creates a frame that encompasses students' personal values and emphasizes true well-being (of which material goods are one part).

A logical next question is, "What supports our well-being?" (CCES, 2003b). Neoliberalism, with its emphasis on material goods, focuses on the role of money and markets. Students are labeled as consumers and firms as producers; a typical lesson might ask students to provide examples. Although this exercise has value, the sustainability paradigm asks students to consider the *multiple* factors that support them as healthy individuals, not just as consumers. In this frame, students consider not only cash markets but also the needs provided by social relationships, community, and the environment. Thus, sustainability is not against the concepts of markets and money, but rather it emphasizes their interdependence within social and ecological systems. Moreover, sustainability challenges deficit thinking by valuing the knowledge and skills students have rather than focuses on the money they might lack.

CEE Standard 3, "Allocation of Goods and Services," can deepen the connection between economics and students' communities. For example, students can conduct a community inventory to determine if and how basic needs are met, as well as the quality of community services (CCES, 2008). Questions might include "Where can people purchase goods and services such as clothing, food, health care, and household goods?" and "If stores or banks don't fill all these needs, what types of exchanges do?" These questions broaden the definition of economic activity and invite students to construct an analysis of how it functions (or doesn't function) in their communities. During these sorts of activities, students likely will raise as many questions as they answer, creating multiple subplots to explore in Stage 2.

Stage 2: The plot thickens. In Stage 2, students investigate specific issues in greater depth. Consider "Trade and Exchange," CEE Standard 5. Students can learn the concepts of imports and exports by identifying the country of origin of everyday materials and the destinations of any goods made locally. To add an equity perspective, students also could examine local, national, or global trade case studies to evaluate if all parties really do benefit from trade. Returning to the issue of food deserts, students could interview people to determine how they obtain food (Do they buy it? Grow it? Barter for it?) and whether the exchanges are perceived as fair and voluntary. Students also can evaluate whether there are enough options for healthy food and enough demand to create healthy markets in which the laws of supply and demand work to regulate prices. If not, what does this mean? Where are the imbalances?

To apply this research to community financial institutions, students can identify options for savings and credit as they compare the advantages and disadvantages of banks, credit unions, and "payday advance" operations. These activities support CEE Standard 10, "Money," and 11, "Financial Institutions."

Lessons throughout Stage 2 of the story should also engage students in continuous reflection through questions such as "How is this all connected?" and "Do the ideas in this textbook hold true in our community? Why or why not?"

Stages 3 and 4: Climax and ending. Stages 1 and 2 have brought students to the point in the story where they must make decisions about how it will end. Stage 3 and Stage 4 lessons do this by having students examine solutions, their impacts, and decision-making structures.

Students might begin by conducting a more thorough survey of the knowledge, skills, and resources in their own communities, including the funds of capital, by asking, for example, "Who in our community knows how to grow food? Fix a bike? Winterize a home?" To develop entrepreneurial skills (so that one truly does have rights to one's own labor), students can identify opportunities to direct these skills and resources toward community problem solving. For example, students might research the demand for a particular product or service (fresh vegetables, weatherization, etc.). Students then can develop ideas for small-scale enterprises based on cash, barter, or even "time banks," exchanges in which individuals trade services on an hour-to-hour basis (Luna, 2010).

Such projects are not only meaningful ways to apply economic concepts such as supply and demand. They also build social-emotional competencies such as relationship skills, responsible decision making, and social awareness (Collaborative for Academic, Social, and Emotional Learning, 2003). This connects academic content with social-emotional skills to develop critical hope and a systems perspective that situates an individual's socioeconomic status within larger social contexts.

Together, Stages 3 and 4 enable students to apply economic knowledge and skills through informed, positive action in the school, community, and larger world. Students thus shape a happy ending to the current story—or set the stage for a new learning adventure.

Conclusion

As we have shown, deficit perspectives of students in poverty are embedded and reinforced through the paradigm of neoliberalism, the dominant perspective in K–12 economic standards. This view one-sidedly equates capitalism with freedom while attributing poverty or success to individual virtue and character. In contrast, the sustainability perspective values social and ecological relationships, recognizes students' experiences, and builds the agency needed to shape a more democratic and sustainable economy.

The implications for educators are clear. To support students in poverty, economics instruction must shift to a sustainability and equity perspective that uses students' experiences as the foundation for analyzing the power dynamics of the mainstream economy. Curriculum and pedagogy must foster a sense of critical hope; further develop students' academic, social, and emotional skills; and support students to apply their knowledge in meaningful ways. This paradigm is necessary to cultivate the capital most vital to democracy: citizens who integrate and apply social, ecological, and economic literacies in ways that serve the long-term well-being of our entire global household.

Note

1. As of this writing (May 2013), economics is not part of the new Common Core State Standards, a set of outcomes developed by the National Governors Association and the Council of Chief State School Officers and adopted by 45 states and the District of Columbia.

References

Anyon, J. (1981). Elementary schooling and distinctions of social class. *Interchange, 12*(2), 118–132.

Apple, M. W., & Beane, J. A. (2007). *Democratic schools: Lessons in powerful education*. Portsmouth, NH: Heinemann.

Barber, B. R. (2004). Taking the public out of education: The perverse notion that American democracy can survive without its public schools. *School Administrator, 61*(5), 10.

Beane, J. A. (1997). *Curriculum integration: Designing the core of democratic education*. New York: Teachers College Press.

Carr, L., Iacoboni, M., Dubeau, M.-C., Mazziotta, J. C., & Lenzi, G. L. (2003). Neural mechanisms of empathy in humans: A relay from neural systems for imitation to limbic areas. *Proceedings of the National Academy of Sciences, 100*(9), 5497–5502.

Collaborative for Academic, Social, and Emotional Learning. (2003). *Safe and sound: An educational leader's guide to evidence-based social and emotional learning programs.* Chicago: Author.

Costanza, R., d'Arge, R., de Groot, R., Farberk, S., Grasso, M., Hannon, B., . . . van den Belt, M. (1997, May). The value of the world's ecosystems services and natural capital. *Nature, 387,* 253–259.

Council for Economic Education. (2010). *Voluntary national content standards in economics.* Retrieved May 16, 2010, from www.councilforeconed.org/ea/standards/

Creative Change Educational Solutions. (2003a). *Defining what matters.* (Document posted in the CCES online Curriculum and Resource Center.) Retrieved from www.creativechange.net

Creative Change Educational Solutions. (2003b). *How do we get what we need?* (Document posted in the CCES online Curriculum and Resource Center.) Retrieved from www.creativechange.net

Creative Change Educational Solutions. (2008). *Community sustainability inventory.* (Document posted in the CCES online Curriculum and Resource Center.) Retrieved from www.creativechange.net

Creative Change Educational Solutions. (2011). *Inquiry as narrative: What story will you and your students shape?* (Document posted in the CCES online Curriculum and Resource Center.) Retrieved from www.creativechange.net

Daly, H. (1980). Introduction to the steady-state economy. In H. Daly (Ed.), *Economics, ecology, ethics: Essays toward a steady-state economy* (pp. 1–31). San Francisco: W. H. Freeman.

Daly, H., & Cobb, J. (1989). *For the common good: Redirecting the economy toward community, the environment, and a sustainable future.* Boston: Beacon Press.

Daly, H., & Farley, J. (2007). *Ecological economics.* Washington, DC: Island Press.

Duncan-Andrade, J. (2009). Note to educators: Hope required when growing roses in concrete. *Harvard Educational Review, 79*(2), 181–194, 399.

Foundation for Teaching Economics. (2012). Retrieved from http://www.fte.org

Friedman, M., & Friedman, R. D. (1962). *Capitalism and freedom.* Chicago: University of Chicago Press.

Hoffman, M. L. (2001). *Empathy and moral development: Implications for caring and justice.* Cambridge: Cambridge University Press.

Keen, S. (2002). *Debunking economics: The naked emperor of the social sciences.* London: Zed Books.

Krebs, D. (1982). Psychological approaches to altruism: An evaluation. *Ethics*, 92(3), 447–458.

Kuhn, T. S. (1962). *The structure of scientific revolutions.* Chicago: University of Chicago Press.

Luna, M. (2010). How to share time. *YES! Magazine.* Retrieved July 4, 2012, from www.yesmagazine.org/new-economy/how-to-share-time

Machan, T. R. (1987). The classical egoist basis of capitalism. In T. Machan (Ed.), *The main debate: Communism versus capitalism* (pp. 139–161). New York: Random House.

Maier, M. H., & Nelson, J. A. (2007). *Introducing economics: A critical guide for teaching.* Armonk, NY: M. E. Sharpe.

Moll, L. C., Amanti, C., Neff, D., & Gonzalez, N. (1992). Funds of knowledge for teaching: Using a qualitative approach to connect homes and classrooms. *Theory Into Practice*, 31(2), 132–141.

Pearl, A. (1997). Democratic education as an alternative to deficit thinking. In R. R. Valencia (Ed.), *The evolution of deficit thinking* (pp. 211–241). New York: Falmer.

Polyani, K. (1944). *The great transformation.* Boston: Beacon Press.

Porter, W., & Mykleby, M. (2011). *A national strategic narrative.* Washington, DC: Woodrow Institute for International Scholars.

Quinn, D. (1992). *Ishmael: An adventure of the mind and spirit.* New York: Bantam Books.

Rothstein, R. (2004). *Class and schools: Using social, economic, and educational reform to close the Black-White achievement gap.* Washington, DC: Economic Policy Institute.

Royce, E. C. (2009). *Poverty and power: The problem of structural inequality.* Lanham, MD: Rowman & Littlefield.

Ryan, W. (1976). *Blaming the victim* (2nd ed.). New York: Vintage Books.

Santone, S. (2012). Ecological economics in education. In R. McKeown & V. Nolet (Eds.), *Schooling for sustainable development in Canada and the United States* (pp. 153–167). New York: Springer.

Smith, A. (2003). *The wealth of nations: Adam Smith.* New York: Bantam Books. (Original work published 1776)

Wood, E. M. (2002). *The origin of capitalism: A longer view.* London: Verso.

Yosso, T. J. (2005). Whose culture has capital? A critical race theory discussion of community cultural wealth. *Race Ethnicity and Education*, 8(1), 69–91.

30

BECOMING UPSTANDERS
Humanizing Faces of Poverty Using Literature in a Middle School Classroom

Wendy Zagray Warren

Tackling an Elephant: A Rationale for Teaching About Poverty

One afternoon, standing in the locker bays of the public middle school where I taught seventh graders, I began chatting with Casey, a student in one of my classes. We often talked during this time, sharing the details of our days. This particular afternoon, seemingly out of the blue, he said, "Ms. Warren, I'm trailer trash. I live in a trailer."

Taken aback, I paused, and drawing on the quick thinking skills teachers so often have to practice, I said, "Casey, to my way of thinking, no human can be trash."

He shrugged silently as he banged his locker closed and waved good-bye to make his way home to the trailer he shared with a mom who loved and protected him. I stood there wondering what had raised this issue for him. How and why he had taken on this stereotype?

I thought back to a 2005 *Phi Delta Kappan* column called "Thoughts on Teaching: And the Winner Is . . ." Author Bobby Ann Starnes offered a poignant description of the effects of class stereotypes that surround us and seep into our pores. She told the story of her niece who lives in the mountains of Appalachia. Starnes wrote, "One day, she [Starnes's niece] was telling her mother about an argument she'd had with a girl at school. 'She's just a piece of white trash living in that junky doublewide on the side of a mountain,' she said, venom dripping from every word" (p. 796). Starnes's sister, horrified, had to remind her daughter that *they too* lived in a trailer on the side of a mountain.

These examples of internalized prejudice reminded me of the power of the media images that surround us. The community in which I taught had many people living in poverty. Where were my students going to learn to counter these stereotypes? I decided my classroom had to be the place. I taught language arts, and, after all, my students had to write and speak about *something*. I could think of no topic more important than one that might shatter their stereotypes, potentially impacting how they treat others in their own community and perhaps the ways they think about themselves.

Finding a Way In

Sometimes I have let teachable moments slip right by. My students have made comments that I recognized as dehumanizing to a group of people, and I chose, in the moment, to ignore them, knowing that stopping to address a slur would change the course of carefully laid curricular plans or lead into difficult conversations I did not feel prepared to handle. I have come to realize, however, that what I allow, I teach. If I choose not to address a comment that I hear in the hallway, the teacher's lounge, or the classroom, I am teaching that the comment is acceptable.

I carried Casey's comment with me but had not yet found the courage, or a point of entry, to ask my students to think and write about issues of class. Then, one day, an opportunity presented itself. It came unexpectedly, as these moments often do.

Students in my classes had been wrestling with the human capacities for love and hate through a study of Nazism and the Holocaust. They were able to cite examples of dehumanization in events leading up to the Holocaust, some of which clearly involved the use of propaganda. I've learned that history has more relevance to my students when concepts are applied to a present-day context, so we also looked at contemporary examples of images that might be considered propaganda, and students were able to identify messages of dehumanization in those images as well. Thinking on my feet, and wanting my students to consider dehumanizing choices they may make regarding their own behavior as well, I asked if they thought there were groups of people dehumanized in our school. What happened next floored me. They produced a list rapid fire, without hesitation and apparently without shame: Mexicans. Asians. Indians. African Americans. Jews. People with brown skin. People who are hurt and in a cast or who are disabled. People with tattoos or piercings. People who drive old cars. Teachers. People who wear ratty clothes. Hobos. People who are fat or skinny. Environmentalists.

The list filled a page. As the conversation continued, I tried to hide my shock. With no more than a nudge, these words usually hidden from the eyes and ears of teachers came pouring out into the daylight of my classroom.

The word *hobo* appeared on the list, and I was puzzled by the connotations seemingly associated with it. Perhaps this was the opportunity I had been waiting for to address the stereotypes associated with poverty that underlay Casey's proclamation that he was trailer trash.

Careful Questioning

I realized that my students must have a very different understanding of the word *hobo* than I did. Rather than rushing to judgment about what seemed to be a misunderstanding of the term, I decided to pose some questions. Asking questions, sometimes even leaving them hanging in the air without expecting immediate answers, is one way I have found to allow space for students to think deeply about their values and recognize their cultural perspectives. With these questions, I hope to challenge students, and myself, to think critically, probing what we see around us, learning to look for perspectives other than our own.

"What do you mean when you say 'hobo'?" I asked. As we talked, I came to understand that my students were using the term to refer to any person who was homeless. And there was judgment attached. A hobo was a person to be feared and scorned. Further answers revealed that the fear was rooted in stereotypes my students had developed about people living in poverty. Somehow, this group had become demonized in their minds, joining the ranks of the "bad guys."

Conversations about class are taboo in many circles. These conversations require people to face hard truths about the United States, to confront the myth of meritocracy as demonstrated in the nation as a whole and in our own neighborhoods, and to think critically about personal responsibility. This conversation would be difficult for many adults, and here I was asking 12- and 13-year-olds to engage in it. Complicating the issue, some of the students sitting in that classroom, perhaps even leading the discussion, *were* poor. Choosing to ignore these topics because they are difficult to navigate, however, comes at a great cost to all of us, especially to students like Casey.

A Step Removed: Fiction as a Teaching Tool

When topics hit so close to my students' lives, I find they can sometimes be approached most tenderly through fiction. By both reading and writing fiction, where actions and consequences are one step removed from the real world, students can think through issues that apply to their own lives. Fiction also provides a way of talking about these issues. We are, after all, talking about characters in a book rather than ourselves.

With this in mind, I arrived in class the next day carrying the illustrated book *Fly Away Home* by Eve Bunting (1991), hoping it would create an entry point for a discussion about poverty. The book's main characters, a six-year-old boy and his father, live in an airport. They try not to be noticed. They dress carefully, all in blue: blue jeans, blue shirts, and blue jackets. They create lists to be sure they sleep in a different terminal each night. Partway through the story, the boy's father boards a bus for his daily commute to work. When his father is away, the boy is cared for by another family that lives in the airport. That family also has a young son. The two boys have a conversation about their longing for a home, vowing that whoever gets one first will invite the other's family to come and live there too. The sting of irony that these boys spend their days watching people arrive from their travels, hugging family members who have come to drive them *home*, is palpable.

I find that open-ended questions reveal the most what my students are thinking. I also try to ask questions that won't embarrass them. Few of us feel comfortable even acknowledging our own rough edges, including the stereotypes we carry, let alone admitting them in public. So rather than beginning by asking my students to name stereotypes they had about homeless people, I waited until after we read *Fly Away Home*, and then I asked what stereotypes about homelessness and poverty were *broken* for them by the characters in the story. They reported that they liked the characters; they didn't find them at all scary. Instead, the characters seemed like people they knew. They weren't dirty; they washed themselves in the airport bathrooms and had a change of clothes. They didn't beg for money; in fact, both the father and the son worked. The tiny boy helped people carry their luggage, and the father worked as a janitor. And they wanted a home.

We struggled together to find a working definition of *poverty* and agreed on this: People who are poor are not consistently able to meet at least one of their basic needs. I began to tread lightly, sensitive to the fact that some of my students' families currently were in that very position, whereas other students would be shocked to learn that poverty might be experienced by people they knew.

The story helped us talk about reasons people might become homeless. The boy's mother had died; we considered the cost of medical emergencies. As the conversation evolved, the examples my students shared came increasingly from their home lives and personal experiences. Several of their fathers recently had been laid off and were away from home, working in oil fields on the Montana–Wyoming border or in Alaska or anyplace they could find a job. During our weekly sharing time, I heard the excitement in their voices on the rare weekends when their fathers were able to come home for a visit.

Bearing Witness: The Role of Nonfiction

In the midst of difficult conversations about poverty, sometimes the dominant, deficit-laced narrative appears in student reactions, as it did when one of my students called out, "Hobos are lazy. They *choose* to be homeless!" Statements like these are, perhaps, attempts to find a way out of discomfort, allowing students, as well as adults, to absolve themselves from taking responsibility for issues like homelessness. Those of us who have never experienced poverty may never have had opportunities to hear the stories of people for whom poverty has been all too real. So although reading a fictional story like *Fly Away Home* is often a safe starting point for conversation, some students might dismiss it as a work of fiction.

Had my students not so easily named groups that are dehumanized in our school community, I may never have considered the possibility that the pedagogical strategies I used when studying the Holocaust might also be applied to facilitate inquiry into other issues of inhumanity. Once that connection was made, however, I began to find more ways to transfer pedagogical techniques and terminologies.

Testimony, for example, is a common way of encouraging students to personalize the stories of Holocaust survivors. It can be easy to dehumanize people with whom we have had no experience. Hearing personal testimony, nonfictional stories of people's lives, makes this kind of dismissal more difficult. I wondered how to apply this model so that the student who thought he "knew" that people chose to be homeless might be invited to consider poverty from a different perspective.

I had limited access to speakers who had survived the Holocaust, so I relied on testimony from the DVD included in *Echoes and Reflections* (2006), a Holocaust curriculum that is a joint effort of the Anti-Defamation League, the University of Southern California Shoah Foundation, and Yad Vashem. I have found that these sorts of video and audio recordings provide an opportunity to hear from, rather than conjecture about, the lives of people who might not be sitting in the room.

I didn't know anyone who was homeless who might actually speak in class. It didn't seem likely that any of my students would speak about their experiences with poverty—the attitudes that had been expressed clearly didn't make that a safe thing to reveal. One morning on the way to work, I heard an episode of NPR's StoryCorp about a woman who lost her job with the state suddenly and unexpectedly, just before retirement (NPR, 2011). Unable to find another job, she lost her home. During this short audio broadcast, she described being in a position in which she never thought she would find herself; she asked people on the street for money in order to buy her daughter a birthday card.

My students listened attentively to this story. Then I asked them to write a short response about what stereotypes had been broken for them in what they just heard. One student wrote, "It makes me realize that everyone has a story, homeless people too." Another wrote, "It makes me think of the hard times I know a lot of families are going through right now."

A common stereotype about seventh graders is that they are egocentric, that few are capable of feeling or expressing empathy. Perhaps the truth is that on the basis of this assumption, we too rarely select content that might invite middle school students to tap into their own capabilities to practice empathy.

Recognizing Our Power: The Roles We Choose

Returning to one of my original hopes for our inquiry into issues of class, I drew on another pedagogical strategy from Holocaust education. I wanted my students to come to understand their own agency in the choices they made regarding their interactions with the people around them. When we see someone asking for money on the street, for example, we have choices to make. When confronted with a person different from us in some way, we choose how we treat him or her. When we hear others around us engaged in name-calling or dehumanization, we alone control how we react. To facilitate this discussion, I introduced four terms commonly used in Holocaust education, terms increasingly also used in bully-prevention curricula: *perpetrator*, *ally* (or *upstander*), *target* (or *victim*), and *bystander* (Anti-Defamation League, 2006). To familiarize students with these terms, I asked them to use them to describe people's actions or inactions during the Holocaust. The truth is that people rarely enact just one of these roles. Instead, we make choices, every minute of every day, about which role we will play in relationship to another person. I wanted my students to understand that if they choose the role of perpetrator one minute, in the next minute they have the option of making a different choice. These choices represent one source of our personal power.

During the Holocaust, many people acted as bystanders. My students often are critical of the fact that so many people made this choice, but when they examine their own behavior, they often realize that they frequently make the same choice. It takes courage to speak truth to power. Taking such a risk sometimes comes at great personal cost. Again, there are plenty of examples of people who took this kind of risk during the Holocaust. But how often do we show our students similar examples of people or groups acting as upstanders in issues of conscience facing our world today? Who are the people making choices to end poverty in our world, our nation, and our own communities? How might our students imagine themselves making similar choices?

Teachers can bring in the director of the local food bank or a nearby homeless shelter; we could show video of protestors occupying Wall Street—a movement that spurred protests all over the country. We can address a serious omission in how students tend to learn about Martin Luther King, Jr., who had come to realize that issues of racial injustice and economic injustice were inextricably linked. In fact, before his assassination, Dr. King had been planning the Poor People's Campaign, an interracial gathering of poor and working-class people from across the country. Ralph Abernathy and the

Southern Christian Leadership Conference continued with the plans, and a protest that became known as Resurrection City was held on the mall in Washington, DC, in June 1968 (Kelly, 2011). I have used websites like one created by Tavis Smiley and Cornel West called *The Poverty Tour 2.0: A Call to Conscience* (2012).

Sitting in our classrooms are future leaders. How might these young people ever be able to imagine themselves solving issues like poverty if they don't come to recognize the power they have in their daily lives? Asking students to examine the roles they choose in their daily lives might help them envision taking a leadership role in the school yard and as they continue out into the world.

Owning Our Imperfections

Educators can play an important role in helping students understand their personal power. We also serve as role models, and we need to recognize that we teach by example at every moment. If we sponsor an assembly or a "spirit day" where we allow, or even encourage, students to enact stereotypes by dressing in ways that stereotype groups of people like "hillbillies" or "hobos," we are teaching that it is acceptable to dehumanize others. We should not be surprised, then, when we hear slurs in our hallways.

I will confess that, in the past, I sometimes have stood silently by or, worse, laughed as these stereotypes were perpetuated. At times I have not even recognized a stereotype in the moment because it reflected my own bias.

In *The Courage to Teach*, Parker Palmer (1998) wrote that we teach who we are, for better or for worse. I, for one, have work to do. Beverly Tatum (1997) explained that if we are not actively engaged in antiracism work, then we perpetuate racism. Thanks to Casey, I have come to recognize that the same is true for class inequality. I understand, as well, that I must engage students with these important topics. As with all good inquiry, my students and I can move forward together, recognizing the power we have to act, both individually and collectively.

As a result of our work in class, Casey must have gained the confidence to claim at least some of his power. One day he came into class and loudly proclaimed, "Yes, I live in a trailer, but I am *not* trailer trash!" I smiled, buoyed by his courage. He continued, "Neither are most of the people in my trailer park. In fact, there's only one person who is."

Oh, dear.

I smiled, knowing young people are, like the rest of us, navigating the complexities of their worlds the best ways they can. Changes to their thinking won't happen in a day. My hope, as a teacher, is to nudge them into imagining the kind of world they'd like to see and the kind of human they'd like to be.

References

Anti-Defamation League. (2006). *Echoes and reflections: A multimedia curriculum on the Holocaust*. New York, Los Angeles, Jerusalem: Anti-Defamation League, USC Shoah Foundation, Yad Vashem.

Bunting, E. (1991). *Fly away home*. (Illustrated by R. Himler.) New York: Clarion Books.

Kelly, J. (2011, December 3). Before occupy D.C., there was Resurrection City. *Washington Post*. Retrieved October 14, 2012, from www.washingtonpost .com/local/before-occupy-dc-there-was-resurrection-city/2011/12/01/ gIQAoNqcPO_story.html

NPR. (2011). *Homeless at 60: "A bullet I didn't see coming."* Retrieved from www.npr.org/2011/12/16/143771611/homeless-at-60-a-bullet-i-didnt-see -coming

Palmer, P. (1998). *The courage to teach: Exploring the inner landscape of a teacher's life*. San Francisco: Jossey-Bass.

Smiley, T., & West, C. (2012). *The poverty tour 2.0: A call to conscience*. Retrieved October 14, 2012, from www.povertytour.smileyandwest.com

Starnes, B. A. (2005). Thoughts on teaching: And the winner is . . . *Phi Delta Kappan, 86*(10), 795–796.

Tatum, B. D. (1997). *Why are all the Black kids sitting together in the cafeteria? And other conversations about race*. New York: Basic Books.

31

LITERACY LEARNING AND CLASS ISSUES
A Rationale for Resisting Classism and Deficit Thinking

Peggy Semingson

People from poor families are <u>not always presented in positive ways in</u> <u>mainstream discourses about education</u>. The major problem, as I see it, is the prevalence of deficit thinking and stereotypes about poor people in these discourses and, in particular, within the broader context of education (Bomer, Dworin, May, & Semingson, 2008; Gorski, 2012). Like many educators, I often find myself wondering <u>what I can do to resist the discrimination and</u> <u>inequity that result</u>, in part, <u>from this sort of deficit thinking</u>. <u>I want to challenge</u> <u>myths about poor families and to resist stereotypes rather than perpetuate them.</u>

To resist and interrogate this deficit paradigm about poor families, teachers and teacher educators need to <u>design curriculum and select</u> materials that <u>deliberately incorporate content about class and poverty</u>. I have found that learning experiences that use authentic materials about the poor can have a twofold purpose: (a) <u>to expose and question the structural conditions that underlie poverty</u>, such as overarching issues of racism, classism, and inequity, and (b) <u>to challenge</u> <u>negative and persistent stereotypes about poor people</u>. As our current economic climate shifts and more families encounter poverty, these goals become even more urgent for our schools and society.

In this chapter I advocate for and describe critical literacy practices (Freebody & Luke, 1990) with which I have attempted to resist classism in PK–12 settings, as well as higher education. Building on the critical literacy paradigm (Vasquez, 2004), I focus specifically on matters of class and classism and on resisting and interrogating mainstream stereotypes about poor people. With this goal in mind, I share methods and materials that can be modified for and implemented in PK–12 classroom settings, after-school programs, home contexts, and teacher education programs.

As a first step, we can select curricular materials and methods that embrace critical literacy (Morrell, 2008; Stevens & Bean, 2007; Vasquez, 2004, 2010). These texts, when carefully chosen, provide possibilities for transformative and dialogic pedagogy. Stevens and Bean (2007) drew on Freebody and Luke (1990) in defining critical literacy as one of the four processes that readers should employ when encountering text. Along with the more familiar practices of code breaker (coding competence), meaning maker (semantic competence) and text user (pragmatic competence), we need to consider the practice of reader as text critic. (p. 5)

Critical literacy is impactful because when we adopt that "critic" perspective, it pushes us to reflect on and disrupt popular deficit perspectives about poor people. As an example, a deficit perspective might assume that poor people don't often use language in the proper, formal register (Payne, 2005). Critical literacy can question this belief, examine the claims and premises that purport to support it, and offer counterexamples in which the poor skillfully use formal and stylistic language in essays, oral speech, poetry, and other forms.

I begin this exploration with a commitment to dialogic pedagogies that value discussion and input from students, which I have found to be most effective as the basis for transforming student thinking (Nichols, 2006). I point to specific literary materials that are aligned with a critical literacy framework and the need for open discussion, these becoming the core underpinnings of my curricular suggestions. I also suggest specific children's books and young adult novels that can be used in both PK–12 and teacher education settings to spur discussion about poverty, class, and economic justice and challenge deficit views. Meanwhile, throughout the chapter, I pose reflective questions that can be used to deepen our own and our students' thinking and to bolster our beliefs about students from families in poverty.

The Deficit Approach

A deficit approach assumes that poor students and families are to blame for economic and other circumstances that surround them (Valencia, 1997, 2010). Unfortunately, this approach often is reflected in teacher professional development programs. For example, one popular program offered by Ruby Payne and associates, and based on her book *A Framework for Understanding Poverty* (2005), has been analyzed in terms of content and the way it characterizes poor students and their families (Bomer, Dworin, May, & Semingson, 2008). By examining Payne's language, truth claims, and ideologies, researchers discovered that many of the claims she makes about poor families depict a deficit view. More specifically, the researchers found that Payne made claims about the poor that can be divided into four main categories: social structures, daily life, language, and characteristics of individuals. Her claims, they found, often were inconsistent with decades of scholarship. However, the program and its premises about poor families remain widely popular in the United States and, increasingly, internationally.

One function of the deficit perspective is to inscribe poor students and families as lacking knowledge of "middle-class values" (e.g., Payne, 2005). In contrast, an additive viewpoint values the student, her or his family, and their knowledge as valuable assets and not as something to be "fixed." Additive models recognize the learning that happens in poor families and communities as valuable (Moll & González, 2004). On the basis of this additive view, educators, scholars, and activists have debunked the deficit premises of Payne's approach. A good synthesis of these efforts can be found in Gorski's "Peddling Poverty for Profit" (2008).

Challenging the Deficit Perspective

What, then, are the positive and additive alternatives to deficit thinking? We can begin by examining popular approaches to working with low-income students, watching out for deficit assumptions along the way. To do this effectively, we must be familiar with larger structural issues regarding poverty such as joblessness, inadequate housing, and low wages and how they affect our students and their families. Only then will we be prepared to draw on an ecological (Bronfenbrenner, 1979) or holistic viewpoint of children and families and focus on educating the "whole child," which requires familiarity with the broader context and material conditions in which she or he lives. This is not just fluffiness. After all, according to Henderson, Mapp, Johnson, and Davies (2007), schools that address larger issues that impact poor children and families have a positive effect on student retention, achievement, and family engagement.

Once we acknowledge and help address these larger concerns, we can design curricula that challenge deficit perspectives about poor students and their families. Next I discuss the components of one approach for doing just that: critical literacy pedagogy. I also describe specific resources that can be used to challenge deficit views in PK–12 and teacher education contexts.

Creating a Space for Dialogue

Educators at all levels can design curricula that involve open dialogue (Bomer & Bomer, 2001). Open dialogue provides a safe space for critical literacy learning; it opens, for example, a time and place to explore stories from poor students and families that challenge deficit views. In fact, this type of dialogue can help facilitate mutual understanding of a wide range of difficult topics such as classism, racism, and sexism.

Even a popular practice like reading workshop (Atwell, 1998; Calkins, 1994) can provide a space for students to engage in this practice. Reading workshop is a literacy teaching structure that supports students in developing reading skills while allowing them to select their own reading materials. Teachers can engage students in reflective conversations about the texts through the written journal the students in reading workshop keep, providing time for conversation among classmates or working with them directly in personalized conferences. Because reading workshop also includes opportunities for teachers to read *to* students, teachers can select stories about poverty and model the types of open dialogue techniques before, during, and after the class experiences such a text.

Conversations That Support a Critical Literacy Framework

It might be easy to assume that critical literacy and open dialogue should be reserved for older students. However, in a classroom in which open dialogue and conversation are supported, even the youngest students can participate in conversations that question mainstream perspectives (Vasquez, 2004). Bomer and Bomer (2001) argued that teachers at all levels should talk about topics such as money, class, race, peace, and nature, among others, in order to model and teach critical reading and thinking. They explained,

> To read critically, one needs to pay attention to concepts that, although they are ever-present in daily life, usually go unexamined in most communities—things that seem to be the way they are necessarily, as if nature had made them this way. (p. 27)

Dialogue about these sorts of topics can be enhanced through the posing of thoughtful open-ended questions. These questions can connect to themes like poverty and social class in children's books or young adult novels that students read. The questions I list in Table 31.1 are centered on the crucial concepts described by Bomer and Bomer (2001) and focus on three poverty-related concepts: money, class, and labor.

When topics related to class and race are incorporated explicitly into PK–12 classrooms, the resulting dialogue can combat stereotypes and, as a result, create the opportunity for deeper learning about larger structural issues related to poverty and social class.

Similarly, when teacher educators model these pedagogies, teacher candidates learn how to incorporate dialogue strategies into their own literacy instruction. Among the best tools I have found for this are children's books and young adult novels, as well as nonfiction texts that address social class, classism, and the lives of poor people. Specifically, in both PK–12 and higher

TABLE 31.1
Critical Questions About Topics Related to Social Class and Poverty

Concepts From Bomer and Bomer (2001)	Possible Spin-Off Questions That Can Be Incorporated Within Literacy Instruction
Money	• What is the purpose of money? • Do we need money? • Why do we need money? • Who controls the money and/or goods in the text we are reading? Why?
Class	• Why are poor people poor? • How are poor people treated in society? • What representations of poor people do you see in the media? How accurate are they, and how do we know?
Labor	• Why do some people earn more money for the work they do? Is this fair? • What does it mean to have a "living wage"?

Note: Adapted from concepts from Bomer and Bomer (2001).

education contexts, I have tried to incorporate these sorts of books into read-alouds, guided reading, book clubs, literature circles, and writing workshop.

In the next section I share some examples of specific ways to integrate class-specific children's books and young adult novels into literacy learning at a wide range of age levels.

Children's Literature and Class-Based Critical Literacy

Children's books and young adult novels combined with authentic class discussion can transform learning, encouraging students to engage in dialogue about important topics (Bomer & Bomer, 2001). Of course, when selecting materials we shouldn't select books that explicitly or indirectly stereotype poor children, children of color, or other groups. On the other hand stories that incorporate characters from a variety of racial and class backgrounds can provide opportunities for especially rich discussions about the complexities of race and class such as the racial dimensions of social class. This intersection is explored in Faith Ringgold's poetic and artistic picture book *Tar Beach* (1991).

All of the texts I describe here were helpful to me during my eight years teaching in public schools in California and Texas, working primarily in bilingual education contexts. Grounded primarily in the genres of realistic fiction and personal narrative, they portray concerns related to class, poverty, and hardship. Of course, despite my focus on these two genres, other types of expository literature, such as biography, autobiography, and memoir, can expose students to similar concerns.

Stories That Counter the Idea of Poor People as "Lazy" or Uncaring Parents

As Stephanie Jones (2008), who writes about education, social class, and literacy learning, argued, "Books offer visions of who we can be, who we are, who an ideal person is and how lives are lived and dreams are dreamed" (p. 44). It is particularly important for disenfranchised students to see their identities reflected in books—to see positive and empowered storybook characters experiencing lives of poverty without a sense of shame. The goal of these experiences is to challenge stereotypes without presenting the world through rose-colored glasses, not wanting to present a sensationalized or glamorized view of poverty that is oblivious to the real issues such as joblessness and inadequate housing, among others. It is a way to bring the voices of those who often are marginalized to the forefront of literacy learning.

Books That Represent Perseverance Amidst Poverty

The goal of critical literacy reading instruction isn't to reproduce the social class structure or to encourage all students to aspire to the consumerist values of capitalism. Students need to be able to hear, read, and otherwise have access to stories that represent narratives that challenge those that are rooted primarily in middle-class voices as filtered through consumer culture. Three picture books that accomplish this task, depicting working-class families who persevere despite difficult financial circumstances, are *Coming on Home Soon* (2004) by Jacqueline Woodson, *A Chair for My Mother* (1982) by Vera Williams, and *Uncle Jed's Barbershop* (1993) by Margaree King Mitchell.

In all three books, characters face challenges trying to make ends meet but find virtue in their work ethic, the support of family, and the values of the broader community. The picture book *Coming on Home Soon* (Woodson, 2004) is set during World War II when, in the era of Rosie the Riveter, women assumed traditionally male jobs. An African American mother, who the reader can infer is a single wage earner, heads to Chicago to work not only to support her family but also to support her country. Such positive portrayals of women of color and working-class women offer insight into the reasons people work as well as the hardships they face. The text suggests a strong sense of family values amidst the nuances of a working-class life, challenging deficit views that portray poor families as dysfunctional and poor parents as lazy. Teachers can use this book to encourage discussion about the ways that class intersects with race and gender.

A Chair for My Mother (Williams, 1982) focuses on the theme of perseverance in a working-class family. It depicts a working-class mother who saves money for a chair she can enjoy after a fire destroys many of her family's material belongings. Although the text does not focus explicitly on poverty, it implicitly offers a positive portrayal of industrious working women, single mothers, and families of color.

Similarly, *Uncle Jed's Barbershop* (Mitchell, 1993) takes place during the Great Depression, when many people from a variety of identity groups faced poverty, financial hardship, and other difficulties. Uncle Jed, an African American man, works hard to reach his dream of owning a barbershop. The barbershop is more of a community gathering place than a purely for-profit business. Uncle Jed is vitally connected to his community and makes financial sacrifices to help others, challenging perceptions that poor people are lazy, don't care about their children, and do not want to work. About Uncle Jed's dream, the author wrote, "He had been saying the same thing for years. Nobody believed him. People didn't have dreams like that in those days."

This book opens opportunities for exploring a wide range of important questions. I often ask students, "Why didn't anyone believe in Uncle Jed's dream?" This steps us toward an opportunity to discuss important historical intersections of race and class. I might ask, "How were African Americans denied access to the 'American Dream'?" Other aspects that might be explored through *Uncle Jed's Barbershop* include the life of a sharecropper, the Great Depression, and the role of barbershops in African American communities.

Young Adult Books for Older Readers

Older students (Grades 5–12) may benefit from reading Sandra Cisneros's *The House on Mango Street* (1989). This collection of realistic vignettes, or short "slices of life," is built on the narratives of a young Latina girl in Chicago who is facing poverty and a variety of other challenges related to mobility, gender and sexism, family, friendship, religion, and the coming-of-age process. For instance, in the title story, a character named Esperanza is shamed by a nun from her school who ridicules the house she lives in and asks her incredulously if she really lives there. Open-ended questions that will help readers explore counternarratives to the sense of shame that is imposed on Esperanza might include "How does Esperanza respond to the shaming of her poverty?" and "What strength does she find in herself to resist the shame and stereotype of poor families and their houses?"

Other books that present characters that face poverty in complex ways include *Out of the Dust* (1997) by Karen Hesse, *Buried Onions* (1997) by Gary Soto, and *The Skin I'm In* by Sharon G. Flake (1998). *The Hundred Dresses* (1944) by Eleanor Estes is an excellent book for introducing ways poor students can be targets of bullying and how inaction in response to bullying can be just as devastating as the cruel actions of the bully. The complexity of the character Maddie, who is poor, and her fears that she will be the next victim of bullying are compelling fodder for discussion, as is her complicitous silence that enables the main character, Peggy, to continue taunting Wanda. This point of tension in the book presents an opportunity to discuss ways our silence perpetuates racism, classism, and other forms of discrimination.

Memoir, Biography, and Personal Narrative

Memoir and biographical picture books and novels can provide alternate narratives, some with inspiring endings and others with the gritty reality of what life can be like for people who are poor. An example of just such a memoir-like picture book is *La Mariposa* (1998) by Francisco Jiménez, which depicts moments in the life of the immigrant narrator, who is poor. The text touches on additional themes like culture shock, cruelty from classmates, and the challenge of learning a new language. Francisco, the main character, finds meaning in art, his inner life, and his own culture and family. Educators using *La Mariposa* can connect themes of racism, classism, and linguistic isolation; the metaphorical transformation of the butterfly (*mariposa*) emerging from the chrysalis represents Francisco's emergence from shame, alienation, and disconnect. Amidst poverty, and despite the deficit views others had of him, Francisco found strength in family, culture, and his awareness of his own strengths and talents. This text, based on the life of the author, offers a complex and nuanced perspective of a student and family living in poverty.

Conclusion

As the poet and activist Audre Lorde (1984) stated, "The master's tools will never dismantle the master's house" (p. 123). We must hear and share voices from people who experience what it is we are trying to understand. One place to find these voices is in children's books and young adult novels that depict people who have experienced poverty in ways that highlight their resiliency, determination, and strength in the face of systemic classism. Even better, we can teach and learn from texts written in the voices of the resilient communities themselves.

Teachers and teacher educators must create a dialogic space to foster the sharing of these voices, validate silenced perspectives, and encourage students to think in just, rather than deficit-laden, ways about social class and poverty (Bomer & Bomer, 2001). A critical literacy framework (Bomer & Bomer, 2001; Morrell, 2008; Vasquez, 2004), in particular, can foster critical examination of the larger economic and political systems through which social injustice and inequities such as poverty persist.

By reading storybook texts, novels, and memoirs that focus on class, students can gain insight into the nuanced complexities of the lives of people in poverty. Jones (2004) suggested creating classroom environments in which students' voices and experiences are validated as they share, write, and participate in the classroom community. Of course, the teacher must carefully facilitate such an environment, and this takes time, energy, and intentionality.

Acknowledging stereotypes is not enough. We also need to challenge the structural inequities at work in poor and working-class children's lives. By acknowledging and examining the broader social and economic justice concerns that impact poor families, including racism, the scarcity of living-wage work, and unequal access to quality health care, we position ourselves to offer clearer counternarratives to those that blame poor students and families for the conditions that press on them the hardest.

Children's Literature Cited

Cisneros, S. (1989). *The house on Mango Street*. New York: Vintage.
Estes, E. (1944). *The hundred dresses*. New York: Scholastic.
Flake, S. G. (1998). *The skin I'm in*. New York: Hyperion.
Hesse, K. (1997). *Out of the dust*. New York: Scholastic.
Jiménez, F. (1998). *La mariposa*. Boston: Houghton Mifflin.
Mitchell, M. K. (1993). *Uncle Jed's barbershop*. New York: Simon & Schuster.
Ringgold, F. (1991). *Tar beach*. New York: Crown Publishers.
Soto, G. (1997). *Buried onions*. San Diego: Harcourt Brace.
Williams, V. (1982). *A chair for my mother*. New York: HarperCollins.
Woodson, J. (2004). *Coming on home soon*. New York: G.P. Putnam's Sons.

References

Atwell, N. (1998). *In the middle: New understandings about writing, reading, and learning*. Portsmouth, NH: Heinemann.
Bomer, R., & Bomer, K. (2001). *For a better world: Reading and writing for social action*. Portsmouth, NH: Heinemann.

Bomer, R., Dworin, J. E., May, L., & Semingson, P. (2008). Miseducating teachers about the poor: A critical analysis of Ruby Payne's claims about poverty. *Teachers College Record*, *110*(12), 2497–2531. Retrieved June 15, 2012, from www.tcrecord.org/content.asp?contentid=14591

Bronfenbrenner, U. (1979). *The ecology of human development*. Cambridge, MA: Harvard University Press.

Calkins, L. (1994). *The art of teaching writing*. Portsmouth, NH: Heinemann.

Freebody, P., & Luke, A. (1990). Literacies programs: Debates and demands in cultural context. *Prospect: Australian Journal of TESOL*, *5*(7), 7–16.

Gorski, P. C. (2008). Peddling poverty for profit: A synthesis of criticisms of Ruby Payne's framework. *Equity and Excellence in Education*, *41*(1), 130–148.

Gorski, P. C. (2012). Perceiving the problem of poverty and schooling: Deconstructing the class stereotypes that misshape education practice and policy. *Equity and Excellence in Education*, *45*(2), 302–319.

Henderson, A. T., Mapp, K. L., Johnson, V. R., & Davies, D. (2007). *Beyond the bake sale: The essential guide to family-school-partnerships*. New York: New Press.

Jones, S. (2004). Living poverty and literacy learning: Sanctioning the topics of students' lives. *Language Arts*, *81*(6), 461–469.

Jones, S. (2008). Grass houses: Representations and reinventions of social class through children's literature. *Journal of Language and Literacy Education*, *4*(2), 40–58. Retrieved July 29, 2012, from http://jolle.coe.uga.edu/archive/2008/representations.pdf

Lorde, A. (1984). *Sister outsider: Essays and speeches*. Santa Cruz, CA: Crossing Press.

Moll, L. C., & González, N. (2004). Engaging life: A funds of knowledge approach to multicultural education. In J. Banks & C. McGee Banks (Eds.), *Handbook of research on multicultural education* (2nd ed., pp. 699–715). San Francisco: Jossey-Bass.

Morrell, E. (2008). *Critical literacy and urban youth: Pedagogies of access, dissent, and liberation*. New York: Routledge.

Nichols, M. (2006). *Comprehension through conversation: The power of purposeful talk in the reading workshop*. Portsmouth, NH: Heinemann.

Payne, R. K. (2005). *A framework for understanding poverty* (4th ed.). Highlands, TX: RFT.

Stevens, L. P., & Bean, T. W. (2007). *Critical literacy: Context, research and practice in the K–12 classroom*. New York: Sage.

Valencia, R. R. (1997). Conceptualizing the notion of deficit thinking. In R. Valencia (Ed.), *The evolution of deficit thinking* (pp. 1–12). London: Falmer Press.

Valencia, R. R. (2010). *Dismantling contemporary deficit thinking: Educational thought and practice*. New York: Routledge.

Vasquez, V. (2004). *Negotiating critical literacies with young children*. Mahwah, NJ: Lawrence Erlbaum.

Vasquez, V. (2010). *Getting beyond "I like the book": Creating space for critical literacy in K-6 classrooms* (2nd ed.). Newark, DE: International Reading Association.

32

IMAGINING AN EQUITY PEDAGOGY FOR STUDENTS IN POVERTY

Paul C. Gorski

I was incredulous when my friend Susan, the principal of a middle school in the southwestern United States, told me that she was being forced by the district to cut her art and music programs. "Test scores," she lamented. "Our scores are not where we want them to be, and certainly not where the district wants them to be." As a result, the district insisted that Susan share her music and art teachers with two other middle schools. "It should work out," she told me, "because more than half of our students will be spending an extra hour each day in math and writing instruction. We're trading art and music for math and writing, like almost every other school on this side of the district."

By "this side of the district," Susan meant the *poor* side of the district. Nearly 90% of her students were eligible for free and reduced lunch. Their parents and guardians epitomized the working poor, often piecing together two, three, or four minimum-wage jobs just to pay the rent and put food on the table.

The district's decision to cut the art and music programs in its lower income middle schools and Susan's capitulation (understanding, of course, that she had little choice but to capitulate) to that decision illustrate what, to me, is the most formidable barrier to the realization of class equity in the U.S. public education system: a serious, if not delirious, case of beneficent shortsightedness on the parts of, well, just about all of us. Susan, like the individuals in her district office, and probably like you, is no ravaging "classist." In fact, she's an outspoken advocate for low-income students and their families. Why, then, was she willing to deny her most struggling, most economically disadvantaged, students access to art and music education—important components, by most any measure, of a holistic liberal education?

The list of educational absolutes is relatively short. There are very few things that we know, and have known for decades, work well for virtually all students. We know, for instance, that students learn more effectively when what they are learning is made relevant to their lives. But we also know this: Students who have access to art and music education perform better in school, and are more likely to graduate, than their peers who do not have access to art and music education (Landsman & Gorski, 2007).

In fact, in-school access to art and music education is especially important to poor and working-class students (Heath & Roach, 1999; Pogrow, 2006).

This stands to reason, of course, because poor and working-class families are less likely than their more economically advantaged counterparts to be able to afford to provide their children with these experiences outside of school (Bracey, 2006). Interestingly, according to Stacey Joyner and Concepcion Molina (2012), who synthesized a broad range of research on how extending instructional time affects student learning for the Southwest Educational Development Laboratory, there is scant evidence that simply lengthening instructional time for math or writing increases student achievement. More important than instructional *time*, they found, was instructional *quality*. This is an important point, and we will return to it momentarily.

Irrationality: A Bad Approach for Educational Equity

First, though, consider this: Why, given what we know, would anybody with the best interests of low-income students at heart think it's a good idea to eliminate art and music education as a strategy for bolstering their academic achievement? A good bit of the trouble, in my estimation, stems from the pressure of high-stakes testing and the heaviness of hyperaccountability. The pressure and heaviness appear to be making some education folks in powerful places a little irrational, willing, or at least hesitantly agreeing, to do all manner of things that we know, and that research shows, are bad for youth and especially for low-income youth. But then, when each of us, from students to teachers to administrators, is being judged on irrationally narrow assessments that don't account for conditions over which we have no control—disparities in school funding, access to health care, access to living wage work, and more—and when our integrity or our job is under attack, we can be forgiven a bit of irrationality.

One sign of this irrationality is the way so many of us, knowing how the obsession with standardized testing—an obsession so out of whack that in some states *kindergartners are given standardized tests*—deteriorates our own agency as educators and, as a result, students' access to fulfilling learning experiences, still somehow get sucked into talking about student success on the basis of test scores. Today I hear much, much more about raising poor students' test scores than about creating equitable schools. Worse, I hear people using the goal of "raising test scores" as a proxy for creating equitable educational opportunity.

To be clear, I know *why* this happens. I understand that all this talk about test scores is a setup for teachers. I recognize that livelihoods are at risk, especially for people who work at high-poverty schools.

Many of the educators with chapters in this book talk about deficit ideology or the deficit perspective. Deficit ideology is a view that sees low-income youth and families as deficient, as "the problem." Deficit ideologues fail or refuse to see low-income people as resilient—as citizens who have to overcome a lot, including the denial of basic rights like access to health care, in order to survive a society in which the odds are stacked against them.

Well, I believe schoolteachers and administrators, and particularly those who choose to work at low-income schools, also are targets of a kind of deficit ideology. The media, informed mostly by people who never have experienced the challenge or delight of engaging a roomful of 30-some young people with all manner of gifts and needs and curiosities, love to target teachers and ignore shrinking budgets and the pressures of high-stakes testing, not to mention the resegregation of schools by socioeconomic status. Political commentators and policy wonks love to compare test scores between schools that are resourced at vastly different levels while remaining devastatingly silent on the inequitable distribution of pristine science labs, AP programs, athletic fields, school nurses, and computer labs. Teacher unions are particularly popular targets.

Given this scorn, I fear that many of my educator friends are buying in largely as a matter of survival. One such friend, an elementary principal at a high-poverty school, explained, "If we don't raise those scores, we risk the state taking over our school, firing our teachers, and stealing from us whatever integrity we have left in the face of this No Child Left Behind and Race to the Top craziness." Test scores, test scores, test scores.

Obviously, all of us want all students to succeed. Really—who would dedicate their lives to teaching if they weren't committed to so basic a goal? Not an ounce of me questions the desire of teachers, teachers' aides, counselors, administrators, and others who spend their lives surrounded by youth to create equitable schools. There are plenty of careers whose workers are less underpaid and underappreciated for people who think they want to be teachers but then decide they just aren't invested enough in the well-being of disenfranchised youth to stay in the profession. Those folks don't tend to stick around very long—at least not in low-income schools.

However, after spending the past several years studying low-income families' experiences in public schools, I am concerned with what we are and are not doing when it comes to realizing the goal of equitable schools for poor youth. The problem, as I have come to see it, is not that we don't *want* to create more equitable classrooms and schools but that we spend tremendous amounts of resources pursuing strategies for doing so that either do not work or, worse, widen the gaps we so desperately want to eliminate.

My intention for the remainder of this chapter is to identify a few of these popular but ineffective strategies and then to turn to what research has shown in a variety of contexts to be effective strategies for strengthening engagement and learning among low-income youth. I am careful, in both cases, to cite studies from the hefty and growing mounds of research on poverty and schooling in order to demonstrate, first of all, that there *is* evidence for what does and does not work. But I also do so in order to show how popular perceptions and even "common sense" often conflict with reality, so that we can't always rely on what "feels right." In fact, sometimes common sense or what "feels right" can be more a reflection of our biases than a blueprint for effective teaching.

First, though, I feel compelled to emphasize a sad but important-to-acknowledge reality: We never will realize educational equity in any full sense until we address bigger economic justice concerns. The symptoms of economic injustice infest schools in a variety of ways. Those of us who have worked in or with poor communities or their schools tend to be pretty well attuned to this reality because we see in youth and their families the implications of food insecurity, the scarcity of living-wage work, unequal access to health care, and the grinding effects of class bias. In a society that prides itself on being a meritocracy—a myth dispelled by several chapters in this book—we haven't even managed to guarantee equitable access to what we call the "great equalizer": education. This is a notable failure for the wealthiest country in the world. Educators should not be held more responsible for the effects of these injustices than anyone else; obviously, the changes required to address them are long-term projects.

It also is true that we can't afford to wait, and poor families can't afford to wait, for an economic revolution. Even as I commit to bigger forms of societal change, I have to commit *now* to doing what I can do to address the repression people are experiencing in this moment, right before me. Of course, to do so effectively, I have to know that what I'm doing actually works—that it doesn't perpetuate the inequities I abhor.

Ineffective (but Popular) Strategies for Educating Poor Youth

I already have pointed out the irrational strategy of eliminating art and music education in order to carve out additional instructional time in math and science. Unfortunately, this is only one of the ways schools unintentionally do harm to poor youth in the name of raising test scores. Two other common and ineffective strategies for strengthening class equity include (a) foregoing engaging pedagogical approaches for lower order pedagogies and (b) tracking or "ability grouping."

 ### *Direct Instruction and Other Lower Order Pedagogies*

Teaching to the test. What does it say about the state of public schooling when a phrase like this becomes part of the education lexicon? As with most bad pedagogical approaches, low-income students are more subject than their wealthier peers to *teaching to the test* and the equally troubling practice of spending class time teaching test-taking strategies. As a matter of fact, poor youth are subject disproportionately to low-level thinking, disengaging, rote, and skills-and-drills pedagogies (Barr & Parrett, 2007; Luke, 2010)—what Martin Haberman (1991) called the *pedagogy of poverty*.

Especially prevalent in low-income schools and low-track classes in economically diverse schools (usually composed predominantly of low-income students) is direct instruction. The direct instruction model, according to the National Institute for Direct Instruction (2012), replaces "teacher creativity and autonomy as high priorities" with "a willingness to follow certain carefully prescribed instructional practices" (para. 2). Notice in this description the double-whammy deficit ideology. An implicit assumption appears to be that students need their teachers to follow "carefully prescribed" practices in order to learn. An explicit assumption is that teachers are incapable of teaching effectively when given the latitude to use their expertise and creativity.

More to the point, research shows that although some amount of direct instruction can be effective for teaching initial skills, an overreliance on direct instruction simply does not produce deep learning. For instance, in their studies on literacy instruction, Elaine Garan (2002) and Stephen Krashen (2009) found that although direct instruction can improve reading mechanics, it fails to improve reading comprehension or scores on tests that "require children to *understand what they read*" (emphasis added; Krashen, Lee, & McQuillan, 2010, p. 28). And this—teaching for lower order rather than higher order learning—is the common denominator for instructional practices that compose the pedagogy of poverty (Haberman, 1991). Like eliminating art and music programs, embracing these approaches is simply irrational, as explained by Stanley Pogrow (2009):

> Reteaching specific discrete skills all the time creates a sense that learning means memorizing. So more advanced learning skills and cognitive processes aren't developed, and these students never understand what learning actually is—even though they have as much potential for academic success as others. (p. 409)

Tracking and Ability Grouping

Tracking, or organizing students into groups or classes based on perceived or assumed capabilities, has become so much a part of the common sense of schooling that most education professionals struggle to imagine the possibility that we might organize students in any other way. In fact, scholars concerned with educational equity began to study tracking practices not out of concern that the overall approach couldn't work but rather out of a concern that the approach, in effect, was being used as a mechanism for segregating students within schools (Losen, 1999). They were right to worry, as tracking systems have been found almost universally to be inequitable by class and race, among other identifiers (Oakes, 2005; Orfield, Frankenberg, & Siegel-Hawley, 2010). Sometimes, as evidenced by some of the narratives in this volume, all it takes for somebody to be tracked into "low-ability" classes or groupings is tattered clothes, brown or black skin, or an accent or dialect stereotyped to belong to a scorned community.

Beyond unjust tracking practices, though, research has shown since the 1980s that tracking simply does not work for a vast majority of students. There is some evidence that the practice can be just a bit beneficial to a tiny percentage of the highest achieving students, but the overall effect is null or negative, especially for low-income students, who most often are placed in lower tracks (Oakes, 2005). In fact, and not surprisingly considering the discrepancies in access to engaging instruction detailed earlier, tracking *increases* gaps in rates of student achievement (Hattie, 2002; Huang, 2009). On the other hand, research has shown that a vast majority of students, and especially those who otherwise would be assigned disproportionately to lower tracks, benefit from learning in mixed-ability groups (Thrupp, Lauder, & Robinson, 2002). In other words, tracking is another illogical response to inequitable educational opportunity for poor youth.

Promising Practices, Preceded by a Caveat

Here's the caveat: Low-income students and communities are infinitely diverse. You know your students better than I do and better than researchers do. It's important to remember that no matter what anybody says and no matter how prettily packaged it might be, there is no set of perfectly scripted strategies that work for *all* low-income students *everywhere* (Balfanz & Byrnes, 2006). In fact, aside from advocating, in any way we can, for the social change necessary to alleviate the very existence of poverty, the most important thing any of us can do in the name of educational equity is to draw on the expertise of people within poor communities as educational partners in order to coconstruct community-specific strategies (Kezar, 2011).

In this spirit, the strategies I describe should be seen not as a prescriptive blueprint for eliminating class inequity or raising test scores but rather as a non-exhaustive, research-supported sample of strategies that, with context-specific adaptions, can be valuable components of a holistic plan for making schools more equitable for low-income families. Please note, as well, that individual strategies might appear more or less relevant based on your job description and sphere of influence.

Instructional Strategies

→*Incorporate art and music components into classroom instruction, regardless of the subject you teach.* As detailed earlier, exposure to art, theater, and music education bolsters learning, engagement, and retention for all students but particularly for low-income students, whose families are less likely to be able to afford to provide access to these experiences outside of school (Catterall, Chapleau, & Iwanaga, 1999; Pogrow, 2006).

→*Adopt higher order, engaging, rigorous pedagogies rather than lower order, rote, skills-and-drills pedagogies.* Recognize that expectations often are communicated pedagogically. What are we communicating to low-income students when they disproportionately are subject to the most disengaging pedagogies? Lee and Burkam (2003) found that students labeled "at risk" who attended schools that combined rigorous curricula with learner-centered pedagogies achieved at higher levels and were less likely to be early school leavers than their peers who experienced lower order instruction. Generally, low-income youth learn best when pedagogy is driven by high academic expectations—when standards aren't lowered based on socioeconomic status or other factors (Ramalho, Garza, & Merchant, 2010)—and when they have access to engaging, dialogic, inquiry-driven, collaborative pedagogies (Georges, 2009; Wenglinsky, 2002). This is the case, as well, when it comes to how they're being taught to use computers and the Internet (Gorski, 2009). The use of critical pedagogies and the development of critical literacies are particularly important for school engagement among low-income students. We can begin by providing opportunities for students to tell stories about their lives that challenge dominant, deficit narratives about poor youth (Dutro, 2009).

→*Communicate high expectations, especially through these higher order pedagogies.* Some people dismiss "high expectations" talk as self-esteem fluff. The reality is that a commitment to high expectations is fluff only when it is all talk and not reflected in the higher-order pedagogies just discussed. When high expectations are reflected in instruction, they can have a tremendous impact on intellectual development (Figlio, 2005; Jessim & Harber, 2005), especially for students unaccustomed to experiencing high expectations from adults in institutional authority positions (Kannapel & Clements, 2005; Kitchen, DePree, Celedón-Pattichis, & Brinkerhoff, 2004).

→*Incorporate movement or exercise into your instruction.* In too many schools, low-income students are losing access to recess and physical education at the same rate as art and music. Because of the lack of recreational facilities in poor communities and the costs associated with recreational sports, many low-income youth experience recess or physical education classes as their only opportunities to exercise. Obviously, students who are physically fit on average fare better in school. In addition, though, childhood physical fitness is an indicator of students' life health trajectories (Fahlman, Hall, & Lock, 2006).

→ *Be conscientious about assumptions regarding the resources to which students have access.* Remember when some teachers would hide a stash of poster board behind a filing cabinet for students whose families could not afford to purchase extra school supplies? Today students often are assumed to have access to computers and the Internet. Many schools communicate with families largely through e-mail and other electronic platforms. Obviously, low-income families are unlikely to have stable access to computers, high-speed Internet, a printer, and other expensive resources and might even struggle to afford cheaper materials like good ol' poster board (Gorski, 2009). Try not to require work that requires access to expensive technologies or extra materials unless you are able to provide access to the resources necessary to complete them during school hours.

→ *Reject the deficit perspective and focus, instead, on student and family assets.* Rejecting the deficit perspective, like having high expectations, is not mere fluffiness. When teachers adopt a deficit view of students, those students' performance declines, and the opposite happens when teachers focus on student strengths—a reality that holds true whether we're talking about socioeconomic status (Haberman, 1995), gender (Johns, Schmader, & Martens, 2005), or any other student identifier. If thinking about this in selfish terms helps, J. Gregg Robinson (2007) found, based on a study of more than 400 teachers in low-income urban schools, that those who rejected a deficit view were happier with their jobs than their colleagues who retained a deficit view. Plus, teachers who understood the societal challenges faced by low-income families were more effective at responding to the needs of students whose families were in poverty.

→ *Engage in family outreach early and often.* Remember that many low-income parents and guardians have experienced schools and a variety of other public systems as hostile environments (Gorski, 2012). So any hesitance you experience as you begin outreach efforts is not necessarily about you. It might be a reflection of very reasonable distrust for the system you represent. Or it might be about long work hours or a lack of access to a telephone at work. So we need to be persistent. We need to establish and build and sustain trust and, perhaps most important, to demonstrate our trust in low-income families (Hoy, Tarter, & Hoy, 2006) by nurturing positive relationships (Patterson, Hale, & Stessman, 2007). Some ways to build trust may include facilitating consistent two-way communication (Barr & Parrett, 2007) rather than reaching out only when something negative has happened, demonstrating an understanding of the challenges faced by low-income families and a commitment to creating an equitable classroom environment across all dimensions of diversity (Weiner, 2003), and refusing to invalidate students' and families' concerns about school inequities (Hamovitch, 1996).

→ *Analyze learning materials for class bias.* In her analysis of picture books, Stephanie Jones (2008) found that poor and working-class families regularly were depicted in stereotypical ways. The books understated the proportion of White people in poverty while overstating poverty in communities of color. A variety of useful tools exist to help us uncover these and other sorts of class biases, including the National Association for the Teaching of English Working Party on Social Class and English Teaching's (1982) checklist for class bias. Better yet, engage students in an analysis of and discussions about the biases you uncover together.

Promote literacy enjoyment. According to Mary Kellett (2009), "If we . . . acknowledge that literacy proficiency can be a route out of poverty . . . the most powerful strategy is to create cultures that promote reading enjoyment. This is likely to make the biggest impact on literacy proficiency" (p. 399). This means, consistent with the other strategies discussed here, that literacy instruction should not focus solely on reading mechanics. It also means avoiding practices that give students negative associations with literacy, such as forcing them, in Kellett's words, to "perform" their literacy skills publicly.

Make sure opportunities for family involvement are accessible to parents and guardians who are likely to work multiple jobs, work evenings, not have access to paid leave, struggle to afford child care, and rely on public transportation. Start by providing transportation and on-site child care (Amatea & West-Olatunji, 2007; Van Galen, 2007).

A Few School- and Society-Level Strategies

The following strategies are the sorts of things for which we might advocate as we grow our spheres of influence.

Advocate universal preschool. Among these strategies, investment in early childhood education might be most critical, as gaps in access to early learning opportunities compound throughout a child's lifetime (Bhattacharya, 2010).

Nurture relationships with community organizations and agencies, including health clinics and local farms. On the basis of an analysis of a variety of models for disrupting cycles of inequality for low-income families, Susan Neuman (2009) found that approaches based on coordinated efforts among educational, social, and health services were most effective.

Reduce class sizes. Despite the debate, research shows that class size matters (Rouse & Barrow, 2006). If it didn't, would the wealthiest independent schools make such a big deal of small class sizes in their marketing materials?

Increase health services in schools. Start by broadening vision screenings to include farsightedness, which is related to up-close reading, as with books (Gould & Gould, 2003). Other health services should focus on health risks that are elevated in low-income communities, such as asthma (Davis, Gordon, & Burns, 2011). And for goodness' sake, fight to keep full-time school nurses in low-income schools, where they are needed so much more than in wealthier schools (Telljohann, Dake, & Price, 2004).

Finally, as you continue to expand your sphere of influence, fight more generally for economic justice—for living-wage jobs, equitable access to health care, equitable school funding, and workers' rights—and against policies that hasten wealth and income inequality in the United States and around the world.

A Final Reflection

These strategies, although not exhaustive, provide points of departure that, when used in partnership with low-income communities, have been effective in many contexts. I understand—believe me, I do—that seeing all of these strategies gathered in one place can feel a little overwhelming. And that is why I encourage each of us to take stock of our spheres of influence. We can't control everything, and that is why it's so important to know that what we are doing in the name of class equity will get us closer to that goal.

References

Amatea, E. S., & West-Olatunji, C. A. (2007). Joining the conversation about educating our poorest children: Emerging leadership roles for school counselors in high-poverty schools. *Professional School Counseling, 11*(2), 81–89.

Balfanz, R., & Byrnes, V. (2006). Closing the mathematics achievement gap in high-poverty middle schools: Enablers and constraints. *Journal of Education for Students Placed at Risk, 11*(2), 143–159.

Barr, R. D., & Parrett, W. H. (2007). *The kids left behind: Catching up the underachieving children of poverty*. Bloomington, IN: Solution Tree Press.

Bhattacharya, A. (2010). Children and adolescents from poverty and reading development: A research review. *Reading and Writing Quarterly, 26*, 115–139.

Bracey, G. W. (2006). Poverty's infernal mechanism. *Principal Leadership, 6*(6), 60.

Catterall, J., Chapleau, R., & Iwanaga, J. (1999). Involvement in the arts and human development: General involvement and intensive involvement in music and theater arts. In E. B. Fiske (Ed.), *Champions of change: The impact of the arts on learning* (pp. 1–18). Washington, DC: Arts Education Partnership, President's Committee on the Arts and the Humanities.

Davis, D. W., Gordon, M. K., & Burns, B. M. (2011). Educational interventions for childhood asthma: A review and integrative model for preschoolers from low-income families. *Pediatric Nursing, 37*(1), 31–38.

Dutro, E. (2009). Children writing "hard times": Lived experiences of poverty and the class-privileged assumptions of a mandated curriculum. *Language Arts, 87*, 89–98.

Fahlman, M. M., Hall, H. L., & Lock, R. (2006). Ethnic and socioeconomic comparisons of fitness, activity levels, and barriers to exercise in high school females. *Journal of School Health, 76*(1), 12–17.

Figlio, D. N. (2005). *Names, expectations, and the Black-White achievement gap*. Cambridge, MA: National Bureau of Economic Research.

Garan, E. (2002). *Resisting reading mandates*. Portsmouth, NH: Heineman.

Georges, A. (2009). Relation of instruction and poverty to mathematics achievement gains during kindergarten. *Teachers College Record, 111*(9), 2148–2178.

Gorski, P. C. (2009). Insisting on digital equity: Reframing the dominant discourse on multicultural education and technology. *Urban Education, 44*, 348–364.

Gorski, P. C. (2012). Perceiving the problem of poverty and schooling: Deconstructing the class stereotypes that mis-shape education policy and practice. *Equity and Excellence in Education, 45*(2), 302–319.

Gould, M. C., & Gould, H. (2003). A clear vision for equity and opportunity. *Phi Delta Kappan, 85*(4), 324–328.

Haberman, M. (1991). The pedagogy of poverty versus good teaching. *Phi Delta Kappan, 73*, 290–294.

Haberman, M. (1995). *Star teachers of children in poverty*. Irvine, CA: Kappa Delta Pi.

Hamovitch, B. (1996). Socialization without voice: An ideology of hope for at-risk students. *Teachers College Record, 98*(2), 286–306.

Hattie, J. A. C. (2002). Classroom composition and peer effects. *International Journal of Education Research, 35*, 449–481.

Heath, S. B., & Roach, A. (1999). Imaginative actuality: Learning in the arts during the non-school hours. In E. B. Fiske (Ed.), *Champions of change: The impact of the arts on learning* (pp. 19–34). Washington, DC: Arts Education Partnership, President's Committee on the Arts and the Humanities.

Hoy, W. K., Tarter, C. J., & Hoy, A. W. (2006). Academic optimism in schools: A force for student achievement. *American Educational Research Journal, 43*, 425–446.

Huang, M.-H. (2009). Classroom homogeneity and the distribution of student math performance: A country-level fixed-effects analysis. *Social Science Research, 38*, 781–791.

Jessim, L., & Harber, K. D. (2005). Teacher expectations and self-fulfilling prophecies: Knowns and unknowns, resolved and unresolved controversies. *Personality and Social Psychology Review, 9*(2), 131–155.

Johns, M., Schmader, T., & Martens, A. (2005). Knowing is half the battle: Teaching stereotype threat as a means of improving women's math performance. *Psychological Science*, 16, 175–179.

Jones, S. (2008). Grass houses: Representations and reinventions of social class through children's literature. *Journal of Language and Literacy Education*, 4(2), 40–58.

Joyner, S., & Molina, C. (2012). *Class time and student learning*. Austin, TX: SEDL.

Kannapel, P. J., & Clements, S. K. (2005). *Inside the black box of high-performing, high-poverty schools: A report from the Pritchard Committee for Academic Excellence*. Lexington, KY: Pritchard Commission for Academic Excellence.

Kellett, M. (2009). Children as researchers: What we can learn from them about the impact of poverty on literacy opportunities. *International Journal of Inclusive Education*, 13(4), 395–408.

Kezar, A. (2011). Rethinking postsecondary institutions for low-income student success: The power of post-structural theory. In A. Kezar (Ed.), *Recognizing and serving low-income students in higher education: An examination of institutional policies, practices, and culture* (pp. 3–25). New York: Routledge.

Kitchen, R., DePree, J., Celedón-Pattichis, S., & Brinkerhoff, J. (2004). *High achieving schools initiative final report*. Albuquerque: University of New Mexico.

Krashen, S. (2009). Does intensive reading instruction contribute to reading comprehension? *Knowledge Quest*, 37(4), 72–74.

Krashen, S., Lee, S., & McQuillan, J. (2010). An analysis of the PIRLS (2006) data: Can the school library reduce the effect of poverty on reaching achievement? *CSLA Journal*, 34(1), 26–28.

Landsman, J., & Gorski, P. C. (2007). Countering standardization. *Educational Leadership*, 64(8), 40–44.

Lee, V., & Burkam, D. (2003). Dropping out of high school: The role of school organization and structure. *American Educational Research Journal*, 40, 353–393.

Losen, D. J. (1999). Silent segregation in our nation's schools. *Harvard Civil Rights-Civil Liberties Law Review*, 34, 517–546.

Luke, A. (2010). Documenting reproduction and inequality: Revisiting Jean Anyon's "Social Class and School Knowledge." *Curriculum Inquiry*, 40(1), 167–182.

National Association for the Teaching of English Working Party on Social Class and English Teaching. (1982). Check list for class bias and some recommended books. *English in Education*, 16(2), 34–37.

National Institute for Direct Instruction. (2012). *About direct instruction*. Retrieved January 3, 2013, from http://www.nifdi.org/aboutdi

Neuman, S. B. (2009). Use the science of what works to change the odds for children at risk. *Phi Delta Kappan, 90*(8), 582–587.

Oakes, J. (2005). *Keeping track: How schools structure inequality.* New Haven, CT: Yale University Press.

Orfield, G., Frankenberg, E., & Siegel-Hawley, G. (2010). Integrated schools: Finding a new path. *Educational Leadership, 68*(3), 22–27.

Patterson, J. A., Hale, D., & Stessman, M. (2007). Cultural contradictions and school leaving: A case study of an urban high school. *The High School Journal, 91,* 1–16.

Pogrow, S. (2006). Restructuring high-poverty elementary schools for success: A description of the Hi-Perform school design. *Phi Delta Kappan, 88*(3), 223–229.

Pogrow, S. (2009). Accelerating the learning of 4th and 5th graders born into poverty. *Phi Delta Kappan, 90*(6), 408–412.

Ramalho, E. M., Garza, E., & Merchant, B. (2010). Successful school leadership in socioeconomically challenging contexts: School principals creating and sustaining successful school improvement. *International Studies in Educational Administration, 38*(3), 35–56.

Robinson, J. G. (2007). Presence and persistence: Poverty ideology and inner-city teaching. *Urban Review, 39,* 541–565.

Rouse, C. E., & Barrow, L. (2006). U.S. elementary and secondary schools: Equalizing opportunity or replacing the status quo? *The Future of Children, 16*(2), 99–123.

Telljohann, S. K., Dake, J. A., & Price, J .H. (2004). Effect of full-time versus part-time school nurses on attendance of elementary students with asthma. *Journal of School Nursing, 20*(6), 331–334.

Thrupp, M., Lauder, H., & Robinson, T. (2002). School composition and peer effects. *International Journal of Education Research, 37,* 483–504.

Van Galen, J. (2007). Late to class: Social class and schooling in the new economy. *Educational Horizon, 85,* 156–167.

Weiner, L. (2003). Why is classroom management so vexing to urban teachers? *Theory Into Practice, 42*(4), 305–312.

Wenglinsky, H. (2002). *How teaching matters: Bringing the classroom back into discussions of teacher quality.* Princeton, NJ: Milken Family Foundation.

PART SIX

Poverty, Education, and the Trouble With School "Reform"

33

STUDENT COLLAGE

Henry Hughes

Dumped in the brambles beneath Portland's freeway, some kid's art project. In this state, he's lucky to even have an art class. They're cutting it all—art, music, gym, and 10 days off the calendar. Now that's an investment strategy. So some kid, just holding it together every morning, hears *Collages due Friday*. Whatever. Glue a bunch of crap to a board. But those circling frames are pretty cool, and the crying photos, the lists, and the grim news layered under the pink-slipped teacher's heady varnish. Maybe this kid knows something we don't, setting it out here in the sun and rain. Signaling the sky that we're in trouble.

34

THE TEACH FOR AMERICA STORY FROM A VOICE OF DISSENT

Mariah Dickinson

"**A**nd he looked at me with a tear in his eye and said, 'Thank you, sir.'"
The tall, blue-eyed young man stood on stage at the microphone, looking earnestly at his audience with a notebook in hand. He was recounting touching and breakthrough moments he experienced with the eighth graders he taught that summer, in 2009. This corps member, along with those of us in the audience, had just completed the Teach For America Institute, a five-week experience during which hundreds of new corps members are "transformed" into teachers through training sessions and a month-long summer school teaching practicum. There was a pervasive sense of accomplishment and pride in the auditorium. But I felt disconnected from the celebratory atmosphere. I felt disappointed and disillusioned.

Teach For America's (TFA's) story is one that co-opts the stories of oppressed communities living in poverty and packages them in marketable themes to recruit young, idealistic college graduates desperate to "help" people less privileged than themselves. For these young idealists who want to "make a difference," it's an attractive storyline with them as the hero, changing the world and "closing the achievement gap" one student at a time. Unfortunately, the real storyline is more complex and troubling than that.

By writing this chapter, I hope to illuminate, through the lens of my personal experience, that other storyline: how TFA undermines the communities it claims to serve and perpetuates the sorts of structures and ideas that sustain inequity.

The Exposition: Setting the TFA Tone

It was like a moment from a horror movie. Imagine walking toward a large building, the kind you see on a college campus. You hear a low, rhythmic hum, and as you draw closer, you begin to recognize the cadence of a chant. The sound is odd, and walking cautiously nearer, you begin to pick out distinct rhythms and tempos, a sound stew of competing vocalizations. With a thudding heart, you open the doors of a large, dim auditorium to see hundreds of people clustered into groups. The individuals in the group at the front of the auditorium are bowing down repeatedly with hands raised above their heads in the form of a triangle, a delta, chanting over and over, "Dellll-taaaaaa." Other groups perform similarly awkward movements and chants. You hesitantly ask a woman by the door, "Is this the TFA Institute assembly?"

"You're in the right place!" She smiles widely and points you to an open seat.

I encountered this scene on the second day of the Teach For America Institute. While my fellow corps members bonded over the regions where they would be teaching by participating in these cultish rituals, I experienced my first visceral reaction to the organization. Already, by that second day, I felt that there was too much indoctrination and elements of a forced "team spirit" in our training and too few critical conversations about how to change an inequitable education system, the latter being the ostensible reason we all were involved in the program.

Perhaps the lack of these conversations reflected, in part, the fact that the majority of corps members can afford not to have these conversations. If most of us were not personally confronted with the struggles of poverty, challenges that the majority of our students would be facing, why would we feel any urgency around these issues? Rather than critically engaging corps members in an evaluation of educational inequities, TFA created a physically and emotionally exhausting experience during Institute to train us to believe that our hard work alone could close the achievement gap.

I vividly remember when I first was introduced to the TFA story. I sat across from the TFA recruiter in the common area of a prominent building on campus. It was the beginning of my senior year. The young blonde woman smiled at me enthusiastically, and as the conversation progressed, I tingled with excitement and energy. According to my friendly recruiter, in TFA I would be taking on an incredible challenge, more difficult and more urgent than anything I had done before. I would be joining a movement to tackle our nation's "greatest injustice," to "close the achievement gap." I would be helping to ensure that TFA accomplishes its mission that "one day, all children will have the opportunity to attain an excellent education." As a student of international development, I saw TFA as an incredible opportunity to participate in domestic development work related to a critical issue.

Naturally, the conversation ended with my excited inquiry, "How do I apply?" Two months later, in November, I had accepted a placement with TFA in the Rio Grande Valley (RGV) of South Texas. I would be teaching seventh-grade special education. I was joining a movement, I thought, that was taking radical steps to create a different education system in America. That was the story I was led to believe.

Rising Action: Questioning the Approach

As the end of my senior year approached and my departure for the RGV drew closer, I connected with another woman in the DC-metro area who would also be teaching in the RGV region come August. Neha and I met on a seasonally warm and sunny day in late April. We sipped cool drinks, talked about what drew us to TFA, and discussed our shared desire to see critical curriculum taught in schools. We saw teaching in TFA as a mechanism for advancing social justice in schools, and we hoped that the organization would provide us with the tools and techniques to do this. I remember leaving that conversation with a warm confidence in having found a kindred spirit. I thought that I must have made the right decision to join the organization if I would be meeting people like Neha and having these kinds of conversations with my fellow corps members. I happily believed I had found myself in the right place.

Fast-forward to the scene from the horror movie a little less than two months later. TFA's culture of indoctrination gave me considerable cause for concern even before I started thinking more critically about TFA's approach to fulfilling its mission. The TFA Institute experience, in summary, felt like an indoctrinating boot camp for privileged idealists. The five weeks were composed of significant daily workloads, a strict training schedule and thorough reprimands for a few minutes of tardiness, the threat and shame of being saddled with a teacher improvement plan if you fell behind in your performance or assignments, and ruthless competition among corps members trying to print out lesson plans in the wee hours of the morning, all on an average of four or so nightly hours of sleep.

One night, several floors in two of the dorms flooded, and although many of us could not return to our rooms to sleep that night, we were reminded via e-mail that we should make sure to finish our lesson plans and turn them in on time. There seemed to be a "break 'em down and build 'em back up in our image" method at work.

Certainly I was not opposed to the hard work. I recognized during Institute that I had a lot to learn before entering the classroom in less than a month, an impossibly hopeful (and, it turns out, impossible) time frame to train an effective teacher. But under what assumptions were we all working so frantically? I began to question the nature of the approach that TFA adopts to close the achievement gap. As I began to question TFA's methods of fulfilling its mission, I often engaged in an internal Socratic dialogue:

Mariah 1:   What is Teach For America's mission?

Mariah 2:   To close the achievement gap, to end educational inequity.

    1:   What is TFA's primary model for addressing this issue?

    2:   TFA recruits mostly high-achieving college seniors from all disciplines to be trained, then placed as teachers for two years in high-need areas. That means areas of the country that are mostly low-income communities of color where students have low standardized test scores and schools have high dropout rates.

1: If this is TFA's model for addressing the problem, what are they identifying as the cause of the problem?

2: Simply put, if teachers are the solution, then it's teachers who are the problem.

1: Why doesn't this jibe with what you believe about the root causes of educational inequity?

2: The root causes aren't simple, that's for sure. They transcend students and schools. They involve the health of communities: the presence of and access to living-wage jobs, access to health care, funding to create safe neighborhoods and community spaces. Of course school is a big part of the issue: It's about the curriculum we teach and which skills we think are important for students. (Do we teach education for liberation through antioppression curriculum and critical thinking or teach students to follow the rules and do as they're told?) It's also about the privatization of schools and the charter movement, the increasing corporate control of public schools, standardized tests and who creates and benefits from them, and the quality of school lunches fed to students on free and reduced lunch programs. It's about the racist, classist, ableist, sexist, heteronormative society that we are all a part of and that does not provide equitable access and opportunity to all people. I don't think anyone would argue that we shouldn't have prepared and effective teachers in the classroom and that wonderful teachers are incredibly inspiring and can change the course of a student's life. But to say that teachers are the cause of or the solution to the achievement gap is absolutely false.

1: Duly noted.

I should mention here that this articulation of my fundamental concerns about TFA did not form overnight or even right after Institute. It grew out of a lot of conversations with other critically thinking corps members and friends, as well as ongoing encounters with TFA, its staff, its trainings, its assumptions, and its language. I continue, a few years after my TFA experience, to deconstruct the TFA story. But my time at Institute was formative in my growing awareness of the trouble with TFA and my dissatisfaction as a corps member.

Climax: The Words and the Method

Listening carefully to the language that TFA uses during Institute is key to understanding the story the organization tells. The fact that we, as corps members, were all united in our work to close the *achievement* gap is, itself, troubling. Achievement is an individual act of effort and skill. Opportunity, on the other hand, is a condition of circumstance. By talking about the achievement gap, are we not blaming the victims, the students, for their lack of access to opportunities? To say that there is a gap in achievement is to say that the students on the wrong end of this gap are failing to perform rather than being set up to fail by an inequitable system. How can an organization effectively mobilize its members to shift a failing education system when the language it uses blames the very group it asserts to be helping?

Already we're off to a bad start. The achievement gap, not the opportunity gap, is a core element of the TFA story. Other language and ideas fall in lockstep with this fundamental belief. I vividly remember an Institute training session that featured a video of a "successful" corps member in his classroom. It was a lesson on classroom management. This corps member had enrolled his third-grade students in a rallying cry, "work hard, get smart," to the point where they begged him for extra assignments. I watched this story unfold and wondered whether *this* is what we should teach our students. What's the message implied here? This corps member was saying that if only his students worked hard enough, they would be smart and achieve in school and life. This suggests that the factor that will lift them out of poverty is hard work. Does that mean that the reason that a student and her family are poor is because her parents did not work hard enough to achieve a "middle-class" life? How classist, over-simplified, and misinformed! The mantra smacks of a "pull yourself up by your bootstraps" mentality that, I thought, underlay the educational inequities we were charged with dismantling.

One popular strategy for motivating students that often was discussed among corps members and in training sessions involved beginning the school year by sharing statistics demonstrating the positive correlation between years of higher education and salary. What we never discussed in formal TFA training was the fact that this approach for motivating students equates the acquisition of money with success, which communicates to the students that they and their families currently are failing. As a result, we were trained, even if implicitly, to reiterate to students that not only are they and their families at the bottom of an economic hierarchy but they are there as a result of their own shortcomings. Of course, this view also ignores the debt that many students incur pursuing higher education and the difficulty they might experience finding a job to pay back college loans in the current economy. While pushing the idea of graduation and college in isolation as the way to a better, more lucrative, future, TFA does not encourage corps members to discuss the barriers, challenges, and inequities built into this path and experienced most harshly by the economically unprivileged. So, again, the bigger picture of inequity is obstructed.

Working hard is not the only factor in success. To teach students to make considerable effort toward an end goal is important. But to teach this in a vacuum, without acknowledging the systemic barriers they face or the tremendous gifts their communities have, is doing them a disservice. It's deceit. This is the point in the story when corps members' privilege comes crashing into the room, wreaking havoc, and TFA averts its eyes and pretends it isn't there.

It's not for a lack of opportunities to discuss these complexities. TFA has diversity sessions during Institute, but we stayed comfortably away from introspection and inequity and focused, instead, on how to work with colleagues, parents, or students who had different ideas or beliefs than we might have. The diversity sessions alluded to race in some fairly simplistic ways, but class was completely ignored. One staff member deflected critical questions by apologetically stating that she was not a trained diversity facilitator. Another staff member admitted that diversity trainings used to be more substantial, but they received feedback that the trainings made corps members uncomfortable. And although we talked about humility, there was a pervasive sense of superiority in the room. We were going into schools to close the achievement gap, but we could not even acknowledge that TFA blamed the local teachers, teachers who were from the surrounding community, for the problems we were supposed to solve. So when it came down to it, was TFA saying that we were being trained to help poor communities because they couldn't help themselves? Is that humility?

Despite supposed efforts to diversify, TFA remains a majority White and economically privileged organization. The communities that it serves are neither predominantly White nor economically privileged. Although the organization recognizes in its diversity statement the need for corps members to reflect the backgrounds of the populations it serves, the composition of the corps indicates how much the organization values this ideal in practice.

At the very least, TFA should encourage corps members to analyze how the organization at large might affect the communities it serves. This is hard to do, and it requires asking difficult questions. For example, might an organization with a majority of White and economically privileged corps members reinforce the colonialist idea that people of color and poor people can't better their own situations? Might it be more effective for these same corps members to work to deconstruct their own views of the world and disenfranchised populations and then work to dismantle the structures that systematically favor Whites and the economically privileged people over people of color and poor people? I'm not asking for TFA to provide answers to these questions, but I am asking for it to facilitate a conversation about them.

Some corps members—although, in my experience, very few—have this conversation, but it's always outside formal TFA trainings. Neha, our friends Rita and Natasha, and I regularly discussed these questions. I found myself, for the first time, consciously confronted with a need to assess my privilege.

As I thought through my own background, I appreciated that my father was an inspirational force.

"Dad, why do you have those bunions on your big toes? They're huge," I would exclaim.

"When you can't afford shoes that fit, you have to wear the ones you have, don't you?" Dad would say. My father grew up poor. One of five children, he was raised in rural Maine. His family was on welfare. He started working at a department store at 14, the same year his father died. After graduating high school, my dad attended the University of Maine with the assistance of financial aid. He earned a degree in computer science and went on to secure well-paying jobs as a computer software engineer, ensuring that his kids grew up never experiencing the struggles of a family trying to make ends meet.

My dad would explain this and then say, "I did work hard, and now I'm not poor. But I had it easy. I'm a White, tall, able-bodied, heterosexual male who was raised Christian. With all of that, overcoming the class barrier wasn't so difficult."

As I thought about my life as a White, economically privileged woman, I wondered about my place in the classroom with my students. I do not speak Spanish, and I had no intimate knowledge of the region in which I was teaching. Furthermore, was it not an injustice that TFA assigned me to be a special education teacher without robust training and education in child psychology? I improved as a teacher in my two years in the classroom and helped many students make academic progress, but then I was gone. What did I offer in those two years that a career teacher from the RGV couldn't?

Although individual corps members have done some wonderful things in the classroom, many of them also set an example of an unsustainable model of teaching. They work incredibly long hours. I knew many corps members who were on the verge of breakdown, and some who had serious mental health episodes. It is an example of privilege to be able to work yourself to the point of burnout, knowing that you don't have a family to support and that you're most likely going to have to hold on only for two years. This is not a model that is beneficial for teachers or for students.

Falling Action: Continuing a Different Story

In the two years that Neha, Rita, and I taught in the RGV (Rita grew up there, making her the rare TFA corps member who teaches close to home), we found ways of telling a different story. Neha quit TFA in August of our first year and worked for a local immigrant rights organization founded by César Chávez. Rita and I attended marches and rallies with Neha to support immigration reform and social justice in the community. I found ways of bringing social justice figures into the curriculum when I could, even when that meant putting coordinate planes on hold to talk about Martin Luther King, Jr., Malcolm X, and César Chávez on MLK Day. Rita and I searched the Internet for slam poetry and spoken word written by youth to share with our students, helping them identify ways to express themselves in English class.

I also attempted to influence TFA as an organization during my time in the RGV. Neha and I embarked on the Border Witness Program one weekend in September of our first year in the RGV to understand "the reality of the border (the struggles, achievements, and challenges—economic, social, cultural, spiritual) through direct experience and personal contact."[1] In several meetings with my TFA program director, who oversaw my progress in the classroom, I indicated my dissatisfaction with the organization and some ideas I had to improve it. My program director suggested that I meet with the executive director, and a few months later, I did. I explained to the ED that TFA could make a more meaningful impact if it worked to address other causes of inequity in education. One important way to do this was to form partnerships with local organizations already doing such work. I took the information from the Border Witness Program with me as a tangible example of a partnership that could involve corps members in issues affecting their students. The ED nodded solemnly and took notes while I spoke. He made copies of the information I brought with me, but in the end, the partnership was not pursued.

During my second year with TFA, the 20th Anniversary Summit was held in Washington, DC. I decided to attend to get a sense for the national movement's current position on its organization and education issues. I received several hundred dollars in funding to attend the conference (whereas requests I made for funding to attend the North Dakota Study Group Conference, a social justice education conference, were denied). The summit was largely what I expected: TFA founder Wendy Kopp and others lauded various charter school movements and spoke about the great progress the organization has made. The root causes of educational inequity and the broad range of issues facing communities in poverty were not addressed.

Resolution: An Ongoing Journey

In the quest for educational equity, TFA is a barrier. The problems in the education system require an approach that eliminates the structures that prevent communities from exerting their power to demand better education and opportunities for themselves and their students. I would argue that TFA works harder in the service of the corps members it employs than the students it claims to help. The organization states that part of its goal is to expose corps members to the state of the education system and the experiences of low-income students. The idea is that, with this exposure, these corps members will continue to fight on their former students' behalf regardless of the sector they choose to enter in the future. This leverages the power of the corps members over the power of the students and their communities, thereby perpetuating a structure that takes power away from oppressed communities and places it in the hands of privileged others to act and make decisions for them. And so far, this approach has accomplished little in regard to changing the economic realities of the communities in which TFA works. Unfortunately, TFA continues to expand its corps and the regions it serves, while an organization focused on closing the opportunity gap should actually be attempting to reduce its numbers and transfer its power to the communities for which it claims to advocate.

I don't know what the solution is to the enduring problem of educational inequity, but I do know that it is not TFA. Through telling parts of my story and experience, I hope to challenge TFA's assertions and grow the voice of dissent. I wrote this chapter from the position of a former corps member, and I do not claim to be speaking as, or on behalf of, anyone else. Ultimately, the decision to accept or reject TFA lies with the students, parents, schools, and communities where TFA has a presence. I hope that by sharing my story, I encourage others to speak up and call to TFA to take a step back and consider on whose behalf the organization really works.

Note

1. See www.arisesotex.org/ariseborderwitness0.aspx.

35

"DO YOU HAVE FIDELITY TO THE PROGRAM?"

Matters of Faith in a Restructured Title I Middle School

Brian R. Horn

In today's public school system, an almost blind faith has been invested in top-down school reform policies, many of which are aimed ostensibly at addressing the needs of poor students, that have created intense competition for public dollars while being exclusively connected to state standardized tests (Kohn, 2011). In the name of catching poor students up with their wealthier peers, policies such as No Child Left Behind (NCLB) and Race to the Top have diverted attention from what happens within the classroom—teaching and learning—and instead perpetuated a "pedagogy of poverty" (Haberman, 1991) that obsesses over memorizing disconnected facts, demands compliance (Kozol, 2005), and fails to close the so-called achievement gap they purportedly are meant to address.

In this chapter I tell a different story of faith—a story about the choices teachers of students in poverty often have to make between their students and top-down curricula. Although my experiences with a specific mandated program may not reflect the experiences of every teacher, being forced into a position to have to choose between having faith in students and having faith in deficit-oriented programs is a common experience for teachers of students in poverty.

"Do You Have Fidelity to the Program?"

"Mr. Horn, could you please come see me in my office?"

"Sure, Mrs. Thomas.[1] I'll be down in a minute."

This was the first time Mrs. Thomas, my principal, had called me to her office, but as I walked through Pioneer Middle School, I was pretty sure why I had been summoned and wondered why it had taken so long.

About a week earlier I had been observed by one of my assistant principals, Mrs. Vaughn. Every teacher at Pioneer was observed regularly by administration, and for language arts and math teachers, observations focused on monitoring our teaching of the prescribed America's Choice curricula.[2] Two years earlier Pioneer had failed to make Annual Yearly Progress for five consecutive years. In accordance with NCLB policy, and because Pioneer was a Title I school, it had been "restructured." A new administrative team had been brought in, 65% of the teaching staff was replaced, and at a cost of over $1,000,000, our district contracted America's Choice, a self-proclaimed "school improvement service" (America's Choice, n.d.) claiming to be intent on turning around failing schools and to provide the language arts and math curricula. America's Choice is owned by textbook publishing powerhouse Pearson, a corporation often criticized for profiting from the sorts of federal education policies that are destroying schools like Pioneer Middle School and deprofessionalizing teaching. Like many of the pedagogical packages imposed on teachers in low-income schools today, America's Choice prescribes predesigned units of study and an adherence to the "workshop model," which has been misappropriated from Lucy Calkins (1986) and organizes instruction into an opening skill-based mini-lesson; a work session with individual work, cooperative work, and/or small group instruction; and a summative closing (America's Choice, n.d.).

Like many teachers in high-poverty schools, I experienced a "narrowing of curriculum" (Crocco & Costigan, 2007) with intense oversight. Mrs. Vaughn had observed the first 30 minutes of one of my classes as students worked with idioms they found in canonical poetry and contemporary hip-hop. To Mrs. Vaughn and anyone familiar with America's Choice, I clearly was not following the mandated units, something I had not done all year, with one exception.

As I continued toward the office, I figured my "insubordination" was going to catch up with me and result in an official admonishment. I imagined having to explain the "radical" content of my teaching, which generally consisted of coconstructing student-led critical inquiry units (Lewison, Leland, & Harste, 2008; Wilhelm, 2007) with my students, most of whom were poor.

When I entered her office, Mrs. Thomas immediately asked me about my knowledge of the "workshop model." She told me that Mrs. Vaughn noted that the opening of my lesson was five minutes too long and asked, "Do you have fidelity to the program—to America's Choice?"

Dumbfounded, I recited a brief monologue consisting mostly of deflections, repeating various forms of "I will be more mindful of the time." I was careful not to affirm my fidelity to America's Choice in the process, while also not saying anything that might warrant additional observations or oversight. I wanted to get out of there as quickly as possible and get back to doing exactly what I had been doing. Mrs. Thomas listened to my muddled answer and didn't press further. I returned to my classroom thinking about matters of faith, trust, and power in her notion of fidelity.

Pioneer: Restructured

Over 90% of the students at Pioneer are eligible for free or reduced lunch. I came to Pioneer while it was being restructured. When I interviewed with Mrs. Thomas, I described my desire to provide students with critical literacy experiences. Mrs. Thomas mentioned America's Choice briefly but told me not to worry because it was to be implemented only in the "Ramp Up" remedial language arts and math classes, which I wasn't assigned to teach.

America's Choice, like many other curricular programs implemented in high-poverty schools, has strict tracking and scripted curricula built on memorization and is devoid of rigor and relevance. According to the program, students in "Ramp Up" were to be given accelerated instruction in phonics, comprehension, vocabulary, fluency, and writing explicitly. Those of us teaching "On Grade Level" and "Advanced" sections were granted professional freedom in our teaching, and I took full advantage of this throughout the school year. My students and I coconstructed and explored critical inquiry units such as "What makes a successful romantic relationship?" and "What is *justice* in the criminal justice system?"

My second year at Pioneer was different. Teachers who had not taught America's Choice during the previous year had been sent to its summer professional development sessions. We were told that "On Grade Level" teachers also were to follow America's Choice curricula. In addition, Mrs. Thomas and the two assistant principals would officially observe us each academic quarter, and Ms. Davis, Pioneer's literacy coach, would observe us weekly. The purpose of these observations, we were told, was to help us implement America's Choice successfully. As the new school year began, I was charged with the task of figuring out how I could continue to teach critical units that reflected my faith in the strengths and desires of my students within the constraints of scripted, universal units that reflected the "expert knowledge" of America's Choice.

"Oh Snaps! That Did Not Just Happen!"

It didn't take long for me to decide that I wasn't going to alter my teaching to meet the programmatic expectations of America's Choice. I had taught my entire career in urban Title I schools and had been expected to do all sorts of things that were not in the best interests of my students. Like the year before, I was going to teach in a way that honored and reflected my students, not America's Choice. But unlike the year before, I was being observed regularly and expected to follow America's Choice curricula.

Instead of following "The First 30 Days" America's Choice unit, which was composed of about 20 predetermined lessons, I had faith in my new students' abilities to chart a rigorous and relevant path forward. After we spent the first few weeks getting to know each other, we began to decide which critical inquiry unit we would pursue first. We decided to pursue the critical inquiry unit "How do you make it in an unjust world?"

"What lesson are y'all on?" was the question I started to hear over and over again from Ms. Davis. I struggled to find the best way to respond, not wanting to lie but not wanting to be completely forthright. I would respond, "We're doing really well, thanks" or "I can't remember" or "Today we did this really cool reenactment." I would explain, "We're not exactly following 'The First 30 Days' per se, but we're hitting on everything good in that unit." I might even nudge, "Since I teach the 'Advanced' section, I really don't want to lesson plan for two different language arts classes. Also, I think if it's good enough for the 'Advanced' kids, it's good enough for the 'On Grade Level' kids."

On the day when most of my students were approaching the shocking climax of the central text of the unit, *The Pearl* by John Steinbeck, the entire administrative team came into my class for my first unannounced observation. My students were spread all over the room in small groups reading, reflecting, and reading some more, and it was clear that what we were doing had nothing to do with America's Choice. I circulated around the room listening to the different groups, soaking up the work of my students, and anxiously awaiting their reading of Coyotito's death.

The hum of the students' reading was building. Fewer reflective conversations were taking place as groups focused their collective attention on the book. As I continued to roam around the room, looking for the group that likely would reach the climax of the story first, the administrative team began roaming, too, interrupting groups to ask students America's Choice questions like, "Do you know what the learning objectives for the day are?"

Annoyed but undeterred, my students pressed on and eventually, one by one, arrived at the chapter's conclusion. I hustled around the room trying to contain the volume of the groups' reactions so they wouldn't distract or dampen other groups' reading. Some students were laughing, appreciative of the suspenseful nature of the story; others were shocked and speechless. Still others were visibly upset, trying to talk me out of Coyotito's fate. "Oh snaps! That did *not* just happen!" one student exclaimed. Other raw expressions of emotion sprang up from all ends of the classroom. Meanwhile, the administrative team rounded themselves up and exited the room.

A few days later I found a note from Mrs. Thomas written on a small scrap of paper in my mailbox. She provided a couple sentences of general feedback: "I really enjoyed observing in your classroom. It is obvious you have a comfortable rapport with your students." She also reminded me that the lesson's learning objectives should be clearly written at the front of the classroom.

"I ♥ Haiti"

When school resumed after winter break, Ms. Davis began talking to Pioneer's language arts teachers about when we would be implementing the America's Choice "Test Taking" unit. The state reading assessment wasn't until March, but Ms. Davis wanted to make sure we would be devoting time to the 20-lesson unit meant to prepare students to pass the test by taking practice exams and learning "tricks" for scoring well.

The message was clear: The only way students at our Title I school could pass the state assessment and "succeed" was for us to follow a decontextualized, generic unit on how to memorize and regurgitate information. The students at Pioneer, most of whom were poor, were viewed through a deficit lens that marginalized their creativity, ingenuity, and intelligence, while disallowing them to work with teachers to coconstruct their own rigorous and relevant academic path. There was no way I was going to "commodify" my students (Kozol, 2005, p. 94) and teach a "Test Taking" unit. Not surprisingly, my students provided an authentic alternative.

On January 12, eight days after the start of the second semester, an earthquake devastated Haiti. Many of my students came to my classes asking about the earthquake and the people of Haiti, and within a few days two students suggested we do something as a school to raise money and awareness, similar to efforts they'd seen on TV. I worked with students in all of my classes to refine this idea and looked for other teachers at Pioneer who would be interested in being part of our burgeoning project. By the end of the week, we had a plan for an "I ♥ Haiti Day."

Utilizing a "problem posing approach" (Freire, 1970), we began to engage students in thinking about the world in which they live, not as a static reality but as a reality in process, in transformation. We reinforced the students as "actors," not "spectators," with power to "transform the world" (Freire, 1970, p. 48) as they build capacity as change agents (Ginwright & James, 2002). In addition, our early dialogue focused on what the students wanted to achieve through this project. They expressed interest in learning more about Haiti in their classes, they wanted to raise money for students in Haiti, and they wanted to make buttons as a lasting and outward sign of solidarity.

From here, my students, colleagues, and I devised a project that would allow for participating teachers to create standards-based units of study focusing on Haiti. The units would be related to the subject matter they intended to teach leading up to "I ♥ Haiti Day" on January 25. Many of my students wanted to raise money so they could feel like they were making a difference. Initially, some students wanted to charge $2 for an "I ♥ Haiti" button as an expression of how much money many Haitians live on each day. Other students didn't like the idea of making a donation mandatory. These discussions allowed us to explore and critique the nexus of charity, power, and social justice and were reminiscent of the many discussions we'd had in class relative to our own communities. In the end, on January 25, participating teachers taught focused lessons on Haiti; donations were accepted, but not required, for Pioneer students and staff to receive an "I ♥ Haiti" button; and the money raised was donated to an organization serving Haitian students.

In my classes we looked beyond the earthquake to explore the rich and oppressive history of Haiti and its people. I attempted to create an asset-oriented narrative that recognized the strengths, talents, beauty, and resources inherent in many of the Haitian people, while also illuminating the presence of historical and contemporary colonialism. This was important to me as a critical educator, because this was not the story being told of Haiti by the media in the aftermath of the earthquake. In addition, I wanted to reinforce the importance of asset-oriented narratives, because they are rarely applied to students in poverty. Social studies classes also explored the history of Haiti, while science classes examined the science behind earthquakes. A local news crew covered the day. A reporter from the National Education Association interviewed me for an article (Rosales, 2010). In all, the event raised over $1,150 for the rebuilding of Haitian schools. But more important, when given the opportunity, students across Pioneer created a thoughtful and politically conscious project that illustrated that they had faith in their collective creativity, ingenuity, ability, and intelligence and also addressed state standards that they would be expected to "master" for the upcoming state assessment.

"How Do You Know They Wouldn't Have Done Better With America's Choice?"

After spring break Ms. Davis's observations and check-ins regarding America's Choice continued, and the tension between the two of us grew. Assessments were behind us, and I became less evasive regarding Ms. Davis's question, "What lesson are y'all on?" I would answer saying that I wasn't teaching an America's Choice unit and explain what we were doing instead. At first, she was a bit surprised and didn't offer much of a response, just writing "not teaching AC unit" in her notes.

Shortly thereafter the official results of the state reading assessment arrived. Although I didn't put much stock in the state assessments as the ultimate measure of my effectiveness and my students' success, I was keenly aware of what the scores meant to my students, who soon would be leaving a "failing" Title I middle school to attend the more economically integrated City High School.

Before learning the scores of my eighth graders, I revisited their scores as seventh graders. Of my 44 "On Grade Level" students who were expected to follow America's Choice, only 21 had passed as seventh graders. As eighth graders, 33 of the same 44 "On Grade Level" students passed with virtually no mandated curricula from America's Choice. I wondered how the scores would be interpreted by administration, especially because I didn't follow the America's Choice curriculum.

I was proud of my students and emboldened by their collective success on the state assessment. America's Choice was imposed as *the* way to ensure students would pass state assessments. Mrs. Thomas and Ms. Davis privileged the state assessment data above all other measures of student proficiency. At best, I hoped my students' successes would garner them and me a newfound respect, a higher level of trust that we could do a better job than America's Choice. At worst, I hoped to be left alone. As it turned out, I got neither.

During what was one of my and Ms. Davis's last debriefings, the tensions between the two of us came to a head. Ms. Davis again asked if we were following America's Choice. When I said *no* she reminded me that I was expected to follow the curricula "like everybody else." I felt somewhat defensive as I explained how rigorous and relevant the units were that my students and I cocreated. I reminded her how my method of teaching engages and empowers students, especially students in a high-poverty school. I got the sense that this line of reasoning wasn't swaying Ms. Davis, so I attempted to compel her with the data I knew she privileged: standardized test scores.

"Less than half of my 'On Grade Level' students passed the state test last year, and 75% of them passed this year."

Ms. Davis interrupted, "And, how do you know they wouldn't have done better with America's Choice?"

It was clear from that point forward that there was little I could say to convince her of the worth of what my students and I had done that year. In the end, according to Ms. Davis, regardless of evidence suggesting otherwise, "fidelity to the program" trumped having faith in and a commitment to my students.

Fidelity: Restructured

Although America's Choice partners with over 1,000 schools, it is not found in every school primarily serving poor students. However, the pedagogy of privileging top-down programs that position corporate power brokers as the solution and poor students as the problem is all too common in many of today's schools. As a result, according to research on the imposition of these sorts of programs on teachers in a diversity of schools, "Teachers in schools with the highest proportion of students from low-income backgrounds—a situation that historically has presented daunting instructional challenges—were more constrained than their colleagues at more affluent schools" (Ogawa, Sandholtz, Martina-Flores, & Scribner, 2003, p. 166).

Another example of this phenomenon is evident in what is happening in the Chicago Public Schools (CPS) regarding their efforts to "turn around" "failing" high-poverty schools. CPS has given control of over 100 high-poverty schools to private vendors such as the Academy for Urban School Leadership (AUSL), which controls 25 schools. The AUSL has been rewarded with multimillion-dollar contracts to fire and replace all staff members in these schools and hand over tight control of the school's operations to a "turnaround specialist" contracted by the organization. In addition, CPS is looking to expand its partnership with AUSL to over 60 schools within the next five years.

Clearly, CPS leaders are embracing corporate dogma as they outsource school reform in high-poverty schools. They are putting faith in programs and so-called reformers and, as a result, doing further damage to poor students, families, and communities. A study (Designs for Change, 2012) comparing "turnaround" schools with 33 high-performing high-poverty CPS schools practicing School-Based Democracy (SBD) illuminates the power of faith in poor communities. SBD is described as a reform that

> emphasizes the involvement of each school community in improving their school through school-based participation by parents, teachers, non-teaching school staff, community members, principals, and students. A central focus of School-Based Democracy in Chicago is an elected Local School Council at each school representing these groups. (Designs for Change, 2012, p. 1)

The study indicated that between 2006 and 2011, the 33 SBD schools started with lower combined test scores on the Illinois Standard Achievement Test (ISAT) than the "turnaround" schools, received less financial support from CPS, and ended with higher combined scores on the ISAT, all while retaining and supporting their original staff (p. 10). The success of these schools that work to collaborate with the poor communities in which they are situated should inspire great hope that similar models can be applied beyond the city of Chicago and extended to other high-poverty schools and communities.

Constrained, hyperstandardized curriculum programs at high-poverty schools stifle teacher creativity and autonomy, impede meaningful relationships between teachers and students, and threaten the professional and personal development of the most qualified teachers (Crocco & Costigan, 2007). As a teacher in a school that was subjected to such curricula, I found I needed to be *pragmatically subversive* in order to meet the needs of my students. This meant I needed to be measured in the ways in which I taught against the America's Choice grain.

I paid particular reverence to the state learning standards, making sure I knew them inside and out and that I could describe and explain how everything we did in the class was connected to what I was technically "hired to teach." In addition, I made certain that my students were fully engaged. Although this wasn't an already held goal of mine, I knew that administration valued classes that were "under control." Our classes were active, and any disagreements or issues within my classes were taken care of "in house" without involving the administration. Last, I made certain not to "bad-mouth" America's Choice to colleagues. Instead I offered respectful critiques publicly and privately so as not to draw extra attention to my teaching. These actions to subvert the curricular pressures were made all the more easy by the fact that I had tenure. Most of my colleagues who were hired after restructuring were first-year teachers eager to fit in and fearful of losing their jobs.

As the editors of this book stated, "The poor are not the problem." In fact, they are the solution. Because of No Child Left Behind and other state and federal education policy, programs like America's Choice are disproportionately implemented in schools that primarily serve poor students and their communities. Instead of further repressing poor students in struggling schools with even more restrictive oversight, a narrow and Eurocentric "traditional" curriculum (Shor, 1992), and a muzzling of student and community voice, the path to strengthening schools needs to place the lives of poor students at the center of the reform process, recognizing them as the solution rather than the problem. Work such as this would involve reimagining the students *as the curriculum* so that the work of learning comes from their lives and interests and not a program, textbook, or corporate entity. Having this sort of fidelity to the students would empower youth and their communities with the academic, social, political, and critical consciousness to act justly upon the world (Freire, 1970).

A common critique of using student-centered, critical pedagogy (Freire, 1970) to engage poor students is that it lacks rigor (Hirsch, 1987; Ravitch, 2000). However, the opposite is true. My teaching was standards-based. But what happened in our classroom transcended the standards. We did the intellectual work of engaged and critical citizens: asking questions, proposing solutions, and coconstructing knowledge. My fidelity in my students ensured that I didn't need fidelity to the program in order for students to succeed and pass a narrow and "violent" test that caused undue stress on students while lacking rigor, validity, and reliability in that they incompletely measure the total child (Janesick, 2007).

So no, I did not have fidelity to the program. I had faith in, a commitment to, and fidelity to my students. I had faith enough to build from their strengths through critical practices. Together we learned to question and act upon the world justly as thinkers, doers, and problem solvers.

Notes

1. The names of all places and people are pseudonyms.
2. America's Choice is now more commonly known as Pearson's School-wide Improvement Model (SIM).

References

America's Choice. (n.d.). *Schoolwide improvement*. Retrieved from www .americaschoice.org/schoolwideimprovement

Calkins, L. M. (1986). *The art of teaching writing*. Portsmouth, NH: Heinemann.

Crocco, M. S., & Costigan, A. T. (2007). The narrowing of curriculum and pedagogy in the age of accountability: Urban educators speak out. *Urban Education, 42*(6), 512–535.

Designs for Change. (2012). *Chicago's democratically-led elementary schools far out-perform Chicago's "turnaround schools" yet turnaround schools receive lavish extra resources*. Retrieved from designsforchange.org

Freire, P. (1970). *Pedagogy of the oppressed*. New York: Continuum.

Ginwright, S., & James, T. (2002). From assets to agents of change: Social justice, organizing, and youth development. *New Directions for Youth Development, 96*, 27–46.

Haberman, M. (1991). The pedagogy of poverty vs. good teaching. *Phi Delta Kappan, 73*(4), 290–294.

Hirsch, E. D. (1987). *Cultural literacy: What every American needs to know*. Boston: Houghton Mifflin.

Janesick, V. (2007). Reflections on the violence of high-stakes testing and the soothing nature of critical pedagogy. In P. McLaren & J. Kincheloe (Eds.), *Critical pedagogy: Where are we now?* (pp. 239–248). New York: Peter Lang.

Kohn, A. (2011, April 27). Poor teaching for poor children . . . in the name of reform. *Education Week*. Retrieved from www.alfiekohn.org/teaching/edweek/poor.htm

Kozol, J. (2005). *The shame of the nation: The restoration of apartheid schooling in America*. New York: Crown.

Lewison, M., Leland, C., & Harste, J. (2008). *Creating critical classrooms: K-8 reading and writing with an edge.* New York: Lawrence Erlbaum.

Ogawa, R. T., Sandholtz, J. H., Martina-Flores, M., & Scribner, S. P. (2003). The substantive and symbolic consequences of a district's standards-based curriculum. *American Educational Research Journal, 40,* 147–176.

Ravitch, D. (2000). *Left back: A century of failed school reforms.* New York: Simon & Schuster.

Rosales, J. (2010). Kansas students and staff open (and sell) hearts for Haiti relief. *NEA Today.* Retrieved from www.nea.org/home/38256.htm

Shor, I. (1992). *Empowering education: Critical teaching for social change.* Chicago: University of Chicago Press.

Wilhelm, J. (2007). *Engaging readers and writers with inquiry: Promoting deep understandings in language arts and the content areas with guiding questions.* New York: Scholastic.

36

THE INEQUITY GAP OF SCHOOLING AND THE POVERTY OF SCHOOL "REFORM"

P. L. Thomas

"With a clamor of bells that set the swallows soaring, the Festival of Summer came to the city Omelas, bright-towered by the sea," opens Ursula Le Guin's (1975) "The Ones Who Walk Away From Omelas."

The reader soon learns about a people and land that leave the narrator filled with both passion for telling a story and tension over the weight of that task:

> How can I tell you about the people of Omelas? They were not naive and happy children—though their children were, in fact, happy. They were mature, intelligent, passionate adults whose lives were not wretched. O miracle! but I wish I could describe it better. I wish I could convince you. (Le Guin, 1975, p. 278)

The narrator offered an assortment of glimpses into these joyous people and their Festival of Summer, and then added, "Do you believe? Do you accept the festival, the city, the joy? No? Then let me describe one more thing" (p. 280).

The "one more thing" is a child, imprisoned in a closet and sitting in its own filth—a fact the people of Omelas "explained to children when they are between eight and twelve, whenever they seem capable of understanding":

> They all know it is there, all the people of Omelas. Some of them have come to see it, others are content merely to know it is there. They all know that it has to be there. Some of them understand why, and some do not, but they all understand that their happiness, the beauty of their city, the tenderness of their friendships, the health of their children, the wisdom of their scholars, the skill of their makers, even the abundance of their harvest and the kindly weathers of their skies, depend wholly on this child's abominable misery. (Le Guin, 1975, p. 282)

And how do the people of Omelas respond to this fact of their privilege? Most come to live with it: "Their tears at the bitter injustice dry when they begin to perceive the terrible justice of reality, and to accept it" (p. 283).

But a few, a few:

> They leave Omelas, they walk ahead into the darkness, and they do not come back. The place they go towards is a place even less imaginable to most of us than the city of happiness. I cannot describe it at all. It is possible that it does not exist. But they seem to know where they are going, the ones who walk away from Omelas. (Le Guin, 1975, p. 284)

At its core, Le Guin's story is about the narcotic called *privilege*, but this parable also highlights a message rarely acknowledged in any culture: *Privilege always exists at someone else's expense*. The horror of this allegory is that the sacrifice is a child, emphasizing for the reader that privilege comes to some at the expense of marginalized *others* through no fault of the closeted lamb.

In the United States, we cloak the inequity of privilege with a meritocracy myth (Fielding, 2008), but unlike the people of Omelas, we embrace both the myth and the cloaking, rarely taking that painful step of opening the closet door to face ourselves. What's behind our door in the United States? Over 22% of our children living in poverty through no fault of their own—as well as a cultural narrative that identifies people living in poverty as "the problem."

Although Le Guin's story ends with some hope that a few have souls and minds strong enough to walk away from happiness built on the oppression of the innocent, I feel compelled to long for a different ending, one in which a few, a few rise up against the monstrosity of inequity to speak and act against it rather than merely walk away.

A Rotting Apple?

The meritocracy myth is powerful in both society and popular views of what public schools mean and can offer: "We like to believe all students have an equal opportunity to learn," explained Liz Dwyer (2012), "regardless of the color of their skin or the amount of money their families have." The meritocracy myth claims that the United States has achieved the status of meritocracy and that our public schools perpetuate that reality.

But *A Rotting Apple: Education Redlining in New York City* has prompted Pedro Noguera to argue that public schools are in fact "evidence of blatant disparities [that] amount to Apartheid-like separations" (Holzman, 2012, p. vi).

A Rotting Apple focuses on New York City, but the patterns exposed here are typical across the United States in public education, a system currently under siege by "no excuses" reformers (Thomas, 2011b) from the U.S. Department of Education (USDOE) to each statehouse across the country.

The data in *A Rotting Apple* connect housing prices and patterns as they correlate with school attendance and measurable outcomes for those students. The patterns exposed by the report's examination of opportunities to learn reveal the following:

> While 46% of the city's White, non-Hispanic students and 47% of the city's Asian students are enrolled in top quartile high schools, only 18% of Black and 16% of Hispanic students are enrolled in those schools. Seventeen percent of students who, because of their family's low income, are eligible for free or reduced price lunches, are enrolled in those schools. Here, again, *the family income metric corroborates those for race and ethnicity.* Nineteen percent of the city's few American Indian students were in the highest quartile schools.
>
> When we look at the racial/ethnic distribution for the lowest quartile, where the average student has a 29% or less chance of graduating in four years with a Regents diploma, we find that a Black or Hispanic student is nearly four times more likely to be enrolled in one of the city's poorest performing high schools as is an Asian or White student. (Holzman, 2012, pp. 15–16; emphasis added)

Broadly, then, the report documents that any child's access to equitable educational opportunities is determined by the coincidence of that child's home and community. In short, the inequity of a child's home drives the inequity of a child's schooling:

> Most, if not all, students in majority middle class Asian and White, non-Latino Queens Community School Districts 25 and 26 . . . have an opportunity to learn in a high-performing school, where most students are able to achieve at high levels. None of the students in Harlem, Bronx and Brooklyn Community School Districts 5, 7, 12, 13, 16 and 19 . . . have the opportunity to learn in a high-performing school. The latter districts serve some of the poorest children in the city.
>
> Students who live in neighborhoods that are overwhelmingly Black, Latino, or impoverished White or Asian have little opportunity to learn the basic skills needed to succeed on state and national assessments, attend one of the city's selective high schools, or obtain a high

school diploma qualifying them for college or a good job. (Holzman, 2012, p. 4)

A Rotting Apple, then, also reinforces the broader issue of in-school inequity detailed by Peske and Haycock (2006), exposing inequitable teacher assignment correlated with student characteristics associated with measurable student outcomes (family income, race, native language, special needs). Peske and Haycock unmasked a tradition in education that exposes how public schooling tends to perpetuate, not counter, social inequity: "Unfortunately, rather than organizing our educational system to pair these children with our most expert teachers, who can help 'catch them up' with their more advantaged peers, we actually do just the opposite" (p. 2).

The inequity of housing, work, health care, and food security paired with the inequity of public school are the child in the closet in Le Guin's story. These inequities are real, and privilege is gained on the backs of the oppressed, but the American people, unlike the people of Omelas, are unwilling to open that closet.

"New York needs a renewed commitment to equity to insure that the opportunity to learn is not determined by the census tract where a child resides," argued Noguera (Holzman, 2012, p. vii), but recent evidence suggests that the entire United States shares the same need for a "commitment to equity."

New York City and Across the United States: Education as Inequity

Although critical and progressive educators, as well as activists seeking social justice, tend to acknowledge the need for a "commitment to equity," the essential problem remains a need to acknowledge inequity, something Americans appear hesitant to do. The powerful link between housing inequity and access to education revealed in the report on New York City is only as compelling as those patterns that are evident in the entire United States.

Housing Costs, Zoning, and Access to High-Scoring Schools (Rothwell, 2012) confirms, however, that educational inequity is not unique to New York. This national analysis concludes the following:

- Nationwide, the average low-income student attends a school that scores at the 42nd percentile on state exams, while the average middle/high-income student attends a school that scores at the 61st percentile on state exams.
- Northeastern metro areas with relatively high levels of economic segregation exhibit the highest school test-score gaps between low-income students and other students.

- Across the 100 largest metropolitan areas, housing costs an average of 2.4 times as much, or nearly $11,000 more per year, near a high-scoring public school than near a low-scoring public school.
- Large metro areas with the least restrictive zoning have housing cost gaps that are 40 to 63 percentage points lower than metro areas with the most exclusionary zoning (Rothwell, 2012, p. 1).

Educational inequity as a reflection of social inequity is the norm throughout the United States because "economic segregation . . . [as] a function of zoning practices" feeds an inequitable public education system (Shah, 2012).

Patterns of in-school inequity pose significant problems for current education reform narratives and initiatives coming from political and public leaders in the United States—all of whom blame people living in poverty and suggest schools are a mechanism for *fixing* the people while ignoring the cultural inequity. The meritocracy myth that blames people in poverty is especially significant against the evidence on income equity prompting Noah (2010) to ask, "Today, the richest 1 percent account for 24 percent of the nation's income. What caused this to happen?"

If children in the United States are experiencing growing inequity of income in their homes and communities, as well as inequity of opportunity in their community schools, how do the current education reform commitments match the weight of evidence concerning what sort of reform U.S. public education needs? Fundamentally, the most high-profile reform claims coming from political leadership and the media simply fail to confront the child in the closet:

> While all of these efforts deserve careful consideration, none directly addresses one of the central issues that limit educational opportunity for low-income and minority children: *their disproportionate concentration in low-performing schools.* In particular, limiting the development of inexpensive housing in affluent neighborhoods and jurisdictions fuels economic and racial segregation and contributes to significant differences in school performance across the metropolitan landscape. (Rothwell, 2012, p. 2, emphasis added)

The education reform narratives, then, that speak to the meritocracy myth and also allow the public not to look at the child in the closet create an ironic dynamic whereby self-proclaimed education reformers acknowledge poverty by ignoring it. As long as our social gaze is fixed on the people and children trapped in poverty—along with the solution being couched in mantras of "work harder"—the social and educational dynamics that perpetuate inequity are never confronted.

Ignoring Poverty as Education Reform

As secretary of education, Arne Duncan represents both the discourse and the policy currently driving education reform in the United States. Duncan (2009) often speaks about equity and education reform. For example, in a speech about the reauthorizing of No Child Left Behind, and typical of his discourse throughout his tenure as secretary of education, Duncan explained,

> I heard their voices—their expectations, hopes and dreams for themselves and their kids. They were candid about their fears and frustrations. They did not always understand why some schools struggle while others thrive. They understood profoundly that great teaching and school leadership is the key to a great education for their kids. (para. 4)

Building on the framework for reform endorsed by Obama and Duncan, self-appointed reformers—including Joel Kline, Michelle Rhee, and Paul Vallas—directly announced a manifesto that asserted, "As President Obama has emphasized, the single most important factor determining whether students succeed in school is not the color of their skin or their ZIP code or even their parents' income—it is the quality of their teacher" ("How to Fix Our Schools," 2010).

Duncan's implication that the public doesn't understand variations in educational outcomes (as well as his misinformation about the singular power of teachers and school leaders to overcome social forces) and reform rejecting the impact of race and zip codes is directly refuted by the reports from the Schott Foundation and Brookings discussed earlier. The conclusions of these two studies highlight that America's faith in a level playing field is not fulfilled in either society or public schools. Furthermore, both studies suggest that the current education reform movement is fundamentally flawed because politicians and the public have committed to addressing poverty and inequity by ignoring poverty and inequity (Thomas, 2012a). The problem is not people living and learning in poverty but the patterns of inequity that stratify those people in their lives and their schools.

The reform agenda speaks to and depends on the meritocracy myth that informs a "no excuses" ideology behind most elements of that education reform. In light of the research, then, several components of "no excuses" education reform are likely to increase the current problems with social and educational inequity instead of address them: charter schools, school choice, Teach For America (TFA), and teacher quality.

Charter schools. The Obama administration and states across the United States are promoting and expanding charter schools, yet the growing body of research on charter schools (Center for Research on Education Outcomes,

2009) shows that student outcomes are little different from outcomes in public or private schools. Essentially, the increased support for charter schools
fails to identify what the problems are confronting education or how charters
embody some unique features that make them uniquely able to address those
unnamed problems. In fact, Di Carlo (2011) explained, "There is nothing
about 'charterness' that leads to strong results." Yet, charter schools, notably
charter chains such as Knowledge Is Power Program (KIPP), are being supported as a primary mechanism for addressing the achievement gap among
racial and socioeconomic subgroups. As Rothwell (2012) concluded earlier,
charter schools do not address the inequity of children's homes and schools.
Instead, the one key pattern shown in the growth of charter schools is that
they are mechanisms for segregating education (Miron, Urschel, Mathis, &
Tornquist, 2010) and that they focus on *correcting* the children trapped in
poverty and not the root causes of that poverty.

School choice. The school choice movement gained momentum in the
1990s, and then initiatives such as vouchers lost steam. But in the past few
years, choice, vouchers, and other types of choices (such as charter schools)
have all regained political popularity, despite the lack of evidence that choice
itself addresses social inequity, educational inequity, or educational outcomes.
Choice—and specifically parental choice (Thomas, 2010)—is a powerful argument again refuted by current reviews of Milwaukee's extensive voucher program. Cobb's (2012) reviews of vouchers in Milwaukee show why both the
choice mechanism and the research (as well as reporting on that research) are
yet more reform solutions that fail to address inequity:

> The results are not particularly useful beyond providing a snapshot of
> how MPCP students and a comparison group of low-income MPS stu-
> dents perform on a battery of state exams. The report correctly cautions
> readers not to make causal inferences about the effects of either sec-
> tor, given the descriptive rather than analytical nature of the analysis.
> (Cobb, 2012, Think Tank Review of Report #32, p. 4)

Typical of research on the impact of choice to reform educational outcomes,
data from the Milwaukee initiative, on balance, fail to show that choice is effective as a mechanism for improving measurable education outcomes or for eradi-
cating the social and educational inequity that is rarely acknowledged as an
outcome of free market dynamics.

The entire argument about choice is driven by a belief in the United States
as a meritocracy and a faith that market dynamics are themselves cleansing
paradigms instead of the mechanisms for inequity that choice proves to be.
Few Americans are willing to look in the closet to see that *privileged choice* is
the result of some *others* being marginalized. For example, "In New York City,

openings in coveted preschools go to parents able to pay for them," explained Walt Gardner (personal communication, April 23, 2012). "The same advantages persist throughout the entire educational process. The results call into question Milton Friedman's claim that choice will provide a quality education for all."

Teach For America. Like charter schools, TFA has gained a great deal of support from the Obama administration and states and school districts across the United States. Because TFA recruits are college graduates without teacher education or teaching experience, however, commitments to TFA fail to address the inequitable distribution of quality teachers to high-needs populations of students (Heilig & Jez, 2010). In fact, TFA perpetuates the inequitable practice of assigning inexperienced and unqualified or underqualified teachers to high-poverty, minority, English-language-learning, and special needs students.

Teacher quality. Promoting TFA is a subset of the broader move to shift the accountability movement away from students alone (the standards and testing movement spawned in the early 1980s) and to include teachers as well. Calls for recruiting the best and brightest to teach are being coupled with value-added models (VAMs) for evaluating, paying, and dismissing teachers. All of these policies, however, fail to acknowledge that out-of-school factors dwarf the impact of teacher quality, that VAM evaluations and merit pay are unstable and ineffective, and that none of these policies address what we know is most inequitable about teaching in the United States: Affluent students are assigned the most experienced and qualified teachers, whereas poor and minority students are assigned new and unqualified or underqualified teachers.

The reality of "no excuses" reform is that political and public leaders have begun to ignore poverty and inequity by directly mentioning poverty and inequity to keep the closet door closed on policies that fail to create equity and often increase inequity.

Addressing Inequity as Education Reform

The Schott Foundation and Brookings reports are evidence that U.S. social and education reform must be reimagined in order to address not an achievement gap based on test scores that tells us what we already know—the out-of-school factors of a child's life are more powerful than that child's school (Berliner, 2009)—but *the equity gap that exists in our society and is reflected in and perpetuated by our public schools.* Social and educational inequity are cross-pollinating forces that must be confronted simultaneously, while setting aside hollow faith in rugged individualism and the imagined and singular power of public schools to reform society.

Much of the current reform language, notably, includes persistent references to that *achievement gap*, but as Gardner (2010) explained, even if in-school equity were achieved, "Don't forget that advantaged children are not standing still in the interim. They continue to benefit from travel and other enriching learning experiences. As a result, the gap will persist."

America's clinging to the meritocracy myth and trust in "no excuses" education reform and policy is not shared in countries that have opened the closet in order to confront inequity and the price of privilege. For example, Sahlberg (2012), director general of Finland's Centre for International Mobility, explained how the United States must confront the equity gap:

> First of all, although Finland can show the United States what equal opportunity looks like, Americans cannot achieve equity without first implementing fundamental changes in their school system. The following three issues require particular attention.
>
> *Funding of schools*: Finnish schools are funded based on a formula guaranteeing equal allocation of resources to each school regardless of location or wealth of its community.
>
> *Well-being of children*: All children in Finland have, by law, access to childcare, comprehensive health care, and pre-school in their own communities. Every school must have a welfare team to advance child happiness in school.
>
> *Education as a human right*: All education from preschool to university is free of charge for anybody living in Finland. This makes higher education affordable and accessible for all.
>
> As long as these conditions don't exist, the Finnish equality-based model bears little relevance in the United States. (para. 4–8)

Education reform is, then, a subset of social reform, not the lever of social reform. But acknowledging inequity is certainly not enough. If America can confront inequity and the social and educational practices that perpetuate that inequity, we must then implement equity-based action.

A Rotting Apple offers recommendations that likely must be applied to the national education reform movement: restoring full funding of education, instituting equitable access to schools and programs for all children, providing school resources linked to need rather than competitive models, ensuring students with identified literacy needs have full social (including health and eye care, as well as food security) and educational support, evaluating schools based on student opportunities to learn ("access to high-quality early childhood education, highly prepared and effective teachers, college preparatory curricula, and policies and practices that promote student progress and success"), and addressing teacher experience and pay equity within and among schools (Holzman, 2012, p. 19).

As well, here are some of the foundational and holistic reforms needed to shift the United States away from a "no excuses" paradigm and toward an equity-based action plan for reform:

- Provide universal health and eye care for all people age 25 years and younger.
- Enact policy to ensure food security for all people age 25 years and younger.
- Provide universal child care for all families in the United States.
- Endorse policy to support and reform workers' rights in the United States. This policy must address wages, health care, retirement, and due process. Currently, workers have dramatically reduced leverage against employers because too many basic human rights are linked entirely to their work status. To be a worker should be a subset of being a human, not the other way around.
- Reform the power and role of the USDOE away from issuing mandates and toward functioning as a mechanism of oversight, specifically in terms of equity. Form regional USDOE sites that monitor equitable school funding, for example, based on the unique cost of living standards within each region.
- Eliminate all high-stakes accountability mandates (standards-based reform) from schools and implement mechanisms of transparency whereby schools are guaranteed autonomy but required to make all practices and outcomes transparent to the public.
- Eliminate high-stakes testing and tracking in schools, policies that are reflections of and perpetuate inequity.
- Identify and reform teacher assignment by addressing the historical and inequitable assigning of teachers that allow experienced and accomplished teachers to serve privileged students while inexperienced and struggling teachers are assigned to students who suffer under the weight of inequity in their home lives.

Social and educational reform built in the pursuit of equity—and not distorted by meritocracy and "no excuses" paradigms—is genuine reform that confronts enduring cultural myths and acknowledges that no single social institution (including public schools) can succeed without understanding the powerful influence of inequity in the life of any single person.

We must remind ourselves that women's rights and civil rights in the United States did not appear on the back of claims that gender and racial equity already existed. Equity comes only when we acknowledge where it does not yet exist. America is not yet a meritocracy, and our schools reflect and perpetuate that regrettable reality. This admission is the first step to equity-based reform that can succeed where our "no excuses" culture is failing us.

Noguera ended his foreword to the NYC report with, "Let us hope that the policymakers who read this report understand its implications and have the courage and foresight to act upon the recommendations" (Holzman, 2012, p. viii).

If leaders and policymakers are willing to confront the evidence of social and educational inequity, this hope may lead to the changes promised by the current president now trapped in "no excuses" reform commitments that offer no hope or change but blame people in poverty for their disadvantages. If people are to blame for poverty, then we must look to those people with power in our society and our schools. People living in poverty are not the problem, but people living in privilege certainly are.

Note

This chapter is partially based upon two of the author's previous works: "Le Guin's 'The Ones Who Walk Away From Omelas': An Allegory of Privilege" (Thomas, 2011a) and "Studies Suggest Economic Inequity Is Built Into, and Worsened by, School Systems" (Thomas, 2012b).

References

Berliner, D. C. (2009). *Poverty and potential: Out-of-school factors and school success*. Boulder, CO, and Tempe, AZ: Education and the Public Interest Center & Education Policy Research Unit. Retrieved from http://epicpolicy .org/publication/povertyand-potential/

Center for Research on Education Outcomes. (2009, June). *Multiple choice: Charter school performance in 16 states*. Stanford, CA: Author. Retrieved from http://credo.stanford.edu/reports/MULTIPLE_CHOICE_CREDO.pdf

Cobb, C. (2012, April). *SCDP Milwaukee Evaluation Report #29, #30, #32*. Boulder, CO: National Education Policy Center. Retrieved from http://nepc .colorado.edu/thinktank/review-Milwaukee-Choice-Year-5

Di Carlo, M. (2011, November 16). Explaining the consistently inconsistent results of charter schools [Web log post]. Shanker Blog. Retrieved from http://shankerblog.org/?p=4229

Duncan, A. (2009, September 24). *Reauthorization of ESEA: Why we can't wait*. U.S. Department of Education. Retrieved from www.ed.gov/news/ speeches/reauthorization-esea-why-we-cant-wait

Dwyer, L. (2012, April 8). *Why America's education system is like apartheid.* Good Education. Retrieved from www.good.is/post/why-america-s-education-system-is-like-apartheid/

Fielding, S. (2008, April 9). *Inside the middle class: Bad times hit the good life.* Washington, DC: Pew Research Center. Retrieved from www.pewsocialtrends.org/2008/04/09/inside-the-middle-class-bad-times-hit-the-good-life/

Gardner, W. (2010, September 20). Poverty rate and the achievement gap [Web log post]. Walt Gardner's Reality Check. *Education Week.* Retrieved from http://blogs.edweek.org/edweek/walt_gardners_reality_check/2010/09/

Heilig, J. V., & Jez, S. J. (2010). *Teach For America: A review of the evidence.* Boulder, CO, and Tempe, AZ: Education and the Public Interest Center & Education Policy Research Unit. Retrieved from http://epicpolicy.org/publication/teach-for-america

Holzman, M. (2012, April). *A rotting apple: Education redlining in New York City.* Cambridge, MA: Schott Foundation for Public Education. Retrieved from http://schottfoundation.org/drupal/docs/redlining-full-report.pdf

"How to fix our schools: A manifesto by Joel Klein, Michelle Rhee and other education leaders." (2010, October 10). *The Washington Post.* Retrieved from www.washingtonpost.com/wp-dyn/content/article/2010/10/07/AR2010100705078.html

Le Guin, U. (1975). *The wind's twelve quarters.* New York: Harper Perennial.

Miron, G., Urschel, J. L., Mathis, W. J., & Tornquist, E. (2010). *Schools without diversity: Education management organizations, charter schools and the demographic stratification of the American school system.* Boulder, CO, and Tempe, AZ: Education and the Public Interest Center & Education Policy Research Unit. Retrieved from http://epicpolicy.org/publication/schools-without-diversity

Noah, T. (2010, September 3). The United States of inequality. *Slate.* Retrieved from www.slate.com/articles/news_and_politics/the_great_divergence/features/2010/the_united_states_of_inequality/introducing_the_great_divergence.html

Peske, H. G., & Haycock, K. (2006, June). *Teaching inequality: How poor and minority students are shortchanged on teacher quality.* Washington, DC: Education Trust. Retrieved from www.edtrust.org/sites/edtrust.org/files/publications/files/TQReportJune2006.pdf

Rothwell, J. (2012, April). *Housing costs, zoning, and access to high-scoring schools.* Washington, DC: Brookings Institution. Retrieved from www.brookings.edu/~/media/research/files/papers/2012/4/19%20school%20inequality%20rothwell/0419_school_inequality_rothwell.pdf

Sahlberg, P. (2012, April 17). What the U.S. can't learn from Finland about ed reform [Web log post]. The Answer Sheet. *The Washington Post.* Retrieved

from   www.washingtonpost.com/blogs/answer-sheet/post/what-the-us-cant
-learn-from-finland-about-ed-reform/2012/04/16/gIQAGIvVMT_blog.html

Shah, N. (2012, April 19). Study links zoning to education disparities. *Education Week*. Retrieved from www.edweek.org/ew/articles/2012/04/19/29zoning.h31.html

Thomas, P. L. (2010). *Parental choice? A critical reconsideration of choice and the debate about choice*. Charlotte, NC: Information Age Publishing.

Thomas, P. L. (2011a, October 30). Le Guin's "The ones who walk away from Omelas": Allegory of privilege. Daily Kos. Retrieved from www.dailykos.com/story/2011/10/30/1031651/-Le-Guin-s-The-Ones-Who-Walk-Away-from-Omelas-Allegory-of-Privilege

Thomas, P. L. (2011b, December 30). Poverty matters! A Christmas miracle. *Truthout*. Retrieved from http://truth-out.org/index.php?option=com_k2&view=item&id=5808:poverty-matters-a-christmas-miracle

Thomas, P. L. (2012a). *Ignoring poverty in the U.S.: The corporate takeover of public education*. Charlotte, NC: Information Age Publishing.

Thomas, P. L. (2012b, May 15). Studies suggest economic inequity is built into, and worsened by, school systems. *Truthout*

37

HOMAGE TO TEACHERS IN HIGH-POVERTY SCHOOLS

Moriah Thielges

As a middle and high school student, I never noticed the seamless nature of my teachers' work. I certainly had "more important" things to worry about. When my teachers first introduced No Child Left Behind (NCLB) in my classrooms in 2001, it seemed pretty inconsequential. As far as I knew, all it meant was that we were going to be taking yet another set of tests to prove what we learned. What was one more test to a teenager whose educational experience had been defined by tests?

As my years as a student progressed, and NCLB began to change education, it became apparent that it would not be "just another test." My school had been achieving decent academic results, but it slowly dipped into the category of schools not meeting adequate yearly progress. I remember pizza parties promised to us by high school administrators if we did well on the tests; celebrations and motivations that, as a teenager, seemed silly. The real consequence, which the teachers seemed to understand all along, was something bigger than a metaphorical Mr. Yuk sticker placed on our school.

My high school and community were known particularly for their support of the arts. We had an award-winning theater program in which students performed in a variety of successful shows and international tours. Our band and orchestra brought home trophies from local and national competitions. The community is expanding its local arts scene, and I think it's no coincidence that the local schools have very strong visual arts programs for students. As an artist myself, I know I would not have followed the path I have followed without a strong foundation in the exploration and understanding of all facets of art.

Out of all the tests, studies, and goals of NCLB, there seemed to be a very strong focus on the fundamentals of memorized skills on a very narrow spectrum of subjects. As a student of education, I learned quickly that the current structure of schooling concentrates on the facts of the "what" and the "how many"; it leaves no room for the amazing concept of "why." The Partnership for 21st Century Skills (2011) lists critical thinking and problem solving, communication, collaboration, and creativity and innovation as necessary skills students should learn in school. There are schools that are fortunate enough to receive the funding to explore this concept through the arts.

Now imagine the schools without these resources—schools that do not have enough computers in their one lab for the average class, especially not with increasing class sizes. These schools might have students who can understand the significance of "why" but fail to provide the "where" and the "what." The reward these schools receive is a Mr. Yuk sticker right on top of that glorious "why" and further budget cuts, ensuring another year without the resources to have a fair chance at passing the biased exams or a fair chance at almost anything else.

The National Assembly of State Arts Agencies published a report called *Critical Evidence: How the Arts Benefit Student Achievement.* It embraces and promotes art advocacy in education. By referencing a collection of studies, the document provides evidence of how art helps provide skills necessary to the 21st century, including thinking and social skills, motivation, and a positive school environment (Rupert, 2006, p. 10). A May 2005 Harris Poll found that 93% of people agree that "the arts are vital to providing a well-rounded education for children" (p. 5). Including art in school helps ensure that students are learning skills that have been deemed necessary for the 21st century.

While student teaching I experienced a variety of schools with different levels of funding for the arts. Despite a variety of resources and instruction available, I found that students in each school held the same capacity for creativity. Some of the most spontaneous examples of ingenuity came from students who attended Title I schools, students who were thought to be "disadvantaged." The district already had decreased the amount of art instruction because of a lack of funding. Skills deemed necessary for the 21st century that are fostered in the art classroom such as problem solving, creativity, and innovation were slowly eliminated from classrooms.

As an educator in the 21st century, I do not believe it will be the "how," "when," and "where" that are the most important lessons to teach. In 10 seconds, I could search online for sumi-e paintings. A simple PowerPoint I created for third graders from my student teaching experience explained where the paintings originated, when the art form developed, and how a painting is created. The depth of the lesson, however, truly lay within *why* the art form was so original and *what* it hoped to convey. Students discovered minimalist art and developed the idea that the *concept* of art could be more important than all the fine details. Students developed ideas in groups on unique ways to share ideas. They created very nice drawings, but the more important result was the new way of thinking that they were able to incorporate into their lives.

I remember, again, the school that I attended. My high school had a "happy" ending; it found the key to adequate yearly progress and has been receiving increased funding for its programs. This is not always the case; with so many schools simply not having resources to keep up, the divide between "haves" and

"have-nots" keeps getting wider. Paul Gorski (2008) stated that the only way to remove this gap is to "stop trying to 'fix' poor students and start addressing the ways in which our schools perpetuate classism" (p. 35). My contribution to this discussion about educating all students to the level they deserve is to propose the power of "why." I believe that using 21st-century tools and promoting the enriched curriculum of discovery is the key to enabling every individual to learn to her or his full ability.

When Dr. Tack, my Foundations of Education professor, approached me about contributing to this book, the idea for the piece of art I share here entered my mind immediately. I wanted to convey not only the individual, who can be beautiful, elaborate, involved, and unique, but also *how* the individual's learning is much more important than the established system of rewards and division. On the basis of my personal journey from student to student of education to educator, I can say for certain that access to deep learning is a greater reward than a pizza party. Educators who encourage the depth and the "why," instructors like Dr. Tack who push students to embrace their voices and offer those voices to the world, are the foundations for the success of every student. Looking back, I understand why rewards were offered to entice us to pass high-stakes tests. But I want each of my future students to have an equal opportunity to succeed in their education with resources and support. I also have learned through my journey that this pattern of rewards for having the "right answer" is perpetuating the wrong educational ideals.

I intended that the three lenses of my journey—as the middle and high school student, student of education, and educator—could be used in viewing my art. I wanted to give a voice to the wonderful students with fantastic abilities who are being overlooked in the current system of standardized testing. The depth of each individual student can be found only by asking questions that elicit rich answers. This painting is homage to the teachers whose schools might fail to reach adequate yearly progress but who succeed in inspiring their students to greatness. Most important, I hope that my painting shows that no individual should be confined by a test, no matter how high the stakes, but that students can use the strengths they possess to break free and succeed.

References

Gorski, P. (2008). The myth of the "culture of poverty." *Educational Leadership, 65*(7), 32–37.

Partnership for 21st Century Skills. (2011). *A framework for 21st century learning.* Retrieved August 29, 2012, from www.p21.org/

Rupert, S. (2006). *Critical evidence: How the arts benefit student achievement.* Retrieved from the Arts Education Partnership at www.aep-arts.org/wp-content/uploads/2012/08/Critical-Evidence.pdf

38

QUESTIONING EDUCATIONAL "REFORM" AND THE IMPOSITION OF A NATIONAL CURRICULUM

Mark Brimhall-Vargas

There is always an easy solution to every human problem—neat, plausible and wrong. (Mencken, 1920, p. 158)

Equal funding for unequal needs is not equality. (Kozol, 1992, p. 54)

Whether one agrees or disagrees with the way school reform happens, current debates over standardized tests and test-driven curricula fundamentally are about a desire to bring about some kind of *fairness* or *justice* through education, particularly on behalf of children who grow up in poor or working-class homes. But I wonder whether we as policymakers and educators adequately question or reflect on whether our decisions actually bring *fairness* or *justice* to students.

In an era in which all educational goals are considered legitimate only if they can be measured empirically, I am left with questions that I would like the reader to join me in considering. Do we know what actually creates justice or fairness in a child's education? Does closing or reducing the achievement gap (more appropriately termed an *opportunity* gap or an *access* gap) necessarily imply that we have created a fair or just educational experience for students? What social conditions, especially around socioeconomic class, are fundamental to making fairness or justice a real possibility? And most important, have we assumed, perhaps naively, that educational *sameness* (often interpreted as equality) is synonymous with *fairness*? Our current educational approach in the United States insists that every child learn the same thing at the same time regardless of preparation, resources, or social conditions. I wonder whether this approach may be overly prescriptive and paternalistic.

In what follows, I seek the roots of our current national love affair with standardized tests and hope to disentangle real "achievement" gap reforms from testing standards altogether, because these policies disproportionately affect poor and working-class people. Instead, I question what we currently call reform, because I do not see that it considers the disparate effects of socioeconomic class at school. To do so, I (a) evaluate the assumption that "sameness" and "fairness" are synonymous, (b) establish a process to consider various options around education reform and subject matter choice, and (c) suggest that real educational reform must come from a diverse, liberal arts curriculum emphasizing the use of critical thinking and an analysis focused on social justice.

Isn't "Sameness" Fair?

In a recent *Time* magazine article, Walter Isaacson (2009) suggested that America's public schools need national standards as benchmarks to ensure that all students receive an adequate education; in his view, adequate education is equated with "same" instruction. Isaacson suggested, "A growing coalition of reformers—from civil rights activist Al Sharpton to Georgia Republican governor Sonny Perdue—believe that some form of common standards is necessary to achieve a wide array of other education reforms" (p. 32). Fundamentally, Isaacson is saying that the *same* instruction will provide educational *fairness*.

However, he did not suggest a national standard for *all* courses and subjects. Instead, Isaacson decided, not surprisingly, to focus on reading and math based on an assumption that these subjects can be taught in an objective way. Only in the fine print did he say that we could postpone a serious conversation about fully standardizing "more subjective subjects like history" (p. 35).

Though I disagree with his assumptions, I do appreciate Isaacson's proposal, because it provides an opportunity to investigate the idea of national standards for academic subjects. It raises important questions: What makes standardization so attractive? Why are we so ready to impose these standards on poor and working-class students? In response to Isaacson's call for sameness, I return the following questions: Whose interests are served by standardization? And what unintended side effects, if any, are ignored? What values or interests inform what we decide to standardize? When we transform our national curriculum to focus almost exclusively on "the basics" (reading, writing, and 'rithmatic), what important aspects of education do we inadvertently?

To explore these questions about what creates a *fair* and *good* education, I start with Isaacson's biggest idea that nationalizing standards necessarily needs to begin with reading and math. Unremarkably, Isaacson's two preferred academic subjects also happen to be two of the three preferred subjects within the No Child Left Behind Act of 2001 (hereafter called NCLB) and its subsequent reauthorizations.[1] The relevant statutory language is as follows:

> NCLB. Section 1111.B.1.C: SUBJECTS—The State shall have such academic standards for all public elementary school and secondary school children, including children served under this part, in subjects

determined by the State, but including at least *mathematics, reading or language arts, and* (beginning in the 2005–2006 school year) *science,* which shall include the same knowledge, skills, and levels of achievement expected of all children. (No Child Left Behind Act of 2001, 2002, p. 21; emphasis added)

A casual read of Isaacson's article against the NCLB language suggests that he prefers what already is preferred in federal education policy. He supports standardization for that which is already mandated for standardization, a somewhat circular argument but also one that I think evades a deeper concern. What if Isaacson is not quite so mercenary as this first analysis suggests? Could it be that both Isaacson's and Congress's preferences are merely reflections of an already broadly held assumption that mathematics and language arts are somehow more important than other worthy skills in preparing a citizen of society? With full information, would a typical, rational person choose these subjects above all others or even choose to privilege any subjects at all? And how do these subjects help children who need the most support in education? I suspect that it is attractive to think that math and reading are obvious choices, but I believe this assumption needs to be investigated.

Reflective Equilibrium: Evaluating Two Possible Paths

To delve into these questions, I use the work of John Rawls (1971) and Ronald Dworkin (1994), who offer process and content guidance, respectively. Rawls is particularly helpful in providing a sensible *process* through which competing ideas and values can be weighed against one another through a self-questioning method he calls *reflective equilibrium*. To describe this approach of "self-examination," Rawls said that a person engaging in reflective equilibrium strives to reach a state where a "person has weighed various proposed conceptions and he has either revised his judgments to accord with one of them or held fast to his initial convictions (and the corresponding conception)" (pp. 48–49). Basically, Rawls suggested that for reflective equilibrium to work, one must be open to being wrong. In this case, I must be open to the possibility that my initial ideas may, in fact, be less defensible than I presume. I mention this to assure the reader that I am aware of this expectation of openness and take its mandate seriously.

For *content* guidance, I revisit a similar thought experiment that was done in regard to health care. This experiment was conducted by Dworkin (1994), who attempted to find a middle ground in the policy debates surrounding the Clinton health care reform agenda (not to be confused with the current "Obamacare" national debate). Dworkin distinguished between two principles that he believed would be useful in achieving fairness within health care reform: the "rescue principle" and the "prudent insurance principle." In what follows, I apply these principles to considering what makes good education reform, especially in light of the fact that reform often (at least ostensibly) targets poor and working-class students.

First, some definitions relevant to the reflective equilibrium experiment should be considered. The "rescue principle" in health care, largely accepted as valid by the medical establishment and most of the U.S. public, has two components: (a) Health care is so important that costs should not be considered when saving the life or health of the individual (i.e., medical expenses and insurance should *not* be weighed or evaluated against other social goods in a competition for resources), and (b) all individuals, regardless of ability to pay, are entitled to this kind of treatment. In contrast, the "prudent insurance principle" seeks to do the opposite with a key assumption. The prudent principle seeks to consider what a rational individual (and, thus, a rational group of individuals) *would likely choose within a context of (a) full information and (b) real social and economic justice*. Thus, following the prudent principle would logically lead us to a rational outcome in which (a) health care costs *are* weighed against other considerations and (b) not all health care measures are equally applied to all people. The key issues I seek to lift and repackage from Dworkin's experiment are reflected in the following crucial questions:

- Should a particular social commodity such as health care or, in this case, public education *ever* be weighed against other social goods?
- Should that standard be applied to *all people in all circumstances*?

Weighing Education Against Other Social Commodities

When mapping Dworkin's principles from health care reform to the current education argument, I find that the two principles being weighed in reflective equilibrium map well to education, with one glaring exception. In Dworkin's health care model, the rescue principle openly suggests that we should spend every last dollar necessary to achieve the goal of health rescue. Simply, "rescue" demands positive results, even if it means redistributing limited funds away from other social interests. In other words, health care spending under the rescue principle is so important that it can demand dollars intended for other social priorities.

And here is the key difference. In the current educational conversation around closing the achievement gap, this rescue principle still boldly demands positive results *but plainly avoids the logically corresponding necessity to redistribute funds to achieve these results*. Thus, the public rhetoric about education reform clearly insists that it should follow the rescue principle—that it should achieve results, no matter what—but remains silent on the need to pull funds from other social commodities to make that possible. Correspondingly, people who support nationalized standards to close achievement gaps (a laudable goal) suggest that these standards will solve a crucial social ill, but they never seriously address the real costs associated with achieving this goal. In Dworkin's health care example, though the rescue principle was certainly extreme, it was at least open and honest about its extreme nature and fiscal demands. A push for nationalized standards in education, however, is not similarly honest about the real costs to achieving the goal of educational excellence for all. It demands rescue for all without the *means* to rescue.

To answer whether we should employ this rescue principle in education, we need to know how much it actually would cost to "rescue" education for everyone. Richard Rothstein (2004) plainly quantified this, explaining,

> All told, adding the price of health, early childhood, after-school and summer programs, this down payment on closing the achievement gap would probably increase the annual cost of education, for children who attend schools where at least 40% of the enrolled children have low incomes, by about $12,500 per pupil, over and above the $8,000 already being spent. *In total, this means about a $156 billion added annual national cost to provide these programs to low-income children.* (p. 144; emphasis added)

The important point of Rothstein's quote is that the $156 billion is really the open application of the prudent principle at work, not the rescue principle, because the figure itself implies a sense of being weighed against other social needs.[2] In other words, if we spend $156 billion on education, it necessarily means we do not spend that money elsewhere. It is also important to note that Rothstein based his assessment on attempting to address the needs of the *average* low-income child (a composite that includes higher and lower performing children from a variety of socioeconomic backgrounds). The reason this is important is that the achievement gap is also based on the performance of the average child. Thus, Rothstein's proposed solution has a good chance of success, because it, like the achievement gap, targets the average (which includes the needs of the most needy).

In contrast, Isaacson's national standards (the first half of the rescue principle) imply that all children should meet set standards all the time, everywhere, regardless of the costs. However, I conclude, as Rothstein did, that the current rescue principle (a mandate of national standards without necessary resources) does not and cannot create a socially just outcome, because it fails to adequately define the problems in realistic terms (where large social goals require adequate resources to be accomplished). This backdoor rescue principle does not allow us to weigh educational goals against other social goals, because it never seriously considers other options for resource allocation.

I do want to give Isaacson's rescue principle the benefit of the doubt in this process. Perhaps Isaacson would consider substantial redistributions of resources to achieve his national goals in math and language arts. For the moment, I will assume so. It still evades the question of whether these uniform standards should be applied to all people in all circumstances. Would a diversity of rational people choose an educational experience for their children beyond reading and math? And most important, would poor and working-class families choose to focus on reading and math or opt for a broader and more diverse curriculum?

Educational Wins and Losses

Although a philosophical argument can be made that poor and working-class families might choose a focus on math and reading, I firmly believe that the opposite is true. The fact of the matter is that common sense and reams of research suggest that a broad, comprehensive education produces the best academic results for all students. This kind of education would focus on the development of the whole person (including classes such as physical education, music, art, etc.) in addition to the preparation for the retooling that arises when there is an inevitable shift in demand for different labor skill sets. For these reasons, poor and working-class families would choose a robust, broad, liberal arts education, because they know that it is the best education for their kids. They also know that it is the education that their wealthier peers give to their kids. Thus, it appears that everyone knows what a good education is, but despite this, we do not provide it.

Clearly, there exists a dynamic, perhaps deep and unconscious, that prevents us from naming the obvious. To uncover this dynamic, we must openly ask, Who benefits by maintaining the current system? The idea here is that education (particularly for poor people) is currently structured in such a way to focus on the production of employees (not vibrant members of our society) who are suitable to low-skilled jobs. This pupil-to-plebian curricular pipeline emphasizes giving students basic skills but not a critical consciousness about how to apply those skills, especially when times change. And without a critical consciousness, these students would continue to struggle to adapt to a changing labor market, making them very responsive to their employers. Indeed, who benefits from this situation?

Longtime activist and educator Bill Ayers unpacked what is perhaps the best explanation for why current "educational reform" tends to appear rational in the public square. Following the reelection of President Obama, Ayers (2012) revealed the plutocratic education reform oligarchy by overtly naming names:

> The [education reform] efforts of the last several administrations are
> now organized into a coherent push mobilized and led by a merry band
> of billionaires including Bill Gates, Michael Bloomberg, Sam Walton,
> and Eli Broad. Whether inept or clueless or malevolent—who's to
> say?—these titans have worked relentlessly to take up all the avail-
> able space, preaching, persuading, promoting, and, when all else fails,
> spreading around massive amounts of cash to promote their particular
> brand of school change as common sense. (para. 2–3)

It is precisely this infusion of vast amounts of capital into the public discourse that has largely shaped or determined what masquerades as educational
reform today. This tidal wave of money also explains why common sense and
academic research can be regularly ignored or silenced when considering what
makes good education.

Thus, it appears that we are really left with two choices, broadly speaking: We can (a) give people the freedom to choose the curriculum that makes
sense for their children in their communities and circumstances, or if we are
truly wedded to a single, standardized curriculum, we can (b) implement the
sort of curriculum offered in schools commonly attended by the economic elite
with mechanisms to ensure that all students are able to genuinely participate in
this curriculum. Essentially, if we want a single curriculum, then morally and
ethically we should demand that all students experience the kind of education
currently reserved for their wealthiest peers, a curriculum including everything
from a variety of physical sciences to robust choices in the humanities. Otherwise, we need to reject national baselines.

In our rejecting a national curriculum, I do believe, however, that it is
important to connect the ideas of having locally responsive, broad, liberal arts
education with seriously addressing the disparities in education that create the
achievement gap. How then should it actually be closed? And what might a
nonstandardized, liberal arts curriculum actually contain? I discuss each of
these questions next.

Finally Closing the Achievement Gap

If we, as a society, wish to actually close the achievement gap, we have to be
realistic about what the actual *causes* of the problem are. Rothstein (2004)
appropriately emphasized that gaps in educational achievement cannot be
solved solely within the school, because the problems do not largely *originate* in
the school. In other words, the achievement gap is not an educational problem
in the strictest sense, and schools do not need to be the only vehicles for social
change. Rather, the achievement gap is a larger problem that is the result of

social inequality in every sector of our society. To effectively tackle this problem, we must take a multipronged approach (including affordable low-income
housing, local health care clinics, educational intervention at early ages, and
programs to keep children learning after the school day or during the summer)
as a way to comprehensively address the problems that create and perpetuate
the "opportunity" gap rooted in socioeconomic class disparities.

Lee and Burkam (2002) pointed out that *race is not primarily the decisive
factor* in the achievement gap:

> Once children's SES is taken into account, effect sizes for race/ethnicity
> *decline about 40%.* . . . Thus, the fact that, on average, Black and Hispanic
> children's families are lower SES "explains away" a substantial proportion
> of the initially observed racial/ethnic achievement gaps. (p. 49; emphasis
> in original)

This suggests that one problem of the achievement gap fundamentally rests in
an inaccurate diagnosis of the problem; that is, we strictly measure race outcomes when we should be measuring a more complex intersection of race, class,
language, and so on.

In addition, the achievement gap is also understood as the disproportionately disadvantaged nature of *the schools* in which children of lower socioeconomic class attend. According to Lee and Burkam, "The least advantaged
of America's children, who also begin their schooling at a substantial cognitive disadvantage, are systematically mapped into our nation's worst schools"
(2002, pp. 76–77). Thus, if our goal is to close the achievement gap, we must (a)
use other social institutions to combat class inequality, (b) measure performance
gaps with an intersectional lens instead of relying solely on the proxy of race,
and (c) provide schools that serve low-income children appropriate resources so
their students can obtain the skills they need.

The Ingredients of a Good Education

If a nationalized standard "common denominator" approach is unlikely to seriously address the achievement gap (and is not good education, in general), then
what kind of education would I suggest? Perhaps the most powerful critical
curriculum is one that struggles with the very topic of this chapter: fairness.
Students will be more prepared to manage their own future when they are given
a broad curriculum that encourages *critical evaluation of existing social circumstances* from a variety of disciplinary subjects (including ones not immediately
obvious such as the arts or the sciences). By engaging *any* particular issue of
inequality, students can learn to build a fair society with the skills they gain

through the development of equally important subjects like history, chemistry, sociology, civics, biology, and, yes, language arts and mathematics.

The reason a focus on inequality from a variety of disciplines is important is that it teaches students about how much in our society is socially constructed, an essential idea that Kozol (1992) summed up like this: "What is fair is what is determined . . . to be fair" (p. 84). This approach is different from Isaacson's curricular suggestions, because it (a) develops disciplinary skills beyond reading and math to triangulate the ways social constructionism manifests and (b) has the added benefit of contextualizing those skills for future application in solving social problems.

I would also suggest that it is not enough for even a broad, liberal arts education to construct a social self-awareness and global awareness. A good education should also plainly speak to the logical inconsistencies and hidden political agendas that prevent real reform in education. In other words, students should reflect on and critique their own educational experiences using what they learn in various disciplines. When considering what "educational reform" actually does, Kozol (1992) said,

> But, when the recommendations of such studies are examined, and when we look as well at the solutions that innumerable commissions have proposed, we realize that they do not quite mean "equity." What they mean, what they prescribe, is *something that resembles equity but never reaches it*: something close enough to equity to silence criticism by approximating justice, but far enough from equity to guarantee the benefits enjoyed by privilege. (p. 175; emphasis in original)

Essentially, in addition to a diversity of subjects that examine broader social context, the best curriculum would also examine the educational process itself. This approach provides a robust education *and* enables students to name the kinds of serious social changes necessary to provide *real* equity in their own education.

Full Circle?

Returning to my initial questions about the achievement gap and national standards, I find linkages to Kozol's (1992) idea that we care about education reform only because we would rather focus on the educational manifestations of a racially and socioeconomically segregated society than address the segregation itself. If we cannot get the children in the same classroom, the logic seems to go, we will bring the same classroom to each child, assuming, again, that sameness will solve differences in educational outcomes that are far more attributable to socioeconomic class conditions. I raise this point at the end of my chapter, because I wish to remind us that our endless discussions about eliminating the achievement gap with naive debates about "standards" can seem like a desperate attempt to ignore our underlying social reality. We live in a society that is not socially just and does not appear to be heading in that direction, and it is one that encourages us to live under the illusion that woefully underresourced and overwhelmed schools serving desperately disenfranchised children can miraculously erase social inequality (and thereby ease our collective conscience). Indeed, Kozol (1992) captured this delicious national hypocrisy when he heaped scorn on self-described "pragmatic" approaches to poor student achievement, like nationalized standards for math and reading. He stated, "First we circumscribe their destinies and then we look at the diminished product and we say, 'Let's be pragmatic and do with them what we can'" (p. 75).

We need to be vigilant against reforms that appear progressive on the surface but masquerade very regressive ideas. Frequently, political parties and ideologies seem to be vastly different when, in fact, they express a singular conservative worldview that has sedimented in our imagination. As Selden (1999) explained,

> The continuing belief on the part of many of today's educators that Progressivism was a period of solely liberal motives, actions, and consequences seriously limits our critical abilities. . . . Early programs for gifted children exemplify this point. Both conservatives and liberals supported such programs, but for divergent reasons. Conservatives' support for gifted education was consistent with their commitment to a natural *elite*, while liberals did so in terms of their belief in natural *merit*. (p. 26; emphasis in original)

Thus, I submit this chapter as a way to disrupt the assumptions around education "reform" that continually permeate right- *and* left-wing ideology. Only by critically examining this issue can we achieve an accurate diagnosis of, and remedy for, this protracted educational disparity.

Notes

1. *Science* is the third subject contained within NCLB, but it is strangely left undefined, though presumably it refers to physical sciences such as physics, chemistry, and biology as opposed to human or social sciences such as the humanities, government, sociology, education, and so on.
2. Rothstein's estimate, $156 billion, is given in 2004 dollars. In 2012 dollars, this figure would be $191.1 billion.

References

Ayers, W. (2012). *An open letter to President Obama from Bill Ayers*. Retrieved November 12, 2012, from www.good.is/posts/an-open-letter-to-president-obama-from-bill-ayers

Dworkin, R. (1994). Will Clinton's plan be fair? *New York Review of Books, XLI*, 20–27.

Isaacson, W. (2009, April 27). How to raise the standard in America's schools. *Time, 173*, 32–36.

Kozol, J. (1992). *Savage inequalities: Children in America's schools*. New York: Harper Perennial.

Lee, V., & Burkam, D. (2002). *Inequality at the starting gate*. Washington, DC: Economic Policy Institute.

Mencken, H. (1920). *Prejudices: Second series*. New York: Knopf.

No Child Left Behind Act of 2001, Pub. L. No. 107-110, 115 Stat. 1425 Stat. 670 (January 8, 2002).

Rawls, J. (1971). *A theory of justice*. Cambridge, MA: Belknap Press.

Rothstein, R. (2004). *Class and schools: Using social, economic, and educational reform to close the Black-White achievement gap*. Washington, DC: Economic Policy Institute.

Selden, S. (1999). *Inheriting shame: The story of eugenics and racism in America*. New York: Teachers College Press.

39

LOCAL EDUCATION FOUNDATIONS AND THE PRIVATE SUBSIDIZING OF PUBLIC EDUCATION

Richard Mora and Mary Christianakis

Public schools operate using public moneys, right? Well, not exactly. Today, because of the lack of sufficient public moneys from state governments, many public schools and school districts in the United States are being subsidized with private funds from businesses, PTA fund-raisers, and local education foundations (LEFs), which are tax-exempt nonprofits. Although these sources of private funding can help schools and districts secure additional educational resources, not all communities have successful education support organizations (ESOs). More often than not, it is the well-resourced, wealthy, and less diverse schools and districts that bring in private dollars (Mattison, 2012). Compared to parents in small and poor districts without fund-raising infrastructures, parents in moneyed school districts can tap into wide networks of professionals in order to finance and support a fund-raising machinery that protects against state budget cuts (Sattem, 2007). Hence, LEF dollars may bolster district budgets, but a reliance on private donations undermines the principle of equity central to public education (Cuatto, 2003).

In this chapter, we argue that by assuming the public function of funding public schools, LEFs, which are typically independent of school districts and raise private donations for a school or district or several adjacent school districts, reproduce the funding inequities that already exist and, as a result, reiterate inequities. To illustrate the impact of the financial disparities among public schools in the United States, we draw on evidence from California, where more than 600 public schools are members of the California Consortium of Education Foundations, an association formed to provide support for in-state LEFs. We close by calling for a redistribution of state funding to public schools.

Local Education Foundations

Looking to supplement budget cutbacks, school districts, principals, and parents established nonprofit funding arms, LEFs, to raise private dollars (Neill, 1983). Over the past three decades, hard financial times have given rise to hordes of new LEFs (de Luna, 1995; Sattem, 2007). Prior to 1979 there were fewer than 25 LEFs in California, and now there are hundreds (Zimmer, Krop, Kaganoff, Ross, & Brewer, 2001).

Because more affluent districts tend to have more effective LEFs that can attract larger contributions, the expansion of LEFs has contributed to existing resource inequities among schools and among school districts (Duncombe & Yinger, 2006). Consider the stark difference in resources of two districts in Northern California that are within 10 miles of one another: the well-to-do, predominantly White Woodside School District, a district composed of one elementary school with fewer than 500 students, and the predominantly Latino Ravenswood City School District, which serves approximately 4,500 students, most of whom receive free lunch. Between 1998 and 2003, the Woodside School District increased per-student spending by thousands of dollars and added music and computer programs after receiving over $10 million from the Woodside School Foundation, which has raised money for these sorts of ventures since 1983 (Reich, 2005). On the other hand, the Ravenswood City School District, which is in need of textbooks, supplies, and building maintenance, has no LEF to supplement its budget (Reich, 2005). The glaring inequity between Woodside and Ravenswood City highlights three sobering truths. First, most LEFs contribute to schools and school districts that are wealthy and small (Brunner & Imazeki, 2003; Brunner & Sonstelie, 2003; Mattison, 2012). Second, many districts serving disadvantaged families have no LEFs. Finally, the majority of the moneys raised by LEFs are spent on students attending schools or districts with little, if any, need for additional resources (Mattison, 2012).

Making matters more unequal, in California wealthy districts with successful LEFs often couple private donations with school parcel taxes, or special taxes voted on by local residents for the purpose of raising additional local school funds. Studies have revealed that in California, "foundation contributions increase by approximately $0.30 per pupil for every additional dollar of parcel revenue" (Golebiewski & Yinger, 2008, p. 4). A more concrete example is in San Marino, California, where the median household income was $154,962 in 2010. Residents voted for two parcel taxes—Measure R and Measure E—to make up for shortfalls in state funding. On March 6, 2007, voters approved Measure R, which renewed a parcel tax of $295 to be used for attracting and retaining excellent teachers, maintaining support programs in math and science, reducing class sizes, and maintaining all educational programming. Just two years later, on May 5, 2009, voters approved Measure E, a $795 supplemental parcel tax for each of the following six years. As a result the San Marino Unified School District receives $1.5 million annually based on Measure R and $3.5 million annually based on Measure E, for a total of an additional $5 million per year to educate the district's approximately 3,250 pupils.

As is currently the case in many wealthy districts, the revenues raised by the local San Marino LEF are far greater than the discretionary additional revenues raised from a local parcel (Cuatto, 2003). The San Marino Educational Foundation, one of California's oldest educational foundations, has raised $29 million since 1980. In 2003, the foundation, whose mission is to "provide supplemental financial support for San Marino Public Schools to achieve its educational objectives," launched a "Save Our Schools" campaign to make up for California's budgetary shortfall. Between 2005 and 2009, the foundation, which is run by volunteers, raised $14,582,996. These LEF funds combined with the funds raised from local taxes more than make up for financial shortfalls.

In addition, San Marino schools, like other wealthy districts, received significant funds from the local parent-teacher association (PTA). In recent years, the PTA has raised approximately a half million dollars per year from a carnival and posh silent auctions. An analysis of voluntary contributions (VCs) by ESOs—PTAs, booster clubs, and LEFs—to over 500 California school districts finds that, similarly, the wealthy Laguna Beach Unified School District is a beneficiary of many private contributions:

> For the Long Beach Unified School District, where the average household income is $40,000, there are 47 ESOs that each raise over $25,000 per pupil and their average per pupil revenue is $39. Down the coast in Laguna Beach Unified School District, where the average family income is $146,562, a total of nine education nonprofits raise enough VCs to contribute an additional $858 per pupil. (Mattison, 2012, p. 41)

In 2005, Jonathan Kozol highlighted these growing funding inequities in public education in the best-selling book *The Shame of the Nation: The Restoration of Apartheid Schooling in America*. He wrote that because of private dollars in public education, we now have "hybrid institutions which are public schools in that they benefit from the receipt of public funds but private in the many supplementary programs that are purchased independently" (p. 49).

Kozol is right. Districts and schools that amass private contributions are freer to invest in their children by using funds in a targeted way and without the restrictions that may come with state and federal moneys (Mattison, 2012). At the school level, the additional financial resources provided by LEFs in wealthy communities help keep teachers in the classrooms, protect electives that otherwise would be cut, and provide teachers with material support to accomplish their instructional goals. Woodside Elementary, for example, has used the millions of dollars from their LEF to establish programs in the arts, physical education, and technology (Reich, 2005). As mentioned earlier, San Marino Unified used parcel tax and LEF dollars to hire more teachers and reduce class sizes.

Similarly, many higher income districts in Oregon use the additional funds from LEFs to reduce their teacher-to-student ratios (Sattem, 2007). The blurry line between public and private funding programs in public schools ensures that public schools will reproduce the economic disparities among school districts. What is more, privately financed public schools "enable parents of the middle class and upper middle class to claim allegiance to the general idea of public schools" when, in reality, their allegiance is more local and they make "sure their children do not suffer gravely for the stripped-down budgets that have done great damage to poor children" (Kozol, 2005, p. 49).

While richer districts use LEF dollars to enrich their students' educational experiences during difficult economic times, disadvantaged districts and their schools cut physical education and art and music programs, lay off teachers and staff, and rely on parents willing to provide "help labor" to accomplish teacher-assigned work related to the day-to-day curricular and clerical responsibilities of teachers (Christianakis, 2011). Reliance on parents becomes an additional challenge for less resourced schools serving low-income Latinas and Latinos and African Americans. Unlike San Marino parents who can provide significant parental involvement, which is "key to [the] fundraising capacity" of LEFs (Sattem, 2007, p. 56), low-income parents face impediments to their parental involvement, such as having long work hours, holding multiple jobs, and contending with other familial responsibilities that conflict with the hours urban schools tend to make available for parent involvement. They must also contend with the lack of community safety, transportation, and child care (Christianakis & Mora, 2012; Coots, 1998; Drummond & Stipek, 2004; Lareau, 1987, 1994; Peña, 2000; Smalley & Reyes-Blanes, 2001; Waanders, Mendez, & Downer, 2007; Zarate, 2007). So not only do economically disadvantaged parents lack the financial security to provide their children with many, if any, of the sorts of outside-of-school educational experiences that wealthier families might take for granted, they also lack the time and social networks to secure monetary and in-kind donations for their schools.

An infusion of unrestricted dollars comparable to those received by wealthier schools would allow poorer schools to target some of their students' greatest educational needs. Yet, the unequal access to private moneys is rarely accounted for when school districts' academic performances are compared, even though it is clearly a factor. All else being equal, schools can "obtain a 10 percent increase in student performance as measured by the [Academic Performance Index]" with an additional "7.1 percent increase in spending" (Duncombe & Yinger, 2006, p. 32). Given this fact, it is not at all surprising that while Ravenswood City schools are singled out for being among the lowest performing schools in the region (Reich, 2005), Woodside Elementary and San Marino schools have been recognized by the State of California for their high API scores. The economic inequities that segregate society by class produce drastically different educational experiences for children and belie suggestions that the United States is a meritocracy and that its public schools are great equalizers. The much-discussed achievement gap between students of differing socioeconomic and racial backgrounds is an inevitable outcome of an educational resource gap due partly to the activities of LEFs.

Funding Schools Most in Need

The very existence of LEFs reveals a significant truth about public education: Dollars matter, and money makes a difference. To increase the educational and, as a result, the *life* chances of our poorest students, we need to resource the schools that serve them. But how, when most states are experiencing budget crises resulting from the great recession coupled with the imposition of neoliberal policies that favor the diversion of public funds away from public goods like public schooling? In fact, in today's political climate, with the neoliberal push toward privatizing public education, the popular discussion on education is not focused on securing additional resources for the most disenfranchised students. Instead, poorer schools are threatened with closure or restructuring while teachers and administrators risk losing their jobs when students, denied the educational opportunities of their wealthier peers, do not perform well on high-stakes tests.

In addition, public education is being viewed more and more as a private investment that parents make in order to secure their own children's financial futures (Labaree, 1997), a view that spurs private donations to the schools attended by the children of well-resourced families. So, although there is anecdotal evidence of wealthy Philadelphia parents in a multiethnic community using their schools' LEF to secure outside funding to support both their local elementary school and a neighboring school that was less resourced and "ill-equipped to do its own fund-raising" (Hicks, 2003, p. 231), such generosity is as rare as it is commendable. The reason is that public school funding inequities "have been accepted with apparent equanimity by those who are their beneficiaries" (Kozol, 2005, p. 48).

Our society should not abdicate its obligation to provide all children with a well-financed public education. Even if wealthier families recognized that financial "allegiance" to their children's schools and school districts "encourage[s] unacceptable inequalities" (Reddy, 2004, p. 265), our neediest children should be dependent on private dollars raised by their own communities to receive an equitable education. Instead, the state and other local communities should support those schools through public moneys and regulated foundation fund-raising.

To help finance schools in poorer neighborhoods, we recommend a redistribution of school funding at the state level so that poor families no longer subsidize the education of middle- and upper-class children. There are three ways that states can redistribute funding. First, states and the federal government should increase funding for public schools by closing corporate tax loopholes and using the resulting funds to finance the public schools in most need of educational resources. Second, we should reconfigure the way that property taxes are distributed. Currently, all states require that individuals and businesses pay taxes on the property they own, and in many states these taxes are the primary revenue source for schools. Property taxes collected in wealthier communities typically produce revenues greater than those collected in poor communities, which creates financial inequities. States should redraw the funding districts such that wealthy school communities are paired with less wealthy communities in the distribution and receipt of state property tax funding. In this way, districts with lower property values will gain some of the benefits of the property taxes collected from the higher priced homes in wealthy communities.

A third means by which states can raise money for schools in impoverished areas is through state lottery systems. Presently, states with lottery systems contribute a (rather small) fraction of lottery revenues to public education. These dollars typically are incorporated into the public education coffers and are distributed rather equally. We propose that funds raised from state lotteries be distributed proportionately, based on the proportion of revenue raised in a given school district in the previous school year. Such redistribution would greatly advantage poorer school districts, as there is ample evidence showing that poor families, with the hope of improving their life chances, spend significantly more money on lottery purchases than individuals with higher incomes. Citing Hansen's (2004) analysis, Wisman (2006) pointed out that "in absolute terms, households with incomes under $10,000 spend almost three times as much as those with incomes above $50,000" (p. 959). If school districts serving poor students received a greater percentage of lottery funding, the additional dollars would go to the very poor communities preyed on by state lotteries hawking dreams of immediate riches (Wisman, 2006) and where children are in most need of additional educational resources. This stream of public dollars resulting from small expenditures in private spending would narrow the resource gap between poor schools and those in wealthy communities that receive private donations via LEFs.

We understand that there would be resistance to changes in state funding of education. Wealthier school districts would probably balk at their local property taxes being shared with schools in less wealthy communities. Similarly, corporations would likely balk at the idea of having to give a percentage of gross revenues to fund schools. And, finally, wealthier school districts may not want to lose funding, and many would likely mobilize parents and LEFs to maintain their access to lottery funds. Still, it may be possible to win enough support for our proposals with a public campaign calling for greater equity and fairness in education—a campaign directed at state governments and headed by superintendents and progressive local leaders in the neediest school districts who understand that equitable funding of poorer schools continues to be a civil rights issue. Poor children should benefit proportionately from the state lottery, which is in effect a regressive tax imposed on the poor (see Wisman, 2006), while wealthier children benefit from their parents' tax-deductible donations to their public schools.

In addition to redistributing public school funds, states must redistribute some of the private dollars. States should intervene by passing legislation that regulates the amount and distribution of private moneys that LEFs are allowed to raise. States could tax a certain percentage of LEF funding for all school districts and redistribute that money to school districts serving predominantly working-class and poor students, who have a constitutional right to an "equal" education.

Conclusion

In difficult economic times, and in the context of growing neoliberal influence and state and federal budget cuts, the resource differences between wealthy and poor school districts become starkly apparent when local revenues are compared. LEFs ensure that children in wealthier districts have more resources than children in poor school districts without the ability to raise comparable amounts of private dollars. Residents in well-to-do districts like San Marino Unified readily tap into the fund-raising culture common in wealthy communities in order to raise substantial tax-deductible charitable contributions to ESOs, including LEFs, in order to improve their schools and increase their property values. The donated private dollars, unrestricted by state and federal mandates, are prioritized to meet districts' needs, such as keeping teachers in the classroom and arts and music programs in schools. On the other hand, low-income districts, like Ravenswood City, are at the mercy of their states' budgets. With no LEFs, or with unsuccessful ones, few additional ESOs, and residents with less disposable income, these districts cannot adequately augment or supplement their budgets (Mattison, 2012), which accounts for their students' relatively lower test scores. So we call on states and the federal government to redistribute tax dollars in order to provide poorer districts with greater access to funds and, thus, uphold the right to equitable treatment found in the 14th Amendment.

References

Brunner, E., & Imazeki, J. (2003). *Private contributions and public school resources* (Discussion Paper 07-03). San Diego, CA: Department of Economics, Center for Public Economics, San Diego State University.

Brunner, E., & Sonstelie, J. (2003). School finance reform and voluntary fiscal federalism. *Journal of Public Economics*, 87, 2157–2185.

Christianakis, M. (2011). Parents as "help labor": Inner-city teachers' narratives of parent involvement. *Teacher Education Quarterly, 38*(4), 157–178.

Christianakis, M., & Mora, R. (2012). Urban Latino parents' narratives of parent involvement. In R. Verdugo & B. Gastic (Eds.), *The education of the Hispanic population: Selected essays.* Charlotte, NC: Information Age Publishing.

Coots, J. J. (1998). Family resources and parent participation in school activities for their children with developmental delays. *Journal of Special Education, 31*(4), 498–520.

Cuatto, E. V. (2003). Not your average PTA: Local education foundations and the problems of allowing private funding for public schools. *Philosophy of Education Yearbook*, 220–229.

de Luna, P. (1995). The education foundation: Raising private funds for public schools. *Oregon School Study Council (OSSC) Report, 36*(1), 1–11.

Drummond, K. V., & Stipek, D. (2004). Low-income parents' belief about their role in children's academic learning. *Elementary School Journal, 104*(3), 197–213.

Duncombe, W., & Yinger, J. (2006). *Understanding the incentives in California's education finance system.* Syracuse, NY: Education Finance and Accountability Program, the Maxwell School, Syracuse University.

Golebiewski, J. A., & Yinger, J. (2008). *Who gives? The determinants of contributions to education foundations, booster clubs and PTAs in California.* Syracuse, NY: Center for Policy Research, Syracuse University.

Hansen, A. (2004, October). *Lotteries and state fiscal policy* (Tax Foundation Background Paper 46). Washington, DC: Tax Foundation.

Hicks, M. A. (2003). Beyond the missiles or music debate: Re-thinking local education foundations. *Philosophy of Education Yearbook*, 230–232.

Kozol, J. (2005). *The shame of the nation: The restoration of apartheid schooling in America.* New York: Crown.

Labaree, D. F. (1997). Public goods, private goods: The American struggle over educational goals. *American Educational Research Journal, 34*(1), 39–81.

Lareau, A. (1987). Social class differences in family-school relationships: The importance of cultural capital. *Sociology of Education, 60*(2), 73–85.

Lareau, A. (1994). Parental involvement in schooling: A dissenting view. In C. L. Fagnano & B. Z. Werber (Eds.), *School, family, and community interaction: A view from the firing lines* (pp. 61–74). New York: Westview Press.

Mattison, C. (2012). *Voluntary contributions to public schools in California: Growth, distribution, and equity* (Master of Public Policy Student Research Papers). Corvallis: Oregon State University.

Neill, G. (1983, May). *The local education foundation: A new way to raise money for schools* (NASSP Special Report). Reston, VA: National Association of Secondary School Principals.

Peña, D. C. (2000). Parent involvement: Influencing factors and implications. The influencing factors and implications. *Journal of Educational Research*, *94*(1), 42–54.

Reddy, R. (2004). Private donations to public schools: Testing the scope of community. *Philosophy of Education Yearbook*, *258*–266.

Reich, R. (2005, Winter). A failure of philanthropy: American charity short-changes the poor, and public policy is partly to blame. *Stanford Social Innovation Review*, 24–33.

Sattem, J. L. (2007). *Publicly funded, privately assisted: The role of giving in Oregon K–12 education* (Master of Public Policy Student Research Papers). Corvallis: Oregon State University.

Smalley, S. Y., & Reyes-Blanes, M. E. (2001). Reaching out to African American parents in an urban community: A community-university partnership. *Urban Education*, *36*(4), 518–533.

Waanders, C., Mendez, J. L., & Downer, J. T. (2007). Parent characteristics, economic stress and neighborhood context as predictors of parent involvement in preschool children's education. *Journal of School Psychology*, *45*(6), 619–636.

Wisman, J. D. (2006). State lotteries: Using state power to fleece the poor. *Journal of Economic Issues*, *40*(4), 955–966.

Zarate, M. A. (2007). *Understanding Latino parental involvement in education: Perceptions, expectations, and recommendations*. Los Angeles: Tomás Rivera Policy Institute.

Zimmer, R., Krop, C., Kaganoff, T., Ross, K., & Brewer, D. (2001). *Private giving to public schools and districts in Los Angeles county: A pilot study*. Santa Monica, CA: RAND Education.

ABOUT THE EDITORS AND CONTRIBUTORS

Editors

Paul C. Gorski teaches in the social justice and education concentrations in George Mason University's New Century College. He is the founder of EdChange and the Social Justice Friends network.

Julie Landsman is a retired public school teacher and the author of many books on education and race. Her work centers on issues of equity and social justice. She is a frequent speaker on these and other topics.

Contributors

Scot Allen is a proud father, loving husband, elementary school teacher, and University of Georgia alumnus.

Stacy Amaral taught bilingual classes in Worcester, Massachusetts, for 40 years. She finished her school career as a counselor for foster and homeless students. Now she works as an interpreter and writer.

Mark Brimhall-Vargas is the deputy chief diversity officer at the University of Maryland. His expertise relates to multicultural organizational development, interpersonal engagement through intergroup dialogue, and conflict resolution.

Iabeth Galiel Briones is a graduate of the Los Angeles Unified School District. He's had many experiences through various programs in the district that he hopes to turn into something positive.

Kristen L. Buras is assistant professor in educational policy studies at Georgia State University. Her books include *Subaltern Speak*; *Rightist Multiculturalism*; *Pedagogy, Policy, and the Privatized City*; and *Charter Schools, Race, and Urban Space*.

Russell Carlock is a doctoral candidate in the Harvard Graduate School of Education's Culture, Communities, and Education program and coordinator of international and ESOL (English as a Second or Other Language) programs at Albemarle County Public Schools.

Mary Christianakis is an associate professor in the Department of Critical Theory and Social Justice at Occidental College. Her current research interests include inequality, literacy development, and juvenile justice.

Joy Cowdery is an associate professor and coordinator of diversity initiatives in the Education Department at Muskingum University. She holds an EdD in Educational Leadership and Critical Pedagogy from West Virginia University.

Mariah Dickinson is a former Teach For America corps member. She currently is working for a government contractor to fulfill a Chinese language scholarship she received while attending American University.

Curt Dudley-Marling is a professor in the Lynch School of Education at Boston College. His scholarship focuses on the social construction of school failure and school success.

Sherrie Fernandez-Williams is a Minnesota State Arts Board Grant recipient, SASE Jerome Grant recipient, Loft Mentor Series winner, and Givens Fellow. She teaches career and English courses at Hamline University and MCTC.

Tricia Gallagher-Geurtsen teaches, writes, and presents about how to meet the needs of culturally and linguistically diverse students.

Whitney Gecker is a graduate student in applied sociology at the University of Massachusetts Boston. She thinks about these things: urban spaces, food systems, human interactions, and what cats dream about.

Steve Grineski teaches Educational Foundations at Minnesota State University Moorhead. His most recent book, coedited with Julie Landsman and Robert Simmons, is *Talking About Race: Alleviating the Fear* (Stylus, 2013).

Nicholas Daniel Hartlep is an assistant professor of educational foundations at Illinois State University. He is author of *The Model Minority Stereotype: Demystifying Asian American Success* (Information Age, 2013).

Lisa Hoffman is an assistant professor of graduate studies in education at Indiana University Southeast. Her teaching and research focus on curriculum, action research, and culturally and linguistically diverse students.

Carolyn L. Holbrook is a writer, educator, and long-time advocate for the healing power of the arts. She teaches composition and creative writing at Hamline University and Minneapolis Community & Technical College.

Brian R. Horn is an assistant professor in the School of Teaching & Learning at Illinois State University (ISU) and the faculty liaison for ISU's Chicago-based Professional Development School programs.

Henry Hughes is an Oregon Book Award–winning poet and frequent contributor to *Harvard Review*. He teaches at Western Oregon University.

Diamond Dominique Hull is a student of Los Angeles Unified School District and a conscious citizen of the Earth.

Janet Kesterson Isbell of Coalfield, Tennessee, is an assistant professor at Tennessee Technological University, where she teaches secondary English and qualitative research methods. She holds a PhD in exceptional learning and literacy.

Taharee A. Jackson is the founding faculty member of the Center for Urban Education at the University of the District of Columbia, which prepares teachers for the nation's most severely undersupported public schools.

John N. Korsmo is associate professor of Human Services at Western Washington University. He consults on issues related to youth and family work and privilege inequality throughout the United States.

Ok-Hee Lee is an associate professor in the School of Teaching and Learning at Minnesota State University–Moorhead. She teaches early childhood education courses and advises graduate students' action research.

Richard Mora is an assistant professor of sociology at Occidental College. His research interests include education, gender, and juvenile justice. His work appears in numerous edited volumes and journals.

Lenny Sánchez is an assistant professor at the University of Missouri. His current research involves schools in South Africa, Ghana, and Missouri. Additionally, his family of six keeps him abundantly entertained.

Susan Santone is the founder and executive director of Creative Change Educational Solutions. A former classroom teacher, she specializes in instructional design and professional development on sustainability and cultural issues.

Jeff Sapp is a professor of education at California State University, Dominguez Hills, in Carson, California. His body of work can be found at www.jeffsapp .com.

Shari Saunders is a clinical associate professor in teacher education at the University of Michigan–Ann Arbor. Her work includes preparing future teachers for their roles as transformative educators.

Peggy Semingson is an assistant professor at The University of Texas at Arlington. Her research focuses on students who face challenges in literacy as well as digital pedagogies and teacher education.

Bobby Ann Starnes currently teaches in the Education Studies Department at Berea College, where she works to prepare teacher activists and change agents committed to social justice, equity, and democratic principles.

Buffy Smith is an associate professor of sociology and criminal justice at the University of St. Thomas. She writes on policy issues regarding mentoring, access, retention, equity, and diversity in higher education.

Shifra Teitelbaum is the director of youTHink, a program of the Zimmer Children's Museum. Diamond Hull and Iabeth Briones were youTHink program participants while in high school.

Jaye Johnson Thiel is a PhD candidate at the University of Georgia. Her research focuses on educational equity, social class-consciousness, and the representation of the working class in children's literacies.

Moriah Thielges graduated from Minnesota State University Moorhead with a degree in Art Education. She currently resides in St. Paul, Minnesota.

P. L. Thomas, associate professor of education at Furman University in Greenville, South Carolina, taught high school English in rural South Carolina before moving to teacher education. His work can be followed via Twitter: @plthomasEdD.

Sandy Nesbit Tracy, a first-generation college graduate (Tarkio College 1967), earned an MA from Stanford University (1995) and a PhD from Colorado State University (2005). She's a writer, artist, and grandmother.

Lori D. Ungemah taught high school English in Brooklyn and is currently a founding faculty member of the New Community College at the City University of New York.

Elizabeth E. Vaughn, a Louis Brandeis School of Law graduate, was appointed Henderson, Kentucky's first Family Court judge. As assistant county attorney, she now prosecutes dependent, neglect, abuse, and juvenile public offenses.

Wendy Zagray Warren taught in public schools for 25 years, most recently in Columbia Falls, Montana. Recently relocated to Berea, Kentucky, Wendy now teaches education studies at Berea College.

INDEX

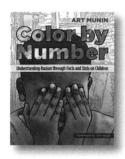

Color by Number

Understanding Racism Through Facts and Stats on Children

Art Munin
Foreword by Timothy A. Wise

"I welcome this addition to the literature already extant on race and racism. It is long overdue."—**Tim Wise**, *Author*, White Like Me: Reflections on Race from a Privileged Son, *and* Dear White America: Letter to a New Minority

By presenting the impact of racism on the most innocent and powerless members of society—children of color—in the form of statistics, this book aims to change attitudes and perceptions.

Children have no say about where they are born or what school they attend. They have no control over whether or not they get medical treatment when they fall ill. They can't avoid exposure if their home is in a community blighted by pollution. The questions this book poses are: What responsibility do we expect children to take for their life circumstances? Do those conditions blight their futures? If they aren't responsible, who is? Are some in society privileged and complicit in denying people of color the advantages and protections from harm most of us take for granted?

Sty/us

22883 Quicksilver Drive
Sterling, VA 20166-2102

Subscribe to our e-mail alerts: www.Styluspub.com

Also available from Stylus

Talking About Race
Alleviating the Fear

Edited by Steven Grineski, Julie Landsman,
and Robert Simmons III
Foreword by William Ayers

To overcome the common fear of discussing race, of saying "something wrong," this book brings together over thirty contributions by teachers and students of different ethnicities and races who offer their experiences, ideas, and advice. With passion and sensitivity they cover such topics as the development of racial consciousness and identity in children, admit their failures and continuing struggles, write about creating safe spaces and the climate that promotes thoughtful discussion, model self-reflection; demonstrate the importance of giving voice to students, recount how they responded to racial incidents and used current affairs to discuss oppression, describe courses and strategies they have developed, explain the "*n*-word," present exercises, and pose questions.

For any teacher grappling with addressing race in the classroom, and for preservice teachers confronting their anxieties about race, this book offers a rich resource of insights, approaches, and guidance that will allay fears and provide the reflective practitioner with the confidence to initiate and respond to discussion of race from the preschool and elementary classroom through high school.

Cultivating Social Justice Teachers
How Teacher Educators Have Helped Students Overcome Cognitive Bottlenecks and Learn Critical Social Justice Concepts

Edited by Paul C. Gorski, Nana Osei-Kofi, Jeff Sapp, and Kristien Zenkov
Foreword by David O. Stovall

"Few challenges in teacher preparation are as salient as teaching the central, troubling concepts of social justice that many profoundly resist learning. With theoretical nuance, pedagogical savvy, and highly relate-able examples and self-reflections, *Cultivating Social Justice Teachers* shows the possibilities for doing what often seems impossible. This book is one that no teacher educator—or any educator—can or should do without."—*Kevin Kumashiro, author of* Bad Teacher!: How Blaming Teachers Distorts the Bigger Picture

Frustrated by the challenge of opening teacher education students to a genuine understanding of the social justice concepts vital for creating an equitable learning environment?

Do your students ever resist accepting that lesbian, gay, bisexual, transgender, or queer people experience bias or oppression, or that their experiences even belong in a conversation about "diversity," "multiculturalism," or "social justice?"

Recognizing these are common experiences for teacher educators, the contributors to this book present their struggles and achievements in developing approaches that have successfully guided students to complex understandings of such threshold concepts as White privilege, homophobia, and heteronormativity, overcoming the "bottlenecks" that impede progress toward bigger learning goals and understandings.